From Normativity to Responsibility

From Normativity to Responsibility

Joseph Raz

OXFORD
UNIVERSITY PRESS

OXFORD

UNIVERSITY PRESS

Great Clarendon Street, Oxford OX2 6DP

Oxford University Press is a department of the University of Oxford.
It furthers the University's objective of excellence in research, scholarship,
and education by publishing worldwide. Oxford is a registered trade mark of
Oxford University Press in the UK and in certain other countries

© Joseph Raz 2011

The moral rights of the author have been asserted

First published 2011
First published in paperback 2013

British Library Cataloguing in Publication Data

Data available

Library of Congress Cataloging in Publication Data

Data available

Published in the United States of America by Oxford University Press
198 Madison Avenue, New York, NY10016, United States of America

ISBN 978-0-19-969381-8 (Hbk)
ISBN 978-0-19-968761-9 (Pbk)

Contents

Acknowledgements

Nine of the chapters in this book are based on previously published articles. All of them have been changed to improve their arguments, to integrate them in the scheme of the book, and to minimize repetition. Another chapter borrows some ideas from an earlier publication. The places of publication of those articles were: Chapter 2: C. Sandis (ed.), *New Essays on the Explanation of Action* (Basingstoke: Palgrave/Macmillan, 2009). Chapter 3: D. Sobel and S. Wall (eds.), *Reasons for Action* (Cambridge: CUP, 2009). Chapter 4: S. Tenenbaum (ed.), *Desire, Practical Reason, and the Good* (New York: OUP, 2010). Chapter 5: R. Shafer-Landau (ed.), *Oxford Studies in Meta Ethics*, vol. 5 (Oxford: OUP, 2010). Chapter 8: *Journal for Ethics and Social Philosophy* 1 (2005) (http://www.jesp.org/). Chapter 9: P. Bauman and M. Belzler (eds.), *Practical Conflicts* (New York: CUP, 2004). Chapter 10: P. Stratton-Lake (ed.), *On What We Owe to Each Other* (Oxford: Blackwell, 2005). Chapter 11: borrows some ideas from a lecture entitled 'The Force of Numbers' published in *Royal Institute of Philosophy Lectures 2003* (Cambridge: CUP, 2004). Chapter 12: borrows from two papers: 'Being in the World', *Ratio* (2010), and 'Agency and Luck', in U. Heuer and G. Lang (eds.), *Themes from the Ethics of B. Williams* (Oxford: OUP, 2011). Chapter 13: *Oxford Journal of Legal Studies* 30 (2010), 1.

Drafts of various chapters were presented at various conferences and colloquia including the following: Chapter 3 at a conference on practical reason at Bowling Green, 7–9 April 2006. Chapter 4: conference organized by D. Enoch in Jerusalem 2008, and The Moral Philosophy Seminar, Oxford 2009. Chapter 5: philosophy workshop in Leeds, and the annual conference of the British Society for Ethical Theory at CUNY's Graduate Center, in 2006, at a conference in Santa Barbara in 2008, and at the Metaethics Conference in Madison, Wisc., in 2009. Chapter 8: the Warren Quinn Conference at UCLA in November 2004 where I had the benefit of comments by T. Shapiro, and at a conference at the University of Maryland in 2005. Chapter 10: conference at Reading 2003. Chapter 11: Royal Institute of Philosophy & Philosophy Colloquium Sheffield, 2003. Chapter 12: a philosophy conference at Reading 2009, a conference on themes from the work of B. Williams 2009. Chapter 13: Hart Lecture, Oxford 2010. Several of the chapters were presented at C. Korsgaard's seminar at Harvard 2007, and others at M. Smith's seminar at Princeton 2008, both of which generated challenging and rewarding discussions.

I am grateful to participants in those occasions. I owe a special debt for comments and advice from Nico Kolodny, David Owens, Ulrike Heuer, David Enoch, Kieran Setiya, Barbara Herman, Anthony Price, Doug Lavin, Tom Pink, Stephen Everson, Rebecca Prebble, Nandi Theunissen, Peter Railton, and Geoff Sayre-McCord. I also benefited from comments by J. Adler, A. Archer, J. Broome, J. Brunero, P. Bloom-field, G. A. Cohen, J. Finnis, L. Green, M. Kalderon, P. Kitcher, R. Kumar, J. Lenowitz, B. Lewis, T. Macklem, A. Marmor, M. Martin, V. Mitova, V. Munoz-Dardé, C. Peacocke, D. Priel, C. Redondo, A. Reisner, S. Ripon, I. Rumfitt, S. Shapiro, G. Sela, S. Shiffrin, M. Smith, J. Stapleton, Gary Watson, L. Wenar, J. Wolff, G. Yaffe, and two anonymous referees for OUP. Above all I am grateful to P. Bulloch who read and discussed with me the book in its entirely, and whose help was invaluable.

1

The Hope

This is not the book I intended to write. It is part of that intention. As I came to realize what the intended book requires I saw that it would be too sprawling and too long in the writing. This chapter is in part about what the book I have written does not include. Perhaps there will be another. In any case, in rough form much of what is missing here exists in other publications.[1] But let me try to explain what the book offers.

There is no compelling starting point, especially as the journey is long, and I visit many ports en route. So I will start with action. I really want to start with our Being in the World, though the phrase may bring associations, helpful or unhelpful. Action is just one aspect of our Being in the World, a much wider topic that includes how we feel about our bodies, how we feel about where we are and how we got there. It encompasses our thoughts, imaginings, feelings, emotions, and other attitudes to how we are, and to how the world is. Much of what will be said can be applied to these broader matters. But, to have a starting point, I will start with actions, and those aspects of mental life directly involved with actions and activities.

This choice, like any other, is not neutral in its orientation. Our actions and activities are many and diverse. The terms connote being active. But actions are not the only way we are active. So are some of our thoughts, beliefs, imaginings, and emotions. Besides, not all our actions and activities are active, at least not to the same degree. They shade into passivity. For example, we digest what we eat, but digesting is something that happens within us, something that happens to us, rather than something we do, at least if what we do implies being active. In this case it is our bodies that are active, but they are active in the way that trees are active when they grow (and passive when they sway in the wind), that flowers are active when they bloom (and passive when they feed the birds). There are actions and activities that are ours not merely in virtue of being the actions or activities of our bodies, or perhaps without being the actions or activities of our bodies at all (even if they are necessarily accompanied by some bodily processes).

We also breathe, and breathing, while being partly like digesting, something that happens within us without our active involvement, is not altogether so. We can

---

[1] Esp. in *The Practice of Value* (Oxford: OUP, 2003); the second part of *Engaging Reason* (Oxford: OUP, 1999); and *Value, Respect and Attachment* (Cambridge: CUP, 2001).

breathe at will, perhaps following doctor's instructions to breathe deeply, quickly, hold our breath, etc., but only to a limited degree, and only for a limited time. Breathing becomes our activity when we intentionally control it. Intention and control are among the marks of the distinctive activity that is the focus of this book. Its claim is that we are active when we control our thoughts, emotions, or actions, by our rational capacities, when these capacities function well. We could also say that we are active when our thoughts, emotions, or actions are controlled by our rational powers. Putting it in this way recognizes that some of our mental processes are ours, that we are active regarding them, even though we do not attend to them at the time, even though it is as if our faculties act automatically on our behalf, provided again that they function well—because some mental processes cannot function well except when controlled by our rational powers, even if below the threshold of our awareness. A second major claim developed here is that our rational faculties function well when they non-accidentally respond to reason. That applies to the various aspects of our active life, to our thoughts, imagination, beliefs, emotions, intentions, and actions. Action will be our starting point, and the book has much more to say about action than about other aspects of our active nature.

Even when we act intentionally many aspects of our actions are not deliberate, often we are unaware of them, and like breathing they are only partially under our control. They may reveal much about us, but they do not do so because we aim to reveal those things in what we do: thus our facial expression, bodily disposition, and tone of voice may communicate as much as our words when we converse with people, but unlike what we say they are only partially (if at all) under our control, only partially (if at all) guided by our rational powers. Perhaps there is no aspect of them that we cannot control, but we cannot control all of them at the same time. Similarly we learn much about people from the way they walk, their choice of a table at a restaurant, or a spot on the beach; we may learn more than they know, let alone intend to convey. I mention all this to locate my starting point, while conceding its partiality, in both senses. First, it is inescapably incomplete, and second, it is deliberately biased towards one aspect of our Being in the World, that which is active in the sense of being within our control.

The reason for this second partiality is the thought that while in many ways the aspects that are not under our control, or only partially under our control, are more fundamental, more basic and pervasive, revealing more about how we are and what we are, we are aware of them and react to them through those aspects of our being that we control, and that are therefore active and intentional, namely through directed, controlled thought, through emotions that 'put us in touch' with ourselves and with others, and through our intentional actions. Of those, intentional actions are a central case, which is why I start with them and the aspects of our mental life that are essential to them.

There are exceptions, but generally speaking intentional actions are taken either to preserve or to modify something in the world or in ourselves and our position in the world.

Before I continue let me interpose two observations about possibly puzzling questions that the previous statement and others I made may have raised. First, I obviously feel free to assert perfectly trivial points known to everyone. Second, I note that there are exceptions to my generalizations, but do not stop to deal with them. I proceed as if they were not there. The reasons for both are roughly the same. My purpose is to explain general and essential features of our experience. I claim neither that the ways I describe them are the only ways to describe them, nor that the concepts I use are the only ones that make thinking about them possible. I claim only that I (aim to) describe and explain essential aspects of our experience, using concepts that we commonly use in thinking about them, when we do. The inescapability and pervasiveness of those features, the fact that they can be described using common concepts, and their availability to everyone, means that what I say, is, if true, trivial in being generally known. This does not mean that it is beyond dispute. Inescapable and pervasive as these features are, they may escape notice; they may be misdescribed, or misunderstood, in themselves, or in their relations to one another and to other phenomena. What may appear trite to some may appear obviously false to others. What I say appears trivially true to me. But I may, of course, be wrong.

All this is complicated by discussing these matters using the very concepts we aim to explain when explaining the features of our experience that the concepts are employed to describe in non-philosophical discourse. In ordinary communication, the versatility of language and the robustness of communication secure understanding of the core message, or perhaps I should say a rough understanding of what is said even when we somewhat misstate what we intend to say, and even if the background assumptions that lead us to express ourselves in the way we do are not familiar to the people we converse with. That utterances are only roughly understood is not necessarily a disadvantage to the speakers, especially if they know their audience well enough to be able to predict which way the understanding or misunderstanding will tend. Often they do not want to commit to anything very precise. This robustness has, however, some less appealing effects. For example, it does not help with communicating subtle points, except for ambiguities and evasions. Precise articulation of subtleties often requires extensive discourse, and two-way exchanges to remove misunderstandings. This helps explain why generalizations of the kind I have been stating allow, inevitably, for exceptions. Such generalizations are commonly used in contexts that determine their scope, or at least determine what kind of exceptions would undermine the truth or reliability of what the speaker says. In abstract philosophical discussions the aim is to reduce dependence on contextual features, to achieve greater literal articulation of the ideas in ways that make them available to a wide audience.[2]

---

[2] Hence another purpose of this first chapter, and of the introductions to the different parts of the book: to introduce the terminology I will use. I will try to minimize relying on technical terms. But two factors often lead to terminological misunderstandings. First, while English offers a rich array of phrases and devices for discourse about normative phenomena, philosophers commonly tend to concentrate on a few of them,

To return to the topic: when acting intentionally (and unless otherwise indicated when talking of action I will have intentional action in mind) we react to the world (ourselves here included as part of it) aiming to change or to preserve some of its features. Those features (existing or to be brought into existence) are therefore part of the explanation of our actions. But they contribute to the explanation in a special way. Many aspects of the world can contribute to the explanation of our actions (be they intentional or not). Imagine Jerry, feeling uncomfortably hot in the overheated room, opening the window to bring in some fresh air and reduce the temperature, and doing so lethargically because the heat enervated him. In this hypothetical situation, the heat figures in two ways in the explanation of Jerry's action. It affected his movements. And it gave a point to his action, as he saw it. This is our starting point: Practical philosophy connects with theory of action in that both are concerned with the way intentional action is what we do in light of and because of how things are, and how we take them to be.

The explanation of intentional action is an explanation of the intentional component of the action, and, generally speaking, it consists of two facts: Those features of the world, as it appears to the agent, which make the action appear worth doing, or at the very least make it appear as having a point, and facts about the agent that made him respond to those, perceived, features of the world. I will describe this polarity by saying that agents' rational capacities enable them (fallibly) to identify some values in some options and to respond to them, i.e. to recognize that those aspects of the option that make it valuable are reasons for taking it, and they enable them also to do so, to take that option for those reasons.

If we turn from action to belief the basic pattern is similar in displaying a duality between features of the world relating in some way to other features, and thus providing reasons for a certain response by rational agents, who through the use of their rational powers can become aware of them and respond to them, except that here it is not that the goodness of an option makes actions that realize it good, thus providing a reason for agents to take the actions, but that some facts are evidence for the existence of others, thus providing agents who can be aware of them with reasons to believe that those other facts obtain as well. A similar structure is discerned when we turn our attention to the emotions. Some features of some events (e.g. success in a demanding task one was keen on) make certain emotions appropriate (satisfaction,

assuming that should the need arise the others can be explained by reference to the chosen few in philosophically relatively uncontroversial ways. Since different writers sometimes focus on different terms, spurious disagreements may emerge, disagreements that are mainly terminological. Besides, the plethora of available expressions expresses the language's recoil from very general terms. Every expression brings nuances of its own. Philosophers while not wishing to ignore differences of substance strive to generalize, and inevitably resort to employing the phrases they choose to focus on in a way wider than their common use. Here lies a source of further apparent disagreements often having little substance. One of the purposes of this chapter is to make familiar my terminological choices, hoping that they will be seen in part as reactions to the need to provide general explanations in a language that resists generality.

pride) and rational agents using their rational powers can become aware of the fact and respond by having the emotion for which that fact is a reason.

In all these cases some features of the world make appropriate the existence, or the coming into existence, of another feature of the world. More specifically they make some reactions by agents appropriate, and—given that we are rational agents—they constitute reasons for those reactions. The explanation of normativity is the explanation of all features of the structures I point to.

You can understand why I saw the broader topic, the one I cannot discuss in this book, as Being in the World. The explanation of normativity is about the way we are in the world, the way our understanding of the world guides reactions to it in our emotions, thoughts, beliefs, and actions. Yet discussing this aspect of our Being in the World, that is discussing the way our rational capacities shape our Being in the World, is liable to distort the greater picture by overrating the role of our rational capacities. My hope, however, is that in forming a clearer view of the nature of reasons we will also be better able to see the limit of their reach. But that too will be no more than implied in the book. It is a subject deserving much more exhaustive examination than the one general hint offered here would suggest. The hint is that the primary significance of reasons, for emotions, beliefs, actions, or whatever else, is to make certain responses eligible, appropriate. Sometimes the presence or absence of additional facts in any particular situation may make the response non-optional, may make one response the required response. That is more likely in the case of reasons for belief and for action than of reasons for the emotions. But on many occasions, I am inclined to say in normal circumstances, there would be more than one response supported by reasons, with none of them supported to a higher degree than any of the others. Needless to say, in all situations our actual response is more definite than that. That is it goes beyond what reasons require of us. And that is the key to the understanding of the limits of reasons, and of the richness of the sources of our responses to the world, which include very much more than our rational capacities.

I should explain what I mean by saying that a response is required by reason— roughly speaking in part it means that when knowledge of the facts that require it is available to the agents concerned then failure to react as required renders their reaction irrational. There are exceptions. These matters belong to the part of the explanation of normativity that is offered here. It must explain what is the connection between normativity and rationality, and how it yields the conclusion that failure to do as reasons that we can know of require renders one's reaction irrational (unless one of the exceptions applies) and why, or more accurately how, it matters that one's reactions are irrational.

That question is at the heart of the explanation of normativity, and will be the subject of Chapter Five. I underlined, a couple of paragraphs above, the role of reasons in making certain options eligible. But all reasons also have a requiring aspect, they also rule out responses as ineligible. The explanation of normativity is the explanation of reasons, and of the way they function to make some responses eligible and others ineligible, thus requiring their omission and the realization of some alternative (if only the alternative consisting in the disjunction of all responses that are not ruled out). The explanation will relate reasons to Reason, to our rational capacities, as well as to rationality. All these notions are explained through their interrelations with one another.

The explanation of normativity encompasses much more than the explanation of the basic structure I pointed to, the relationships of features of the world and the responses they make appropriate, which rational beings, persons, can discern and follow through. The additional parts of the explanation of normativity, or so I join various other writers in assuming, relate other normative concepts to reasons. Explaining rights and duties, property and status, authority and promises, virtue and justice, the law and the normativity of language, and the rest of the normative phenomena, includes much more than explaining reasons. But the explanation of their normativity consists in pointing to the way they are related to reasons. And that is a task that cannot be undertaken here. It belongs with the investigation of these different topics, with the analysis of justice, virtue, and so on.

You may well think that there is something forced in insisting that the account of reasons is the focal point in the explanation of normativity. After all, many illuminating discussions of, say, justice, or of virtue, never as much as mention reasons. It is possible, of course, that they simply avoid some fundamental questions. That would not be surprising given that we do not explore the foundations of every normative phenomenon that we investigate. But it is also possible that they explore the foundations along different, broadly parallel lines. I have already acknowledged that possibility above. In explaining the phenomena each account takes a few concepts to be pivotal to the explanation. Their choice is far from arbitrary, but that does not make it inevitable, or show that there could not be alternative successful explanations—all it shows is that if there are such then they are compatible with the offered explanation. Moreover, inevitably the key concepts are used beyond the contexts in which we find them in normal discourse, or in alternative theoretical accounts. This is not to say that the concepts are distorted. They are given explanations that are true to their fundamental character as manifested in the contexts of their standard use (subject to the observations above, regarding the diverse sources of these concepts and their tendency to be understood in inconsistent ways by people coming from different traditions). But the explanations allow for their application in a wide variety of contexts in which they are not commonly applied, to facilitate the theory of normativity offered, which rightly aspires to a high degree of generality, and which has to bring out the features that unite normative phenomena (as well as to mark significant divergences among them).

One concept that plays a central role in many accounts of normativity and normative phenomena is 'principles'. Its absence from the present book is no accident. I believe that it does not help, and that its invocation is often misguided. Principles are, roughly speaking, general propositions, in our context general normative propositions, which are thought to be particularly illuminating, or central, relative to a certain normative view or theory (a religion or a 'moral system', etc.). Principles of rights and duties or of what one is to do are normally presented as entailing conclusive reasons for action or belief. We rarely encounter principles of the form: that an action may deceive is a reason against it. Principles are much more likely to state that 'One may not deceive', sometimes allowing for an exception or two ('except to save one's life' etc.). Given that what one has conclusive reasons to do or believe depends on what reasons for and against the action or belief one has, principles are conclusions from the existence of reasons, and cannot themselves occupy a fundamental role in an account of normativity.

It appears otherwise to supporters of some theoretical views, mostly descending from Kant. So their demotion in this book is not theoretically neutral. The reasons for rejecting the theories that place principles at the forefront of normative thought cannot, however, be discussed here.[3]

There are various sources of difficulty in explaining normativity. The most important is that normative thought is a very basic and pervasive, perhaps inescapable, part of our thought, and normative phenomena are pervasive elements in our experience, and famously the more basic and pervasive a concept or an aspect of reality is, the more elusive its explanation. When thinking of such concepts it is not even clear what needs explaining. After all, their pervasiveness means that we are familiar with them and with their meaning. When forthcoming explanations consist of articulating some of the necessary relations between concepts, or between the phenomena they apply to, such explanations are by their nature somewhat circular: there is no standpoint independent of, outside the phenomena explained, from which they can be explained. All that can be done is to clarify necessary connections, and remove misguided conceptions. It is also possible to vindicate the criteria for the application of such concepts by *reductio ad absurdum* arguments that refute the negation of these criteria.

All of this is widely appreciated. When it comes to normativity, however, additional difficulties arise. One is sometimes identified with the need to get round an objection raised by Mackie, namely that normative properties (such as being of value or having a point, or being appropriate, or required) are queer properties.[4] A second is that these properties are causally idle and therefore there is no way we can come to know of their existence even if they exist.[5] And a third is that the rational capacities that allegedly enable us, persons, to identify and respond to reasons that apply to us cannot exist, for their existence cannot be explained by evolutionary theory, which is the true and

---

[3] 'Rules' is sometimes used interchangeably with 'principles', in which case the above comments apply to rules too. At other times the term is used to refer to rules set up by authorities or custom. Personal rules are general resolutions one adopts for one's own conduct (to brush one's teeth every evening). In that sense the content of different rules, say one valid in the US, the other in France, may be expressed by the same proposition. I have discussed rules of this second kind in *Practical Reason and Norms* (1975; current edn. Oxford: OUP, 1999), ch. 2, and *Between Authority and Interpretation* (Oxford: OUP, 2009), ch. 8.

[4] J. L. Mackie, *Ethics* (Harmondsworth: Penguin Books, 1977), 39ff.

[5] The first to raise a variant of this objection in modern times may have been G. Harman in *The Nature of Morality* (New York: OUP, 1977), ch. 1.

adequate explanation for the emergence of intelligent life.[6] Finally, there is the objection that an account of normativity has to explain how reasons cause persons to change their beliefs, emotions, or conduct, but that reasons are causally inert and therefore cannot figure in the explanations of our beliefs, emotions, and conduct.

Of these only the fourth and last problem is taken up in this book (and only to the extent that it is independent of the others). The third problem is largely a scientific problem. It appears that current scientific theories may be unable to explain the emergence of rational powers. There is much else that they have not yet managed to explain, and many explanations one finds in writings about evolutionary theory are speculative. There may be issues that will have to be faced when the biological sciences develop further. At the moment all we can say is that we do not yet know. While I do not deal with the first two problems in this book I think of it as preparatory to their discussion. I have offered what I take to be the building blocks for their solution in previous writings.[7] But there is much work to do before they are tackled head on, and that is the task ahead.

Two ideas often used in explaining normativity and rationality play only a secondary role in this book. One focuses on the relations among our attitudes, or rather on favoured sets of conditions that those relations must conform with, the other on the powers of and the activities of reasoning. According to the first approach, normativity manifests itself in the requirement to have one's attitudes conform to a set of conditions, and they are rational if they do, and irrational if they do not. The requirements that our beliefs should be consistent and that our beliefs and intentions should comply with the so-called instrumental principle (roughly that we should intend what we believe to be the necessary means to our ends) are prominent examples. According to the second approach, and the two can be used to supplement each other, normativity manifests itself in reasoning well, and we are rational so long as we do so, and our attitudes are the products of (or are responsive to) the conclusions of well-conducted reasoning. Both approaches have been developed with great care and subtlety, and my description of them would be a caricature of these views were it meant as anything more than a way of identifying the two families of theories.

It falls to Part Two of the book to explain the role of these two approaches within my account (though Chapter Five offers the general structure of the explanation). The book is heavily tilted towards problems to do with practical thought, and action in its light. In all its parts, however, I tried to keep the wider manifestations of normativity and rationality in mind, and not only because of their intrinsic interest. It seemed illuminating to compare and contrast theoretical with practical thought, normativity and rationality. One clear example of the benefits is the challenge that the contrast between practical and adaptive reasons (the subject of Chapter Three) poses, in that

---

[6] For example along lines suggested by Sharon Street in 'A Darwinian Dilemma for Realist Theories of Value', *Philosophical Studies* 127 (2006), 109.

[7] Esp. in *The Practice of Value* (Oxford: OUP, 2001), but see also ch. 9 in *Engaging Reason*.

epistemic and other adaptive reasons are not provided by the value of the response that they require: are practical and theoretical normativity species of (one kind of) normativity? It is common to take this view nowadays. But that often depends on assuming that epistemic normativity depends on the value of knowledge, or of some related epistemic condition. I share the view that normativity is one in all its manifestations, but not that explanation of the fact.

Another example of the importance of discussing theoretical and practical reasons and normativity in tandem is central to Part Two of the book. I criticize common views that practical reasoning is a distinctive kind of reasoning (rather than merely a reasoning about a different subject matter). That may be thought to distort the nature of practical reasoning. Part Two aims to explain some of its special features, and establish that they are consistent with the fact that all reasoning is the same kind of activity.

The discussion in Part One is exclusively about people looking towards the future. That is so even when they react to the past. But reasons have a double life. They do not merely guide our course (in thought and action) for the future, they also serve to assess how we are doing at present, how we did in the past. To ask whether our thoughts or actions conform or conformed to reason is more or less the same as to ask not how we should act or be in the future, but whether the way we are, or the way we acted in the past, are justified. Even as you read this you are bound to notice the intricacies of various distinctions I am gliding over: is the question whether we are justified in having those thoughts or having acted in those ways, or is it whether the thoughts and actions are justified? Are these essentially the same question? Are they the same as the question whether we, or our thoughts and actions, were justified when we had them or took them? And why did I smuggle in talk of justification, a notion absent from the previous discussion? How does justification relate to the reasons that apply to us? Or to our rationality?

It is again time to underline the fact that we cannot seek answers in the meaning of these words or phrases. First, on most (really on all but highly regimented) occasions we grasp the meaning of statements through our understanding of the context of their utterance, and the purposes of the discourse. Second, on most occasions what we grasp is ambiguous, but most often in ways that do not matter for successful reflection or communication. Quite often ambiguity facilitates communication. In any case, it means that the aim of the discussion in Part Two is not to clarify the meaning of 'justification' but to distinguish a variety of propositions people often make using 'reasons', 'ought', 'justification', and similar words and phrases (e.g. that there is a reason for X, that X has a reason), and to explain their interrelations, thus explaining the relations between what we have reason to do, what we are justified in doing, and the role of reasoning in determining both.

The topics of Part Two, reasoning and justification, lead naturally to Part Three, for they raise the question of responsibility. We can think of responsibility for unjustified actions or attitudes as a precondition of the blameworthiness of a person for an attitude or an action, or perhaps for a whole set of actions, intentions, beliefs, and the like. Responsibility for justified actions or attitudes may be a precondition of praiseworthiness. Either way responsibility may point to further consequences of being justified or unjustified, rational or not. But crucially, responsibility attaches to people in a more holistic way. Some people are responsible for their actions, while others are not. In this way the end is in the beginning, in understanding how people are subject to normativity, namely how it is that there are reasons addressed to them, and what is the meaning of that for our Being in the World.

PART ONE

On Normativity

A Brief Introduction

An explanation of normativity is offered in Chapter Five. This may be an overstatement: It explores what an explanation of normativity could look like, and offers an explanation of the kind possible. The explanation is an explanation of how it is that (the facts that are) reasons are reasons, namely call for a response, and how it is that we can and do respond to them. Of course, we do not respond to reasons perfectly and that too will be explained in that chapter.

This focus on normative reasons as the key normative phenomenon, whose explanation explains normativity more generally, is popular, but not with everyone. Chapter Two defends that approach, clarifying the relationship between two senses of 'reasons'—that is the difference between explanatory and normative reasons. It aims first to establish that normative reasons are not merely explanatory reasons explaining a special range of phenomena. That is, it rejects the view that there is only one sense to 'reasons', that of explanatory factors, and that so-called normative reasons are not really normative, that they are merely explanations of normative phenomena. But the chapter acknowledges that there is a necessary relationship between normative reasons and explanations, namely that normative reasons provide explanations of conduct, of beliefs, and other attitudes, which are of a distinctive kind. It offers an explanation of the kind of explanations normative reasons provide, and advances the thesis that all normative reasons can feature in such explanations.

Chapter Three continues that theme. In distinguishing between standard and non-standard reasons it explains why standard reasons must be capable of explaining conduct in that special way. Non-standard reasons for one action or attitude are standard reasons for another—so this general lesson applies to them too. The second main theme of Chapter Three is the explanation of three fundamental differences between two kinds of normative reasons, practical and adaptive (my name for the second kind, which includes epistemic reasons and others). One of the differences is that practical reasons derive from the value of what they are reasons for, whereas epistemic and other adaptive reasons do not. That means that normativity cannot be explained by reference to value.

The dependence of practical reasons on value is further explored in Chapter Four. It starts from the ideas explained in the previous two chapters, i.e. that practical reasons are essential for making sense of intentional action, and since practical reasons are grounded in the value of what they are reasons for, that intentional action is necessarily action aiming at some good. The thesis goes back to Socrates, and is fundamental to the way both Plato and Aristotle understood our rational nature. My discussion of it shows how complex and qualified it has to be, but that nevertheless it is true in a way that underpins both the normativity of practical reasons, and the nature of intentions and intentional actions.

2

Reasons: Explanatory and Normative

Scepticism and puzzlement about normativity tend to focus on practical normativity, on the status and interpretation of reasons for action. Indeed some writers have tried to diffuse the sense of mystery by pointing to the secure position of normativity regarding beliefs.[1] I will not follow that route, but rather explain how the very existence of intentional actions involves belief in the existence of reasons, both practical and epistemic. That does not entail that there are such reasons, but it makes belief in their existence pretty safe, as its denial leads to the (self-defeating) conclusion that all our intentional actions are based on a mistake. I am pointing of course to a thesis familiar through being as often disputed as defended, namely that intentional action is action for a reason. The thesis will be examined in Chapter Four, where a weaker thesis will be defended, namely: Acting with an intention or a purpose is acting (as things appear to the agents) for a reason. This thesis is weaker in two respects: (a) One would be acting intentionally if one Φs for the reason that P even if it is not the case that P or not the case that P is a reason to Φ, provided that one takes it to be the case and to be such a reason, and (b) while all actions with a purpose or intention are intentional actions, not all intentional actions can sensibly be said to be actions done with an intention. Before we get to examine the thesis some ground clearing is required. In the next chapter I will defend a typology of reasons, with far-reaching implications regarding their normativity. The task of the present chapter is to vindicate the distinctness of the concept of normative reasons, and separate it from another, that of explanatory reasons. I will discuss practical reasons, though the lessons drawn here can readily be translated to apply to other normative reasons.

A normative practical reason is a fact that actions of a certain kind have properties that can give a point or a purpose to their performance, properties that make it possible for people to perform those actions because they possess them, and where actions so undertaken are intelligible because of that fact. Reasons, and this is a common view

---

[1] An early example is R. Edgeley's *Reason in Theory and Practice* (London: Hutchinson University Library, 1969). Another is H. Putnam. See e.g. his *Reason, Truth and History* (Cambridge: CUP, 1981), and various of the essays collected in *Realism with a Human Face* (Cambridge, Mass.: Harvard UP, 1990). For a more recent argument see J. Hampton, *The Authority of Reason* (Cambridge: CUP, 1998).

among writers on the subject, have a dual role here. They are both normative and explanatory. They are normative in as much as by endowing an action with a point or purpose they guide decision and action, and form a basis for their evaluation. They are explanatory in that when there is a reason for which an agent acted then that reason explains (features in an explanation of) that action. 'Reasons' has two meanings. When the term is used in one meaning it refers to a normative consideration, when used in the other it refers to an explanatory factor. I will start by trying to make good this claim (Sections 2 and 3), and (in Section 4) defend it against Broome's view that normative reasons are factors explaining 'ought-facts'. Finally, I will consider the way normative reasons figure in the explanations of action (Section 5). But first Section 1 introduces some preliminary background considerations in the shape of terminological conventions.

1. Background: mostly terminological

Our reason-related thought and discourse is supple and replete with distinctions, which almost always remain implicit. Even philosophers rarely try to make them explicit. There is no need to introduce completely articulated definitions. Our implicit under-standing of them would suffice for most purposes, and further clarifications will be offered only where needed. My purpose in this section is merely to draw attention to a few of those distinctions.

Think for example of the following three propositions: 'The beauty of its buildings and canals is a reason to visit Venice'; 'The art treasures in its museums are a reason to visit Venice'; 'The risk of pollution and flood damage is a reason to visit Venice'. I will assume that all three are true. Yet we have here only two, not three, reasons to visit Venice. The beauty of the city and the treasures of its museums are each an indepen-dent reason to visit it. The risk to the city and its treasures is not in itself an additional reason, not in itself a reason at all, one may say. Rather, it is part of each of the other two. We can analyse in different ways the effect of the threat to Venice on a more precise specification of the reasons for visiting it. But such classifications of elements in reasons have limited use, and different classifications would be appropriate for different purposes. So none will be offered here.[2] The important point for our purposes is that when stating that the risk of pollution and flood damage is a reason to visit Venice one is not presenting the risk as a 'complete' and independent reason to visit Venice. Rather, one is referring to a reason of which this is an element. The statement can be taken as equivalent to saying 'There is a reason to visit Venice and part of it is the risk...' with the implication that the reason is for a visit in the near future.

By the same token when I say 'The treasures in its museums are a reason to visit Venice' I refer to a reason of which the fact that there are treasures in the museums in Venice is but a part. It follows, given reasonable assumptions, that I may not know all

---

[2] I did offer a general scheme in *Practical Reason and Norms* (1975; current edn. Oxford: OUP, 1999). J. Dancy suggested a somewhat different one in *Ethics Without Principles* (Oxford: OUP, 2004).

the details of the reasons. For example, when you ask me: 'do you mean that we have reason to go there next week' I may well reply that I do not know. Next week is Easter week and possibly the museums (or a number of them) will be closed. But clearly the reason is a reason to visit Venice in order to visit its museums, so that there is no reason to visit it if doing so cannot facilitate visiting its museums.

The example shows that we possess an implicit understanding of criteria for identity of reasons. It does not follow that we possess a complete set of criteria for identity of reasons. If 'a complete set of criteria' means one which provides either a yes or a no answer to any question of the form 'is this reason the same as that reason?' then we do not possess such a set because none exists. While many questions of the form: 'do these propositions refer to one reason or to two?' have a ready answer, others have none at all. The identity of reasons is not fully determined. For practical purposes this makes no difference and that is why no criteria exist.[3] This observation reflects the fact that the concept we are trying to elucidate is a common concept, not a philosophical term of art, and while theoretical reflection involves making explicit much that is only implicit in the way the concept features in thought and discourse, it has no business reforming the concept, or reshaping it, except to the extent that this is inevitable.[4]

The incompleteness of the criteria for identity not only makes counting the number of reasons present a pointless and often an impossible exercise, it makes any reference to 'a complete reason' somewhat suspect. If I use the expression occasionally it is to say that certain elements belong with any complete reason (or any complete reason of a certain kind) meaning that they are necessary parts of any reason (or any reason of that kind).

One important kind of relations among reasons that may contribute to the incompleteness of their criteria of identity is their transitiveness. Why is it the case that (a) the beauty of Venice is a reason to visit it? Because it means that (b) being there is being in a beautiful place, and one has reason to be in beautiful places. On the one hand (b) explains (a). It explains in virtue of what (a) is a reason. On its face (b) is a second reason. However, the force or strength of the reason we have to visit Venice is not the combined force of (a) and (b) but is the same as the force of either one of them (and—other things being equal—they are of equal force). That inclines one to think of them as but one reason. The case for neither view is conclusive. An aspect of a reason can explain why it is a reason (given the puzzle that generates the need for an explanation) and the force of two different reasons is not always greater than the

---

[3] The same is true of intentions, a significant analogy given that action with intention is action for a (supposed) reason.

[4] A feeling for a properly regimented landscape encourages a philosophical propensity to avoid ambiguities, and reduce multiplicity of forms to one. For a subtle example see S. Everson's 'What is a Reason for Action' (in C. Sandis (ed.), *New Essays on the Explanation of Action* (Basingstoke: Palgrave Macmillan, 2009)), 22, considering whether reasons are states or events, etc. In this, as in previous writings, I remain indifferent to the systematizing propensity, when it does not yield illumination. I refer to many things, events, states, etc., as (practical) reasons, assuming always that such formulations when true are so in virtue of their relations to properties of the action for which they are reasons (e.g. that they facilitate actions with those properties).

force of the stronger among them. We are again confronting a case where identity criteria are incomplete, because there is no real issue that depends on them.

2. On explanatory reasons

Whatever provides a (correct) answer to questions about the reasons why things are as they are, become what they become, or to any other reason-why question, is a Reason. Reason-why questions seek explanations and whatever provides or constitutes an explanation is the reason why whatever it explains is as it is. Needless to say I am not proposing a grammatical test. Reason-why questions can be asked without using those words. We can ask 'what is the reason for the deformation?', or 'what explains the deformation?', or use other words. What is important is the distinction between providing (or purporting to provide) information ('It is 4 p.m.', 'She is in Sydney') and providing (or purporting to provide) explanations. Reasons provide explanations. Some writers take propositions to provide explanations, and therefore to be reasons. As false propositions explain nothing I will join those who take facts to be explanatory reasons. One reason to take propositions (rather than facts) to be explanatory reasons is that logical and conceptual relations hold among propositions regardless of their truth. But, as such relations also hold among facts, it is well worth preserving the core idea (that reasons explain) even at the cost of occasional complexity (due to the inability to rely on unrestricted inferential relations) or awkwardness of expression.

Facts are reasons why; that is, they are not reasons in themselves, but reasons why something is thus and so. They are reasons in as much as they provide an explanation. Possibly, any fact is a reason for something or other. For every fact there may be a reason-why question, in a correct reply to which it figures non-redundantly. To refer to a fact as an explanatory reason is to refer, at least implicitly, to a relation it has to something else: it is a reason why this or that happened, and so on.

Arguably, explanations are also relative to the person(s) for whom they are intended. An explanation is a good one if it explains what it sets out to explain in a way that is accessible to its addressees, that is in a way that the addressees could understand were they minded to do so, given who they are and what they could reasonably be expected to do in order to understand it. However, there is a clear distinction between the two relativities. No useful information is conveyed by a proposition of the form: this fact is a reason. One needs to specify something about what it explains to convey any useful information (e.g., 'this fact explains something about the origin of life'). On the other hand, while the criteria for an explanation being a good one are relative to its addressees, its character as an explanation is not. An explanation of the nature of laser radiation suitable for university students is an explanation of laser radiation, even when addressed to primary school children for whom it is not a good explanation. Explanatory reasons are so in virtue of their relations to what they explain, and stating that a fact is a reason is stating that it stands in the explanatory relation to what it is a reason for.

As can be seen I am using 'reason' to refer to any fact that figures (non-redundantly) in an explanation, and not merely to the totality of facts all of which figure (non-redundantly) in an explanation. It is tempting to call the totality of all the facts that figure non-redundantly in an explanation a complete reason. I may occasionally use the term in order to avoid complex formulations. But if taken literally it implies more than is established and possibly more than is true: it implies that there is at least one comprehensive way of individuating facts, such that relative to any such scheme of individuation and object of explanation, it is either true or not, regarding each fact, that it belongs to the explanation of that object. There is reason to doubt that the explanation relation is such that it is ever true that regarding any object of explanation there is a set of explanatory facts such that it explains that object, and that adding any other fact to it is redundant so far as that explanation goes. It seems that our ways of individuating facts and the notion of explanation are such that any explanation can always be non-redundantly amplified, clarified, and expanded.

We should therefore take talk of complete explanation with a pinch of salt. There are, however, two important points. First, that even if there are no 'complete reasons' there may be alternative reasons, that is alternative successful explanations of the same object, which are not in competition with each other, so that each is an independent explanation of the object. Second, that normally in advancing or citing reasons, non-trivial parts of 'complete' reasons are cited as (asserted to be) reasons, and by so citing them the speaker implicitly refers to 'a complete reason' (or to a disjunction of complete reasons), of which they are a constituent part, as the reason (for whatever they are meant to explain). We can state this point while avoiding reference to the completeness of any reason: In stating 'that R is the reason for P' we refer to a (possibly complex) fact {R} which includes R, and state that it explains P.

Suppose I say: 'The heat wave was the reason for his collapsing', and you reply: 'That is not so. He would not have collapsed had it been less humid'. What sort of disagreement is this? You are probably pointing out that the heat does not explain his collapse by itself. It explains it only in the context of certain other facts, and it may be useful to mention some others of them (or not, as the case may be). So we do not disagree about the explanation, merely about which features of it are worth mentioning. It would have been otherwise had you said: 'No. He collapsed because he was struck by a bullet.' In that case we would have been advancing rival explanations. As it is we both referred to the same explanation by citing different parts of it.[5]

3. Normative reasons

The preceding observations explain why explanatory reasons are not much discussed by philosophers. Whatever one can say about them is better explored when studying

---

[5] All these considerations apply, *mutatis mutandis*, to normative reasons.

explanations, a voluminous philosophical subject. Explanatory reasons are mostly discussed, or at least mentioned, by philosophers interested in normativity, who consider whether there is a second sense to 'reasons', such that in that sense 'reasons' refer or purport to refer to what I will call normative reasons. Is there a second sense to 'reasons', and if so are there such reasons? Put in different terms: are there normative reasons, and are normative reasons, if there are such, reasons independently of being explanatory reasons? Are they reasons of a different kind?

This is not the same as to ask whether all reasons are explanatory reasons. I have already acknowledged that they are: it is likely that all facts, I said, can figure in some explanation or another. I will continue to assume that all reasons are facts, and when we refer to other things as reasons, the references can be recast as references to facts,[6] hence all reasons are explanatory reasons. That does not, however, establish the univocality of 'reasons'. It is possible that there are facts that are reasons in a different sense while being also explanatory reasons. That they are reasons in a different sense can perhaps be established by the fact that they can explain (at least some of) what they can explain because they are reasons in a different sense of the word.

I will argue that there is a second sense to 'reasons'. When the context requires disambiguating my meaning, I will refer to reasons in this second sense as normative reasons. I will suggest that their character as normative reasons enables them to play a certain explanatory role, and thus that the way they function as explanatory reasons presupposes that they are also reasons in a different sense.

It is generally agreed that the notion of a normative reason cannot be explained through an eliminative definition. That is, any explanation of it in which the word 'reason' does not occur will include another term or phrase whose meaning is close to that of 'a reason', so that those who puzzle over the nature of reasons will not be helped by the definition. It will raise similar puzzles in their minds. We explain the notion of a normative reason by setting out its complex interrelations to other concepts. Not to explain, but to minimally locate what we are talking about, we can say that normative reasons, if there are such, count in favour of that for which they are reasons. They have the potential to (that is, they may) justify and require that which they favour.

Those who wish to deny that normative reasons are a distinct kind of reasons may claim that normative reasons are simply explanatory reasons that differ from others in providing explanations of a special kind of facts. After all, explanatory reasons are often classified by what they explain: individual events, or laws of nature; motivations or pains, etc. The distinctness of the object of explanation does not require different senses of 'reasons'. Reasons are just the facts that explain. Different kinds of facts may explain different kinds of phenomena but they explain them, and are reasons, in the same sense of 'explanation' and of 'reasons'.

---

[6] I do not mean to suggest that we do or should refer only to facts as reasons. I follow this usage for convenience' sake only, but by the same token not only facts can be taken to be explanatory reasons. For example, I refer to hypnosis as a reason in the text below.

If so-called normative reasons can favour, justify, or require, is it not simply a way of saying that they are the facts that explain why it is a fact that something is favoured, justified, or required? That is they are facts explaining why the proposition that this or that is favoured, justified, or required is true. If so does it not follow that there is no different sense of reason here, only a different object of explanation? But normative reasons do not always justify or require what they favour. Nor is it always the case that what they favour is (non-relationally) favoured. That depends on what else is true of it. When they neither justify nor require it, they cannot explain why it is justified or required. And when what they favour is not (non-relationally) favoured they cannot explain why it is favoured.

Can we do better by modifying the suggestion: would not those reasons explain why what they favour is favoured by them? Only if one thinks that a fact can explain itself; or if you like, only in the Pickwickian sense in which that A favours B explains why B is favoured by A. Clearly here talking of explanation is otiose. In any case it does not dispose of the claim that normative reasons do something other than explain. Their explanatory use is secondary, and depends on the fact that they favour what they favour, a fact that sets them apart from other explanatory reasons. The existence of a normative relation: that one thing is a reason for another, is, on this suggestion, the object of the explanation. But for there to be something to explain there must be normative reasons, that is reasons in a sense that is independent of the explanatory sense of 'reasons'.

Does one fare any better by suggesting that 'P is a normative reason for A' just means that P explains why A is favoured (to a degree) by something? And does it explain this by displaying what it is that favours A, namely P? Again, that style of explanation presupposes that there is a normative relation of being a reason for something (in this case for A) and states what that reason is in the instant case (namely that P).[7]

Or consider another tack: if reasons for belief are reasons only in being explanatory reasons, what do they explain? The answer may appear obvious: they explain why the person who has the belief, has it. They explain his believing. If that is meant as a universal truth about explanations of believing, that is of why people who have a belief believe as they do, then it is false. For example, the reason Jamie believes a certain proposition may be neither the reasons there are for his belief, nor the reasons for it of whose existence he is or can become aware. The reason for his believing may be that he was hypnotized to believe it. But hypnotic suggestions are not reasons for belief. So while the reason for his believing may be that he was hypnotized that is not a reason for the belief, it is not a normative reason for believing that proposition.

Nor is it necessarily the case that the reasons to believe a proposition are the facts that explain that belief (that believing) if the belief is rational or rationally held. The reason

---

[7] The same point applies to the suggestion that reasons are facts that would explain why justified or required actions are justified or required. Here too the explanation would presuppose that the reasons which feature in the explanation, or some of them, are themselves normative reasons.

that explains the believing looks back to its causes (the causes of having it or of still having it). The rationality of believing depends on one's openness to critical evaluation of the belief, one's ability and willingness to revise or reject it were the evidence to point that way.

One may say that reasons for a belief are those facts that explain the believing, meaning the acquisition of the belief when it was rationally induced. But this view allows that 'reasons' is ambiguous between explanatory reasons, which, presumably, can explain all beliefs, and normative reasons for belief, which, among other things, explain those beliefs that were rationally arrived at, that is beliefs arrived at because of reasons for the beliefs (and the same can be said of the explanation of why one rationally sustains certain beliefs when the explanation invokes reasons for those beliefs).[8] Regarding the latter kind of reasons their ability to explain the believing depends on the fact that they are normative reasons, reasons that can justify a belief, whether or not they also explain it, and they explain beliefs as rational or justified because they are normative reasons.

It is relevant here that we regularly refer to reasons for belief independently of any explanatory context, i.e. when reasoning about what to believe, which is not the same as reasoning about what would explain the belief once we have it (for reasons given below - reasoning what to believe is not to be confused with reasoning about what one ought to believe).

4. Normative reasons and ought-propositions— Broome's reasons

One concept that is beyond doubt a normative concept and has often been taken as the normative concept par excellence is that expressed by 'ought' (when used in its primary meaning). It is therefore not surprising that if one thinks that reasons are explanations, and nothing but, then one would be tempted to claim that they are nothing but facts that can explain what one ought to do, to believe, etc. That is the line taken by John Broome, and I will consider that hypothesis by considering his view. My discussion of Broome's view has two objects: first, to understand why ought is not the basic concept; second, to explain why Broome's understanding of reasons is partial and misleading.[9]

Broome's view revolves around two theses:[10]

---

[8] This remark assumes that rationality has to do with the ability to discern and respond to reasons, a view explained and defended in Chapter Five.
[9] Broome formulates his thesis with reference to ought-facts. I will use the more common terminology of true ought-propositions, meaning true propositions that can be expressed in sentences contain an ought operator (used in its primary meaning).
[10] J. Broome, 'Reasons', in R. J. Wallace et al., *Reason and Value* (Oxford: OUP, 2004).

A) Some reasons are perfect reasons: 'A perfect reason for you to Φ is... a fact that explains why you ought to Φ'.

B) Other reasons are *pro tanto* reasons: 'A *pro tanto* reason for you to Φ is a fact that plays the for-Φ role in a potential or actual weighing explanation of why you ought to Φ, or in a potential or actual weighing explanation of why it is not the case that you ought to Φ and not the case that you ought not to Φ'. ('Reasons', 41)

The first thing to note about the theses is that they are consistent with the view that 'reason' has two meanings: an explanatory and a normative one. Arguably only facts that constitute normative reasons can explain true ought-propositions.[11] Furthermore, my view of normative reasons is more than merely consistent with the claim that normative reasons explain (that they are part of an explanation of) the truth of true ought-propositions; it entails it.

Broome seems to think that the reasons normally thought of as normative reasons are facts that explain ought-propositions in a special way. He calls them '*pro tanto*' reasons and claims that they feature in weighting explanations:

[T]here are reasons for you to Φ and reasons for you not to Φ. Each reason is associated with a number that represents its weight. The numbers associated with the reasons to Φ add up to more than the numbers associated with the reasons not to Φ. That is why you ought to Φ. ('Reasons', 36–7)

He relaxes these conditions: weight need not be exact and the function of total weight from component weights need not be additive. Even so, Broome's explanation of *pro tanto* reasons combines two elements. First, these reasons come with weights, and what one ought to do is some function of those weights. Second, there being reasons for something entails the possibility of the existence of a reason against that very thing. I am not aware of any ought-proposition that can be explained by reference to weights in the way suggested by Broome. The very notion of an associated weight is hard to make sense of. Be that as it may, it seems plain that weights play no role in our understanding of many reasons for actions which are not conclusive ones, but which contribute to the determination of what to do.

Broome does not offer any justification for the weight-related view of *pro tanto* reasons, unless one takes his reference to the use of weighing and balancing metaphors by various writers as a justification. But metaphors are exactly that. I regularly write about one reason defeating another. But that is hardly a reason to attribute to me the view that conflicting reasons are opposing fighters, who engage in some form of combat. I have suggested that the non-metaphorical point is that in deliberating

---

[11] It is true, though, that all perfect reasons, that is, all explanations of *why* one ought to do this or that, or to believe this or that, will include elements that are not normative reasons. As I will explain below, they all require closure propositions, that is, propositions to the effect that nothing defeats the conclusion, and closure propositions are not themselves propositions of reasons. So, if, as Broome stipulates, 'perfect reasons' explain true ought-propositions then—and this is my view—they include some normative reasons, and some other elements.

about what one ought to do, propositions about various reasons are relevant, and it is by reasoning from them, and about their interrelations and so on, that the conclusion is drawn.[12] Given that the claim about weights is not essential to the thesis that reasons are just explanatory facts, I will ignore it.

The second element in the definition of *pro tanto* reasons is that they are normative reasons that can be defeated. Broome rightly points to a difference in the logical standing of (what I regard as) different normative reasons. Some are such that there cannot be any reasons that conflict with them. Others, his '*pro tanto* reasons', do not have that feature, that is, that being a reason for something is consistent with there being a reason against that very thing. The contrast is real and significant. But so are many other distinctions between types of reasons. Arguably, the difference between epistemic and practical reasons is more fundamental, but both are normative reasons.[13] There is no reason to think that normative reasons are confined to those that manifest either of the features by which Broome defines *pro tanto* reasons. I conclude that Broome's distinction between *pro tanto* and perfect reasons does not contribute to our understanding of normative reasons, and need not be further considered here.

I shall argue that Broome's account misconceives the relations of ought and reasons. First, according to Broome, normative reasons are *mere* explanations of why ought-propositions are or are not true. It is worth remembering that, as Broome rightly points out, the explanation relation between explaining and explained facts is not itself normative. But according to him there is nothing normative in the explaining facts either. Reasons are correctly labelled 'normative' when and because they feature in the explanation of ought-facts, and nothing more. Their normativity, as it were, exhausts itself in being such explanations. One way of describing the point is to say that according to Broome there are no reasons that are in themselves normative. Second, and perhaps as a result, Broome misunderstands the nature of ought-propositions.

Instead of a direct explanation of the ways normative reasons are normative, too large a task for the present chapter, I will illustrate Broome's mistake by pointing to two contexts in which the point of referring to reasons does not depend on their explanatory role. First, in cases of akrasia people act for what they believe to be the lesser reason. For akrasia to be possible it must be possible that they are right in that belief.[14] So imagine cases in which they are right. I knowingly act for a lesser reason. I am not acting as I ought to act, and I know it. But I am acting for a (genuine) reason. It is merely one that, as I am aware, is defeated in the circumstances. The reason for which I act is a normative reason, and it explains my action. Its being a normative reason and its success in explaining my action, which is due to its ability to motivate me, as

---

[12] See *Practical Reason and Norms*, ch. 1.

[13] See Chapter Three below.

[14] While a person who acts on what he thinks is the lesser reason, but is mistaken about this, and the reason he follows is the better reason, is akratic, it seems pointless if not meaningless to attribute akrasia to creatures who are unable to tell which reasons are better, and are inevitably mistaken in all their beliefs about the relative strength of reasons.

normative reasons can, do not depend on its contribution to the explanation of any ought-proposition, not even to the explanation of the falsity of any such proposition. This shows that, even though normative reasons may contribute to the explanation of some true ought-propositions, their relevance in cases of akrasia goes beyond any such contribution.

The second example is drawn from a case recognized by Broome. He mentions that sometimes it is not the case that one ought to Φ, nor is it the case that one ought not to Φ. As he says, such cases may belong to different subcategories ('Reasons', 38–9). In some there are no normative reasons either for or against Φ-ing. In others there are reasons pro and con Φ-ing which do not defeat one another. Here the existence of normative reasons is essential to elucidate the difference between these two types of case, though there is no difference between them regarding which ought-propositions apply to them. Again, we see that normative reasons do more than explain ought-propositions.[15]

These reflections point to the nature of the relations between reasons and ought-propositions, which I will sketch in rough metaphorical terms. Normative reasons are facts that have normative bearing or force. They are called 'reasons' because they can serve as stepping-stones in reasoning about what to believe or what to do. Deliberating from the reasons that apply to us we become aware of the attractions and drawbacks of options. We may reach a variety of conclusions: that we have a duty to do something (and we may have duties that we ought not to fulfil); that we have a right to do something; that certain options are acceptable (we may have a right to do unacceptable things); that it would be prudent to take some actions; that it would be irrational not to take them; and others. One such conclusion, different from any of the ones I mentioned, is that we ought to take some action. Ought-propositions are not the centre of practical thought. Nor are they the foundations on the basis of which we can understand reasons. Rather, they are one of a variety of propositions whose truth conditions include the existence or absence of some normative reasons or others.[16]

There is one particular factor that complicates the explanation of ought-propositions. Let us focus on propositions of the form: 'When C, P ought to Φ' (where 'C' stands for circumstances, 'P' for a person, or a set of people, and 'Φ' for an action, a doing, or an omission). When such propositions are very specific they state what one has conclusive reason to do. For example: that John Doe ought to give Jane Roe £5 by midnight is true only if there is a conclusive reason for John Doe to give Jane Roe £5 by midnight.

---

[15] Chapter Eight will provide further illustrations of Broome's misunderstanding of the relations of reasons and ought, which led to his mistaken explanation of instrumental rationality.

[16] On many occasions there is no conclusive reason to do any of the actions open to us (as naturally presented when debating what to do). We may have undefeated reasons to stay at home and carry on with the novel we started last week, but also undefeated reasons to visit our cousin, or to perform any of a number of other feasible actions. In such cases there is nothing we ought to do.

But this is not true of general ought-propositions. This is particularly clear regarding universal ought-propositions. Here are a few examples: 'People ought to pay their debts punctually'; 'People ought to be kind to their grandparents'; 'One ought to vote in parliamentary elections'. Those who believe these and similar propositions do not necessarily believe that there are always conclusive reasons to be kind to one's grandparents, to repay debts punctually, or to vote in parliamentary elections. At the very least it should be clear that compliance with these three ought-propositions may on occasion conflict: On a particular day it may be the case that one would not be able to vote in the election if one were to pay one's debt punctually and vice versa.

There are two kinds of universal ought-propositions that are true only if there are conclusive reasons to behave as they indicate: First, there are conceptually true propositions of that kind. If murder is unjustified intentional homicide then 'One ought not to murder' is true because there is always a conclusive reason not to murder, and, on our assumption, that is a conceptually necessary truth. Second, there may be some so-called moral absolutes (or absolute reasons of other kinds), namely reasons (or combinations of reasons) that defeat all possible (combinations of) conflicting reasons. For example, possibly it is true that 'In all states the law ought to prohibit torture, without qualification', meaning among other things that all governments ought to see to it that their law prohibits torture. But most universal ought-propositions do not belong to either kind. Are they all false?

One cannot respond that they are implicitly relative. 'One ought to vote in general elections' and 'so far as one's civic duties are concerned one ought to vote in general elections' are distinct propositions, and in any case even the relativized proposition could be true even though it is not the case that in so far as one's civic duties only are concerned one always has a conclusive reason to vote in general elections. Sometimes one's civic duties require abstaining. The same will be true of any non-conceptually necessary relativization.

Nor can one maintain that universal ought-propositions are abbreviations of very detailed propositions that include a complete list of exceptions, all the circumstances in which one does not have a conclusive reason to act as the proposition indicates. It is plausible to think that while one can have complete knowledge and understanding of (the content of) ought-propositions, no one can know all the exceptions (i.e. that no one can know either a list of them or a generalization stating them that is not true merely on logical or conceptual grounds). Hence the propositions normally expressed by universal ought-propositions are what they appear to be. They are not (identical with) detailed propositions listing all the cases, or circumstances, in which one need not do what the proposition states that one ought to do.

It is one of the virtues of the concept of normative reasons that it enables us to think about normatively complex and indefinitely changeable situations, helping us to marshal their normatively significant features into forms that facilitate coherent deliberation. So how are universal ought-propositions related to specific ones and to reasons? I think that propositions of the form 'When C, P ought to Φ' are true only in the case that, and because, there is a reason (or a number of reasons) which applies whenever C is the case, and which in at least some instances of C is a conclusive reason for P to Φ.[17] On this view it is a conceptual truth that there are normative reasons that explain why one ought to Φ, when one ought to. This account of the truth conditions of practical ought-propositions[18] specifies the same truth conditions for specific and for universal ought-propositions. It is merely that as specific propositions apply only to one occasion they are true only if on that occasion there is a conclusive reason to do as they indicate.

It follows that ought-propositions, unlike propositions about reasons, are always sensitive to options available in the situations to which they apply. I have reason to see the new Almodóvar film. Full stop. That is true even if, as it may turn out, I never have the option to see it. But I have a conclusive reason (and thus I ought) to see that film only if there will be an occasion on which seeing the film is an available option, and the reason to see it defeats the reasons (if there are any) for following alternative available options. A conclusive reason is one that defeats all competing reasons (if there are any), namely all the reasons for each of the available options.[19]

It is far from clear whether this account provides an adequate explanation of ought-propositions. It seems to involve a degree of regimentation of the meaning of sentences. It may be too simple to capture the nuanced ways in which 'ought' is standardly used, and therefore to account for the nuanced differences among propositions in whose expression it features (though many of them may be due to conversational implicatures). Possibly the explanation above does provide the core of a comprehensive account of the meaning of 'ought'-propositions, and all that is required to complete it is to identify the various ways in which other 'ought'-propositions relate to it. Think, e.g. of the following: 'Toasters ought to toast bread', 'Acorns ought to grow into oak trees', 'Mature beefsteak tomatoes ought to be large, juicy and fresh tasting', 'The past tense of "fight" ought to be "fighted"'. They differ in many ways: some are about what ought to be—others about 'ought to Φ' where 'Φ' is an action verb; some are about the functioning of artefacts, some about natural kinds, others relate to grammatical conventions. Yet they all share the existence of a norm (i.e. the fact that something, a certain regularity however complex, is normal) in the background, and all express the thought that the norm 'entitles' one to expect something, that in so far as the norm (i.e. the fact of that regularity) is concerned, in so far as one knows nothing relevant but what is normal, one has reason to believe something to be the case.[20]

---

[17] Note that I am referring to simple unqualified ought-propositions (displaying the general form 'X ought to Φ' or 'when C, X ought to Φ'). Their meaning varies when qualified: one always ought to Φ may mean that one's reason for Φ-ing is always conclusive, etc.

[18] First suggested by me in the Introduction to Raz (ed.), *Practical Reasoning* (Oxford: OUP, 1978).

[19] This is one, but not the only, reason why X ought to do A and X ought to do B does not entail X ought to do A&B—doing both may not be an available option.

[20] It need not be sufficient to warrant belief, or it may warrant only the weaker belief that probably something is the case.

Of course, given that, as I know, my toaster has been broken for months I have no reason to believe that my toaster will toast, but even it ought to toast, expressing the thought that had I no other relevant information, what is normal of toasters will have given me reason to think that it will toast. Similarly what is normal of the formation of the past tense would have given me reason to think that 'fighted' is the past of 'fight', had I known nothing else. As it is I know better. I point to the fact that the case deviates from the norm, that 'fight' is an irregular verb, by stating what reason the norm gives one. Intention and context establish that various uses of 'ought'-sentences do convey different information (that the norm is so and so, that the case conforms to it, that it deviates from it, etc.), but in all cases the information is conveyed by expressing the proposition that given the norm on its own one has reason to believe that…I mention these possibilities to indicate the potential of my account to serve as the core of a general account of 'ought'. But whether or not it does, it does explain why practical ought-propositions cannot play any foundational role in understanding practical thought.[21]

5. The normative/explanatory *nexus*

It seems plausible to assume that reasons in both senses are called 'reasons' because of their connection to Reason. But there is a closer connection between them that explains the common name. Briefly, it is that normative reasons provide the standard explanations of beliefs and of actions done with an intention or a purpose. Moreover, it is a necessary condition of any fact being a reason that, when conditions are appropriate, it provides such an explanation. Put another way, epistemic reasons can explain (or figure in an explanation of) beliefs, and practical reasons can explain (or figure in an explanation of) actions performed with an intention or purpose.

This point is generally recognized, though sometimes neglected. It expresses the thought that normative reasons can guide agents, that is that they can move agents, who are aware of them, to action, belief, and the like. Hence they can feature in explanations of such actions, beliefs, and the like.[22] In further exploring that idea I will

---

[21] Broome offers a few examples of explanations of ought-propositions that do not include normative reasons ('Reasons', 43–7). They all depend on his characterization of normative reasons as coming with weights. For example, he writes:

You ought not to believe that it is Sunday and that it is Wednesday. A plausible explanation of why not is that 'It is Sunday' and 'It is Wednesday' are contrary propositions and you ought never to believe both a proposition and its contrary. (ibid. 42–3)

He rightly points out that no weights are involved in this piece of reasoning. But if it were true (which it is not, as will be explained in Chapter Eight) that you ought never to believe both a proposition and its contrary, then there is a normative reason for not believing that it is Sunday and that it is Wednesday. Whatever establishes that you ought not have contrary beliefs is also a reason for not having these two beliefs. Once we use 'reasons' in the normal way, to enable us to refer to all normative reasons, the counter-examples disappear.

[22] The characterization given is imprecise. To give but one example: suppose that a fact cannot guide because it is impossible for people to believe in it, but would be capable of guiding, and therefore of figuring in an explanation of actions, were it possible to believe in it. Is it a reason (at least so far as the stated condition

not be looking for a characterization of the causal or other mechanisms on the existence of which these explanations depend. I will merely try to characterize the kind of explanation involved. We can start the exploration in the company of Bernard Williams, since the point was crucial to his argument for reason internalism.[23]

How do normative reasons explain and what do they explain? Following Williams I will explore this regarding practical reasons only. Similar considerations apply to epistemic reasons. Obviously, reasons for an action do not always explain the action, even when it was performed. It may have happened accidentally, and even when intentional and performed for a reason, the intention may have been motivated by something else, either by some other reason for that action or by a mistaken belief that there is some other reason. So the point is not that whenever one does what there is a reason to do one acts for that reason. Nor is it that there are no other, non-reason-related, explanations for an action (hypnosis, statistical explanations, and others). Rather the point is that normative reasons must be capable of providing an explanation of an action: If that R is a reason to Φ then it must be possible that people Φ for the reason that R and when they do, that explains (is part of an explanation of) their action. Or, as Williams puts the point:

If there are reasons for action, it must be that people sometimes act for those reasons, and if they do their reasons must figure in some correct explanation of their action.[24]

Furthermore, the role reasons play in the explanation must be of a certain form. If that R is a reason to Φ, then it must be possible that awareness that R motivated the agent to Φ, that is: that R motivated the agent (who was aware of the fact) to Φ. Sometimes the phrase 'motivating reasons' is invoked in such contexts. I will not use it myself, for it is liable to confuse. Sometimes the phrase is used to refer to a kind of explanatory reasons for actions, those that explain them by pointing out that they were motivated by belief in the existence of a (normative) reason. That sense is much narrower than the natural understanding of the phrase (motivating reasons being reasons explaining actions by their motivations).[25]

---

is concerned)? Whichever conclusion one comes to on this and similar issues is likely to be stipulative, or if you like, explicative, that is going beyond explaining existing concepts, and involving their modification for theoretical purposes. It need be none the worse for that. The important point is that to say of a fact that it is a reason for an action is not merely to say that it shows the action to have some good, some point to it. It is to say something like that it can rationally guide an agent towards that action.

[23] I will not consider the merits of any form of internalism or externalism about reasons, nor Williams's own argument for internalism. Like some other writers I think that the contrast is more confusing than helpful. My own view will be clear enough. Its classification as a form of internalism or externalism is immaterial.

[24] Bernard Williams, 'Internal and External Reasons', in *Moral Luck* (Cambridge: CUP, 1981), 102.

[25] See J. Dancy, *Practical Reality* (Oxford: OUP, 2000), 6: 'I have characterised the distinction between the reasons why we do things and the reasons in favour of doing them in terms of the motivating and normative. In doing so I have tried to avoid any suggestion that we are dealing here with two sorts of reasons....the same reason can be both motivating and normative. A reason for acting can be the reason why one acted'.

Back to business: what is important for our purpose is not that facts that are normative reasons can explain (that they can figure in the explanation of) actions. Just about any fact *can* (given appropriate circumstances) figure in some explanation of some actions. The normative/explanatory *nexus*—as I call it—requires that the potential explanatory role of facts that are *normative reasons* depends on and presupposes their normative force: it has to be that they can explain because they are normative reasons, and by being normative reasons. That I promised can explain my promise-keeping action in a way in which the impact of low atmospheric pressure cannot. No doubt being in the mountains where atmospheric pressure is low can explain some aspects of my conduct, but the explanation (assuming the normal scenario) is of a completely different kind.

What is this special way in which normative facts figure in explanations? My promise explains my promise-keeping action in the right way when awareness of the fact that I promised includes recognition of it as a reason for the action, and I take the action to be sensible because it is supported, perhaps even required, by my promise. The low pressure affects me independently of whether I am aware of it, and regardless of what I think of it. The **normative/explanatory** *nexus* holds that every normative reason can feature in an explanation of the action for which it is a reason, as a fact that, being recognized for what it is,[26] motivated the agent to perform the action, so that the agent guided its performance in light of that fact.

This last condition, that through awareness of the reason the agent guides the performance, and does not merely initiate it, is taken for granted in common reason-explanations of actions, but is sometimes ignored to their detriment by more formal philosophical accounts. Harry Frankfurt pointed out its importance, and Kieran Setiya suggested that it solves the problem of deviant causation (so far as basic actions are concerned) that afflicts accounts of intentional action such as Davidson's.[27]

Williams explains an important aspect of this *nexus*. To see it we need to remind ourselves how Williams's view differs from that of some other Humeans. First, Williams finds no problem in the fact that reasons may be facts about how things are in the world and not only about the agents' beliefs and desires. Of course in that case they could figure in explanations of the agents' conduct only if those agents are aware of them. But that is consistent with the normative/explanatory *nexus* as he (and I) understand it. Furthermore, Williams does not object to the thought that beliefs can

---

[26] Notice that the *nexus* requires recognition, not mere belief. The belief must be properly related to the fact in virtue of which it is true, it cannot be merely accidentally true. I do not discuss here what that connection is. It is whatever makes it true that the agent recognizes the fact, is aware of it, etc. J. Hornsby takes the connection to require knowledge. See 'A Disjunctive Conception of Acting for Reasons', in A. Haddock and F. Macpherson (eds.), *Disjunctivism* (Oxford: OUP, 2008), 244. For a comment on Hornsby's general account see J. Dancy, 'How to Act—Disjunctively', in Haddock and Macpherson (eds.), *Disjunctivism*, 262. For reasons that will be evident below, my account of acting for a reason is not a version of disjunctivism.

[27] See H. Frankfurt, 'The Problem of Action', in *The Importance of What We Care About* (Cambridge: CUP, 1988), 69, 72ff., and K. Setiya, *Reasons Without Rationalism* (Princeton: Princeton UP, 2007), 31–2.

motivate. He does not endorse the view that only desires can be reasons, since only desires motivate, and therefore only they can explain actions in the right way. This is neither true, nor is it true to Williams's account. He allows, for example, that

there are some cases of an agent's Φ-ing because he believes that there is a reason for him to Φ, while he does not have any belief about what that reason is. ('Internal and External Reasons', 107)

More generally he asks:

Does believing that a particular consideration is a reason to act in a particular way provide, or indeed constitute, a motivation to act?…Let us grant that it does—this claim indeed seems plausible…' (ibid.)

The crux for Williams is not directly in the possibility of being motivated by one's beliefs but in the way one could acquire such motivating beliefs:

the basic point lies in recognising that the external reasons theorist must conceive in a special way the connexion between acquiring a motivation and coming to believe the reason statement. For of course there are various means by which the agent could come to have the motivation and also to believe the reason statement, but which are the wrong kind of means to interest the external reasons theorist. Owen [Wingrave—in James's story] might be so persuaded by his father's moving rhetoric that he acquired both the motivation and the belief. But this excludes an element which the external reasons theorist essentially wants, that the agent should acquire the motivation because he comes to believe the reason statement, and that he should do the latter, moreover, because in some way he is considering the matter aright. (ibid. 108-9)

This is indeed a required element. The initial thought that normative reasons must be capable of explaining is not that (taking the matter beyond Williams's example, but in the spirit of his remarks) one could accidentally come to be motivated by awareness of the reason. Awareness of the reason must non-accidentally motivate, and it must motivate, as Williams puts it, because the agent 'is considering the matter aright'.

But what is that way? Here we have to go beyond Williams, though without conflicting with what he says in the quoted passages. Williams's phrase 'considering…aright' suggests, first, that the explanation relates to rational agents, and depends on their exercise of their rational powers, and therefore (given the implausibility that the motivation can be generated in the right way by some external circumstances surrounding the believing) second, that the way that the belief has to explain the motivation is by having the content it has, by what it is a belief about.

This leads in several steps to the requirement that the reason itself figure in the explanation. *First*, the belief must be belief in the fact that is a reason, and include belief in its character as a reason. Motivations to perform a particular act would not be reliably and rationally brought about by a belief unless the belief was a belief about a reason to perform that act. *Second*, the belief itself must be explained by the existence of the reason, and it must be acquired or maintained in a rational way. Therefore, *third*, the reason itself figures in the explanation of the action. Ultimately one is motivated by the fact that is the reason, through the mediating belief, recognizing it as such. The reason is part of the explanation of the belief, which is why both it and the belief are motivating factors. And finally, *fourth*, the belief, the awareness of the reason (where it is rational and true) must not only prompt, but guide the action.

A typical objection relies on the fact that, as was pointed out at the beginning of the chapter, an act is intentional and done with a purpose even if the belief that motivated it is false. It follows, goes the objection, that the fact that renders the belief true (when it is true) cannot be part of the explanation of the action. It has, of course, to be admitted that when the belief is false (a) the action can be explained, and (b) its explanation as intentional must include reference to the belief that there was a reason for it (as was argued in the first point above), and (c) as that belief is false, no reason can be part of the explanation. So, regarding intentional actions based on false beliefs about the reasons for them, the explanation does not refer to any normative reason for the action. Even if there were such reasons they do not explain why the action was performed. However, the objection continues, if the belief alone is sufficient to explain intentional actions when it is false it must also be sufficient to explain actions when it is true. The further factor, the existence of the reason, is not necessary to the explanation which is, as is shown by the case of false beliefs, adequate without it.

Admittedly, citing the belief, without adding that it is rational and true, does explain the action, and shows it to be intentional. Furthermore, it is plausible to think that 'being an explanation of' is not a transitive relation. Sometimes even if C explains B and B explains A, C does not explain A. So even when the existence of the reason explains awareness of it as a reason, we need something additional to show that it can also explain action for that reason. But that is consistent with the possibility that an explanation that includes the reason among the explanatory factors is a better explanation of the intentional actions to which it applies. To be sure the reason is not part of the explanation of the action just by being an element in the explanation of the belief that prompts the action. It has to play a role in the explanation of the action itself, especially in its explanation as intentional.

The practice of explanation shows that in fact the reason does figure in explanations of actions: Why did I go to Chamonix for my holidays? Because it is so beautiful there. Why am I rushing to my office? Because I promised to meet a student there in ten minutes' time, etc. It is, however, one thing to know that reasons can figure in explanations of action, it is another to understand why this is so. Analogous considerations show that epistemic reasons can be part of the explanation of the belief (the believing) that they are reasons for, and that practical reasons can be part of the explanation of the action for which they are reasons.

Where a belief is held for reasons these reasons are relevant to its evaluation as warranted or otherwise, and therefore properly belong with the explanation of the believing. Analogously, when an action is taken for a reason that reason is relevant to the evaluation of the action, as an acceptable action, a rational or irrational one, and to the evaluation of the action in light of its consequences: is it a step in a direction that should be followed, or discontinued, should one apologize or compensate for it? And so on. Hence, where an action is taken for reasons the reasons contribute to its explanation, deepen our understanding of the action in ways that are relevant for its evaluation.

Nor can it be objected that explanations by reference to reasons are not part of ordinary explanations of believing or acting, that they are special explanations relevant only to those interested in the rationality or justification or some other evaluative aspect of the belief or action. On the contrary, reason-explanations explain action and belief by reference to their inherent features. After all, it is inherent in beliefs that those having them take them to be warranted, and would abandon them had they thought that they were unwarranted. Similarly, by their nature intentions to act involve belief in reasons for the intended action. Hence reason-explanations deepen our understanding of intentions, actions, and beliefs, by contributing to an understanding of whether they have the features that they purport to have.

It may clarify things if we return to explanations of actions done in the belief that there is reason (or that there is undefeated reason) for them when that belief is false. Observing common explanations offered in such cases we distinguish several types:

a) The agent did it because he believed that R
b) The agent did it because he mistakenly believed that R

(where 'R' has the required content for a reason-explanation). It would be a mistake to think that (b) is the same explanation as (a) because the reference to the fact that there was no R is explanatorily idle. Rather (b) is a more comprehensive explanation than (a). (a) is adequate to a certain range of interests in why the agent so acted. (b) is adequate for a wider, perhaps one may say here, deeper range of interests. Similarly when the belief that led to the action was true we still have two possible types of explanation:

a) The agent did it because he believed that R
c) The agent did it for R

((c) entails that he believed that R). (a) is still a good explanation, but for the reasons explained (c) is a better, more comprehensive explanation, one which answers a wider range of interests in the action.

Finally, to the fourth claim, that awareness of the reason must guide the action. I do not mean that otherwise the motivation would be irrational. There are many possible causal routes from a belief in a reason to motivation, which while not irrational, are adventitious. If normative reasons are to meet a meaningful explanatory potential requirement they must be capable of explaining through belief in their existence qua reasons. The element of guidance can be understood by analogy with a negative feedback mechanism: we, automatically and normally without being conscious of the fact, monitor the performance of the intentional action such that if it deviates from the course we implicitly take to lead to its successful completion we correct the performance, bringing it back to the correct path, or interrupt it, when we fail to correct it. So, the claim is that one's action is guided by a reason just in the case that one is motivated by the reason, through awareness of it, in a way that is manifested by the (normally unconscious) self-correcting process of tracking the success of the process of performing the action.

Another possible worry may be generated by my claim that reasons explain actions through the mediation of belief in the reasons *as reasons*. It may be thought that this implies possessing concepts and having beliefs that many people who act for reasons do not have. This worry, if justified, may not disprove the letter of the normative/ explanatory *nexus*. After all it requires nothing more than the possibility of certain explanations. But it would go against its spirit. For surely, the *nexus* is meant to relate to a standard form of explanation of actions undertaken for reasons. The worry is, however, unjustified.

Saying of people that they have certain concepts may mean either of two things. Perhaps it is better to say that there are two standards by which such claims are judged true. The lower standard requires having thoughts, which can be correctly described by propositions that involve the concepts. Having those thoughts is manifested by re-cognizing their implications, and being guided by them, reacting to them appropriately and trying to adjust our responses when becoming aware that they are inappropriate responses to those thoughts. The inferential connections between concepts and be-tween thoughts can be spelt out in general terms. We may say that there are principles that spell out these connections. Knowledge of such principles, however, is not required to meet this basic standard for concept possession. One has the concept if one follows the standards for its correct use even if one does not know what they are. This is typically manifested in 'normative behaviour', i.e. one judges different uses of the concept to be correct or incorrect, etc., without being able to provide a generali-zation (or being able to provide only a partial one). The higher standard of concept possession is one that requires ability to explain the concept, to articulate its implica-tions and inferential connections. That is it requires knowledge of the principles constitutive of the concepts. These are matters of degree. However, the basic standard for concept possession does not require such knowledge. This means that the gap between having concepts and knowing how to employ them, on the one hand, and being able to think about the principles that govern one's understanding of those concepts, on the other, is greater than may appear. I can treat a promise as a reason, and as we may say, implicitly know that it is a reason, without being able to understand any statement of the principle that sets out what I understand when I understand the notion of a promise. We are here in territory that was explored by Brandom, and using his terminology we may say that making things explicit is more difficult than is sometimes thought, for it may require additional concepts, concepts that one need not have to have the implicit knowledge. More fundamentally, Wittgenstein's rule-following argument establishes the priority of the lower standard. It establishes that the lower standard constitutes the necessary basic form of concept possession.[28]

Applying the distinction to normative reasons we could say that action for a reason requires ability to take certain facts to be reasons (e.g. it may require taking promises to be reasons, at least for those having the concept of a promise). It does not require being able to think about reasons in the abstract. I therefore conclude that it is justified to say that the normative/explanatory *nexus* does not require excessive conceptual mastery, nor excessive conceptual knowledge. As was already explained, the requirement that normative reasons explain through agents being aware of reasons as reasons is necessary to ensure that we refer to the right kind of explanation, and the right kind of explanation is explanation mediated by our rational faculties.

A final possible dissatisfaction I will mention here is that none of the above constitutes an explanation of the productive process that leads to awareness of the reason and from there to the motivation and the action. That is, of course, true, but I doubt that it is a drawback. Welcome as such explanations are, they are not needed for an understanding of the normative/explanatory *nexus*. Indeed so far as that goes they may do too much. As stated the *nexus* is sufficient, for those who understand it, to distinguish cases in which an action is done for a normative reason (and can be explained relying on the *nexus*) from other cases. It can be rightly pointed out that the ability to distinguish those cases made possible by the statement of the *nexus* is not sharp, that it leaves us undecided in many cases in ways that no further explanation can resolve. But that is just how things should be. The phenomena are not sharp because they are defined by our concepts, and our concepts are vague, leaving the phenomena they apply to vague.

The *nexus* helps with another puzzling problem that may have tilted some writers in a Humean direction. Is it not the case that if facts about the desirability or value of actions are reasons for actions then beliefs (in the existence of those reasons) must motivate? We can understand how beliefs motivate when they, as it were, attach one to a goal or desire that the agent already has, for example by pointing to a way of satisfying it. It is puzzling, however, how beliefs that are not related to pre-existing desires can motivate. Does it follow that if one is not motivated one does not have the belief? The preceding reflections showed that it is the facts, the reasons themselves that ultimately motivate. I do not deny that there may be difficulties in explaining how facts can motivate, but at least these are different difficulties, to do with the nature of values. As we saw, beliefs in the existence of reasons can also motivate, and sometimes they are the only explanation of the motivation there is (either because there are no reasons, and

---

[28] See L. Wittgenstein, *Philosophische Untersuchungen=Philosophical Investigations*, trans. G. E. M. Anscombe, P. M. S. Hacker, and J. Schulte, 4th edn. rev. P. M. S. Hacker and J. Schulte (Chichester: Wiley-Blackwell, 2009). Cf. G. P. Baker and P. M. S. Hacker, *Wittgenstein: Rules, Grammar and Necessity: Essays and Exegesis of 185–242*, vol. 2 of. *An Analytical Commentary on the Philosophical Investigations*, 2nd edn. extensively rev. P. M. S. Hacker, (Malden, Mass.: Wiley-Blackwell, 2010).

the beliefs are false, or because the agent does not know what they are, though he believes, or knows, that there are some). But the motivating power of these beliefs exists in the shadow of the motivating powers of the reasons. As the agent sees matters, it is as if there are reasons, and they motivate him, even when he does not know what they are, and even though they are not there.

This chapter has been concerned with the relations between explanatory and normative reasons, concerned to show how while normative reasons are explanatory reasons, they explain in a special way, explain by being normative. But it claimed more. The **normative/explanatory** *nexus* states that necessarily normative reasons can explain the actions, beliefs, and the like of rational agents.[29] Why is compliance with the *nexus* a necessary feature of normative reasons? For Williams the answer is simple: only if they comply with the *nexus* can reasons make a difference to agents.[30] If one calls other things reasons those other reasons are irrelevant to agents. This is true, but open to the rebuttal that the difference between normative reasons and other facts may matter in other ways than in being relevant to agents by being capable of guiding them. We need a broader explanation of what normative reasons are to assure us that we miss nothing in subjecting them to compliance with the *nexus*. Furthermore, we need an explanation of why the *nexus* is interpreted to apply to each individual agent and reason, that is it is understood to imply that the reasons an agent has on an occasion are reasons that, given an appropriate understanding of 'can', can explain his action on that occasion. The elements of such an explanation have already emerged. We can examine some of its contours by contrasting three possible situations:

Cold: when cold Rex warms himself by pacing around.

Meteorite: a meteorite struck Rex's neighbourhood just hours after he left. Everyone in the neighbourhood died. The behaviour of that kind of meteorite is well understood: their movements are completely random, and unpredictable. There is nothing that further research can reveal about them.

Rigoletto: Rex admires the opera, and learning that the current production is excellent he goes to watch it.

In all three cases Rex is on the right side, if I may put it so, of what is good. But only in *Rigoletto* does the story make clear that he acts for a reason. Indeed, the facts of the other cases do not even reveal whether Rex is a creature able to act for reasons. In **Cold**, if Rex is capable of acting for reasons he—normal circumstances assumed—paces about for a reason, namely to warm himself up. But animals that cannot act for

---

[29] The *nexus* deals with the vexed question of the relations between reasons and people's subjectivity. In *Engaging Reason* (Oxford: OUP 1999), ch. 5, I criticized claims that recognition of reasons must motivate. The *nexus* is part of an alternative account of the issue. Chapter Five below provides the rest.

[30] The argument is part of his case for internalism about reasons, where I do not follow him. His argument for internatlism relies on additional premises that are inconsistent with the arguments of this book.

reasons do the same, as might people in some conditions even if they are not able to act for reasons. That the action is good does not show that it was taken for a reason.

In **Meteorite** escaping the meteorite was not a reason for Rex to leave the neighbourhood. His escape was a lucky chance. If Rex is a person he may have left for a reason.

He may have believed that the meteorite will strike, in which case his belief may have explained his departure from the neighbourhood. Yet even though the belief would have been true the actual meteorite strike would not have explained his departure in the way required by the *nexus*. Furthermore, given that the motion of the meteorite was random it could not have explained his behaviour in the required way. Therefore, he did not have a reason to leave the neighbourhood in order to escape the meteor. To claim that the impending meteorite strike was a reason for him to leave is to confuse what is good with what one has reason to do. The value of actions is a reason for them, but only when it can guide them, and it can guide them only if it can explain their conduct. Otherwise, we are simply lucky if we do what is good and unlucky if we do what is bad.

The *nexus* requires that reasons can explain agents' beliefs or actions or emotions in a special way: In their exercise of their rational powers, agents are led to awareness of the facts that are reasons qua reasons, and to rational reaction to this awareness. The broader explanation of reasons, and of the *nexus*, must await Chapter Five, in which the relations of reasons, rationality, and normativity are explored.

3

Reasons: Practical and Adaptive

Ultimately the aim is to explain normativity by explaining the character of and the relations between Reason and reasons. Possible obstacles on the road to the goal are the fundamental differences between some types of reasons, differences we notice most readily when comparing reasons for action and epistemic reasons. The present chapter considers some of these differences, using them to illuminate a major division between types of normative reasons,[1] which I will call 'adaptive' and 'practical' reasons. A few clarifications of some aspects of the concept of epistemic reasons will lead to a distinction between standard and non-standard reasons (Section 1). Some differences between epistemic and practical reasons will be described and explained in Section 2, paving the way to generalizing the contrast and explaining the differences between adaptive and practical reasons (Section 3). Sections 4 and 5 further explain and defend the views of the preceding sections. In the course of these discussions the toxin problem and the 'right kind of reason' problem are resolved.[2]

1. Standard and non-standard reasons

Reasons for action, I will assume, are facts that constitute a case for (or against) the performance of an action. Epistemic reasons are reasons for believing in a proposition through being facts that are part of a case for (belief in) its truth (call such considerations 'truth-related'). These maxims (as I shall call them) have proved controversial.[3] Confining myself to the epistemic maxim two clarifications and one argument may help.

---

[1] I will generally use 'reasons' to refer to normative reasons, adding the adjective only occasionally to underline the point. Reasons are inherently relational. 'P is a reason' means that there is someone and some action or belief so that P is a reason for that person to have that belief or to perform that action. The same is true of evidence: 'E is evidence for P' means that there is someone such that at a particular time E is for that person a reason to believe that P.

[2] Though not quite: the 'right kind of reason' issue arose as a problem for a 'fitting attitude' approach to normative properties, which I do not share. What is here resolved is the analogue of the problem as it affects some other approaches.

[3] My formulation of the maxims allows for one asymmetry between them, and merely appears to allow for a second. The real asymmetry is that there can be normative reasons against an action that are not reasons for any other action (not even for an omission, when that notion is given its proper meaning). Any reason against believing that a proposition is true is a reason for believing that it is false. The mere apparent asymmetry is that an epistemic reason in being a reason to believe in some proposition is part of a case for its truth. There is no equivalent in my formulation of the maxim governing reasons for action. That is a mere apparent contrast for

The first clarification concerns the question what determines whether available epistemic reasons are sufficient to warrant belief. It is not my view that only truth-related considerations figure among those determining the sufficiency of the case. However, the factors or principles that determine whether the case for the truth of a proposition is adequate to warrant belief are not themselves reasons for belief. Therefore, the maxim is not affected by this point.[4]

The second clarification concerns arguments that simplicity, elegance, explanatory power, or other such considerations govern rational belief or theory acceptance. The maxim is consistent with such views, so long as theory acceptance is understood for what it is: acceptance of theories, not belief in them. The maxim is about reasons for belief only. It denies that the simplicity of a proposition or a theory is always a reason to believe it. But such considerations may be relevant to acceptance of propositions. As Ulrike Heuer suggested to me, accepting a proposition is conducting oneself in accord with, and because of, the belief that there is sufficient reason to act on the assumption that the proposition is true: acceptance of the proposition that P entails belief, but not belief that P. Rather it entails belief that it is justified to act as if P. Thus acceptance combines epistemic and practical reasons, though its target is action rather than belief. Acceptance dominates many areas of practical thought. The whole system of law enforcement via courts and tribunals is based on acceptance of presumptions, like the presumption of innocence, and on accepting verdicts based on evidence presented in court, while ignoring all other evidence. Juries and judges are not required to believe that the accused is guilty or innocent. They are only required to accept and pronounce verdicts that are correct according to the evidence before them. Often other people who do not believe that the verdict is correct have compelling reasons to conduct themselves as if it were correct, that is to accept its content.

My one argument in support of the maxim is directed against the suggestion that since believing something can have benefits or disadvantages independently of the truth of what is believed there can be epistemic reasons that are not part of the case for its truth. For example, should an evil demon credibly threaten to punish me unless I believe something, would that not be a reason to believe that something? Perhaps it is.

---

to believe that P is to believe that P is true (though those who do not have the concepts are not able to express that fact). There is no concept of sufficient generality to make the same point regarding actions. We could say that the case for an action is the case for the action being worthy of performance. But the idea of being worthy has connotations that do not always apply, and as it is not meant to add anything to the maxim there is no need to introduce it (or alternatives to it) there.

[4] See e.g. S. Stroud, 'Epistemic Partiality in Friendship', *Ethics* 116 (2006), 498–524, in support of the relevance of non-truth-related considerations. It is worth adding that Stroud's observations and arguments are particularly challenging to those who think that epistemic norms divide all epistemic situations into those in which one must, on pain of irrationality, hold a belief and those in which one must not do so. Her views are easier to accommodate in a more sensible understanding of epistemic norms, one that allows for the existence of many epistemic situations in which it is neither rationally required nor rationally forbidden to hold a belief. Perhaps I should also add that contrary to some philosophical opinion degrees of confidence in a proposition are not degrees of belief.

I will return to that question in Section 3. For the moment let us accept a terminological convention and continue to call the truth-related reasons for belief (and only them) epistemic reasons. The others, if reasons at all, are practical reasons, perhaps they are practical reasons for belief. There are fundamental differences between truth-related and non-truth-related reasons for belief which show that the latter are practical.

Among others, truth-related considerations differ from other alleged reasons for belief in two important respects. First, one who believes that there is a conclusive case for the truth of a proposition cannot but believe that proposition (pathological cases[5] apart). There is no gap, no extra step in reasoning, between believing that the case for the truth of the proposition is conclusive and believing the proposition. Similarly, there is no gap between believing that the case for the truth of a proposition is inadequate and withholding belief in it.[6] Call this the No Gap Principle. It requires one important qualification. Perhaps the following is a good way of stating the qualified principle: *Whenever the content of a proposition is within one's immediate reach*, there is no gap, no extra step in reasoning, between believing that the case for the truth of the proposition is conclusive and believing the proposition.[7]

Why the qualification? Imagine that I know that there is conclusive evidence that everything in a certain news report is true, but I have not seen the report, and do not know its content. Suppose that it says that the president has resigned. So, I believe that there is conclusive evidence that the report, which is—though I am not aware of the fact—that the president has resigned, is true. Does the above entail that I (a) believe that there is conclusive evidence for the proposition that the president has resigned? and (b) believe that the president has resigned?[8] If the answer to (a) is negative the unqualified principle can stand. But it may strengthen the principle to qualify it as

---

[5] Pathological cases are ones where some of the conditions which constitute belief are met while others are not. There are many possible pathologies. One simple one is when one manifests all the criteria for such a belief, except in a particular context, say when thinking about one's relations with one's parents, when the belief sort of disappears.

[6] These claims require a more elaborate, qualified, and subtle formulation than I can give them. For an argument for a position a good deal stronger than the two claims I make here see J. Adler, *Belief's Own Ethics* (Cambridge, Mass.: MIT Press, 2002). For various discussions of non-truth-related reasons see Gilbert Harman, 'Rationality', repr. in G. Harman, *Reasoning, Meaning and Mind* (Oxford: OUP, 1999); E. E. Smith and D. N. Osherson (eds.), *Thinking: An Invitation for Cognitive Science*, vol. 3 (Cambridge, Mass.: MIT Press, 2nd edn. 1995–8); D. Parfit, 'Rationality and Reasons', in D. Egonsson et al. (eds.), *Exploring Practical Philosophy* (Burlington, Vt.: Ashgate Press, 2001); J. Olson, 'Buck-Passing and the Wrong Kind of Reasons,' *Philosophical Quarterly* 54 (2004); J. D'Arms and D. Jacobson, 'Sentiment and Value,' *Ethics* 110 (2000), 722–48; W. Rabinowitz and T. Rønnow-Rasmussen, 'The Strike of the Demon: On Fitting Pro-Attitudes and Value', *Ethics* 114 (2004), 391–423; P. Hieronymi, 'The Wrong Kind of Reason', *Journal of Philosophy* 102 (2005), 435–57 at 437. My own view is very similar to that of S. Darwall in *The Second-Person Standpoint: Morality, Respect, and Accountability* (Cambridge, Mass.: Harvard UP, 2006), 66.

[7] Possibly further qualifications are needed to deal with perception. As I walk down the street I perceive many things about the people around—do I come to believe all the propositions that a complete description of what I perceive would include? I have sufficient, sometimes conclusive, reason to believe them. But it is doubtful that I do form all those beliefs there and then. Complex considerations, bear on the case, but they cannot be explored here.

[8] I may believe so on independent grounds. But do I believe it because it is part of this true news report?

I proposed, so that it applies even to cases in which the equivalent of question (a) has a positive answer. The effect of the qualification is that even if I am aware that I have conclusive reason to believe that the proposition in the news report is true, and therefore, as the principles states, I believe that it is true, it does not follow that I believe that the president resigned. I do believe that the news report is true, but that does not give me immediate access to the content of the news report.

Knowledge that testimony is true or reliable etc. provides an epistemic reason that, typically, does not disclose the content of the proposition for the truth of which it is a reason. There are other reasons where this is the case. Being familiar with the experimental procedure in a certain area, I may be able to appreciate that the results of an experiment support the hypothesis it was meant to test without knowing what that hypothesis was. These examples may suggest a stricter qualification: the principle applies only when one knows the content of the proposition for which there are conclusive reasons. But that condition is too restrictive. While belief is not closed under entailment, people believe some propositions simply because they are immediate entailments of beliefs they have. People who believe that British residents have a right to enter Britain also believe that Londoners have that right (assuming they know that London is in Britain) even though that last proposition never occurred to them. We may say that if one believes a proposition one believes all the propositions that it entails which are within one's immediate reach, which are immediately available to one, where the test is that one becomes aware of the fact that they are entailed immediately one's attention is drawn to the fact. The No Gap Principle states that one comes to believe that P upon realizing that there is conclusive evidence for it, provided that it (the content of the proposition) is immediately available to one.

More directly and more generally (and again excepting pathologies), reasoning from (what we treat as) reasons for belief to a conclusion (from: 'the door is open' to 'therefore anyone could have walked in') we acquire the belief as we arrive at the conclusion. As we conclude that therefore anyone could have walked in, we come to believe that anyone could have walked in. By way of contrast, one cannot similarly reason from a non-truth-related reason for having a belief to having that belief. Belief that Bush is a good president cannot be my conclusion in reasoning from the fact (let us assume) that I would get a plum job offer if I did so believe. All that is logically and conceptually possible for me to conclude is that it would be good if I believed that Bush is a good president. But that is a different conclusion. It too is a belief, but a different one. Of course to say that it would be good if I believed that Bush is a good president leads, assuming various further conditions (e.g. that the normative/explanatory *nexus* is satisfied), to the conclusion that there is a (practical) reason to bring it about that I so believe.[9]

---

[9] Ulrike Heuer drew my attention to the fact that given the normative/explanatory *nexus* not everything that makes believing beneficial provides a reason for action. To do so it must be capable of figuring in an

Needless to say belief in the advantages I will enjoy if I believe that Bush is a good president can cause me to deceive myself into believing that there are adequate truth-related reasons to believe that Bush is a good president. But that does not undermine the contrast between truth-related and other considerations to which I pointed.[10]

Second, think of the distinction, familiar from practical reasons, between conforming with reasons and following them. A reason to Φ is conformed with when one Φs, and is followed when one Φs for that reason. In some cases conforming requires following: Some reasons are reasons not merely to perform an action, but to perform it for a reason (this is normally the case when the reason is to perform the action intentionally), and some reasons require performing it for that very same reason (one's love may be a reason to perform actions out of love). Often, however, reasons are reasons to perform the action, regardless of the reason why. I sometimes find myself in my office at a time I promised to be there, even though I forgot about the promise. Still, I did all I promised to do. I conformed to the reason my promise is. Applying an intuitively analogous distinction to theoretical reasons, we see that in coming to believe what one has non-truth-related reasons to believe one conforms to those reasons, but one cannot come to that belief by following them. One cannot come to believe a proposition for the reason that there are non-truth-related normative reasons for having that belief. That cannot be one's reason for holding that belief. By way of contrast one can come to have a belief by following truth-related reasons for it. One can have the belief for which they are reasons, and one can have it for those reasons.[11]

These considerations, especially the second one, suggest a distinction between standard and non-standard reasons for action, belief, intention, emotion, or whatever. Standard reasons are those that we can follow directly, that is have the attitude, or perform the action, for that reason. Non-standard reasons for an action or an attitude are such that one can conform to them, but not follow them directly (and the impossibility is conceptual or metaphysical, not a matter of psychological difficulty).

The importance of the distinction is shown by its relevance to many other issues. Not least that having a belief for adequate truth-related reasons is rational, and having it for non-truth-related reasons (i.e. when one's [belief in] non-truth-related reasons to believe is—part of—the explanation of why one believes), even if useful and desirable, is irrational. This vindicates a familiar thought: epistemic reasons can warrant belief. Non-truth-related reasons cannot. So while it may be best (because it is advantageous, or conducive to the common good, etc.) to believe that, e.g., one's loved ones are in

---

explanation of an action which could be performed for that reason. That condition may not be met. I will discuss the matter further in Chapter Six where the *nexus* will be further examined.

[10] This failure of the simple route to a belief is (a generalized form of) Williams's condition that one reaches the belief 'because in some way he is considering the matter aright' in *Moral Luck* (Cambridge: CUP, 1981), 109. See also Section 5 of Chapter Two.

[11] The same points are at the core of N. Shah's 'A New Argument for Evidentialism', *Philosophical Quarterly* 56 (2006), 481–98.

perfect health, or that one will win a competition, the factors that make it so are not epistemic reasons for that belief. They are non-standard practical reasons for having the belief.

2. Epistemic reasons and reasons for action—some differences

It is time to turn to the differences between reasons for action and epistemic reasons. I will focus on evidence-based reasons. Here are some others: That today is Friday the 17th is reason to believe that Sunday will be the 19th. That the visitor I expect is a bachelor is reason to believe that he is male. That citizens have a right to vote in elections and that you are a citizen, is reason to believe that you have a right to vote. Logical, conceptual, norm-based, expert-based, testimonial and other epistemic reasons differ from evidence in important respects. The crucial differences between practical and epistemic reasons, the first two below, apply to all of them, and that makes it unnecessary to discuss them separately.

a) The first two: pluralism and value

Two fundamental differences between epistemic and practical reasons[12] follow from the maxims. Epistemic reasons are governed by one concern: determination whether the belief for which they are reasons is or is not true. Reasons for a single action may, and typically are, governed by many concerns. A single action can serve or disserve a number of distinct and independent values: It may be an act both of friendship and of justice. Moreover, even when the reasons for an action derive from a single value the action may serve independent concerns: a single act can advance the welfare of several individuals, when the interest of each of them is a reason, an independent reason, to perform it.[13] To the extent that reasons for action represent independent concerns, we have reason to satisfy all of them. When reasons deriving from independent concerns conflict it is impossible to do so. In that case whatever we do some of the concerns that generate reasons for us will remain unsatisfied (by our actions at the time).

Hence when (independent) reasons for action conflict, that is when we have reason to perform several incompatible actions, even when it is clear which action is supported by the better reason, there is some loss, consisting in the fact that even when we successfully do our best there are concerns that we have reason to meet or satisfy which were left unsatisfied. Typically, concerns that remain unsatisfied provide reason for some action in the future, to satisfy them, or if impossible (or unjustified because of further conflicts) to do the second best, to come as close to satisfying them as possible

---

[12] As indicated at the outset I will argue that reasons for action are but one kind of practical reasons. However, to facilitate expression I will refer to them using the generic category, 'practical reasons' rather than the less flexible 'reasons for action'. What I say is meant to be true of all practical reasons.

[13] See Chapter Seven.

(which is what compensation often is). If I have reason to have a relaxed weekend by the seaside and a stronger conflicting reason to work in the office to meet an urgent deadline, then I should work in the office and find a way of taking half a day off on Monday to get at least some holiday.

There is no close analogue of the need to satisfy independent concerns and therefore no close analogue of reasons for compensatory actions in epistemic reasons. Epistemic reasons can conflict, but all of them are about the truth of the propositions for or against belief in which they are reasons. The weaker reasons are just less reliable guides to one and the same end. There is no loss in dismissing a less reliable clue. This is a fundamental difference between epistemic and practical reasons. Noting this difference Susan Hurley[14] compared reasons for belief to rules of thumb, useful when useful, but happily replaced when better ones are available. She used this difference between practical and epistemic reasons to explain the absence of epistemic akrasia.

To put it in my own terms: because there is no possibility that the lesser reason for belief serves a concern that is not served better by the better reason there is no possibility of preferring to follow what one takes to be the lesser reason rather than the better one. The possibility of akrasia depends on the fact that belief that a practical reason is defeated by a better conflicting reason is consistent with belief that it serves a concern that the better reason does not, and that can motivate one to follow it.

So far I argued that practical reasons serve many concerns and epistemic ones can serve only one. It is tempting to explain this by saying that practical reasons derive from many values, whereas epistemic reasons derive from one value only, presumably the value of having true beliefs, or two, the values of having true beliefs and of not having false ones. I think that there is some, though only some, truth in the first half of that proposition: the value of actions constitutes reasons for them and as actions can have many distinct evaluative properties there are many concerns those reasons express. But reasons for belief are not similarly connected to values, not even to a single value.

First, the diversity of concerns manifested in practical reasons is not entirely due to the diversity of values. Diverse values do generate diverse concerns, but so do other factors: For example, being a medically qualified caretaker of sheltered accommodation for disabled people I have a reason to help anyone there who needs insulin injections. There are several such people. So I have a reason to help each of them. Each of these reasons represents an independent concern, and they can conflict with one another, even though they all derive from the same value.

Second, epistemic reasons do not derive from the value of having that belief in the way that reasons for an action derive from the value of that action. It is not the case that there is always (even a *pro tanto*) value in having a true belief, whatever it is. Nor is it the case that it is always a disvalue to have a false belief. If that is so, and since there can

---

[14] S. Hurley, *Natural Reasons* (Oxford: OUP, 1989), 130–5. The argument is not conclusive, but the case for epistemic akrasia is not the current subject. The disanalogy Hurley points to is real enough.

always be reasons for believing at least any true proposition, it follows that reasons for belief are not provided by values in the way that reasons for action are.[15]

There is a large body of writings about epistemic value. It is possible that some of it is influenced by a misleading metaphorical saying that belief aims at truth, or that truth is the aim of belief.[16] But dismissing this saying is not dismissing all thoughts of epistemic value. Some of them arise in the context of an argument, going back to Plato, whose conclusion is sometimes said to be that knowledge has more value than true belief.[17] But unless there are other reasons for thinking that there is value in (all) true belief or in all knowledge there is no need to formulate the conclusion in a way that presupposes such views. It can be expressed, for example, by saying that wherever there is value in having a true belief that P there is greater value in having knowledge that P.[18] Some writers seem to be motivated by (some variant of) the thought that epistemic inquiry aims at acquiring true belief (or warranted belief, or knowledge) and therefore that it aims at some good. Hence there is value in true belief. But that is a non sequitur. It is misleading to say that epistemic inquiries aim at the truth. Each has its own aim: to find out the time of departure of the next train to Oxford, the date of the emergence of *Homo sapiens*, etc. It is at least awkward, and perhaps misleading, to say that the aim is the truth about the time of departure of the next train, etc. But let that be as it may. Nothing follows from the fact that epistemic inquiries aim at some good regarding the value of knowledge or of true belief, any more than the fact (if it is one) that all economic activity aims to make a profit shows that there is always value in making a profit. At best it shows that where there is no value in making a profit or having knowledge or true belief the economic activity or epistemic inquiry is not justified.

Is there no argument supporting the idea that true beliefs or that knowledge have value? The most promising contenders are various ways of building on the thought that truth is a constitutive standard of correctness for beliefs.[19] It is constitutive of beliefs that

---

[15] The same goes for knowledge. There is no value in having knowledge as such, and reasons that underwrite knowledge do not depend on the value of having that knowledge. Since a variety of objects of value are under consideration in epistemological discussion I use 'epistemic value' to cover all and any of them. For a survey of recent writings on the value of knowledge see D. Prichard, 'Recent Work on Epistemic Value', *American Philosophical Quarterly* 44 (2007), 85–110. For a recent collection of work on the topic see A. Haddock, A. Millar, D. Pritchard (eds.), *Epistemic Value* (Oxford: OUP, 2009).

[16] For a critique see D. Owens, 'Does Belief Have an Aim?', *Philosophical Studies* 115 (2003), 283–305.

[17] See for an intriguing recent contribution: J. Hyman, 'The Road to Larissa', *Ratio* 23 (2010), 323.

[18] Note, however, that it is impossible to formulate the general thesis about epistemic value as: in so far as there is any value in having a belief about whether P, it is better to have a true belief rather than a false belief. First, given that the condition applies only in special circumstances this thesis does not have the generality sought by those who believe in epistemic value. Second, it is false. Sometimes there is value in having some belief about whether P, but better to have a false one rather than a true one (winning a bet may turn on it, and the winning may be the weightiest relevant consideration).

[19] In this form the argument does not apply to knowledge. But possibly derivative arguments can then be brought to bear on knowledge; the argument about the superior value of knowledge is one such. Here again I try to characterize and comment on families of arguments, which is why I do not tie the discussion to any single version of the argument. The scope of the family is wide. E. Sosa's argument for the existence of an epistemically fundamental value seems to belong here as well, and is perhaps the best example of the family. See E. Sosa, *A Virtue Epistemology* (Oxford: OUP, 2007). He regards knowledge as the aim of belief and

they are subject to it (not that they conform with it). As will be explained in greater detail in Chapter Five, there are other cognitive-like mental states that are not beliefs precisely because they are not constituted by this standard. Criteria or standards of correctness come cheap. We can stipulate them at will, and for various purposes, good, bad, or indifferent, we do. The standing of truth as the standard for belief is special in at least two vital ways: First, beliefs are automatically self-correcting, meaning that we automatically lose a belief upon becoming convinced that it is false, and acquire it upon becoming convinced that it is true. Second, we do not acquire or change our beliefs at will. While I am awake they are liable to change even without my being aware of the fact. The first point establishes that we cannot change the criterion for belief, and the second point that we cannot choose not to have the mental states of which it is the constitutive standard. That makes the relationship of truth and beliefs vital to an understanding of beliefs and their place in our life. But it does not show that truth is a value in beliefs (that true beliefs have greater value than false ones).

So we can discuss the relationship of truth and belief without relying on the thought that true belief has value. That relationship is not subject to voluntary control—which suggests that it is not a case of the instantiation of value. But perhaps we have missed out on something? One suggestion is that there are counterfactuals that establish the value of true belief. For example, that we willy-nilly rely on beliefs that we have and it is better to rely on true rather than on false beliefs. But sometimes it is better to rely on false beliefs. That proposition lacks the generality required to establish that it is always better, if we have a belief about something, to have a true belief about that something. Of course, sometimes, e.g. when we have absolutely no other relevant information regarding some belief, we would have an epistemic reason to believe that if we rely on it, it would be better if it were true. But (a) that does not establish (on pain of *petitio principii*) that true beliefs have greater value than false ones, and (b) it is not always the case that we have such an epistemic reason.[20]

None of the preceding considerations contradicts the claim that there is value to true belief, perhaps a special kind of value, a view consistent with value pluralism, and supported by the fact that truth is a criterion of correctness for beliefs. For one may say that there is normally a proximate connection between being better and being correct, since it is always better to be correct. Given that, the value of truth in belief is only *pro tanto*; it cannot be refuted by showing that sometimes it is better, all things considered, to have a false belief.

---

therefore that knowledge is better than truth 'is just a special case of the fact that, for any endeavor that one might undertake, it is always, necessarily, proper for one to prefer that one succeed in that endeavor, and indeed succeed aptly, not just by luck'. 'Value Matters in Epistemology', *Journal of Philosophy* 107 (2010), 167 at 189.

[20] Similarly, while the fact that one's beliefs are warranted is evidence that one is functioning rationally, it does not follow, even assuming that it is good to function rationally, that it is better to have warranted than unwarranted beliefs (only that it is a by-product of something good).

It is always difficult to refute claims that something is a *sui generis* good. Is it like other goods? No, but that is because it is *sui generis*. But there is absolutely no good at all in many of its instances. It only appears so because the good is overwhelmed by bad features of that thing, etc. Remember, however, that we are not concerned with words. There may well be contexts in which assertions using the sentence 'truth is of value (or a value)' are assertions of true propositions. The preceding paragraphs may help in identifying what propositions were thus truly asserted. There is no interest in claims that there are epistemic values if they are values in a completely different sense of the word. Can it be shown that epistemic values, to the extent that there are any, are values in the sense here discussed?

Imagine the contrary, that is imagine that in all cases, if we have a belief about a certain matter then it is *pro tanto* better to have a true rather than a false belief, just because it is true. Consider an example:[21] A month ahead of time I believe that Red Rod will win the Derby or that the Social Democrats will win the elections in Denmark. There may be ways to increase the likelihood that my belief is true. Perhaps I could give valuable advice to Red Rod's jockey, or lend my expertise to the Social Democrats. Is the fact that that will make it more likely that my beliefs are true a reason to do so? If there is value in one's beliefs being true as such then there should be no difference between making reality conform to the belief and making the belief conform to how things are.

b) Third difference: presumptive sufficiency

The value-independent character of epistemic reasons has important implications that will occupy much of the rest of this chapter. Here I will argue that it is responsible for another difference between epistemic and practical reasons. Practical reasons are presumptively sufficient. Epistemic reasons are not necessarily so. To see this we need to recall that often what appear to be references to several reasons may be references to one and the same reason. That my mother is in hospital, that there is a rail strike today, that she forgot her slippers at home may all be cited by me as my reason for heading towards the bus stop. But they may all refer to one reason. Facts that are part of a reason are commonly stated as a way of referring to the ('complete') reason of which they are a part.

For a reason to Φ at a particular time to be *presumptively sufficient* is for it to be the case that if there is no other reason either for or against so acting then (a) Φ-ing at that time is justified, and (b) if the agent rationally believes that the reason applies, and that there is no other, then his failing to try to Φ is akratic.[22]

---

[21] I am remaining faithful to ordinary experience, namely that we often have beliefs about future events, while being aware that certain events, some under our control, can make them more or less likely to happen. I see no reason to think that none of these beliefs is rational or warranted.

[22] Michael Stocker and Jonathan Dancy are among writers who reject the second feature. I find their views difficult to sustain, but we need not consider them here. The first feature is sufficient to establish the

Things are different with epistemic reasons.[23] Even if at a particular time there is only one reason for the agent to believe that a particular proposition is true, and no reason against that belief, coming to have that belief on the strength of that reason may be unjustified and irrational, and failing to do so may be justified and rational. Even a good and undefeated epistemic reason may be insufficient to warrant belief. It may support it, but not be sufficient to warrant it.[24]

One may object that it is possible to define epistemic reasons as reasons that warrant belief, thus eliminating the difference between the two kinds of reason. Such a move is, however, too artificial to make any difference. We can identify practical reasons independently of whether they are presumptively sufficient, simply by identifying their normative force. We then show by example or argument that they are presumptively sufficient. If one insists on defining complete epistemic reasons as those that are presumptively sufficient to warrant belief it would follow that there are good, independent epistemic reasons, which are not complete reasons. They nevertheless have normative force and that would be enough to establish the difference between practical and epistemic reasons, as there are no practical reasons with normative force that are not sufficient to warrant action.

This contrast between epistemic and practical reasons is made possible by an important difference between belief and action. We can suspend belief, but not suspend action. Suspending belief means believing neither the proposition nor its contradictory. But, while the opportunity to perform an action exists, there is no third option between doing an action and not doing it.[25] If not performing an action is the contradictory of performing it then suspension of action, that is neither performing it nor not performing it, is not possible.[26] But while this difference between action and

difference between practical and epistemic reasons. See e.g. M. Stocker, 'Raz on the Intelligibility of Bad Acts' and J. Dancy, 'Enticing Reasons', in R. J. Wallace et al. (eds.), *Reason and Value* (Oxford: OUP, 2004).

[23] See *Engaging Reason* and D. Owens, 'Epistemic Akrasia', *Monist* 85 (2002), 381, 382–3.

[24] For a contrary view see D. Davidson, 'How is Weakness of the Will Possible?', in J. Feinberg (ed.), *Moral Concepts* (Oxford: OUP, 1970), repr. in Davidson, *Essays on Actions and Events* (Oxford: OUP, 1980), 21.

[25] One has the opportunity to believe or disbelieve or suspend belief in a proposition while one is in possession of one's rational powers. Not so with action: to be able either to take or not to take an umbrella one needs to have access to an umbrella. One way of avoiding the choice is to deny oneself the opportunity to perform the action. But that possibility does not undermine the asymmetry between belief and action. Sometimes we say that we must choose between A and B because we have had a choice between A, B, and C, and we have already decided against C. William James pointed out that the choice between taking the umbrella or leaving it is 'not forced' because we can stay at home. (See 'The Will to Believe', *New World*, vol. 5 (1896), 327–47.) He seemed to think that that re-establishes the parity of choices whether to perform an action or not, whether to love someone or not and to believe something or not. But that would undermine the disanalogy only if there is always a third option between performing A and not performing it. This does not seem to be the case. I have no third option between continuing to sit as I am or not.

Note that there is a third option between intentionally Φ-ing and intentionally not-Φ-ing (intentionally avoiding to Φ). However, since practical reasons are reasons for actions (and only occasionally for intentional actions) the relevant comparison is between beliefs and actions, not beliefs and intentional actions.

[26] Reports of my beliefs take the form JR believes that the cat is on the mat (or JR believes: the cat is on the mat), while reports of my actions do not normally have a propositional object; they relate me not to a

belief makes room for the possibility of undefeated epistemic reasons that do not warrant beliefs, it does not in itself explain the difference. The explanation lies in the first two differences. Given that epistemic reasons are governed by a single concern, they have, as we saw, the character of clues, and like clues they may be both good clues and insufficient to enable one rationally to form a view about the solution. Analogously, evidence may be good evidence but insufficient to warrant belief. On the other hand, a practical reason exists only if there is some good or some point in performing the action for which it is a reason. This is what it is to be a reason, to be a fact that confers value or point on the action. Hence, a single reason is sufficient to give point or value to the action, and absent any other reason it is sufficient to justify it.

3. Generalizing the contrast: practical and adaptive reasons

Reasons (taken together) determine the ways people should relate to the world, in their beliefs, emotions, actions, and the like. But epistemic and practical reasons do so in fundamentally different ways. Briefly stated the basic difference between practical and epistemic reasons is that practical reasons, taken together, determine what and how, in light of the value of things, we should change or preserve in ourselves or the world.[27] Epistemic reasons do not. They determine the way our beliefs should adjust to track how things are.

There are other normative reasons. Do they divide into two classes of which reasons for action and epistemic reasons are examples? For lack of appropriate terminology I will use 'practical reasons' to designate the class of which reasons for action are an instance, and 'adaptive reasons' to designate the class to which epistemic reasons belong. Reasons which are value-related are practical reasons, even if they are reasons for having a belief or an emotion. Reasons are adaptive if they mark the appropriateness of an attitude in the agent independently of the value of having that attitude, its appropriateness to the way things are. Are there other instances of these types?

proposition but to an action: JR ate the apple. Hence some may claim that there is no asymmetry since report of my state of belief can take the form JR does not believe that the cat is on the mat, which covers both disbelief and suspension of belief. But the asymmetry does not concern reports of beliefs or actions. We can recast reports of my action as: I performed the action: I ate the apple. (It is not the case that I performed the action 'I ate the apple') is the equivalent of (it is not the case that I believe that the cat is on the mat). Now we see that the asymmetry is evident: if it is not the case that I ate the apple then I did not eat the apple. There is no analogue of suspension of belief.

[27] A caveat: I write, here and elsewhere, of practical reasons as constituted by the fact that the actions for which they are reasons have value. But as is implied by the normative/explanatory *nexus*, and will be further discussed in later chapters, there are other qualifications, filters that determine when the value of actions provides reasons for their performance. The famous 'ought implies can' may be—on some interpretations—an example of one such filter.

a) The case of emotions

Standard reasons for belief are adaptive, while non-standard reasons for belief are practical. How about reasons for or against having an emotion? I will just introduce the topic, which is too large to deal with here. The role of reasons in our emotional life is very different from their role in our beliefs. I will mention only two differences. First, reasons allow much greater latitude regarding whether an emotion is required. For the most part even when appropriate there is nothing amiss in not having it. Fear is appropriate when facing great danger, but only exceptionally would its absence when in danger be against reason. Nor is its appropriate degree strictly regulated by reason. Second, emotions do not necessarily respond to reasons with the immediacy that characterizes belief's relationship to reasons.[28] When convinced that a belief is not supported by reasons we lose the belief, but typically realizing that we were mistaken to think that there were reasons for an emotion does not instantly kill off the emotion. A period of adjustment is usually needed. These and other differences notwithstanding, emotions, like beliefs, are subject to at least two kinds of reasons. For we can usefully distinguish between affect-justifying reasons for emotions and practical reasons for having emotions, which are not affect-justifying reasons.

Affect-justifying reasons are part of a case for the emotion being an appropriate response to how things are. Affect-justifying reasons are reasons awareness of which could rationally induce, as well as (other things being equal) establish the rationality of, having an emotion. Having been insulted is an affect-justifying reason for resentment. The fact that anger with one's competitor may, in the circumstances, improve one's chances of winning the competition is not an affect-justifying reason. Absent any other reason for anger, it will be irrational to be angry for that reason.[29] But that anger will help one win the competition gives it value which may provide a practical reason for experiencing that emotion.

Affect-justifying reasons are adaptive. We can test their independence of value as before: Given that I am afraid of the journey (for no reason) do I have any reason at all to make my journey dangerous and make my fear appropriate? Given that I am jealous of Abe, do I have any reason to induce Abe to do something that will give me reason to be jealous of him? Only in jokes. The same applies to other emotions: we have adaptive reasons that they be appropriate given how things stand. But it is not the case that when we have an emotion there is always value in its being appropriate. Sometimes this is so, but sometimes the reverse is the case.

---

[28] In this regard emotions resemble actions, in that the path from reasons to emotions is mediated by the imagination as the path from reason to action is mediated by the will.

[29] Judgements of irrationality are notoriously tricky to analyse. One complication regarding the rationality of the emotions results from the fact that we may have (sometimes conflicting) affect-justifying and practical reasons for them. Anger with my competitor, deliberately induced to help me win the competition, may, in so far as it was so induced, not be irrational, while being irrational in so far as my competitor did nothing to merit that anger. Perhaps the best way to sort out this apparent conflict is to say that my inducing the anger was not irrational, even though being angry is irrational.

To be sure, the very meaning of 'appropriate to the way things are' when applied to emotions, is problematic in ways in which the appropriateness to the way things are of true beliefs is not. Possibly the concept is incoherent. Possibly emotions are appropriate just in case that beliefs, which are part of what makes them the kind of emotions they are, are true. This may be related to the fact that some emotions appear not to have appropriate reasons. A murderous rage, for example, appears never to be appropriate, perhaps because there is no belief that one must have to have the emotion. This would explain why it is not irrational to feel murderous rage. It is just immoral. Generally speaking, an emotion is irrational if one experiences it without there being an adaptive reason for having it. But this is so only if there can be adaptive reasons for it. Where none can exist neither experiencing nor not experiencing the emotion can be rational or irrational, though there can be practical reasons for or against having it. This is not the place to consider these vexed matters. For our purposes suffice it to establish that affect-justifying reasons are not value-related.

This would explain why there can be adaptive reasons for having emotions that it is always wrong to have. For example, some people believe that there is never a good reason to be envious. They must refer to practical reasons, for surely there are adaptive reasons for envy. If you envy someone his victory then you have no reason to envy him if he did not in fact win, if you are mistaken about his victory. If you continue to envy him after your mistake has been corrected, you are irrational. If he was victorious then you may have an emotion that it is bad or wrong to have, but you are not irrational.

So far so similar to beliefs—affect-justifying reasons are the standard reasons for emotions, and they are adaptive. There are, however, also non-standard reasons for emotions, which are practical reasons. Arguably, however, matters are much more complex. As I have already mentioned, given the circumstances reasons for emotions may require an emotion. Not having the emotion in such circumstances may show a deficiency in the people concerned. But we are unlikely to take them to be factors that contribute to a judgement that the person lacking the emotion is irrational. Further-more, at least sometimes the deficiency may be a moral deficiency. Think, e.g., of people who do not feel compassion when it is appropriate, and 'required', as it were, to feel compassion. We are likely to think of this as a moral blemish, but not as a case of irrationality, not even if the person believes that compassion is required. Why not? Does it mean that the reason for the emotion is a moral, therefore a practical reason? That would show that there are standard practical reasons for emotions. But it would not explain why flouting them is not irrational, even if one is aware that one is flouting them.

But perhaps even though the emotion is a moral emotion, and its inappropriate absence or presence is a moral defect, the reason for the emotion is an adaptive reason. We can compare these cases to the moral deficiency betrayed by one's beliefs (e.g. believing that there is no reason not to inflict suffering on non-human animals), which does not show that the reasons for the beliefs are themselves practical reasons. That would explain why the deficiency does not affect judgement of rationality (the reasons are adaptive, and we assume permissive in the cases under consideration) while also explaining how emotions can contribute to the evaluation of the morality of one's life or character.

b) Actions

There seem to be no adaptive reasons for actions, no sense of a reason for action that is unrelated to its value. Does the fact that all reasons for action are practical reasons mean that there are no non-standard reasons for action? Or does it mean that they require some alternative explanation? I think that the latter is the case.

The case for there being non-standard reasons for action arises out of the familiar case of actions that have a certain value only if they are not performed in order to realize that value. Some may say that where the value of an action cannot be realized if it is done in order to realize it then that value does not provide a reason for the action that would have it. The alternative is to take it as providing a reason to perform the action but not for that reason. In other words, the value of the action is a reason that is conformed with only if it is not followed. Performance of the act that manifests the value need not be coincidental. We may create some other reasons (e.g. by an appropriate bet, or by habituation to follow an appropriate rule) for performing the action.[30] (Such manipulation is not always possible, but then not always can we conform to reasons that apply to us.) This suggests that even such values provide reasons for the actions that have them.

These will be, though, non-standard reasons for action. The value of the action cannot be the reason for which the action is done: We cannot successfully perform the action we have reason to perform for that reason (because the action we have reason to perform is 'to perform a specific act but not for that reason'). But the reason is a reason to get ourselves to perform the action. So it seems that there are both standard and non-standard reasons for action, both kinds being practical reasons.

c) Intentions

Intentions present complications of their own. Reasons for action are either reasons for intentional actions, or for actions that need not be intentional. Put another way, practical reasons may be conformed with either only by an intentional action, or by actions that need not be intentional. Either way they are also reasons for intending the action, because performing it intentionally is a way of performing it.[31] If the reason is to perform an intentional action then having the intention is necessary for conforming with the reason. But even if the action need not be intentional intending it is the

---

[30] We may want to distinguish two senses of following a reason: (1) one follows a reason to Φ which applies to one if, for that reason, one does something to facilitate one's Φ-ing, and (2) one follows a reason to Φ if one Φs for that reason. Where an action has value only if performed not in order to realize that value it can be followed in sense (1), but not in sense (2) which is the standard sense of the expression (and to which I referred earlier as 'directly following').

[31] Reasons to perform an action unintentionally are the sole exception to the above.

normal way to secure its performance, and therefore an undefeated reason for the action is also a reason for intending it.

Reasons to Φ are standard reasons for intending to Φ. But there can be others. There can be reasons to intend an action that are independent of whether there is reason for the action. I will call them independent reasons (for intentions). For example, it may be a good thing to reassure some people that I will perform an action, say in a year's time. This may be so even though there is no reason to perform the action.[32] If I now intend to perform the action they will be reassured. So I have a reason to intend to perform an action that I do not have, and I know that I do not have, adequate reason to perform. A few months down the line that reason may disappear (e.g. it may become clear that the action will be performed anyway, if not by this agent then by another). In fact the agent never performs the action. Nevertheless he had a reason to intend it at the time.[33]

Just as a reason to perform an action is also a reason to intend the action so, at least in many cases, an independent reason to intend an action is, *ipso facto*, a reason to perform the action so intended. Sometimes this will be so because it is impossible to intend to Φ without Φ-ing, as is the case when the intention is the one embedded in the action (the intentionality that makes an intentional action intentional); alternatively, and more generally, when performing the action will make it easier to have the intention to perform it we may have a reason to perform the action to facilitate having the intention.

The question is: is it possible to intend to perform an action, which we do not believe that we have any (other) reason to perform, for an independent reason for that intention? We can manipulate ourselves to have such an intention, for example by inducing in ourselves false beliefs about the case for the action, and we can come to have such beliefs through self-deception. We may even be able to create reasons to perform the action (e.g. promise to do so) thus making it possible to intend to perform it. Such cases do not show that it is possible to intend to perform an action for an independent reason. If they are the only ways in which we can follow independent reasons for having an intention then such reasons are non-standard. Like other non-standard reasons they are practical reasons. If so then as with reasons for action, both standard and non-standard reasons for having intentions are practical reasons.

Before we examine the matter we should note that, as always, there are various mixed, or intermediate, cases. For example, on Sunday one may believe that there is an adequate reason to Φ on Friday. Nevertheless, one may not have formed an intention to Φ on Friday. Then an offer of a reward arrives, provided one forms now an intention to Φ on Friday. It seems that in such a case one can form an intention

---

[32] The Toxin Puzzle (G. Kavka, 'The Toxin Puzzle', *Analysis* 43 (1983), 33) raises the question whether when we believe that there is reason against an act we can still respond to a reason for having the intention. The phenomenon here discussed is wider, in not relying on a belief that there are reasons against the act.

[33] Sometimes there may be reasons against having intentions when there is no reason for the action. I will disregard such cases.

(now) for an independent reason. Now suppose that one does not believe that there is an adequate reason to Φ on Friday, but that it is likely that by Friday there will be such a reason. Arguably, one can follow the independent reason for the intention, and form the intention even so. As always, we can push examples to the brink when no answer is compelling, and the cases are indeterminate. But we can focus on the extreme and clear cases.

Suppose that one has an intention that one has only independent reasons to have. Regarding beliefs, emotions, and actions, if they need to be supported by what the agents take to be adequate reasons to be rational then they are irrational if agents believe that they are supported only by non-standard reasons. Emotions and beliefs are irrational in these circumstances because the reasons needed to make them rational are adaptive reasons, and the agents believe that they are supported only by practical reasons. Actions are irrational in these circumstances because while they are supported, as they should be, by practical reasons, these reasons are, as the agents know, followed in a self-defeating way. Non-standard reasons for intentions are practical. So the question turns on whether directly following independent reasons for an intention to Φ, when one does not believe that there is or will be a reason to Φ, is impossible or self-defeating.

Here is an example: suppose that you offer me something worth having (which there is no reason why I should not wish to receive from you) if I intend to move my hand, resting on the sofa, five inches to the left. You do not care whether or not I actually move my hand, and there are no other reasons I am or can become aware of that bear on either action or intention. I ask myself: should I form that intention, and of course that immediately raises in my mind the question about the action: should I move my hand? Yes I say, for if I do, I will be doing so intentionally, thus earning the offer. My deliberation relies on the fact that in the circumstances acting is a way of having the intention, hence the reason for the intention becomes a reason for the action. This kind of independent reason for an intention is therefore a standard reason for it.

Now suppose that your offer is on condition that I intend now to move my hand tomorrow (and that we know that there will be no other reason regarding the intention or the action tomorrow). You care neither whether I move my hand tomorrow nor whether I maintain my intention to move it for more than a few minutes. The difference being that in this case once I now intend to move my hand tomorrow I no longer have reason either to maintain the intention or to perform the action. I have already met the condition of the offer. The question is: can I form an intention now when I now believe that I will not have reason to maintain it or to act on it? If an intention presupposes belief that there is reason to perform the action one intends then I cannot form such an intention for the independent reason, for I do not now believe that there will be a reason to perform the action tomorrow.[34] It is still the case that it would be good to have the independent intention, but that good does

---

[34] A similar conclusion is arrived at by N. Shah in 'How Action Governs Intention', *Philosophers' Imprint* 8 (2008), 1–19 (http://hdl.handle.net/2027/spo.3521354.0008.005) who writes: 'The constitutive norm for

not generate a standard reason for having it. Possibly it does, however, generate a non-standard reason to get myself to have that independent intention (through self-deception, or by securing another reason for the action to be intended, etc.). In conclusion independent reasons to form future-directed intentions can be followed if supported by a separate reason to Φ, but when this is not the case, when unaided they can only be followed indirectly, by making ourselves form them. Therefore unaided independent reasons for future-directed intentions are non-standard reasons. But independent reasons for having the intention embedded in an intentional action are standard reasons for intentions.

4. Standard and non-standard reasons—again

The distinction between practical and adaptive reasons, as drawn here, depends on the prior distinction between standard and non-standard reasons. I identify non-standard reasons as reasons for some action or attitude that cannot be (directly) followed (call this 'The Condition'). In discussion Kieran Setiyah raised an objection, whose exploration will help clarify the nature of the distinction.

Can the standard/non-standard distinction rest on The can-be-directly-followed Condition? Is it not the case that anything that anyone takes to be a reason can be followed by that person? Is that not what we mean when saying that it is taken to be a reason? How can one take something to be a reason without following it as a reason?

Suppose that one replies that The Condition applies only to ('real') reasons. It is not a test by which to determine what is taken to be a reason and is not. There are independent ways of establishing whether a fact is taken by someone to be a reason to do something or to have some attitude. Allowing this point does not altogether resolve the difficulty. Suppose that a certain fact is a reason. For example, imagine that someone promises Jake a large sum of money if he believes that P. By all accounts this makes it good, at least in one respect, that Jake believes that P, and, the *nexus* and other conditions being satisfied, that is a reason to have that belief. I claim that it is a non-standard reason for it cannot be followed. But suppose that Jake does not think that. Suppose that he is philosophically minded (it is possible to develop the example so as to get rid of this assumption) and believes that the promise is an ordinary, standard, reason for believing that P, and that as a result he comes to believe that P. Of course, I will say that he has not followed the reason that the promise gave him, that he deceives himself into believing that he followed the reason and that it is a standard reason for belief. Perhaps. But can that be established by The Condition? I claim that he did not follow the reason because I take it not to be a standard reason. But I have to establish that he did not follow the reason first. I have to establish this independently of assuming that

intention is this: intending to A is correct only if A-ing is the thing to do.' However, he disregards the possibility that independent reasons to intend to A provide reasons to A.

the reason is not standard, for only this way would The following-a-reason Condition establish which reasons are standard.

Could one reply that The Condition is about following-reasons-without-being-guilty-of-conceptual-confusions, whereas Jake is conceptually confused and only because of that can he follow the reason directly? But that reply both concedes too much and does not help. It concedes that Jake did follow a non-standard reason, that his conceptual confusion enabled him to do more than the clear-headed can do. And the reply does not help for the problem is to establish that he is conceptually confused. If he is then the accurate reply is that, just as in the case of 'following' something that is no reason at all, Jake merely thinks that he is following the reason, whereas in fact he is not. He is self-deceived. But what establishes that he is conceptually confused?

The very possibility that Jake is self-deceived in believing that he has followed the reason establishes that the question of whether one follows a reason is not purely a matter of how the agent understands his situation. To follow a reason he must behave in a way that is possible given the nature of that reason. That I am thirsty is a reason for me to drink the water in front of me. But it is not a reason to call my mother. Suppose that I say (bizzarely, but bizarre things happen) that my reason for calling my mother was that I was thirsty. Barring some complicated story to make the claim true, I am (a) confused, either conceptually, or about the nature of telephone calls, or about thirst, and (b) I did not follow that reason, I merely thought that I did. That much follows from the kind of reason that thirst is.

Two questions loom: First, does the nature of a reason also determine what it is a standard reason for (as I shall argue later any non-standard reason for one thing is a standard reason for another)? Second, is the claim that the nature of a reason determines what it is a reason for consistent with taking the possibility of following a reason as a mark of its being a standard reason? The doubt embodied in the first question is that the non-standard reasons for beliefs, emotions, intentions, actions, etc. are reasons for beliefs, emotions, intentions, actions, etc. The distinction between standard and non-standard reasons depends, if you like, on more subtle factors. But are they part of the nature of the reasons?

Both questions can be answered in one by examining the factors that make it impossible to follow reasons, thus rendering them indirect. I can make no claim that the analysis of this chapter is exhaustive, but let me briefly recap the factors here explained, starting from the case of non-standard reasons for action and intentions. Here two kinds of factor may make a reason non-standard. First, if following it is self-defeating. Second, in the case of intentions, if the formation of the intention is impossible, as it violates some necessary condition for having an intention. These conditions are met when the reason for the action is a reason for an action not performed for that reason, and when the reason for the intention does not provide a reason for the action (not even as a way of having or of facilitating the having of the intention). The existence or absence of these conditions does not presuppose any claim about the impossibility of following reasons that meet them. These conditions are part of, or derive from, the character of those reasons, and the claim that reasons that meet the conditions cannot be followed results directly from them.[35]

Turn now to adaptive reasons for beliefs and emotions. Here the case is different. The reasons that are in fact non-standard do not comply with the maxims governing such reasons: they are not part of a case for the beliefs or emotions being appropriate (not part of the case for the truth of the beliefs, and whatever substitutes for truth in the case of various emotions).[36] That too is part of the nature of the reasons. So, anyone who reasons: I will get lots of money if I believe that P therefore P is mistaken, and given the character of the mistake, confused. But is he confused about what it is to directly follow a reason? Not necessarily. In the strong sense of having a concept he may not have the concept of following a reason. He may be following reasons generally in a satisfactory way, but is unable to articulate the nature of that activity. That may sound as if the analysis is stipulative: one just calls directly following a reason for a belief coming to have (or sustaining) the belief because the reasons constitute a case for its truth. But there is nothing stipulative here.

We should not be misled by the ubiquity of 'reason' discourse. My reason for believing that P may be that I confuse two things. That may be a good explanation of my belief, but it does not refer to a normative reason. The distinction, though not its articulation, is available to all competent rational beings. So is the fact that if I believe that P because I think that the fact that it is advantageous for me to believe that P shows that it is true that P I am, in doing so, irrational, whereas if I made myself believe that P in order to gain some advantage I was not irrational in doing so?[37] And perhaps most importantly, competent rational people are familiar with the fact that non-epistemic reasons cannot serve to warrant belief. Similarly competent rational beings are either familiar, or can easily be made familiar, with the experience of being unable to believe something in spite of knowing that it is to one's advantage to believe it. The distinction between the ability directly to follow a reason for belief and being guided by it only indirectly, through making ourselves believe what we have reason to believe, merely expresses these familiar points.

---

[35] Setiya offers the following example: 'If you offer me a lot of money to intend to buy an apple tomorrow, it seems that I can follow that reason, deciding to buy an apple and doing so (so long as I think it is sufficiently likely that I will buy the apple tomorrow).' That seems to me to be mistaken. Whatever happens today, come tomorrow I will not buy the apple. I would not be able to think of a single reason to do so. (There is no problem if I can now think of a reason, independently of the offer, to buy an apple tomorrow—but that is irrelevant to our case.) So I will not buy the apple. If I know that now (as I can do) then I know that buying the apple will not help me in forming the intention now to buy it tomorrow. So I have no reason to buy the apple, and your offer does not constitute one. Hence the offer, though it is a reason for having the intention, is not one that can be followed. Of course, people form intentions when they should know that that is silly so often that we think that we could do so in this case as well. And indeed if we are confused or mistaken we will succeed. But when we do so we merely think that we follow the reason (if we do). We do not in fact do so.

[36] Non-standard reasons for actions and intentions do conform to the maxims governing actions and intentions in being part of the case for the value or point of the actions or intentions.

[37] Whether or not my belief that P is irrational when I made myself have it to gain an advantage, is a separate issue. It may or may not be irrational, depending on further facts.

But how does it apply to self-deception? Think first of ordinary deception: Aware of the advantage of having a belief that I know to be false I may well ask a friend to deceive me into believing it. That would constitute a typical case of indirectly getting myself to believe something. The difference in the case of the self-deceived is that he does not need to ask a friend to deceive him. He has done so himself earlier. That makes it appear as if he follows the reason directly, and that constitutes a genuinely special feature of self-deception and of genuine conceptual confusion about the character of reasons. But their character as deception and confusion can be established by the fact that the self-deceived and confused ignore the distinction referred to in the preceding paragraph. Given that one independently establishes that these are cases of confusion or self-deception it is non-circularly established that the deceived have not directly followed reasons, but merely mistakenly thought that they did. Ultimately, however, the explanation of the force of this point depends on understanding the normativity of reasons, their hold on us, a matter to be discussed in Chapter Five.

5. Special practical reasons for beliefs and emotions?

There is one last question to consider: we saw that there are standard and non-standard reasons for actions and standard and non-standard reasons for having intentions. The question is are the practical reasons for having beliefs or emotions distinct types of practical reasons, on a par with reasons for actions and for intentions, or are they simply reasons for actions (and for intentions)? Surface appearances suggest that practical reasons for having beliefs and emotions are just that. They suggest that it distorts things to regard them as reasons for action. Perhaps they yield instrumental reasons for action, as the way of bringing it about that we conform to the primary reasons to have those beliefs and emotions. But it would merely distort things to deny that there are practical reasons for beliefs and for emotions.

But this argument from surface appearances is suspect. Consider: we have reasons to have efficient transport systems, and good housing. Does it mean that there are distinct transport and housing types of practical reasons? In a way there are, but that is simply to classify practical reasons by the subject matter they relate to. That is not the sense in which epistemic reasons differ from reasons for emotions, or reasons for actions differ from reasons for intentions. These distinctions are based on the thought that reasons are normative and we respond to them through recognizing them as such. Our beliefs respond to reasons: as we recognize epistemic reasons our beliefs change in line with them. With due modifications the same is true of emotions, and of intentions. The basic classification of reasons is a classification of standard reasons, because the fact that they can be followed is what makes reasons into reasons.

We also respond to non-standard reasons for beliefs and emotions, but we do so directly by performing actions and only indirectly by changing our beliefs and emotions. Non-standard reasons for belief are like reasons for having good houses, they are reasons for actions that will have those results. The result is that all non-standard reasons are practical reasons. All non-standard reasons for one thing are standard reasons for another: a non-standard reason to believe that P is a standard reason to bring it about that I believe that P.[38] A non-standard reason to Φ is a standard reason to bring it about that I Φ.

This conclusion helps with some of the points raised in the discussion of the emotions above. For example, if one has an emotion that is not supported by adaptive reasons (where adaptive reasons are possible) it is an irrational emotion to have in the circumstances. But if one has an emotion in defiance of decisive practical reasons against having it one is morally or otherwise deficient, but not irrational. Why not? Is not defiance of (what are taken to be) valid reasons irrational? It is, but since the reasons are not *really* reasons for the emotions, since they are reasons for action to bring it about that one has the emotions, the irrationality is in the failure to try to prevent or suppress the emotions. If one tries and fails one is not irrational at all, but one is still morally or otherwise deficient.

Does that argument prove too much? Does it not show that there are no reasons for actions, only reasons for intending, for we can only respond to reasons to act by intending to act, just as we can only respond to non-standard reasons for belief, or to reasons for having good housing, by acting? We know, of course, that reasons for action are primary, for standard reasons for intentions are reasons for the intended actions. But does not that simply undermine the argument I used in the previous paragraph? To think so is to misconceive the relations of intention and action, imagining that when acting intentionally one acts by forming an intention that causes one to act. In fact the intention of an intentional action is not a mental event separate from the action but an aspect of the action, the way it is performed. One responds to a (perceived) adequate reason to act by acting (intentionally). Sometimes we respond now to (as we see it) an adequate reason to act in the future by forming now an intention to act in the future. Future-directed intentions are separate from the actions. The reasons for them, though normally deriving from the reasons for the actions, are a distinctive kind of reasons simply in virtue of the fact that we respond to them directly by forming the intentions. But reasons for action do not require future-directed intentions. We can respond to them by acting.[39]

---

[38] It is also, and this is true of practical reasons generally, a standard reason to believe that there is a reason to bring about that I believe that P.

[39] Scanlon's discussion of the same issue is similar in some respects, but he mistakenly concludes that 'judgement-sensitive attitudes constitute the class of things for which reasons in the standard normative sense can sensibly be asked for or offered' (*What We Owe to Each Other* (Cambridge, Mass.: Harvard UP, 1998), 21). The mistake leading to this conclusion is his view that 'actions are the kind of things for which normative reasons can be given only insofar as they are intentional, that is are the expression of judgement-sensitive attitudes'. That is at best ambiguous. Of course we respond to reasons intentionally. But it does not follow that reasons are always for intentional actions, that they can be conformed with only by intentional actions. There are plenty of reasons that are conformed with by actions, intentional or otherwise.

6. Conclusion

The distinction between adaptive and practical reasons has important consequences. For example, we may well say that practical and adaptive reasons do not conflict. While we may have epistemic reasons for a particular belief and a practical reason not to have it the two conflict neither in the way that two epistemic nor in the way that two practical reasons conflict. The outcome of 'conflict' between adaptive and practical reasons is not, as in genuine conflicts between practical reasons or between epistemic ones, that the better reason prevails. They are not in competition, and reasons of neither kind can be better than reasons of the other. Rather, adaptive reasons, being the standard reasons for belief or for having emotions, prevail. Practical reasons, being non-standard, can 'win' only by stealth.[40] There is much here that remains to be explored, not least being the question: in what sense are reasons of the two types reasons in the same sense? This is due to their being normative in the same sense, as will be explained in Chapter Five. In this chapter I merely tried to sort out the terrain, to show that normativity is not to be explained by value, and to endorse one implication of Bernard Williams's work, namely that the key to normativity is in the concept of following a reason.

---

[40] Note though that standard and non-standard reasons for action, both being practical, can conflict in a straightforward way. And the same is true of reasons for intentions.

4

On the Guise of the Good

Every action and pursuit is thought to aim at some good

Aristotle

I don't care what's right or wrong

Kris Kristofferson, 'Help Me Make It Through The Night'

In an article that established this phrase[1] as the standard name by which this ancient thesis is referred to these days Velleman rhetorically challenges its adherents:

The agent portrayed in much philosophy of action is, let us face it, a square. He does nothing intentionally unless he regards it or its consequences as desirable....Surely, so general a capacity as agency cannot entail so narrow a cast of mind. Our moral psychology has characterised, not the generic agent, but a particular species of agent, and a particularly bland species at that.[2]

To launch us on our way I will provisionally take **the Guise of the Good Thesis** to consist of three propositions:

(1) Intentional actions are actions performed for (normative) reasons, as those are seen by the agents.[3]

(2) Specifying the intention that makes an action intentional identifies central features of the reason(s) for which the action is performed.

(3) Reasons for action are such reasons by being facts that establish that the action has some value.[4]

---

[1] Which is borrowed from Aquinas, *Summa Theologica* (ST) 1a2ae, 8, 1: what is willed is always willed '*sub ratione boni*'.

[2] D. Velleman, 'The Guise of the Good' (1992) repr. in *The Possibility of Practical Reason* (New York: OUP 2002), 99.

[3] The normative/explanatory *nexus* (see Chapter Two above) establishes that when one acts for the normative reason that P one acts in the belief that P is a reason for the action, and one is motivated by that belief. In the sequel I rely on this result in stating (1) and variants of it. Needless to say, sometimes 'I did A for the reason that P' is true because P is the correct non-normative explanatory reason for the action.

[4] Meaning that that there is some good in the action is the reason for it. This is a brief version of a complex thesis which explains what kinds of values constitute or provide reasons, and spells out when the value of actions does not provide practical reasons. Some such cases will be discussed later in the book.

From these it is said to follow that

> (4) Intentional actions are actions taken in, and because of, a belief that there is some good in them.

For most purposes we can ignore the second proposition, which is often assumed but rarely considered when discussing the Thesis. There are other ways in which the Thesis was understood and formulated. Velleman, for example, assumes a relation between intentions and desires. Explaining the rationale for the Thesis he writes:

The reason is that he acts intentionally only when he acts out of a desire for some anticipated outcome, and in desiring that outcome he must regard it as having some value.[5]

I will remain non-committal about the relations of intentions and desires, and will therefore not discuss desires in this chapter.[6] The above statement of the Thesis presupposes cognitivism about discourse on reasons and values. Trying to state and discuss the Thesis in a way that is neutral between cognitivism and non-cognitivism would unreasonably complicate matters. There should be little difficulty in applying the considerations below to non-cognitivist or other versions of the Thesis.

On the face of it Velleman is blaming supporters of the Thesis for a factual mistake, a mistake about human psychology. Perhaps because they are bland and square they think that all people are. But it is more likely that he is merely teasing his fellow philosophers. After all, the Thesis fits Hitler and religious fanatics more straightforwardly than it does your neighbourhood grocer (as the examples below will illustrate), and they are hardly your common or garden square and bland types. Besides if it is wrong the Guise of the Good is more likely to be wrong about all people some of the time than about only some people all of the time. Commonly alleged counter-examples to the Guise of the Good (for example touching a dark spot on the wall or passing one's fingers through one's hair 'for no reason at all') are hardly actions unknown to the square or bland among us.

The Guise of the Good is best understood as a conceptual thesis; the three propositions constituting the Thesis are taken to be conceptual truths. That underpins the derivation of (4) from (1) and (3): Given that (1) and (3) are conceptual truths, only a conceptual or logical mistake could lead people who act for what they take to be practical reasons to deny that they act in the belief that there is some good in the action. And because their denial rests on such a mistake it does not undermine the conclusion that they do in fact have such a belief.

Section 2 considers the case for the first leg of the Thesis. It will lead to the formulation and defence of a revised version of the first part of the Thesis in Section 3. Sections 4 and 5 will then tackle objections to the third part of the Thesis. But first, in Section 1, some different ways of understanding the Thesis are considered, and a prima

---

[5] 'The Guise of the Good', 99.

[6] In *Engaging Reason* I argued against the view of desires that is required for the correlation between them and intentions assumed by Velleman.

facie argument for it is offered. In the final section I will raise the issue of the significance of the Thesis as it emerges from these discussions. Does it still fulfil the aspirations of its traditional supporters?

1. Initial objections, clarifications, and a prima facie case

What could support the Guise of the Good, given the many apparent counter-examples? Here are two such counter-examples:

A: The miner: The management proposes to close the colliery. The miners vote on whether to accept the proposal and the redundancy pay that goes with it or to oppose it. You talk to one of the miners: 'You are voting to stay put'.—'Sure', he says. 'So you must have some hope [of keeping the mine open]'.—'No hope. Just principles'.

B: The fish: sitting in the bath, Johnny, and it does not matter whether he is a child or an adult acting like a child, says: 'I am a fish' and beats the water with his open palm (presumably pretending to flap it with his tail). 'Why did you do that, Johnny?'—'That's what fish do'.

We can readily imagine how in cases like these it may be difficult to get the miner or Johnny to acknowledge that there was value in the action. The miner may insist that his vote does no good. He just had to vote that way. Perhaps, we may say, it is a matter of integrity for him. Johnny may be altogether puzzled by the thought that there was some value in the action. He was just playing at being a fish.

We know how the argument develops, or one way it may develop. When thinking about their intentional actions agents do not necessarily think of them under the Guise of the Good, and they may not even be disposed to think of them in that way. That is, there may be no ready way, no readily available evidence or argument that would lead them to acknowledge that their intentions express, imply, or presuppose belief in the value of the intended actions. So the Thesis assumes that when such acknowledgement is not forthcoming people nevertheless believe that there is something good about their intentions, or intentional actions (which therefore conform to the Guise of the Good), and are somehow mistaken if they deny that.

But perhaps, contrary to (4) above, the Guise of the Good does not presuppose that agents believe that there is value in their actions. Let us allow, for the sake of argument, that reasons are facts that endow the action with some value. Is action for a reason action taken in the belief that there is value in the action? There may be an alternative. It is difficult to deny that actions are intentional only if and because the agents are aware of some of their characteristics. But need they believe that the characteristics constitute reasons for actions? One alternative suggestion is that action for a reason is action performed in the belief that it has certain characteristics that the agent treats as reasons, that is as good-making. He need not believe that they are good-making, just as someone who accepts a proposition treats it as true, though he need not believe that it is true. The analogy is Velleman's. He thinks that that is the most that can be claimed by supporters of the Guise of the Good. But, he contends, this claim is true only if 'take it as good-making' means that one treats the characteristic in the same way one would if one thought that it is good-making, which can be the case even though one may believe that it is not good-making. Velleman's point is that supporters of the Guise of the Good must resist this interpretation. They must understand 'take it as good-making' to mean take it to be good-making, which—according to this suggestion—describes their attitude to the fact so taken.

A terminological convention may help. Let's say of people that they think that something is the case only when they believe so, and the belief is in their mind at the time. People have many beliefs that are not present to their mind. They believe much more than what they currently think about. Many such beliefs are remote from their thoughts, except on rare occasions. I believe that my mother was 30 when I was born. But it must have been some twenty years or more since I last had that thought. Applying this to the matter in hand I will understand taking a feature of an action to make that action good in some respect to be tantamount to believing that the feature is good-making. We say that the agents take the feature to be good-making rather than that they believe it to be good-making to intimate (a) that they do not necessarily think of that at the time, (b) it further intimates that they may not be able to articulate that belief, at least in that way. It is stated in the report of their beliefs in terms that they may not be fluent in (e.g. 'value' is used in philosophical writing as something of a term of art—see below), at a level of generality they are not comfortable with, etc. When people act because they take the action to have a good-making feature, it is not merely that they have the belief that the action has some value and that they take that action, rather the belief is part of what leads them to take the action, and it guides the action. It is not in their mind, but it is part of the explanation of what they do. There is of course the alternative understanding of what is meant by treating a feature as good-making, but as Velleman points out, that alternative does not support the Guise of the Good. So I conclude that to defend the Guise of the Good one has to accept proposition (4) above, that is that intentional action is action performed because of a belief that the action has some value.

Supporters of the Guise of the Good must, therefore, attribute to the miner and to Johnny, in the examples above, either mistakes about their own beliefs, or mistakes in rejecting certain characterizations of their beliefs. What could explain such a mistake? Two responses help to explain what is at issue. First, the notion of 'the good' or 'value' used in expressing the thesis is not to be confused with the concepts that are normally expressed by ordinary use of these terms. This is evident from the fact that in discussions of the Guise of the Good Thesis 'value' and 'good' are used interchangeably, even though they are neither synonymous nor does their normal use express the same concept. In arguing for and applying the Guise of the Good Thesis philosophers rely on a concept with broader applications than those associated with the normal use of those words. There is no point in trying to describe this concept here. It is familiar from the writings on the subject, and on value theory generally. And of course, one familiar aspect of it is the absence of agreement about its nature.

The second response, made necessary by the first, as well as by other considerations, is that the Thesis does not assume that agents capable of intentional action must have the concepts used in stating the Thesis (the concepts of the good, intention, reason for action), nor does it claim that they believe that these concepts apply to each of their intentional actions. It assumes that they have a belief about their action that can be truly characterized as a belief that the action has a good-making property, one that constitutes a reason for the action, and that reason or their belief in it, explains why they perform the action.[7]

In attributing to the miner, in the example above, the belief that the action is good because, e.g., it is required by principles, we are not distorting his views. We neither attribute to him a concept of value according to which being required by sound principles endows an action with value, nor do we ignore or pervert his distinction between actions that are good because they promote good ends and actions that are required by principles. We are simply describing his views using a broader concept of value, one that allows that an action can have value either because it advances the realization of good ends or because it is required by a valid principle, as well as in other ways.

More, however, is required to deal with Johnny. First, we need to distinguish Johnny the child from Johnny the adult playing at being a child playing at being a fish. We—their parents and others—attribute to children beliefs they do not altogether have, and concepts they do not altogether possess, and our doing so is a vital part of their learning process.[8] Others may also have a defective grasp of concepts, and therefore a defective grasp of the beliefs that they use those concepts to express. Such cases are not counter-examples to this, any more than they are to other conceptual theses.

How about Johnny the adult? Even when prompted he does not endorse the thought that there is something good in acting as a fish would. Possibly he would assent to it if subjected to a lengthy explanation and argument. But that is not the point. The Guise of the Good Thesis claims that he has the belief when he acts like a fish, not that he can be brought to adopt that belief. To maintain the Thesis, to show that it applies to people like Johnny, one has to establish that his pretending to be a fish discloses a belief that there is some good in acting like a fish, perhaps because he believes that imaginative play-acting is good, or for some other reason.

There may be other positive indicators that Johnny does indeed have such a belief. But perhaps there are none. In that case defenders of the Guise of the Good will say

---

[7] See Chapter Two for the discussion of the normative/explanatory *nexus*.

[8] I will not consider the conditions under which animals that do not possess concepts act intentionally, or have intentions, as I believe that those differ radically from the conditions under which animals possessing concepts act intentionally and have intentions.

that the fact that Johnny's play-acting is intentional shows that he believes that there is some good in his action. They will, in other words, take the Thesis to be at least to some extent self-verifying. This may look like a refutation of the Thesis, but it is not. For example, we would not hesitate to attribute to Johnny belief that his brother is unmarried, on the sole ground that he believes that his brother is a bachelor, given that it is a conceptual truth that bachelors are unmarried (and that Johnny is a competent user of the language, or of some relevant segment of it).[9] We do not require an independent ground for the attribution of the belief.[10]

The difference, some will say, is that the Guise of the Good cannot be relied upon until it is established. True. My point was merely that it is no refutation of it, no argument against it that on occasion the Thesis itself is the main ground for the attribution of the appropriate belief. I will return to cases like Johnny's once the case for the Thesis is examined.

But what is the case for the Thesis? It starts from a crucial point, made by Anscombe, and recently emphasized by Setiya,[11] namely that those who act intentionally know what they do (know it under the description under which the action is intentional, as some will add). In itself mere knowledge is consistent with the actions being done unintentionally. Agents may be mere witnesses to what is happening to them, or to what they do accidentally. What marks intentional actions is that they are done because of what their agents believe the action is (including what it may bring about). That means that what the agents believe about the action leads them to do it, and guides their doing of it, all the way (that is, as far as that kind of action can be guided by its agent),[12] and that suggests that they approve of the action, given what they believe about it. They so act because they approve of the action, and that in turn means that they think that it has some value, since value is what we approve of.

Human beings being what they are, their attitude to their intentional actions is often too ambivalent to say that they approve of what they do. They may retain doubts about the wisdom of their actions. They may believe that it would be better to avoid what they are (intentionally) doing. They may even do what they do because it is not the best thing to do, do it in order to hurt themselves, or someone else, or for other (explanatory) reasons. The Guise of the Good is meant to accommodate such

---

[9] It is important for the analogy that 'My brother is a bachelor' and 'My brother is unmarried' are distinct beliefs, just as intending to Φ and believing that there is some good in Φ-ing are distinct mental states or attitudes.

[10] It would be different if one were to say not that Johnny believes that there is some good in his action, but that he was thinking that at the time.

[11] G. E. M. Anscombe, *Intention* (Oxford: Basil Blackwell, 1957); K. Setiya, *Reasons Without Rationalism* (Princeton: Princeton UP, 2007), 24.

[12] I was tempted to write 'guide the action all the way to its conclusion', but when I hit the bull's-eye the conclusion is when the dart hits the board, and that is some time after I stopped guiding it. I intentionally hit the bull's-eye only if I hit it by intentionally throwing the dart and guide my throwing the dart all the way to its conclusion. The qualification in the brackets in the text is not ideal either. Perhaps it is possible to use some remote control mechanism to affect the flight path of the dart. Not doing so does not undermine the guidance condition of intentionality.

ambivalent and akratic conduct by claiming merely that agents see some good in what they do, which they may do even when they are ambivalent or convinced that they are acting for the lesser good (or the greater evil).

The Thesis does not express optimism about human nature. It is meant to accommodate not only mistakes, even gross mistakes about what is of value, but also anomic conduct in defiance of value (though this last point will not be discussed until Section 5 below). Its point is that intentional actions are actions we perform because we endorse them in light of what we believe about them, and that means that we must believe that they have features that make then attractive, or as we say, features that give them value. The thought is that endorsement presupposes an appropriate object. It does not presuppose that the action has endorsable properties, but it does presuppose that it is taken by the agent to have such properties.

Talking of agents endorsing their intentional actions is metaphorical. It is meant to point out a feature of intentional action of which the Guise of the Good is meant to be an account. It assumes that intentions are necessarily accompanied (if not partly constituted) by beliefs about the intended action. They cannot be identified by their felt quality, or by their direction of fit, alone. The thought is familiar: Fear is what it is partly because those afraid think that they are in danger. Envy is what it is partly because the envious believe that the object of their envy is superior in some desirable respect (success, reputation, happiness, possession of some advantages, etc.). Neither can be identified by their 'felt' qualities alone. The Guise of the Good takes a similar view of intentions. They differ from other mental attitudes or states that accompany some of our actions, the Thesis claims, in their necessary association with beliefs about the actions and with their role in the acting. The beliefs have to explain why the agents took the actions, i.e. they must figure in an explanation of their actions that relates to the way they saw the actions, and aspects of themselves and the world, and how that led them to take the actions. Hence the Guise of the Good's claim that intentions must involve a belief that there is something attractive about the action, that it has some value.

The preceding four paragraphs present a case for the Guise of the Good, which is good enough unless there are considerations militating against it. That is what we must examine next.

2. Are intentional actions actions for reasons?

The Guise of the Good is, whatever else it is, a thesis about intentions. How does it relate to intentional actions? There are independent intentions, as I will call them, which are ones one can have at a time one is not doing what the intention is an intention to do. My intention to fly to New York next week is an independent intention, as is my intention to complete this book. I have the second intention while doing what I intend to do, that is while being engaged in the activity of bringing the book to completion, but I can have it while I am eating, sleeping, or gossiping with friends. It is not an intention that I can have only when doing what it is an intention to do.

On the other hand, when I (intentionally) drink some water the intentionality manifest in my action is an aspect of the action, an aspect of the way the action is performed. It could be that I am drinking the water because I have an (independent) intention to drink the water, but it could be otherwise. I may just distractedly pick up the glass of water and sip from it, while thinking about the implications of a flaw in my argument. My action is intentional, but there is no Intention with which I perform it. At other times while there is an independent intention with which I perform an intentional action it is not an intention to perform that action. When talking about my friend's holiday I uttered the word 'went' and did so intentionally, but I was hardly aware that I used that word at that moment. I did it intentionally because I intended (had the independent intention) to describe his holiday experience, and saying 'went' was part of that activity. I did not have an independent intention to say 'went', but I said the word in the course of acting for an independent intention that I did have.

Embedded intentions, the intentions present in all our intentional actions, are aspects of, manners of, acting, and thus distinct from independent intentions even when we act intentionally because we have an independent intention. They consist in facts such as that our actions are guided by beliefs about what we are in the process of doing (what we do if our action is to be intentional), so that at the sub-personal level our movements are continuously monitored and adjusted to fit those beliefs, and in other facts playing a similar role in the performance of the actions.

Given this distinction between independent intentions and embedded intentions, which is the Guise of the Good about? The first part of the Thesis, as stated, is about embedded intentionality, as that is the feature that makes all intentional actions intentional. There can, of course, be a sister thesis to the effect that independent intentions to perform an action involve a belief that there is some good in the action. It may well be thought that this sister thesis is less vulnerable to objections than the Guise of the Good in the provisional form given it at the beginning of the chapter. I will return to this possibility. For the time being let us take 'intentions' in the discussion of the Thesis to refer to embedded intentionality.

Consider Ignatius who placed a bomb on a regular commercial flight in order to destroy incriminating documents being transported on it, knowing with complete certainty that if the documents are destroyed everyone on board will be killed. The bomb explodes, destroys the documents, and kills everyone. I think that Ignatius has murdered the people on the aeroplane, and that he did that by intentionally killing them.

It is sometimes said that one Φs intentionally if and only if one Φs with the intention of Φ-ing. In the preceding paragraphs I suggested that some intentional actions are not performed with an independent intention, and it is natural to say that they are not performed with an intention. They are intentional because of their embedded intentionality, as I called it, that is, because of the manner in which they were performed. But there is no need to make an issue out of a point of linguistic propriety. We can accept that whenever one Φs intentionally one Φs with the intention to Φ, provided it is understood that the intention need not be an independent intention. It may be merely an embedded intention, i.e. nothing other than the intentionality embedded in the action.

Ignatius did not have an independent intention to kill the passengers and crew. He would have been just as happy, or even happier, had the documents been on a pilotless plane with no passengers, or if through a freak chain of events the documents were destroyed, but the passengers and crew were uninjured. Nor was the killing a means to destroying the documents, it was a mere side effect. But given how things were he did kill them intentionally. Therefore—by our terminological stipulation—he had an embedded intention to kill when acting to carry out his independent intention of destroying the evidence. His embedded intention to kill, his intentionality in killing the people, derived from his independent intention to destroy the evidence. More generally:

> **Derived embedded intentions** (definition): whenever one intentionally performs one action by performing a second action, if one has an independent intention to perform the second action, but no independent intention to perform the first, then one's embedded intention to perform the first derives from one's embedded intention to perform the second. Putting it semi-formally: (x) (Φ) (ψ) [If x intentionally Φs by intentionally ψ-ing, and if x has an independent intention to ψ, but no independent intention to Φ, then x's embedded intention to Φ derives from x's embedded intention to ψ]

Does Ignatius' case constitute a counter-example to the Thesis? After all Ignatius intentionally killed people without believing that there was reason to kill them. This is familiar territory, and the responses to the alleged objection are numerous and well known. Some of them are more controversial than others, and there is no point in rehearsing them all. Think of one possible response to the objection, that is that Ignatius has a reason to kill the people, namely that the killing is a by-product of the destruction of the evidence, and Ignatius thinks that he has reason to destroy the evidence. This reply is unhappy as it stands. It does not even purport to show that Ignatius believes that he has reason to kill the people on board the plane. Rather it claims that because he believes that he has reason to destroy the evidence he has reason to perform those actions that he will be performing by destroying the evidence. This cannot be right. One's belief (possibly mistaken) that one has a reason to do one thing cannot, in this way, generate reasons to do other things.[13]

Possibly if Ignatius has a reason to destroy the evidence he has a reason (obviously not necessarily undefeated) to kill the people on the plane, though even this is far from clear. After all killing them is not a means to the end of destroying the evidence. Be that

---

[13] The claim in the text is a generalization of a claim often made regarding instrumental rationality, namely that if you think that you have reason to pursue a goal you really have a reason to pursue the means to the goal. See Chapter Eight.

as it may it is irrelevant to the assessment of the Guise of the Good which is, as it must be, about people's beliefs about their actions. That there was (possibly unbeknown to the agent) a reason to perform an action is no ground at all to think that it was performed intentionally.

So, does Ignatius believe that he has reason to kill the people? He may well not believe that, and if so he would not be mistaken. He believes that he has reason to destroy the evidence. But that, in itself, does not show that he believes that he has reason to do anything else, not even if he does believe that in destroying the evidence he would also be doing those other things.

Nevertheless, the objection fails to undermine the Thesis. Ignatius intentionally killed the people because he killed the people by intentionally destroying the evidence, and he knew it (knew that that was what he was doing while doing it). All that the objection shows is that the first proposition of the Guise of the Good, which says

(1) Intentional actions are actions performed for reasons, as those are seen by the agents

should be augmented to clarify its meaning:

(1') Φ-ing is intentional only if, in the belief of its agent, there is either a reason to Φ or a reason to perform another action such that by performing it he will, as he knows, be Φ-ing.

The question we face is whether the argument for the Thesis, namely that it contributes a vital element to the explanation of intentions, applies to the Thesis in this amplified form. We can reply by considering again the example: Had the embedded intention to kill the people not been derived from the embedded intention to destroy the evidence one might have felt that (1') defeats the promise the Guise of the Good holds of contributing to the explanation of intentions. Had the intention that is not supported by belief in a reason, not been derived from the other intention, which is supported by such a belief, it would have appeared that the Thesis applies to some intentions only. Therefore it is not part of an explanation of intentions generally. But given that the objection relies on derivative intentions that problem is avoided.

The Guise of the Good explains non-derivative embedded intentions, and the derivative ones are explained by being derivative. There is nothing more to them. That is, it is not as if Ignatius has two separate (embedded) intentions. Rather, in the circumstances his (embedded) intention to destroy the evidence is extended, as it were, and counts also as an (embedded) intention to kill. As mentioned above, the intentionality of an action consists largely in its performance being responsive to a belief about what the action is to be. Ignatius' action of killing the people on board is responsive to the belief that the action is to be a destruction of the evidence, and to no other. There is no independent existence to the derivative embedded intention to kill (beyond his knowledge that in destroying the evidence he will be killing the people).

It is instructive to compare cases like Ignatius' with some activities consisting of a sequence of actions,[14] activities such as giving a lecture, singing a song, driving a car, or walking to the door. Here too each of the actions, which in combination constitute the activity, is intentional. But while every one of them could be an action we attend to and think about, our attention to them is intermittent, and of varying degrees of intensity. Typically, agents are not aware of many of the individual actions that constitute such activities (saying 'and then' in the middle of the lecture, or singing an A flat note, or using turn signals when driving, or slightly adjusting one's direction when walking to the door, and so on). Consequently, agents are guided by knowledge of how to produce the sequence, and not by beliefs about the reasons for many of the individual actions constituting the activities.[15]

Yet, these cases differ from Ignatius'. While here too the performance of one action depends on performing the others, the dependence is very different. It is not a case of each of them being performed by performing another of them (though the activity as a whole occurs by performing all of them). Each requires different movements, or their absence, and each is governed and controlled by us separately. Their dependence expresses itself by the fact that later actions are modified in light of earlier ones, so that all are governed (to various degrees of success) by the overall purpose of the activity as a whole. (If in driving I stray slightly to the left at one point I will compensate by turning slightly to the right and so on.)

This suggests that the embedded intentions of each of the actions that constitute such activities are governed by one or more independent intentions that determine the content of the embedded intentions, thus making the activity as a whole intentional: an intention to give that lecture, sing that song, drive home, and the like. It is tempting to go further and to claim that

(5) Every intentional action or activity is governed by some independent intention, which determines the content of its embedded intention(s).

If so, then the relationship of the governing independent intention to the embedded intentionality of the action merits careful exploration, which it cannot receive here. Roughly understood, if intentional actions are not only performed because of their agents' belief in reasons for them, but are also controlled and guided by the agents in light of those beliefs, then the independent intention that involves belief in a reason for

---

[14] To be distinguished from sequences of bodily movements that may constitute one action (e.g. lifting one's arm) but are not distinct actions in themselves.

[15] Is it the case that they have conditional beliefs: that one should say 'went' when that is required to express one's thought in the way that one started to express it, etc.? Any attempt to pursue this thought runs into complications that expose the implausibility of the suggestion. We simply know how to use the language, etc. No specific beliefs of this kind are involved. At the same time we may interrupt, divert, or abort the sequence if we become aware that it requires an action that there is a clear and undefeated reason to avoid—intentional actions, and semi-automatic action sequences are controlled by subliminal monitoring of their progress, both in getting to their goal, and in not involving undesirable actions.

the action determines the content of the embedded intentionality that guides the performance of the action, to make it what it must be to conform to the believed reason. (5) can be supplemented by

(6) Every independent intention involves belief in a reason for the action intended;

and together (5) and (6) can replace (1') in a new version of the Guise of the Good Thesis. Is this new version immune to criticism? (6) seems plausible. I will consider it later on. The weakness is in (5).

We can accept that in the case of many intentional actions their intentionality (their embedded intentions) is governed by independent intentions. Some such relationship between independent and embedded intentions is needed to explain how independent intentions lead to intentional actions. The question is whether all our intentional actions are governed in this way by independent intentions.

We have already seen examples that show this not to be the case. Acts such as passing one's hand through one's hair while thinking or talking, or of idly scratching the surface of the table, and many others, are intentional, but normally the people performing them do not have independent intentions to perform them. This is not because they do not plan or decide on them in advance. Independent intentions, just like embedded ones, can be formed in the acting. They need not precede the action. Nor are they counter-examples merely because the agents are disposed to say that they performed these actions for no reason (or for no special reason). Such utterances can be reconciled with the Thesis by claiming that people mean that there is no reason worth mentioning, that the reasons are too insignificant to mention. It is just that while all the counter-examples of this kind are actions that can be performed with an independent intention, typically they are not. Normally they are on the periphery of their agents' attention, and are genuinely performed idly, for no reason or purpose. But it is at the core of (6) that independent intentions necessarily involve belief in reasons or purposes. It is therefore impossible to endorse both (5) and (6). Since (6) seems plausible, we must take the examples to refute (5), and with it the new version Guise of the Good.

3. Revising the Guise of the Good

Without (5) the thesis of the Guise of the Good must be weakened to apply only to actions that are done with an independent intention. (1) now becomes

(1") Actions performed with an independent intention are actions performed for reasons, as those are seen by the agents.

The rest of the thesis is unaffected:

(2) Specifying the (independent) intention that makes an action intentional identifies central features of the reason(s) for which the action is performed.
(3) Reasons for action are facts that establish that the action has some value.

The problem is that this revised version appears not to be supported by the argument adduced at the end of Section 1 in support of the Guise of the Good. The argument for the Thesis was that it explains what it is to act intentionally, and how intentional actions differ from others. It both supported the Thesis and underlined its importance as a key to the explanation of intentionality in action. The counter-examples establish that there are intentional actions to which the Thesis does not apply, and that undermines its claim to explain the nature of intentional actions. But without this argument what is there to support the Thesis? Besides, if it applies only to a limited range of intentional actions, it loses its promise of providing the key to an understanding of intentionality in action.

One is tempted to dismiss the counter-examples as dealing with insignificant actions. I have sympathy with this response, but it cannot consist simply of dismissing the counter-examples. To sustain the Guise of the Good we cannot rely on the insignificance of those examples. On the contrary, we need to establish their significance, their role in our life as persons, and to show how this is consistent with the claim that the Guise of the Good explains the nature of intentional actions, once the Thesis is adjusted to allow for the counter-examples.

Nor is the task of explaining the significance of the examples likely to be simple. There are other counter-examples, which are very different from the ones mentioned so far. One well-known class of counter-examples is expressive actions, such as kicking whatever is nearby in anger, or uttering swear words in exasperation. Nor do these two classes exhaust the counter-examples. I doubt that there is an informative way of drawing up a comprehensive list of types of counter-examples. But here are two others:

> **Hypnosis:** Acting under the influence of post-hypnotic suggestion Jane goes to her wardrobe, puts on a dress then takes it off and returns it to the wardrobe.
> **Kleptomania:** Rachel, a kleptomaniac, picks up a tin of pickled gherkins in the supermarket, and leaves the shop without paying.

Both Jane and Rachel knew what they were doing, and by all normal tests both acted intentionally. Both acted in a controlled way, tending to ensure that the actions would be successful (namely, that they accomplish what they intended to do). But both deny that they saw any reason to do what they did.

In considering these cases it is useful to return to the case of Johnny playing at being a fish, and of course his example stands for many. There I have suggested he did believe both that there was reason to play-act, and that there was some good in his play-acting. He is, I wrote, mistaken in denying these facts. It would, however, be implausible to think that this is true in the types of cases we are now considering. The intentions manifested in them do not, in the actual circumstances of these cases, reveal a possible reason for their actions in which they might believe. It is not like the case of someone who plays at being a fish, where the obvious reason is that it is fun. Second, we have an alternative explanation of their behaviour that undercuts the case for thinking that they have a belief in a reason for their actions. While in Johnny's case the attribution of belief that there was some good in the action did crucially depend on the Guise of the Good Thesis, it was also supported by these circumstantial, largely negative facts: the availability of a plausible belief to ascribe to Johnny, and the absence of an alternative explanation of his action.[16] So, while I rely on the Thesis in my understanding of Johnny's case, that reliance conforms to the general principle that belief is not attributed on the strength of a single indicator alone. The new types of cases are therefore different. They are real exceptions to the Thesis.

All of this notwithstanding, there is a strong case for not taking Jane's and Rachel's actions as damaging counter-examples. They are clearly exceptional, as the causes of their actions are inimical to the normal exercise of our powers of agency. Some may even challenge whether it is appropriate to call such actions intentional. I think that such doubts are unwarranted,[17] but that does not matter. We can allow that such doubts are natural for the cases are ones in which normal powers of agency are temporarily reduced, and become partially ineffective.[18] That is why even though Jane and Rachel acted intentionally, and their actions do not conform to the Guise of the Good, they do not refute the Thesis.

That means that explanations and theses in the theory of action need not aspire to be exceptionless. I would go further and say that they should not aspire to be exceptionless, and if they are exceptionless that is a worrying sign, a sign that they miss important features of the situation. The examples under discussion bring out that being intentional can be a matter of degree. Actions are characterized as intentional by a variety of criteria, several of which can be realized to various degrees, making it appropriate to speak of degrees of intentionality. There are cases of which one should say: Yes, up to a point, or in a certain respect it was intentional, but in others less so. In some respects Jane and Rachel acted intentionally, but in others they did not. That is why their

---

[16] More needs to be said: First, the mistake I attributed to Johnny is slight. It results from an incomplete mastery of the concepts of reason or the good. It is rather like the mistake of philosophers who reject the Guise of the Good. Second, it may be denied that classifying an act as a case of kleptomania provides an explanation. Kleptomania is a poorly understood condition. But we know enough about it to rule out some explanations, including the attribution of normal independent intentions. We know for example that kleptomaniacs often steal objects they have no need for and that they are eager to get rid of once the episode is over.

[17] To see that it is instructive to compare these cases with H. Frankfurt's description of what he regards as acting under coercion (Frankfurt, 'Coercion and Moral Responsibility', in *The Importance of What We Care About* (Cambridge: CUP, 1988), 80). It does not matter that his characterization of coerced action is unduly narrow. His coerced actions are cases of people whose will is overpowered by the coercing action or circumstances, and they cannot help but do what they are doing. They act intentionally, but their actions are unlike what is normally understood as coerced action, which is action for a (perceived) reason to remove the threat. Frankfurt's coerced person does what is necessary to avoid the threat, but not for a reason. He has lost normal control over his power of agency. I think that in this case it is even clearer that the Frankfurt 'coerced' person is acting intentionally, but there is little reason to distinguish him from Jane and Rachel.

[18] Only partially ineffective for they act, controlling their conduct as they would had they decided to act not under the influences that make them act in the given circumstances.

examples do not refute the Guise of the Good. That is a thesis about intentional actions, and if it is true of all fully intentional actions; and if one can explain the exceptions by showing that the facts that establish that the Thesis does not apply to them also account for the fact that they are examples of diminished intentionality, then they lose their force as counter-examples.

This burden is easily discharged in the case of Jane and Rachel: Their purpose, their goal of performing these actions, is, as it were, imposed on them from the outside, by a hypnotist or by a pathological condition, and that both stops them from conforming to the Guise of the Good, and makes their actions less than completely their own, and therefore intentional only in some respects.

In another place I discussed expressive actions along similar lines.[19] I argued that they do not conform to the Thesis precisely because of ways in which they involve loosened control over the actions, which means that while they are intentional there are respects in which they display diminished intentionality. How about the other counter-examples we noticed, those of idle actions like stroking your hair? I noted the instinctive reaction that they are insignificant kinds of action. There are two ways in which they are marginal or insignificant. First, they are performed when our attention is elsewhere. That, as in other cases, affects their intentionality: in most cases they are actions we routinely perform, and therefore we can perform them without attending to them. But it does not matter to us if they fail, or change their character. Our fingers may slide out of their routine rhythm. The action may be interrupted, and we may still not notice, nor would the agent mind that the action failed, or got transformed from, say, stroking one's hair to gently flattening it. Second, typically these exceptions are relatively simple actions, consisting predominantly of routines of bodily movement. They do not include actions such as giving a party, campaigning in an election, or writing a novel.[20]

The second point shows that these actions are of marginal importance. The first point shows them to be, while intentional, of reduced intentionality. The fact that we do not fully attend to them shows that. It follows from this that the action is unlikely to be one of securing a result that goes beyond the disposition of one's own body. When one kicks a ball or turns on the tap one needs to attend to what one is doing, and one cannot attend to kicking a ball or turning on a tap without believing that there is a point in doing so. Again, these cases are exceptions because they are marginal cases of intentionality, not displaying all the features of intentional actions.

The revised Guise of the Good Thesis has other exceptions. Because I am unable to classify them exhaustively I will mention only one other kind of exception:

---

[19] *Engaging Reason*, 36–44. One can also question whether expressive actions can be governed by independent intentions at all. I will not consider this question.

[20] There are complications and further distinctions. For example, I can find myself operating an ATM without having noticed what I was doing. But in that case, while my movements may be intentional, I did not intentionally withdraw money from my account.

Nibbling after blood:[21] An accident causing horrible injuries and mutilations has just happened outside Jamie's window. The sight will disgust him, and he knows that. There is nothing he can do to help the injured. Yet he is powerfully drawn to the window, and is looking, feeling disgusted, and physically ill, at the sight.[22] There is no doubt that he went to the window intentionally, and is intentionally looking at the injured people outside. I will return in the next section to the question of whether Jamie has a reason to behave as he does. The crucial point is that he does not think he has such a reason, and yet his behaviour is intentional, and does not fall into any of the categories of exceptions so far examined. It should not be assimilated to the case of kleptomania. Jamie's case is meant to be one in which the agent is naturally motivated to act, but can resist. Jamie cannot help but feel drawn to look at the scene but he can suppress the urge, and stay away from the window. His situation is rather like that of someone who has a sweet tooth, and having had lots of chocolate already, is taking another piece, even though he knows that he will feel nauseated.

Jamie is another exception to the thesis, and his case cannot be explained away in the way the others were. It is not a case of diminished or marginal intentionality. Yet I doubt that it can undermine the Thesis. It is possible that Jamie believes that he has no reason for his action because he is conceptually confused about reasons. For example, had he thought that one has reason to satisfy urges, like the urge to look at a gruesome scene (or the urge to have one too many pieces of chocolate) then he would have believed that he has reason to act as he does. Moreover, it seems plausible that if Jamie is mistaken about thinking that he, and people generally, do not have reasons to satisfy urges of these kinds, his mistake is a conceptual mistake, due to an incomplete and somewhat mistaken understanding of the concept of a reason for action.

Whether all these suppositions are true depends to a considerable degree on whether there is in fact a reason to satisfy such urges. I will return to that issue in the next section. For the moment what remains is to explain why exceptions that are due to a conceptual confusion do not undermine the Thesis. Whether or not Jamie's is an apt illustration, the general point is that conceptual truths about the way people use concepts are bound to have exceptions when people misuse concepts. That is, given that the ability to use concepts involves the ability to misuse them, theses about concepts cannot be refuted by examples of their misuse.

---

[21] I am indebted to Ulrike Heuer for this example. My name for it derives from E. M. Forster: 'Of the many things Lucy was noticing to-day, not the least remarkable was this: the ghoulish fashion in which respectable people will nibble after blood' (*A Room with a View* (London: Edward Arnold, 1908), ch. 5).

[22] Cf. '"But," I said, "I once heard a story which I believe, that Leontius the son of Aglaion, on his way up from the Piraeus under the outer side of the northern wall, becoming aware of dead bodies that lay at the place of public execution at the same time felt a desire to see them and a repugnance and aversion, and that for a time he resisted and veiled his head, but overpowered in despite of all by his desire, with wide staring eyes he rushed up to the corpses and cried, 'There, ye wretches, take your fill of the fine spectacle!'"' (Plato, *Republic* IV: 439e).

4. Reasons and value

It is time to examine the third leg of the Thesis, namely that reasons for action consist of the fact that the action has some value. I will now assume that (1″) is correct, that is that actions performed with an independent intention are performed for reasons, as those are seen by the agents, that is, I will assume that independent intentions involve belief that there is a reason for the intended action. The question under consideration is whether reasons for action are that the actions have some value. If they are then (1″) implies that barring conceptual ignorance or mistakes actions performed with an independent intention are performed in the belief that the action has some value.

The argument for this view will proceed in two stages, and be followed by an examination of some objections. The first stage concerns the character of reasons belief in which is necessary for action with independent intentions. Such actions, actions done for a purpose as we can also describe them, are actions that were done by people who had a view of their situation, and in light of that view found some reason to perform the action (so much is established once (1″) is acknowledged). The reason must be something that makes the action one to perform, one that it would be good to perform, and that means that it must be something that renders the action desirable, namely a fact that shows some good in the action. In brief the reason the agent thought he had must be something that shows that the agent knew what he was doing, and not only that he felt, and witnessed himself being, propelled towards acting by some psychological condition. There must be something that he believed to be true of the action and that he took to make the action attractive. There must be something that made him decide to act because what he took to be the reason seemed to him to make the action worthwhile. Note that that the act is desirable, in the sense used here, cannot mean merely that there is a reason for performing it. Rather it is a characterization of the fact that constitutes that reason. One has the reason because the act is desirable. To take it to be desirable or worthwhile in the required sense, the agent's attitude to the reason for which he acts must be capable of sustaining certain counterfactuals: Had the agent been aware (or had he thought that he was aware) of undesirable features of the action he would have formed a view on whether the features that provide, as he believes, a reason for the action still make it the action to perform in spite of its undesirable aspects.[23] Such a view, and that is another conceptual observation, consists in a judgement on the relative importance of the good and bad features of the action.

Setiya did more than anyone else in recent times to challenge the Thesis. He thinks that intentional actions are taken for reasons but not in the belief that there is something good about the action. We need to address objections to the Guise of the Good advanced by him and others. But there are aspects of his view that reinforce my belief that the Thesis is right. In particular, he underlines the fact that agents who act intentionally know what they are doing and why:

---

[23] Though, as we must always remember, he might have acted for what he took to be the lesser reason.

It is sufficient to be acting for a reason that one meets the demand for an explanation of what one is doing and why. One need not also believe that the reasons for which one is acting are reasons to act in that way.[24]

Setiya recognizes the difference between reasons explanatory of an action and a normative reason for the action. Explanatory reasons of actions are facts that explain the actions. The following are three such reasons, possibly all truly explaining the same intentional action:

> Jill did it because she was jealous of Jim.
> Jill did it because she felt a sudden rage; a sudden rush of blood to her head made her do it.
> Jill did it in order to inherit Jim's wealth, as she knew that she would after Jim's death.

Only the last one explains the action by reference to a normative reason. Setiya insists, and is surely right, that whenever one acts intentionally one believes in some explanation of one's action. He is also right to insist that the explanation need not incline us, the spectators, to believe that the action was justified. Any and all of the above explanations can be available to the agent and none of them inclines me to believe that the action was justified. It is also right that because they are explanations of intentional actions they point to factors that (metaphorically speaking) pushed or pulled the agents towards the actions. But while there can be a number of (compatible but distinct) explanations of every intentional action, there must be for every action performed with an independent intention at least one explanation that meets an additional condition: it must explain why the agent decided to perform the action, rather than resist the pull towards it. Of the three examples only the last, only the explanation via a normative reason, does that. Depending on the circumstances the other explanations may be more revealing of the action, or they may constitute the more illuminating parts of a more comprehensive explanation that includes all three as elements. But only the third, killing to inherit, even establishes that the action was intentional (jealousy and a sudden rush of blood to the head, together or separately, may explain loss of control leading to accidental killing).

Setiya's account lacks the resources to distinguish between the first two explanations and the third one. Doing that is essential for an account of independent intentions. And, the suggestion is, what marks actions done with independent intentions is that they are ones that their agents believe to have some value in them, and thus the agents have available to them explanations by reference to what they take to be normative reasons, namely explanations purporting to show that there is some good in the action.[25]

---

[24] *Reasons Without Rationalism*, 12.

[25] It is not clear whether Setiya's own view (that necessarily when acting rationally one acts under the Guise of the Good, but irrational agents do not always do so) is inconsistent with the Thesis here defended. Irrational actions are by their nature deviations from the norm, and if those who do not conform to the Thesis

The second stage of the argument is required to counter one alternative understanding of actions for a purpose, and of normative reasons. According to it the argument thus far shows only that in acting for a purpose one believes that some feature of the action constitutes a normative reason for it. It does not follow that the agent believes that there is some good in the action (thus rejecting the tail end of the previous paragraph).

If, however, a fact cannot be a reason for an action unless it establishes that the action possesses some value, then in believing that there is a reason for an action one believes that the action has some value, unless one is mistaken or confused about the concepts of a reason, or of having value. So to deny that to act for a purpose involves acting in the belief that the action has some value one has to deny that to be a reason a fact must establish that the action for which it is a reason has some value. How would the argument proceed? Imagine the following conversation:

Jumping: Ben is in a building which is going up in flames. He jumps out of it. Abe: Why did you jump?—Ben: It was the only way I could save my life. Abe: I can see that but is there any good in that?

Or, imagine a different conversation:

Job: Ben: Why should I go to the interview?—Abe: It will get you the job.—Ben: Why is that a reason to go to the interview?—Abe: Because if you have a job you will earn a living and will not starve.—Ben: I can see that, but is there any good in not starving?

The last question in each exchange appears out of place, and redundant. The suggestion is that reasons can be just ordinary, i.e. non-normative facts. What is special about them is that they stand in a normative relation to an action, being a reason for it. To say of them that they establish that the action has some value is superfluous. It does not contribute to the fact that the reason is a reason. Therefore, acting for a reason need not involve belief that there is some good in the action. It is enough if it involves belief that one has reason to perform the action.

This view, I will argue, ignores rather than replies to what the first stage of the argument established. To be relevant to our discussion Ben's (I will focus on his example) reply must be understood to explain what he did by reference to normative reasons. But the understanding of the examples implied here fails to show that. To examine this claim I will focus on Ben and his Jump, and consider it in light of two further hypothetical situations:

are irrational (in part) because of their failure to act under the Guise of the Good then, as explained above, while their actions are exceptions to the Thesis they are not damaging counter-examples.

Torture (and death): If Ben would be saving his life by jumping he would be immediately seized by people who would first subject him to severe torture and then kill him.

Betrayal: suppose that to save his life Ben has to reveal the whereabouts of a document which will inform the evil regime of the identity of his colleagues in the opposition, who will be tortured and killed.

Let us assume that Ben rightly thinks that were he in **Torture** he would have no reason to jump, and that had he been in **Betrayal** he would have had a reason to betray (i.e. to save his life), but a stronger reason not to do so. It seems reasonable to assume that in **Jump** Ben not only believed that jumping is the only way to save his life, but also that in the circumstances of the case that it would save his life is a reason to jump, i.e. that he is not in a situation like **Torture**, and that belief was relevant to his action, as he would not have performed it had he believed that his situation is one in which he has no reason to save his life. Similarly, we can assume that he believed that the situation is not similar to **Betrayal**, that is that it is not one in which while he has a reason to jump it is defeated by other considerations. The suggestion is not of course that Ben considers and rules out the possibility that he is in many specific situations where he would have no reason to save his life, or would have defeating reasons. Rather, the suggestion is that he entertains a general belief that he has an undefeated reason to save his life.

The first stage of the argument above showed that in order to have that belief Ben needs to have and use certain conceptual capacities. Broadly speaking he must be able to judge that certain situations constitute reasons and others do not, and that sometimes more than one reason bears on the cases for and against performing an action. It was further argued that we individuate reasons by the good they do, the good that actions instantiate. An action that saves the life of Abe, and protects some beautiful picture from destruction, is one that we have two mutually reinforcing reasons to perform. They are two because the action instantiates two distinct good-making properties. For the purpose of the current argument we can accept that reasons are or can be ordinary facts, such as that jumping will save your life. That does nothing to undermine the argument that reasons are individuated by the good that conforming to them secures, and therefore that mastery of the concept of a reason requires some understanding of the notion of value. Therefore, given that action for a reason is action motivated and guided by belief that there is a reason, it also involves belief that there is some good in the action.

As we saw earlier, this argument does not establish that all actions with independent intentions are undertaken with such beliefs. It merely establishes that (a) given the direct conceptual connection between reasons and value one is justified in attributing a belief that there is value in an action on the basis of a belief that there is reason for it, so long as there is no evidence that the agent does not have such a belief; (b) evidence that the agent does not believe that there is value in the action in spite of there being a reason for it establishes some conceptual confusion on the part of the agent; and

(c) given that action with an independent intention involves belief in there being a reason for the action, any serious conceptual confusion about the nature of reasons means that the action is intentional in some deviant way only.

Let it be accepted that the facts that constitute a reason for an action also establish that there is some good in it. The rejection of the Guise of the Good now comes to rest on an additional contention: that the action has some value is not a reason for it. Stating that it has some good is nothing but another way of stating that there is a reason for it. For necessarily 'There is some good in Φ-ing' is true if and only if there is a reason to Φ. It now seems that rejecting the third part of the Guise of the Good (that reasons for action are such reasons by being facts that establish that the action has some value) depends on accepting some version of what is known as 'buck-passing'.

Some of the reasons why 'buck-passing' accounts of the good are false have been explained elsewhere,[26] and the matter cannot be fully examined here. In rejecting the view I will say no more than that the good of inheriting, surviving, getting a job, having friends, etc. does not depend on there being a reason to bring them about. We can establish their value without raising the question of whether there is reason to bring them about, and if we conclude that there is reason to bring them about that is because they are valuable. Hence, on cursory examination buck-passing fails to grasp the nature of value. But without it the alternative to the third leg of the Thesis fails.

5. Some objections considered

That concludes my two-step argument for the Thesis. Can it be sustained against the objections it faces? One of them has to do with value inversion, namely the fact that sometimes people sincerely take themselves to be acting against value, choosing actions because they are evil, bad, or worthless, and doing so with open eyes.[27] Such cases hold many fascinations for the theorist as well as many horrors for those at the receiving end. I have discussed them elsewhere,[28] where I explained that another reason for many theses in theory of action not being exceptionless is the ability to deviate from any norm, including those of meaning and rationality. Not all deviations are possible, but (given that determination of our beliefs, intentions, emotions, and so on is governed by multiple criteria) much is possible. I will not return to that discussion here. There are other objections:

[26] e.g. U. Heuer, 'Explaining Reasons: Where Does the Buck Stop?', *Journal of Ethics & Social Philosophy* 1/3 (2006) (http://www.jesp.org/).
[27] Compare Augustine's desire to steal the pears which, he said, he 'loved only for the theft's sake' and 'Doing this pleased us all the more because it was forbidden....I was being gratuitously wanton, having no inducement to evil but the evil itself' (*Confessions*, trans. Albert C. Outler (Philadelphia: Westminster Press, 1955), Book II, ch. viii, sec. 16), or Dostoevsky in *Notes from the Underground*: 'I got to the point of feeling a sort of secret abnormal, despicable enjoyment in returning home to my corner...acutely conscious that that day I had committed a loathsome action again'.
[28] *Engaging Reason*, ch. 2.

One objection has to do with cases where agents do believe in normative reasons for their actions, but in ones that do not establish any value in the action (for example, that it was undertaken to preserve racial purity).

Second, there are those alien cultures whose normative reasons seem to be entirely unrelated to anything we can make sense of.

Third, there are familiar cases in which the agent's judgement that there was no value in the action or that there was no reason for it is hard to dismiss as a case of being mistaken about his own beliefs. **Nibbling after Blood** belongs here.

The first of the objections requires us to revisit some of the ground already covered. Think of Jill who kills her uncle to inherit his fortune. We can assume that she will deny that there is any value in her action, and dismiss this as irrelevant because she is likely to be applying a different concept of value, perhaps one in which only moral values are values. But why impute to her a belief whose articulation requires a concept she does not have? Because she takes the fact that as a consequence of the killing she will inherit from her uncle as a fact that explains her action, in the required way, that is by being a feature of the killing that determines her to kill, not merely one that makes her kill. It guides her deliberation and is subject to rational constraints.

This shows that inheriting is a rational factor in her mind, that it does not explain her action in the way that the influence of alcohol might. And as a rational consideration militating for the action it is capable of being seen to be in competition with still further considerations. For example, the fact, should she learn of it, that if she kills her uncle she will sleep no more will give her pause, and may or may not lead her to desist.

Jill furnished us with the outline of an argument of why it is right to attribute belief in value to a person who explains his action in non-normative terms and declines to apply normative concepts to it. But it was an easy case, because it makes sense to think that she has the belief we attribute to her at least in as much as the feature of the action she points to (inheriting from her uncle) has value (even though not one justifying killing anyone). Now suppose that you see Brian punching and kicking a person in the street. You ask him why and he says: 'he is a bloody foreigner'. 'But what reason do you have to beat him up?' 'That is the reason: he is a foreigner.' 'Why is that a reason?' 'It just is.' End of conversation, and end of Brian's own thoughts about the subject.

Here there is no value at all in the action. What can justify attributing to Brian belief in the value of his action in this case? In spite of this difference, in all essentials Brian's case is like Jill's. He regards the fact that his victim is a foreigner as a normative reason. He too recognizes other reasons, and can reason which of them, if any, prevails when they conflict. Patient inquiry will show the contours of his beliefs, and disclose what normative concepts are apt to describe his views, and they will be concepts that show what, in his eyes, is good in this or that action.

It still remains unclear how the Guise of the Good can be reconciled with the possibility of mistakes. There is no difficulty if the mistakes are purely factual. The claim that Jill kills her uncle because (let us assume) she thinks that she will have a better life if she inherits from her uncle is consistent with her being mistaken about the prospect of inheriting. Maybe her uncle changed his will the week before, etc. There is no difficulty in reconciling such mistakes with the Thesis. But is it consistent with normative mistakes? Imagine someone who explains that this person deserves better treatment than that because he belongs to a superior race so that his interests count for more than the interests of members of inferior races, or that sex with people of inferior races is wrong because it dilutes the purity of the race, and so on. If he shares our concept of the good, and believes that racial purity is good, then that is his mistake. But assume that, as in our previous examples, our racist does not have our philosophical concept of the good. He does not admit to a belief that preserving purity is of value. In fact preserving racial purity has no value. What grounds do we have to attribute to him a belief that neither he nor we admit to?

The answer depends on our racist's grounds for his racism. He may believe that racial mixing leads to strife, or that it causes members of both races to fail to excel in the use of racially specific talents that he believes them to have. Such reasoning shows that he takes racial purity to be instrumental to genuine values such as the avoidance of strife, or the development of one's talents. He is wrong about the relationship between the ideals of purity, harmony, and fulfilment of one's potential. But given that he subsumes the mistaken value under real ideals or values it is plain that he believes that his racist actions have some value.

A difficulty exists only when the agents under discussion do not defend their belief in their false values by reference to any genuine values. They take them to be ultimate considerations, which cannot be justified by reference to any others. But even in such cases there may be direct evidence that these agents take their reasons, however misguidedly, to show that there is some value in their actions. For example, they are likely to recognize the relevance of questions of consistency, logical or factual, between their alleged consideration and others, which are genuine values. They may also acknowledge that at least in principle attaining some other goods may be impossible given their actions. They may, of course, believe that their reasons are consistent with those (genuine) values, and that they in fact lose no (other) goods by their actions. And it may be impossible to convince them otherwise. That is neither here nor there. In acknowledging the relevance of the issue to decisions about what to do, or to whether their reasons are sustainable, they show that they treat their reasons as facts that contribute to the value of actions.

What if the agents are indifferent to the relations of their racial reasons to genuine values? They may have some priority rules, avoiding the need for reasoning about the relative case for one or another consideration. This scenario is even clearer when we turn to the second of the classes of cases I listed above, the case of thoroughly alien cultures. In the nature of things there are no examples to give. We imagine a culture where the concepts used in stating reasons for action are alien to us, and have no equivalents among our normative and value concepts. Possibly such a culture is not possible, at least not among humans. Be that as it may the general argument given earlier, namely that independent intentions are formed for believed reasons, and that reasons relate to value, applies. The alien culture is not a counter-example. To be that we need to understand it. All we can say is that it is a culture of concept-using people, who can act intentionally. That, given the general argument for the Guise of the Good, is enough to establish that the Thesis applies to them, and our ignorance prevents us from finding anything to challenge or undermine the conclusion.

There will be the inevitable charge that in claiming that the Thesis applies to alien cultures we distort their meanings, and impose on them 'our' concepts which are not suited as tools for understanding their culture. But the charge is unwarranted. No claim to understand alien cultures was made. The concepts used in the Guise of the Good are 'our' concepts, and there is no pretence that they are not. Nor are they used to interpret aliens' world view, or their ways of justifying actions. Only two claims about the alien cultures are made: one is that the people there use concepts (or it would not be a culture) and that sometimes they act with independent intentions. The Thesis is true of them for no other reason than that it states part of what is involved in having independent intentions, and in acting intentionally.

Finally we have to address the third kind of objection, illustrated by the nibbling after blood type cases. Jamie, you will remember, intentionally goes to the window to look at the gruesome sight that makes him sick. He thinks that looking at it has only disvalue, and that he should not act as he does. How can we say that in spite of this he really believes that there is value in his action (or for that matter that there is a normative reason for it)? The answer is in the details of the case. One misguided objection to the Thesis points out that sometimes we act in pursuit of desires that arose in us neither by deliberation nor in response to recognition of the value of their satisfaction. Hunger, thirst, and sexual desires are examples. In many such cases we recognize the value of satisfying such desires once they arise, thereby recognizing that there are reasons (not always undefeated) for satisfying them. These cases are therefore not counter-examples. The value of satisfying such desires is sometimes the value of having the desire and satisfying it. Food and sex are among the good things in life and they are better if we have them when we desire them. Even with food and sex the desire for them does not always come when it would be good to have them. Sometimes the only value in satisfying the desires is to get rid of them.

In his own eyes Jamie's case is rather like that. He thinks that there is nothing intrinsically good in looking at gruesome sights whether or not that is done in response to an urge to do so. That is what he is telling us when he denies belief in the value of the action. But he could have resisted the urge, and he did not. He decided to go to the window and look at the sight. That shows that he takes it that there is some value in his action. It will relieve him of the tension of wondering what things are like, wanting to see them, regretting not having done so. It will probably also give him some satisfaction, some pleasure, which he does not understand and probably does not want to understand. He looks out in order to rid himself of the urge and the tension it produces, and probably also in order to get that pleasure.

Perhaps, you will say, but that does not establish that he believes that there is some value in his action, given that he denies having the belief in its value. I think that his denial shows that he disapproves of his own action even while he is so acting. But that is typical of cases of akrasia, and Jamie's is one of them. In acting with an intention to see the gory sight he is acting in the belief that there is some good in so doing. But his disapproval of his own action leads him to be less than completely honest with himself. He is reluctant to admit to the satisfaction he derives, and confines himself to referring to the nausea he feels. His emphatic disapproval overpowers any recognition of the value of relieving his urge, which he does not want to acknowledge as a benefit, even though he knows that it is.

6. Concluding remarks

Velleman complained that the Guise of the Good takes people to be square and bland. I suggested that it applies not only to larger than life fanatics like Stalin whose reasons we can understand but also to people who defy comprehension. Moulay Ismail was supposed to have said: 'My subjects are like rats in a basket. And if I do not keep shaking the basket, they will gnaw their way through.'[29] By all accounts he behaved accordingly. I doubt that Moulay Ismail was square or bland. Those who read the quotation as simply expressing concern for his continued rule underestimate him by ignoring the attitude to other people that it expresses. I do not think that I can understand many of his actions. Of course, we have learnt to expect the worst of people. We may be shocked by stories of his conduct, but are not surprised. Something like that is what we expect to happen from time to time. That does not establish that we understand his reasons. Yet we have reason to think that the Guise of the Good was true of him, for even though much of his brutality was spontaneous, his actions were commonly informed by independent intentions.

Of course, the Thesis that I was defending is neither the one that Velleman or Setiya and other critics objected to, nor the one that others upheld. The question arises whether the modified Thesis retains the philosophical interest and the promise that the criticized Thesis held. In particular, can it still be seen as providing a key to the understanding of rational agency by explaining the nature of intentions? A brief survey of the modifications made and of one or two other points put in the course of argument suggests an affirmative answer.

The revised Thesis presupposes a distinction between embedded and independent intentions. It does not claim to apply to embedded intentions except in as much as they depend on and their content is determined by independent intentions. Hence it applies only indirectly (if at all) to derived embedded intentions, and it does not apply to intentional actions not governed by independent intentions. Even regarding indepen-

---

[29] Sultan Moulay Ismail was the founding father of the Moroccan royal Alawite dynasty. For our purposes it does not matter whether the attribution is true. It is enough that people can believe it to be true.

dent intentions it allows for exceptions, provided they can be explained as deviations from the norm, either by being cases of less than complete intentionality or as anomic inversions of the norm. Finally, I emphasized that the Thesis attributes to agents belief that the action has some value-endowing property and that they recognize it as value-endowing. They need not be able to express that belief in words, and they certainly need not have the more general belief that their reason for the action is that it has some value (rather than that it has the specific value they take it to have).

This last clarification is vital to make the Thesis plausible. It would be absurd to assume that intentional actions presuppose possession of abstract concepts, nor does the purpose of the Thesis require it to assume that. This clarification does not undermine the claim of the Thesis to express a central element of intentional action. The other modifications and clarifications are not ad hoc. They arise out of the general nature of theses about concept-employing attitudes and actions. They apply to the full or mature form of the attitude, allowing exceptions in other cases, so long as the fact that the case is an exception explains why the case is less than paradigmatic of full intention, and allows for the possibility of people playing with the norms, twisting them in a variety of ways, a phenomenon very familiar from creative ways of using language, which achieve an effect by deviating from the norms (of meaning or grammar, etc.).

So the revised version of the Thesis retains its role in the explanation of action and of intentionality. From its earliest origins, whatever version of the Guise of the Good was viewed with favour was the keystone keeping in place and bridging the theory of value, the theory of normativity and rationality, and the understanding of intentional action. Its success in fulfilling this key role makes the version here defended a variant of the traditional Thesis, serving the same role in establishing the interconnections of those wider theories.

5

Reason, Rationality, and Normativity

We are now in a position to employ the view that all normative phenomena are normative in as much as, and because, they provide reasons or are partly constituted by reasons. It makes the concept of a reason key to an understanding of normativity. To see how it yields an explanation of normativity I will outline an explanation of the connection between reasons and Reason and between Reason and normativity.

1. Reasons and Reason

Why are the facts that constitute reasons reasons? What about those facts makes them reasons? As expected the answer is that there is an inherent relation between reasons and Reason—understood as our rational faculties or abilities. But what is it? Think of it this way (and I will focus here on practical reasons): that I am hungry is a reason to eat. But what has **Reason** to do with it? Would I not eat, if hungry and if food were available, anyway? Do not animals of species that do not possess Reason eat when hungry? If reasons do not call for Reason why are they reasons?

The facts that are reasons are reasons because they are part of the case for a certain response, for a belief or an action or an emotion. The example of hunger shows that there can be, and sometimes there are, capacities and processes that reliably lead to appropriate responses to facts that are reasons, without the mediation of rational powers. Nor are these absent in humans.[1] So why are the facts that are reasons reasons if there are processes that align us with them independently of our rational powers? We cannot claim that in all domains reliance on rational capacities is better at bringing us into conformity with reasons than other processes. Often the automatic, Reason-bypassing processes are best. Though there need be no rivalry between them, and often rational capacities regularly interact with Reason-bypassing processes.

---

[1] The point is probably limited to practical reasons and reasons for emotions, and does not apply to epistemic ones. The reason is conceptual: ACTION is a generic concept, covering acting for reasons, as well as other actions, whereas BELIEF is the specific concept that marks one of various broadly cognitive states that essentially involve our rational capacities, being essentially responsive to reasons (not necessarily in being generated by the realization that there are reasons for them, but rather in being modified upon awareness that there are sufficient reasons against them), as some of the others, like guesses and hunches, are not.

Of course, some reasons can neither be brought into existence nor recognized except through the use of Reason. This is the case with most reasons that are cultural creations. But even in their case, the explanation why they invite certain responses need not invoke that fact. For example, some epistemic reasons that can only be recognized as reasons by rational creatures can nevertheless be identified as facts *calling for belief*, because they are *evidence for the truth of that belief*, and their standing as evidence can be explained without invoking the way that they are identified.

So why are they reasons? Because Reason is our general capacity to recognize and respond to reasons. There are other capacities that also do that. But Reason is the universal capacity to recognize reasons, one that in principle enables us to recognize any reason that applies to us, and to respond to it appropriately. A little later I will say more about the way Reason enables us to recognize reasons. In particular that it enables people *reflectively* to recognize that the facts that are reasons are reasons. Here I will add just one observation: that Reason is a capacity reflectively to recognize reasons does not entail that every exercise of reason involves reflection, reasoning, or deliberation. With experience we learn to identify and respond to reasons instinctively, though in ways that depend on and presuppose first, reliance on past reflection, and second, the monitoring presence of rational powers that control and stand ready to correct mis-identifications or misdirected responses.

Even so the statement that Reason is the general capacity reflectively to recognize and respond to reasons may appear formal and uninformative. Is not saying that Reason is the universal capacity to identify and respond to reasons like saying that we dream dreams? Since 'dreams' are defined as the objects of dreaming, saying that we dream dreams is a mere formal statement. But the analogy with Reason and reasons ignores the normative aspect of the relations between them. Reason can malfunction. There-fore, reasons cannot be defined as what Reason recognizes and responds to. As Reason may fail there are criteria by which success and failure are determined, and they determine what reasons there are to be recognized. Put another way: our rational powers are a general capacity to recognize and respond to facts that make certain responses appropriate, and such facts are reasons because they can be recognized and responded to by our rational powers. The second half of this statement is a conse-quence of the *nexus*: when certain responses are beneficial or otherwise appropriate or welcome but they cannot be recognized by Reason, they are not reasons.

In conclusion we can say that Reason does not make reasons into reasons (Reason is not a source of reasons). But they are reasons because rational creatures can recognize and respond to them with the use of Reason. Needless to say, there are features of the world that we respond to, where the response cannot be secured via using our rational powers. Such responses are involuntary, and the triggering features are classified as stimuli. Because the response cannot be secured by our rational powers, that is because it cannot be guided reflectively, those stimuli are not reasons, even if the response is sensible, beneficial, etc. Being the general reflective capacity to recognize reasons distinguishes Reason from other processes like hunger, or the instinctive avoidance of fire, which recognize some specific kinds of reasons. To be a reason a fact must be one that we can respond to using our rational powers, whether or not on any specific occasion that is how we do respond to it.

The last sentence basically repeats the normative/explanatory *nexus*. It, and the argument leading to it, also help vindicate the *nexus*. Features of the world constitute a case for certain responses (actions, beliefs, emotions). But to be such a case it is not enough that a certain response to them is welcome or apt. It is necessary for rational creatures to be able to respond to those features by using their rational powers to recognize them for what they are. This relationship of reasons to our rational powers has far-reaching consequences. The one that will feature later in the book is the knowability requirement it implies: only features of the world that we can in principle come to know can constitute reasons. Because only they can be responded to using our rational powers, and as we saw, that is what makes reasons into reasons.

2. Reason and reasoning

The thesis that Reason is the power to recognize reasons will be finessed and somewhat modified in Section 3. First, I will relate it to the more common view that Reason is the power of reasoning. Paul Grice combines both views:

No less intuitive than the idea of thinking of reason as the faculty which equips us to recognize and operate with reasons is the idea of thinking of it as the faculty which empowers us to engage in reasoning.[2]

Grice thought that the two ideas harmonize. He proceeds to explain:

Indeed if reasoning should be characterisable as the occurrence or production of a chain of inferences, and if such chains consist in (sequentially) arriving at conclusions which are derivable from some initial set of premises, and for the acceptance of which, therefore, these premises are, or are thought to be, reasons, the connection between these two ideas is not accidental.[3]

I will basically follow Grice, though my understanding of the way the two ideas harmonize is somewhat different from his. Reasoning is Reason's main way of recognizing reasons. But Reason includes more than the power to reason, and since not all reasoning aims at identifying or operating with reasons the relationship of Reason and the power to reason is more complicated than may at first appear.

I have already noted that some mental activities that depend on past reasoning are manifestations of our rational powers even though they do not involve present reasoning, and that activities guided and monitored by Reason in the background are also manifestations of rational powers not involving reasoning. But there is much more: Sometimes it is irrational for people to fail to engage in reasoning, as when they have an overriding reason to reason, and are in a position to know that. Such

---

[2] P. Grice, *Aspects of Reason* (Oxford: OUP, 2001), 5.   [3] Ibid.

irrationalities are non-derivative. Even when, as is only sometimes the case, failure to deliberate is a result of a decision, the irrationality of failure to deliberate does not depend on such prior decisions, and does not derive from their irrationality. Likewise, sometimes the very activity of reasoning, even when one is reasoning flawlessly, is irrational. There may be conclusive reasons, which are known or should be known,[4] not to reason, thus rendering one's reasoning irrational. One can also be non-derivatively irrational in continuing deliberation for too long, failing to come to a conclusion. Besides, weak-willed intentions show that intentions can be non-derivatively irrational. They are intentions one forms against one's own better judgement. It follows that the irrationality of a weak-willed intention does not derive from failure to reason correctly.

These considerations suggest that Reason consists of more than the power of reasoning, and includes at least the power to form intentions and decisions. Two further considerations support this view. First, reasoning being an intentional activity, the power to form intentions and decisions is intimately involved in it, and given that their faulty use can render the whole activity of reasoning on a particular occasion irrational there is a case for counting the power to form intentions and decisions among our rational powers. Secondly, and more generally, I have been implicitly relying on a test that I will call the *irrationality test*. It says that if the exercise of a capacity can be non-derivatively irrational (that is irrational not because something else is irrational) then the capacity is one of our rational powers. I will further consider the test in the next section.

Still, the ability to reason is at the core of our rational capacities. How so? Some, like Harman, think that reasoning 'is a process of modifying antecedent beliefs and intentions'.[5] But that should not be taken to provide a test for identifying reasoning. It is doubtful whether reasoning has to lead to modification of belief or intention. I may, for example, examine one of my beliefs, and, not having new information, I consider again the considerations I considered before and do not find grounds to change my mind.[6] My reflections seem a straightforward case of reasoning, but they need not involve a change of belief or intention. There are other cases in which one reasons without changing beliefs or intentions. The reasoning may have been tentative, not reaching any final conclusions.

In such cases the reasoning, though not leading to their change, is undertaken *in order* to examine the case for a modification of one's beliefs or intentions. This is commonly the case, but it need not be. One may indulge in reasoning in order to pass the time. One may playfully examine hypotheses and their consequences, doing so as a game, a

---

[4] Or at least one should accept the proposition that there are such reasons and behave accordingly.

[5] 'Practical Reasoning', in *Reasoning, Meaning and Mind* (Oxford: OUP, 1999), 46. His later paper 'Rationality', ibid., allows for reasoning which does not change judgement.

[6] Nor need such cases yield a belief that the beliefs or intentions one examined need no revision, at least they need not yield a belief to that effect different from the one one had before. It depends how much one trusts the reasoning just concluded.

pastime, possibly doing so carelessly, offhandedly. It does not matter. Nor does it matter if one's reasoning is affected by wishful thinking. One would not change one's views as a result, for one does not take the activity, the reasoning, seriously. It is just an amusing pastime. One is not irrational on such occasions, even though the reasoning is faulty, and may display a propensity to commit fallacies, which may give grounds to believe that one would be irrational when reasoning 'seriously'.

Bad reasoning, I conclude, is[7] irrational when and because one non-accidentally fails to respond appropriately to reasons, and the failure is, is due to, a failure or malfunction of one's rational powers. When one has reasons to form beliefs or to consider the merits of beliefs or actions, then if one does so irresponsibly, carelessly, or negligently, or if one's reasoning is affected by motives that should not affect it, that is if one is guilty of one or another form of motivated irrationality, and if these failures are due to an entrenched disposition to fail in that way, which afflicts one's rational powers, then one is failing to respond properly to those reasons in a way which renders one's flawed reasoning irrational. Motivated irrationality is a form of belief-formation contrary to reason and so is negligent reasoning. Negligence is not merely carelessness. It is carelessness (for which we are responsible) when we have reason to be careful.[8] We can only reason negligently when we have reason to form beliefs or seriously to consider the merits of beliefs or of actions. The examples support the conclusion that mere bad reasoning does not constitute irrationality. I will return to the point below.[9]

This leads to the main point: While not all reasoning aims at identifying and operating with reasons, the power of reasoning is essentially a power whose purpose is to identify and respond to reasons. Reasoning is an intentional mental activity, and a norm-guided activity in that it is governed by criteria of correctness. This is true of both 'serious' and 'non-serious' reasoning. Reasoning playfully is reasoning governed by the same norms, and mistakes remain mistakes (though their commission does not show that we act irrationally).

The norms of correct reasoning show that the point of reasoning is to enable us to detect and respond to reasons. The constitutive standards of reasoning determine both what is reasoning and what is successful reasoning. Reasoning is an activity that is held responsible to those standards, an activity whose success is judged by them.[10] They

---

[7] Perhaps I should say 'deserves to be regarded as' irrational—one may well claim that the boundaries of the concept of 'irrationality' are vague on this point. It is the theoretical account of Reason that ultimately drives this view. So at most one can claim that it is not at odds with firm features of the concept.

[8] See Chapter Thirteen.

[9] Note that there are two kinds of mistake in reasoning which do not render it irrational. In the text I focus on one of them, i.e. when one is not reasoning 'seriously', one is not reasoning in response to a perceived adequate reason to reason. The other is when the mistake is due to a lapse of either memory, attention, or another of one's ancillary powers, which are not among the rational powers, or to an occasional rather than entrenched malfunction of one's rational powers.

[10] This gives rise to the question: when is an activity governed by those standards? I will not consider this issue here. It seems reasonable to suppose that it is so when either the person engaging in the activity is one who has the capacity to reason and takes himself to be so governed, namely accepts the legitimacy of judging

determine the success of reasoning as a generic activity, though the actual reasoning one engages in on this occasion or that may be undertaken for some other purpose, and may be successful—though not as reasoning—for some other reason even when flawed as a piece of reasoning.

This, then, is the difference between 'serious' and 'non-serious' reasoning. Serious reasoning is meant to serve its point, and, therefore, to be successful according to its constitutive standards. Non-serious reasoning is the use of the same capacity, performing an activity of the same type, but detached from its normal purpose. The activity is still held responsible to its constitutive standards, but the reason that led to engaging in it may be served regardless of its success as reasoning. So non-serious reasoning is a marginal case of reasoning. It is understood and is broadly conducted as serious reasoning, but, as it is detached from its point, failure to conform to the norms governing the activity is not necessarily, on that occasion, a fault.

Reasoning's constitutive standards are ones that ensure that, when followed, the conclusion of the reasoning is warranted, namely one that we have adequate reason (though not always a conclusive reason) to accept. Directly they warrant belief, indirectly they warrant actions, emotions, and other reason-sensitive attitudes. To be more accurate we need to take note of the fact that in most instances of reasoning one relies on some propositions whose credentials are not examined during that reasoning episode. Hence successful reasoning assures reasoners that the conclusion is warranted, on the assumption that so are the unexamined propositions relied upon. Its purpose is to establish that given that assumption, certain beliefs, intentions, and the like are warranted.

The norms of correct reasoning determine the point of reasoning, and since the norms of correct reasoning are norms that warrant acceptance of the conclusion of a correct reasoning the purpose that they serve is to guide us in judging which beliefs and intentions we have reason to have. This establishes the connection between Reason as the capacity to respond to reasons, and reasoning.

3. The scope of Reason

Characterizing Reason as the general reflective capacity to recognize reasons raises the question of which mental capacities belong with it, which belong with our rational powers? I will say little on the subject. It is not my aim to suggest criteria capable of adjudicating various borderline cases, either between animal species that typically have Reason and those that do not, or regarding the boundaries within a species between those who have Reason and those lacking it. The fate of borderline cases may well

his activity by those standards, or if that person behaves in a way which is reasonably understood as presenting himself to others as someone who is reasoning. But much more needs to be said.

depend on additional considerations not canvassed here. But a few further observations on the core concept, relying on our general knowledge of it in a way that ties it to the account here proposed, may be helpful.

Various connections between Reason and other concepts can be called upon in clarifying the concept. One is between Reason and personhood: creatures that do not have rational powers are not persons. A second is between Reason and accountability, which marks one sense of responsibility. Creatures that do not have rational powers are not responsible (accountable) for their actions.[11] And a third is with the notion of irrationality. It led to the irrationality test suggested above.

The irrationality test suggests demarcations of Reason that are not dictated by its characterization as a general power to recognize and operate with reasons. Decline in some mental capacities like the powers of memory and of concentration affects one's ability to detect and respond to reasons. But we do not stop being persons simply because of loss of memory and of concentration (at least not while we retain them to a minimal degree). Hence these powers do not belong with our rational powers. But if so, given that our success in recognizing reasons depends on our powers of concentration and memory, can Reason be identified with the reflective power to recognize reasons? This identification of Reason is correct, so long as it is understood to represent the core of the concept of Reason, and is not expected to set its limits.

The irrationality test is one of a number that offer more help with marking the limits of our rational powers. It too suggests that memory and the power of concentration are not among them because failures of memory and concentration, however bad, are not irrational. They are among many mental capacities that are ancillary to our rational powers, enabling them to function well. Some provide the input on which the rational capacities rely through perception, sensations (including those that are accompanied by drives: like hunger, thirst, discomfort at the surrounding temperature, sexual arousal, and more), or memory.

By the irrationality test the powers of reflection, deliberation, and decision are rational capacities. Interestingly the irrationality test suggests that the capacity to have some emotions is among our rational capacities because some emotions can be non-derivatively irrational.

The test relies on a distinction between derivative and non-derivative irrationality. Something is derivatively irrational if it is irrational only if and because something else is irrational. For example, actions are irrational only if and because the intentions or decisions that render them intentional are irrational.[12] Cases of non-derivative irrationality are cases where the irrationality of what is irrational does not logically or

---

[11] This does not mean that we are only responsible for or accountable for the exercise of our rational powers—see Chapter Thirteen.

[12] One interesting result is that only intentional actions can be irrational, and not even all of them, since not all intentional actions are actions undertaken with an intention.

conceptually depend on nor is it due to some other irrationality. If a flawed exercise of a capacity can only be derivatively irrational that capacity is not part of Reason. If, on the other hand, a flawed exercise of a capacity can be non-derivatively irrational then that capacity belongs with our rational capacities, is part of our Reason.

Arguably emotions can be irrational when and because they are founded on irrational beliefs. Fear based on an irrational belief that the shadow on the wall is the devil about to kill one is an irrational fear. But emotions can be irrational when they are disproportionate reactions to rational beliefs. In such cases their irrationality is non-derivative, and therefore by the irrationality test, emotional capacity is part of our rational powers.

This conclusion will not surprise some, while seeming preposterous to others, who will take it as a reason to reject the irrationality test. There is, however, an independent case for including the capacity to have some emotions among the rational powers. For example, empathy is crucial for understanding other people, as well as animals of other species, and arguably emotional responses are essential to our ability to understand that we have reasons of certain kinds, and to the ability to understand[13] what response to various reasons is appropriate, as well as to motivate us to respond as we should. There are also separate reasons for confidence in the irrationality test. It seems natural to think that only failures of the power of Reason could be irrational, except when the irrationality is derivative, that is, when it derives from failure of powers of Reason. However, these matters require a more detailed exploration of the role of the emotions in our make-up as persons, in our motivations, and in our cognitive powers.

There is one important clarification, indeed modification, of the slogan that Reason is the general reflective capacity to recognize reasons. The slogan may give an unduly passive image of rational powers, just tabling reports, as it were, of what reasons are to be found where. The slogan should be augmented to say that Reason is the general capacity to recognize and respond to reasons. Clearly that is so regarding theoretical reasons: recognizing a sufficient case for a belief whose content is immediately available to the agent is adopting the belief. There is no separate step involved, no transition that, pathological cases apart,[14] can fail. Properly recognizing epistemic reasons is properly responding to them.

Things are somewhat different when it comes to practical reasons (including reasons for mental acts). Action may require interventions in the world, regarding whose success agents have less control than over the response to epistemic reasons or to reasons for mental acts, intentions, and omissions (on most occasions). Except for the capacity to reason, decide, form intentions and a few other capacities essential to be able to act with intention that are part of our rational powers according to the

---

[13] We can learn of those reasons, and of the response they make appropriate, from testimony or other indirect means. But arguably we can understand them only because we have emotional capacity ourselves.

[14] A reminder: psychological phenomena are 'pathological' when they meet some of the criteria determining their attribution (or existence), while failing others.

irrationality test, the capacity to act is not part of our rational capacities. This has to be borne in mind in interpreting the extended slogan.[15]

Nevertheless the extended slogan, properly understood, is correct. For even regarding practical reasons, rational capacities must involve response to them if they are to involve recognizing them. People who recognize a conclusive reason to Φ (to eat, or whatever) and who fail to respond to it at all, fail (when the time comes) to form an intention to Φ, have no positive attitude at all towards Φ-ing, do not respond appropriately to other people Φ-ing, etc., are non-derivatively irrational. Thus, the irrationality test shows that capacity properly to respond to reason is part of our rational capacities.

Furthermore, people who fail to respond appropriately in any way at all do not fully recognize the existence of the reasons. Attribution of belief depends on the existence of a variety of criteria of belief, and they include not only avowing the belief, and attesting to reasons for it, etc., but also responding to it appropriately: those who would not put an apple on a table (assuming normal circumstances), for fear that the apple may fall to the floor show themselves not to believe that there is a table there. At best theirs is a pathological case of belief. Hence recognizing reasons involves responding to them, and the mental capacities involved in setting ourselves to respond, the powers of decision and intention, are part of our rational powers.

4. Irrationality

Reason, i.e. the rational powers or capacities, is involved in activities such as choosing, deciding, reasoning. These activities, and therefore their results[16], are rational so long as the rational powers guiding them function properly. They are irrational when these powers malfunction. It is possible, by accident, for the result to be a happy one, that is the person concerned may accidentally choose or decide as reason directs. But when the result is the outcome of a malfunctioning rational power it is happy but irrational.

This line of thinking allows for a distinction between mistakes (in reasoning, choosing etc.) that render the activity irrational, and those that do not. The latter are due to malfunctioning of powers relied on in these activities that are not among the rational powers. For example, they may be due to lapses of memory, failures of attention, or failures of perception, etc. Possibly, the account has to be modified somewhat to allow for additional kinds of mistakes that do not render the activities irrational. (For example, cases where the malfunction is accidental may not render the

---

[15] A capacity to act, while not part of the rational capacities, is an essential part of the wider group which constitute the capacity for rational agency. They are pivotal in determining responsibility. See Part Three of this book.

[16] Using the term in the technical sense given it by von Wright (*Norm and Action* (London: Routledge & Kegan Paul, 1963)), i.e. as the state that defines the completion of the process or activity.

activity and its outcome irrational. Arguably, they are irrational only if due to a persistent condition.) I will not examine that possibility here.

This view of rationality—the view that we are rational so long as we are properly guided by well-functioning rational powers—has been followed by various writers, e. g. Michael Bratman. Others, e.g. John Broome, have taken a different view: according to them rationality relates to the occurrence or non-occurrence of certain relations among mental states. For example, and to simplify, our beliefs are irrational if they are contradictory.[17] By way of abbreviation I will call the first view dynamic and the second static.

How do the two views relate to each other? They would be in harmony if it turns out that they coincide in their judgements about the rationality of beliefs, intentions, emotions, etc. But they do not. We may reach conditions condemned as irrational by the static view by reasoning as we must according to the dynamic view. For example, there may be overwhelming evidence for a certain proposition and once aware of that I believe that proposition. I have no choice, and I am dynamically rational. But it is possible that I am also aware that the proposition contradicts some of my other beliefs. I am therefore aware that either this or some other of my beliefs are false, but I dynamically-rationally think that the fault is in the others. I do not know which of the others is the guilty one. I only know that the proposition concerned contradicts one or another of my other beliefs. Nor do I know how to improve my other beliefs (one of them is false, but it may approximate the truth). This may occur in conditions in which it would be dynamically irrational for me to abandon any of my current beliefs, but dynamically irrational not to add to them a belief which, as I know, is inconsistent with them.

If situations like this are possible then the two approaches to rationality conflict. They also conflict because one can satisfy the static conception without satisfying the dynamic conception (e.g. via a string of mindless accidents).[18] It is possible to say that there is no conflict for these are not two rival accounts of rationality. Rather they are explanations of two different concepts of rationality. I cannot examine this possibility here, so let me simply record that I suspect it to be mistaken, i.e. I suspect that the two accounts do conflict, and that at least one of them is mistaken.

5. Normativity and personhood

Finally, I turn from the relations between Reason and reasons, to the relations between Reason and normativity. First, I will reject two tendencies sometimes found in discussions of normativity. One is to identify it with an orientation towards value,

---

[17] Broome lists a number of more carefully formulated relations between mental states whose occurrence renders them irrational. For Broome's criticism of some inadequate views of the nature of rationality, see 'Does Rationality Consist in Responding Correctly to Reasons?', *Journal of Moral Philosophy* 4/3 (2007), 349–74.

[18] A point made to me by Niko Kolodny, whose letter to me I am here quoting.

the other with the demands of rationality. I will suggest that the value of a thing provides some reasons, but not all, and in any case does not explain the force of reasons. I will also suggest that there is no reason, and no need for a reason, to be rational.

The difference between practical and epistemic reasons is central to the attempt to understand the normativity of reasons. It defeats any attempt to explain normativity as having to do with the influence of value on us. Epistemic reasons have nothing to do with value. One way to persist with the view that normativity is tied to value is to claim that reasons for belief are only conditionally normative, which means that they are only conditionally reasons. They are reasons when it is good to have that belief, but not otherwise. Epistemic reasons help towards having true beliefs, and this matters only when there is a reason to have them. Epistemic reasons are a type of instrumental practical reasons.

This view flies in the face of the fact that all judgements that go with reasons apply to epistemic reasons unconditionally. To mention but one: we are not irrational for failing to conform to a conditional reason until the condition is met. But it is irrational not to have the beliefs one has adequate reason for whether or not the condition obtains, that is whether or not there is value in having them.

Next, a few words about Rationality and normativity. First: neither the question of the hold epistemic reasons have on us nor the question of their normativity is the question 'why be rational?'. We can fail to conform to reasons that apply to us and still be rational. That would be the case so long as our failure is not due to a malfunction of our rational powers, for example, so long as our failure is due to non-culpable (e.g. non-negligent) mistakes and ignorance, or to failing memory. There is no normative standing to being rational as such. There is no reason to be in a state in which one failed to identify reasons through a non-culpable mistake, even though the failure is not a failure of rationality.[19]

There are two common mistakes that may be responsible for some writers' focusing on reasons to be rational. *First*, they fail to notice that we need no reasons to function rationally, just as we need no reason to hear sounds in our vicinity. So long as we are conscious our powers of hearing and our rational powers are engaged, though not always successfully.[20]

---

[19] Of course we do not commend a person for failing non-negligently to identify reasons that apply to him, and therefore we do not say to him 'you were very rational in what you did'. But that is a point about the implications of what we say. At other times we may say so: 'Oh, I have become totally irrational' he exclaims in despair, and we reassure him: 'You are perfectly rational, you just made a mistake'.

[20] In a comment on an earlier version Kolodny explains the point better than I did: 'True, my believing that 2+2=4, knowing what I know, is not (i) under my voluntary control. Nevertheless, my believing it can be (ii) the direct upshot of deliberation, of reflection on reasons (and this amounts to a kind of control over my beliefs, . . .). By contrast, not even the latter is true of the *functioning of my rational powers as a whole*. There is no question of deliberating, "Shall I function rationally?" and then directly proceeding, on the basis of an affirmative or negative answer, to continue functioning rationally, or to cease to. I could not *follow* such a reason, in the sense Raz emphasizes in "Reasons: Practical and Adaptive" (in D. Sobel and S. Wall, *Reasons for Action* (Cambridge: CUP, 2009) 37)' [on which Chapter Three is based].

Second, as I have noted above, some writers confuse conformity to some logical principles with being rational. Most commonly avoiding contradictions (or known contradictions) is mistakenly said to be a condition of rationality. To be sure those who have contradictory beliefs have some false beliefs, but that does not show that they are irrational, or that they ever did something irrationally. One can come to endorse a set of contradictory beliefs without ever committing an irrationality.

The quest for an explanation of normativity is not the question 'why be rational?', and neither is it the question of the reasons for conforming with reasons. Such reasons do not explain the hold reasons have on us, as these supporting reasons need as much explanation as the supported reasons.

There is, of course, another question: what is the point, one may ask, of being successfully rational, of functioning rationally well? The point is obvious: it is a way of identifying and responding to reasons. There can, of course, be non-standard reasons for functioning rationally well, or badly. One can bet that one will not fail or that one will fail to function rationally and so on. Such bets then provide (practical) reasons to try to do what it takes to win them. Clearly the question of normativity is not about the existence of such occasional reasons.

These preliminaries illustrate the difficulty in locating the question we are after. Perhaps the following illustrates the difficulty: suppose one defies an epistemic reason, what is wrong with that? The answers seem to be internal to the concepts involved: we say—if you defy reason you are irrational. So what? Your beliefs are incoherent—well suppose they are, what of if? And so on. The temptation to say: 'if you disregard reasons you will fall down and break your neck', or point to some other adverse practical result, is overwhelming. And as we saw has to be resisted.

We, some of us, want to step outside the conceptual web, and find an explanation for the hold that reasons have on us. This we can do since their hold on us depends on the fact that responsiveness to reasons is constitutive of personhood.

I should immediately make clear that I do not share the thought of some philosophers that a constitutive account of reasons will settle what reasons there are. Thinking of practical reasons, Korsgaard, e.g., claims that 'Action is self-constitution and accordingly,...what makes actions good or bad is how well they constitute you.'[21] She suggests that all practical reasons can be derived from this insight: we have a standard of being a good person, and you have reasons for actions that will constitute you as one, or something which includes this idea. My constitutive account of personhood can yield no such results. It is a mere formal account, and we will have to consider whether such a formal account is, even if true, of any significance.[22]

---

[21] C. Korsgaard, *Self-Constitution: Action, Identity and Integrity* (Oxford: OUP, 2009), 25.

[22] This makes it immune to the criticism of constitutive accounts advanced by David Enoch in 'Agency, Shmagency: Why Normativity Won't Come from What is Constitutive of Agency', *Philosophical Review* 115 (2006), 169–98.

Here is the formal constitutive story: Reasoning and deliberation are mental activities that we can decide on. There are practical reasons for or against reasoning and deliberating. But we cannot decide how to respond to epistemic reasons. It is constitutive of belief that it is governed by our responsiveness to epistemic reasons, governed gaplessly, automatically as it were. Responsiveness to epistemic reasons is constitutive of believing.

Responsiveness to reasons can, of course, fail: through mistakes, fallacies, wishful thinking, self-deception, and more. How then are these standards constitutive of belief? Does not failure establish that conformity to reason is only contingently related to belief?

Conformity to reason is indeed contingent. What is essential to belief is, *first*, its subjection to the normativity of reasons, its being subject to evaluation as warranted or unwarranted depending on its conformity with reasons; and, *second*, the fact that it is automatically, as it were, self-correcting. Failures to conform to reasons are self-correcting when we become aware of them. Again, no gap exists, no decision to correct is required, no involvement of the will.

That is why the responsiveness to epistemic reasons is a form of constitutive normativity, normativity built into the very possibility of belief.[23] Not all our mental states are responsive to reasons. I may think that I am a feathered bird, and not respond at all to evidence that I have no feathers nor beak, etc. But then that kind of thinking is fantasizing, imagining, daydreaming, or the like; not believing.

There are two lessons here: first that we recognize the difference ourselves. We know the difference between belief and imagination, and we know that it consists in part in that belief is, while imagination is not, subject to the full discipline of reasons (though imagination may be partially subject to it, in a variety of different ways). I say that we know that, meaning not that we would, or even could, articulate what we know in these terms. We may not be that reflective, we may have false philosophical

---

[23] One worry, raised by Veli Mitova, is that as responsiveness to reasons is constitutive of the capacity to form beliefs when that capacity malfunctions its product is not a belief at all. If it is constitutive of beliefs that they respond to reasons, non-responsive beliefs are not beliefs. However, that misinterprets the way in which responsiveness to reasons is constitutive of beliefs. Each belief is responsive to reasons not by being a successful product of our rational powers, but in being automatically and gaplessly subject to their functioning, and that is manifested by its self-correcting potential discussed above. Naturally, the full story is much more complex. One point in particular is crucial for the coherence of my account: some conditions of rationality, i.e. some conditions of responsiveness to epistemic reasons, are universally constitutive of belief, so that there is no (non-pathological) belief that does not conform to them. Some of these apply when agents are aware of their application. An example of these may be the condition that one cannot, in full awareness of the fact, believe a proposition and its negation (though one can oscillate between them, or display other pathologies). We are sensitive to some conditions of rationality even when we are not aware of them as conditions of rationality, in that they tend to increase the degree to which we hold beliefs only if warranted through consciousness bypassing processes. But generally, firm belief that something is a condition of rationality (whichever way it is conceived, i.e. even if one is not aware of it under this description) will have a more direct effect on our belief formation. That enables us to improve our understanding of rationality, and of the conditions of rationality, and thereby improve the processes by which we form and maintain beliefs.

beliefs, or we may lack the concepts I am using. What I mean is that the statement I made correctly describes what we know, regardless of whether or not we are aware of this.

The second lesson is that our control over belief differs from our control over various forms of imagination. Regarding the imagination control consists entirely of voluntary control. It depends on the degree to which we can imagine at will. Not so with belief.

We cannot always imagine things at will, and when we do we cannot always make ourselves stop imagining at will, and, most noticeably, even when we imagine something at will our voluntary control over the details of the imagining is very limited. In all these respects our voluntary control over belief is generally similar (we can decide what to deliberate about, have some ability to remember, i.e. to recall, at will, can often decide to stop considering a matter, and so on). But distinctively, we have little voluntary control over the way our beliefs respond to reasons we think we have. We also have limited voluntary control over whether to have beliefs. We can shut our eyes, but when open we cannot just refuse to believe what we see (whatever we say) without believing that we have some reason to doubt what we see.

What is important is that the limits of our voluntary control over our beliefs are not the limits of our control over them: we are in control over our beliefs by functioning properly as rational agents, that is, we are in control, and active, so long as, and to the degree that our beliefs are governed by Reason, by our rational powers.[24] That is what makes us persons. Roughly speaking we are persons so long as we have rational capacities, and by and large our beliefs and actions are governed by them, which is the same as saying so long as we have beliefs.

In brief outline: responsiveness to practical reasons is also constitutive of being a person, for without it there is no action with the intention of doing it. While not all actions are performed for a reason, when we do something with the intention of doing it, which is roughly when we have a purpose in doing it, see a point in doing it, we act for a reason, that is we act in the belief that there is a reason for the action.

Such actions, which I will somewhat inaccurately refer to as intentional actions, are governed by reason somewhat less directly than beliefs. Both intentional action and belief are subject to failures correctly to identify reasons, failures to follow through with the implications of reasons one identified (as in failures of memory or lapses of attention) as well as to irrationalities, including motivated irrationalities. In both cases we recognize such failures for what they are in principle, thus acknowledging that beliefs and intentional actions are inherently governed by Reason. There is, as we know, a keen debate about the difference between the conditions for rationality of belief and of intentional action, e.g. whether there is epistemic akrasia. For our purpose suffice it to note that whatever differences there are they are secondary to the basic point that we cannot, while acting intentionally, but act for a (perceived) reason (albeit

---

[24] Compare my discussion of the matter in *Engaging Reason*, ch. 1.

not always the one we believe to be the best reason).[25] Rationality, namely respon-siveness to reasons, is thus constitutive of being persons.

The relationship of Reason and reasons has been the thread going through this chapter. Trying to understand what motivates one to search for the foundations of normativity, we realize that the search cannot even as much as be stated from 'inside' as it were. From 'inside' we can only look for reasons for reasons, or note that disregard-ing reasons is, under appropriate circumstances, irrational, that is a symptom of the malfunctioning of our rational powers. All such internal investigations inevitably move in a circle, and do not reach the puzzle.

So we went outside, and raised a question about reasons, stated in non-normative terms: what is the hold reasons have on us? The answer was that we cannot ignore them because we are persons, or more precisely, because rational powers are constitu-tive of personhood, and because they are powers whose use does not depend on our will. That is, these powers are engaged and active willy-nilly, independently of any decision to use them, so long as we are awake and do not suppress them. They are like our hearing rather than like our ability to speak. Hence, so long as we are persons we engage with reasons, generally trying to do it well, however imperfect our success.

Now, you may object that even if true these observations do not explain norma-tivity, let alone justify its standing. They say something about rational powers, but nothing at all about reasons. I emphasized early on that explaining why reasons call for a certain response need not invoke our rational powers, which are merely powers to recognize and respond to what is there independently of them—well, at least some-times, given that some reasons would not exist but for the powers and activities of rational creatures.

In a way the objection is justified. Rejecting the feasibility of a reductive explanation means that once we step outside, as it were, and examine normativity as a whole we lose the ability to explain it. That explanation is inevitably internal—reasons are what we should follow, disregarding them is unjustified, etc. But we can explain from outside the inescapability of normativity, the hold reasons have on us. We do so, to be sure, by pointing out features of rational powers, but rational powers are essentially powers to recognize and respond to reasons. So in explaining their place in our life we also point to the hold that reasons have on us, though that hold is subject to mistakes and irrationalities.

Still, disquiet may persist: does any of this amount to more than saying that we are boxed into treating certain considerations as if they were reasons? Does it not fail to vindicate them as reasons? Are reasons normative in the deeper sense that there is a point to being guided by them, that being guided by them is not an arbitrary, albeit a natural response? Is our responsiveness to reasons just a fact rather than a response to a

---

[25] I have discussed challenges and exceptions to this view in Chapter Four, and in chapter 2 of *Engaging Reason*.

normative consideration? Is it not like saying that we are persons only so long as we breathe, a fact that we must acknowledge, but can find arbitrary, and are free to resent?

I'll say nothing about breathing. But reasons are different. Here, I think, the fact that the account is confined to their formal characterizations is—far from being a short-coming—a key to its success. Reasons are governed by *maxims* stating that *a reason for belief is a fact that is part of a case for having that belief*, and *a reason for action is a fact that is part of the case for performing that action*. Such characterizations are relatively formal in that they do not directly yield a way of establishing what is a reason for what. But they focus discussion about what properties make for reasons: Such investigation may yield that beliefs, though not thoughts generally, are without flaw if true, and actions done with intentions to do them, though not actions generally, are without flaw if they are adequately valuable. Hence reasons for beliefs are truth indicators, and reasons for actions are their value properties. Truth indicators are truth indicators even if there are no rational creatures who can rely on them to form beliefs. Values, those whose existence does not depend on the culture of rational creatures, are values, and have instances whether or not there are persons able to perceive and respond to them as values. Our rational capacities enable us to recognize and respond to reason-constituting facts, and being reflective powers they enable us to improve our understanding of what makes those facts what they are, and how best to identify them for what they are. Do all values derive from the well-being of some agent? Is there some property that constitutes some facts as moral reasons, and so on? The formal characterizations serve to focus and frame thought about which more substantive properties constitute reasons, properties whose standing does not depend on our rationality.

This, some will say, is a very surprising view to end up with. Does it not mean that normativity resides in our rationality; that values, and truth indicators, etc., are not normative in themselves? It depends on what you mean by in themselves. Barometric pressure is evidence of weather that we, using our rational capacities, have come to recognize and we form beliefs on its basis. No doubt some other animal species, lacking rational powers, respond 'automatically' to variations in barometric pressure. They do not take it to be a reason for anything. They do not recognize its normative aspect. But it has it. It has it in virtue of the ability of rational creatures to recognize that it is evidence of forthcoming weather. Or think of our dependence on food for survival. We forage for food using our rational capacities. Some other animal species seek food independently of any rational powers. It is no reason for them, but it is of value to them. We depend for survival on our ability to adjust our pupils to light levels, our ability to adjust our breathing and blood circulation to prevailing conditions. We do so as other species react to barometric pressure: the features are not reasons for us. But they are good for us. Does all this show that value and evidence are not normative? At most it shows not that they are not normative, but that what makes them normative is their ability to function as reasons, that is to be recognized as such by creatures using their rational powers.

But, some will say, the question remains: Assume that I am right in emphasizing (a) that subjection to the discipline of reasons is semi-automatic, (b) that it is normative in being an adjustment of our beliefs and intentions in light of reasons; and (c) that the capacities manifested in these adjustments are constitutive of being persons. But having conceded that this is so only shows that a general rational capacity is constitutive of personhood, and not that reasons or normativity are constitutive of personhood: the three points fail to vindicate normativity. It is not enough to point out that creatures with no rational capacities are not persons. Clearly there is nothing amiss with pigeons, even though they do not (I assume) have rational capacities. A vindication of normativity has to show what is amiss with failing to conform to reason on this or that occasion.

At this point I have to admit that I no longer understand the sense of puzzlement. What is amiss with failing to conform to reason is just that. It can be specified further: it may be defrauding a person of his money, or it may be wasting one's talent, or missing an opportunity to make a lot of money, or remaining confused about black holes. It all depends on the nature of the reasons one flouted. But clearly that is not the puzzle. It has something to do with vindicating reasons or normativity in general, without assuming their cogency. So what is it? We do know that people who flout reason sometimes prosper. Is the desire for some further vindication of reasons a hope that philosophical argument can show this to be an illusion? But there is no illusion there.

PART TWO

On Practical Reasoning

Introduction

Reasoning is central to the way we recognize and come to respond to reasons. It is thus central to our capacity, as rational agents, to appreciate and respond to normative considerations. Reasons are facts, aspects of the world. But our reaction to them is necessarily mediated by awareness of them. Chapter Six provides a transition from the discussion in Part One to the concerns of Part Two by considering some of the familiar difficulties in understanding that relationship: the relationship between the facts that are reasons and our beliefs or knowledge of what reasons there are.

Thinking of practical reasoning brings in a crucial factor, so far ignored: that reasons conflict, and much practical reasoning is about the proper response to such conflicts. Ignoring this fact undermines the value of Aristotle's practical syllogism, as will be argued in Chapter Seven. Some additional terminology (some of it briefly used in Chapter Two) will be explained as the need arises. Reasons will also be referred to as *pro tanto* reasons, to underline the fact that they may conflict, while avoiding commitment as to whether they defeat conflicting reasons. Reasons which are not defeated by all the conflicting reasons will be referred to as sufficient, or adequate, and if they also defeat the conflicting reasons they are conclusive. This last clarification brings out an important ambiguity, usually left to the context to resolve, namely whether one refers to the reasons for a particular action in the plural or singularly: sometimes when saying that the reason for an action defeats all the conflicting reasons one means that all the reasons for that action, taken together, defeat the conflicting ones. Chapter Eight will suggest that at least in some respects that notion, the notion of the case for an option (without differentiating its different components, the different reasons that make it up) is the primary one. But before we get there Chapter Seven considers the distinctness of practical reasoning.

Ever since Aristotle, theories arguing that practical reasoning has peculiar features, that it is a *sui generis* form of reasoning, abound. Being a sceptic on this point I examine the question in Chapter Seven. The question of the special character of practical reasoning is not a very sharp one: how special is special? Does the fact that assertions about quantum phenomena do not feature in practical reasoning show that it is special? Or that there is a special form of reasoning for quantum mechanics? Clearly we have no interest in verbal disputes. The interest is in identifying ways, if there are such, in which practical reasoning differs from other forms of reasoning. Chapter Seven argues that there is one way in which it is not special: the conclusions of practical reasoning, like the conclusions of all reasoning, are beliefs. Therefore, there is no good argument to the special character of practical reasoning from the fact that it has special kinds of conclusions. This has significant implications for the relationship between reasoning and rationality, since the fact that intentions and actions can be irrational seems to be among the motivations for claims that intentions or actions are the conclusions of practical reasoning. But these depend on the mistaken belief that irrationality can result only from some failures of reasoning, a mistake exposed in Part One.

One way in which we identify different domains of thought is by their concern with different kinds of properties. Practical thought and practical reasoning are concerned with a variety of normative properties. As in the rest of the book, I consider only what I take to be the most basic and simplest normative property, being a reason, or more specifically, being a practical reason. Practical reasoning, at this elementary level, is concerned with two fundamental phenomena. One is the conditions of transmission of that property, namely under what conditions is it the case that necessarily if A is a reason so is B (or, more narrowly, when is it the case that B is a reason because A is)? Second, when reasons conflict which, if any, prevails?

The first of these topics includes the hallowed subject of instrumental reasons. It forms the topic of Chapter Eight, which argues that while many recent writings about the subject (by Korsgaard, Broome, Wallace, for example) improve considerably our understanding of the issues involved, they are still in the grip of the myth of instrumental rationality, which misconceives the relevance of our goals to our reasons, as well as the conditions under which we have instrumental, or facilitative, reasons.

I argue that: (1) When we have an undefeated reason to take an action we have reason to perform any one (but only one) of the possible (for us) alternative plans that facilitate it; (2) The rationality or lack of it displayed in our reactions to our own ends—in particular adopting what we believe are means to their realization, or our failure to adopt such means—consists in the exercise or failure to exercise properly the same capacity, and in conforming with or violating the same principles of rationality, which we exercise or fail to exercise, conform to or fail to conform to in other contexts. The supposition that there is a special type of rationality, or of rational principles, to which 'instrumental rationality' refers is the myth of the title of my chapter. The two theses provide an alternative to a familiar account of these matters, which is rejected in the third thesis: (3) The fact that one has an end does not provide reasons for its realization, nor for taking the means for its realization.

Chapters Nine to Eleven turn to the second cluster of issues, those involved with conflicts of reasons. First, in Chapter Nine, I identify two different and important types of, or senses of, conflicts of reasons, and discuss some of their implications. Chapter Ten builds on that analysis to explain the relations between 'we have reason to Φ', and 'we have reasons to Φ', showing how that implies a limited degree of aggregation. The aggregation sanctioned by this argument is consistent with the treatment of aggregation by Scanlon. The second half of the chapter criticizes Scanlon's reasoning about aggregation both in these cases and more generally. Chapter Eleven deals with the degree to which aggregation may be justified. It explains why talk of promoting value is misleading, and argues that aggregation is in place in certain domains, but is misconceived when applied as a principle of reasoning or rationality or an implication of the concepts of practical reasons or of value.

6

Epistemic Modulations

Naturally, for the most part our success in reacting to reasons depends on establishing which ones apply to us. Some of our opinions about what reasons we have are bound to be mistaken. And some of these mistakes are blameless. Even when we are, and act as, competent and responsible epistemic agents, some of our views, including our views about what reasons we have, are liable to be false. How does that affect what we have most reason to believe or to do? Or, what we ought to believe or to do? Or, what we would be rational to believe, or to do? Or, what beliefs or actions would lay us open to criticism of various kinds? We have to face these diverse questions separately, as the answers may not align neatly. I will discuss the issue as it relates to practical reasons.[1]

Observing normative discourse and the way it deals with these matters reveals the usual picture: Our use of language is highly flexible and context-dependent. We use the same sentence or word to say one thing on one occasion, and another on a different occasion (e.g. 'I did what I should have done, given that I believed that that action would avoid the accident', and—on another occasion—'of course I should not have done what I did, for even though I thought that it would avoid the accident in fact it made it worse'). Besides, our discourse heavily depends on conversational implicatures, and other pragmatic principles. For example, when asked why I took my umbrella I may say that rain was forecast, or that my new hat would be damaged if rained upon. Both are presented as explanations of my action by reference to a normative reason. (Assuming we are thinking of one occasion) both refer to the same reason. But neither statement states its content in full. We never do. More to our point, the first states a reason to believe that there is reason to take the umbrella; only the second directly refers to a reason for action. Semantic and pragmatic theories formulate principles that govern the correct linguistic behaviour and its understanding. The following reflections (like the rest of the book) do nothing of the sort. Rather, relying on the conclusions of Part One, they explore the relations between the reasons we have and our beliefs about what reasons we have (given that whenever we act with intentions we rely at least implicitly on a view of how both epistemic and practical reasons apply to us at the time) and how they can reasonably be related to our familiar

---

[1] For the most comprehensive discussion of these issues see M. J. Zimmerman, *Living with Uncertainty* (Cambridge: CUP, 2009); for other instructive discussions see J. J. Thomson, *Normativity* (Chicago: Open Court, 2008) ch. 11; N. Kolodny and J. MacFarlane, '"Ifs" and "Oughts"', *Journal of Philosophy* 107/3 (2010).

concepts, with the aid of conservative explications. Nothing here said establishes that there are no plausible or cogent alternative ways of handing these matters. The aim is merely to illustrate that the general approach here pursued is supple and robust enough to cope with these questions, thus indirectly supporting it, and lending credibility to the answers to these questions that are here provided.

Some of the required work is merely clarificatory or classificatory. But some deals with substantive questions. There are two main substantive tasks: First, to mark the difference between conduct and attitudes that are open to criticism and those that are not. Second, to provide a way of representing the structure of deliberation about what to do or believe. Ultimately the account offered has to be judged by its success in meeting these tasks, and its integration in a wider account of practical thought. The argument to follow will occasionally turn on examples of people's deliberation and conduct. In considering them I will assume that they deliberate and act rationally. Not because people invariably do, but because the account we are looking for is an account of rational deliberation and conduct.

A simple account (or framework for one) is that there is a strict separation: the reasons agents have (which, as explained in Chapter Two, determine what they ought to do) are not affected by their beliefs as to whether they have those reasons (namely, whether they have a reason to Φ is not affected by whether or not they believe that they have a reason to Φ).[2] The reasons they have determine whether they did what they ought to have done (or believed what they ought to have believed), while whether their actions were justified,[3] namely free from criticism, depends on whether their beliefs that these were the actions to perform were warranted, and given further considerations—which will not be explored here—this determines whether they are praiseworthy or blameworthy.[4] Does the simple account, as it applies to practical reasons, survive scrutiny? The simple account can be understood in various ways. Sections 2 to 6 defend a somewhat attenuated interpretation of its application to reasons. Section 7 examines the degree to which it applies to ought-propositions and to justifications.

1. A short detour: ought of rationality?

Reason, it was argued in the last chapter, is the power to detect and respond to reasons. It is not a source of reasons. There are no reasons of rationality, is one way of putting it.

---

[2] I am grateful to Gabe Mendlow and Ruth Chang for advice on the formulation of the thesis. I take the simple account and the cases for and against it to apply to all beliefs (doubts, and uncertainties) be they factual or other. That is they apply to beliefs and doubts about morality, beliefs and doubts about what to do when one is in doubt about morality, and so on. As every fact that is a reason for action has both evaluative and non-evaluative properties the thesis applies to both kinds of beliefs about facts that are reasons.

[3] I use 'justified' here in a natural but restricted sense. Section 7 elaborates and explains.

[4] As elsewhere in the book, being sceptical of the success of global formulae for reaching right conclusions about what to do or what to believe, I offer none.

To be sure, in some conditions people, or their beliefs, intentions, or actions can be irrational. But that fact is not a reason to avoid being in those conditions.

That avoids one of the conundrums generated by one common view. According to it practical reasons determine a so-called objective ought. We objectively-ought to do what we have best practical reasons to do. The epistemic reasons for believing that we ought to do this or that determine a so-called ought of rationality. We rationally-ought to do what we have best reason to believe we have best reason to do, or something like that. Faced with two potentially conflicting verdicts about what to do, we are hard pressed to determine which one to follow. The very meaning of the question 'which one am I to follow?' is elusive. Does it mean the same as 'which one ought I to follow?'? And is this 'ought' the objective one or the rationality one? And what help would it be to know what either of those tells us? We already know that.

The ought-of-rationality view is right to point out that if one believes that one's best reason is to Φ then failing to Φ may be (depending on additional conditions) irrational. To many it appears obvious that we ought to do what would avoid irrationality, or, as they are more likely to put it, what rationality demands of us. But that endorses the mistaken view that rationality is a source of reasons rather than a power to discern and respond to reasons. Given the inconclusiveness of most arguments for philosophical theses, and their semi-holistic nature, the fact that my understanding of rationality avoids this particular conundrum counts in its favour.[5]

2. Reasons for action

A practical reason to Φ, you will recall, is a fact constituting a defeasible but presumptively sufficient case for Φ-ing. Reasons have, in the current parlance, *pro tanto* force, though that does not mean that *pro tanto* reasons are different reasons from conclusive reasons. Rather, conclusive reasons are *pro tanto* reasons that defeat all their conflicting reasons, even given their combined force. 'Adequate reasons' is the term I will use for (*pro tanto*) reasons that are not defeated by conflicting reasons, even when taken together. I will also, however, freely use alternative expressions, like 'sufficient reasons', or 'undefeated reasons'.

When considering the effects of ignorance, mistakes, and uncertainty on what we are to do we need to consider first their effect on what reasons we have and then their effect, if any, on the adequate or conclusive reasons that we have, that is on the status of those reasons as adequate or conclusive.

The simple account meets here its first test. Notice, however, that the account does not imply that identifying what practical reasons there are must not rely on epistemic conditions. For example, possibly an unknowable fact cannot be a reason for anything.

---

[5] Cf. N. Kolodny in 'Why Be Rational?', *Mind* 114 (2005), 509; 'How Does Coherence Matter?', *Proceedings of the Aristotelian Society* 107 (2007), 229; 'The Myth of Practical Consistency,' *European Journal of Philosophy* 16 (2008), 366; 'Why Be Disposed to Be Coherent?', *Ethics* 118 (2008), 437.

This would seem to follow from the normative/explanatory *nexus*: since an unknowable fact cannot guide us, it cannot feature in the (normative-reason based) explanation of conduct and therefore cannot be a reason. I will be assuming that this epistemic filter is individuated to people (though not necessarily to people at a moment in time). That is, if some people cannot know of a fact it does not constitute a reason for them, even though other people can know about it.[6] The epistemic filter is analogous to what I will call the possibility filter that we encountered in Chapter Two. I will never have the option to acquire a magic cure for all illnesses. The value of acquiring it, being altogether impossible to realize, provides no reasons. Agents can have a reason to do only what is 'in principle' possible for them to do (and, just as with the epistemic filter, the nature of the relevant possibility remains to be explored). Both possibility and epistemic filters follow from the *nexus*, and mark the difference between what is of value and what one has reason to do (see further below). This epistemic filter regarding what reasons we have will turn out to be of vital importance in what follows. For the moment the claim is merely that *ordinary* (vague, as it has to be in the absence of criteria for the epistemic conditions that affect what reasons we have) ignorance, uncertainty, and mistakes do not change the reasons we have. The argument for the simple account at this juncture is that ignorance, mistakes, and uncertainty presuppose something about which we are ignorant, uncertain, or mistaken. The relevant objects of our ignorance, mistakes, and uncertainty are the practical reasons we have. So, ignorance, mistakes, or uncertainty indicate a flawed grasp of the practical reasons we have, reasons that are independent of our grasp of them. (To reiterate an earlier point: the claim is merely that saying that reasoners try to establish what reasons apply to them is a correct description of what they do. It is not that they necessarily do or even could formulate the aim of their deliberations in that way.)

Can it be otherwise? We can imagine two possible alternatives. According to one, reasoning about whether there are any reasons to Φ is done in two stages. In the first stage we try to establish whether there is a reason for Φ-ing that is independent of our beliefs about whether there is such a reason. Having concluded the first stage we can examine the belief about reasons for Φ-ing we now have and, perhaps only if it meets certain conditions, conclude that that belief is true because it is self-realizing, that we have the reason that we believe we have because we believe that we have it. A second way of avoiding the simple argument is to claim that in reasoning about whether to Φ, we are not trying to establish the existence of belief-independent reasons at all. We are

---

[6] To make the argument sound one needs fully to describe the kind of unknowability involved. Does it mean 'impossible to know given the laws of nature'? Perhaps even a weaker condition will do: no one at the time would have found out about it regardless of their best efforts. What is needed is some measure of robustness of the unknowability, a distinction between it and more ephemeral types of ignorance or mistake. The filter, and the distinctions on which it rests, may be needed to cope with the arguments pressed by J. Lenman, 'Consequentialism and Cluelessness', *Philosophy & Public Affairs* 29 (2000), 342–70. I will not consider the matter here.

following a prescribed procedure, and the outcome to which it leads us creates a reason for Φ-ing. That is, if we reached a certain result then we have a reason, and if not—not.

Neither suggestion carries any credence. There are views of practical reasoning that see it as following a certain procedure. The Kantian test of the first categorical imperative is often understood in such a way. But no one suggests that the outcomes we reach, whatever they are, determine what reasons we have. We must follow the reasoning process correctly, relying on no false premises, and only if we reach correct conclusions do they determine our reasons.

The two-stage suggestion is no more plausible. It includes one stage too many. We act using our thoughts, intentions, etc. How else could we act? But our reasons remain those represented by the content of our thoughts and intentions. It is not having the thought that the dish would be tasty that seems to us to recommend eating it, it is that it would be tasty. If we make a mistake it remains a mistake. The mistake is not self-correcting, meaning that it does not change the reasons we have (though it is relevant to an assessment of various aspects of our responsiveness to reasons, such as our rationality, responsibility, or blameworthiness).

3. Conditional goods and the case of insurance

One particular kind of reasons worth special consideration is that consisting of conditional goods. It is easy to illustrate it by considering insurance policies. Here is an example:

> **Bicycles**: Beth has just given up on having bicycles. She had bicycles for the last ten years, and throughout the period she had insurance against theft of her bicycles. As it turns out the bicycles were never stolen. She paid the premium for ten years, but never made a claim under the policy.

The question is: did Beth have a reason to insure the bicycles? Let us agree that she had a warranted belief that she has an adequate reason to insure her bicycles, and that no fault can be attributed to her in virtue of having taken out insurance. But did she really have reason to do so, or was her belief that she has such a reason a (blameless) mistake? Let us put to one side whatever psychological benefits (peace of mind, etc.), or other incidental benefits (being seen by her friends to be responsible, etc.) she may have derived from having the policy. We can easily imagine cases in which no such benefits exist. Furthermore, the question is merely whether she had *a* reason to have cover, not whether she had *an adequate* reason to be covered. So we do not need to inquire into her general financial situation, etc.

It may be argued that unless one recognizes that beliefs that there are reasons, or some of them, are themselves reasons, Beth did not have reason to insure the bicycles. She would have had such a reason only if there were some good in insuring the bicycles. There would have been good in the insurance had there been a valid claim under it. Given that there was no such claim, the policy cost her money and brought no benefit. Therefore, as it turned out there was no value in having it, and therefore no reason to have it.

That is a bad argument. For one thing it misrepresents Beth's belief about the reasons she had to take out the insurance. It suggests that she believed that the bicycles will be stolen, and therefore the policy has value. But she did not, nor is that a belief typical of people who take out insurance. If Beth had any belief on the matter, which is unlikely, she believed that her bicycles would not be stolen. Of course she knew that she would benefit greatly from having the policy were they to be stolen. But she had another benefit in mind, and it determined her to get the insurance: it was belief in the conditional good of being covered if her bicycles are stolen. That, securing that good, was her reason for taking out insurance.

Typically, conditional value is derivative value. That is, it is valuable only if and because of the good mentioned in the consequent. Once your bicycle is stolen it is good to be covered and that is why it is also good to have the conditional good. That may incline people to think that the only value is the one that materializes when the condition is met. After all, one may think, a conditional good is just that: conditionally good. It is not unconditionally good. But that is a mistake. Conditional goods can be unconditionally valuable. Insurance policies are only one example. Options are another.

In fact (some) conditional goods are among our most treasured possessions, as can be seen by the store we put on being ready, and on having options. We acquire skills, just in case we may need them, we live in circumstances that will enable us to take advantage of various options should they come along, and so on. We feel rewarded just by living in an environment where good things may happen, and we derive strength and a sense of our own achievement just by being open to new valuable opportunities, and capable of taking advantage of them. Needless to say, we would be disappointed, and our lives impoverished, if only few valuable options came our way. But that does not mean that the value that conditional goods have for us is a purely conditional value, i.e. that they have no value until the condition obtains, or none if the condition never obtains. The unconditional value of (some) conditional goods is a common feature of all our lives. It does mean that actions that secure it may have a double value. Some conditional values (like insurance policies which expire once a successful claim is made under then) terminate once the condition is realized. Others can continue even when the condition materializes (my option to visit my neighbourhood museum remains even while I actually visit it). In such cases one can enjoy the unconditional value of the conditional good, and the value that accrues when the condition is realized at the same time. That need not be a source of puzzlement, and it does nothing to deny the unconditional desirability of the conditional good itself.

The unconditional value of those conditional goods that have it is partially explained by the facilitative principle. They are the facilitative goods discussed in Chapter Eight. The principle is broad enough to allow for the current value of facilitative goods, and for the fact that they have value even though they end up not leading to the good they derive from. But I hope that the preceding observations suggest that some conditional goods have additional value, deriving from their contribution as constitutive elements of the lives that people—sensibly—aspire to have.

4. Adequate reasons

While the practical reasons we have change over time, propositions affirming that we have a (non-facilitative) reason to do this or that do not inherently assume a specific occasion or class of occasions to which the reasons apply. If I have reason to get a present for Jim for his 40th birthday then I have it throughout the period from now till, at the very least, his 40th birthday. By way of contrast, saying that I have reason to catch a bus to the shop to buy him a present presupposes a situation, or a class of situations, in which catching the bus would be (as I believe) a good step on the way to having a present for Jim. Similarly, having an adequate reason to do something presupposes an occasion or a class of occasions on which it is true that the reason is adequate. That is a consequence of the fact that the adequacy of a reason indicates something about the way it fares given other—possibly conflicting—reasons, and other considerations that may affect the importance of conforming to it on this or that occasion (for example, that this is or is not the last opportunity to conform to it). The very same reason may be adequate on one occasion but not on others.

So, adequate reasons are relative to different occasions or situations, and those are defined by (a) the options available to the agent, and (b) the considerations that bear on their relative desirability. My situation changes as my options and/or those other considerations change. Availability itself is taken here to be independent of knowledge. An option is available to me if, given how things are, then if I know what would constitute trying to perform it I can succeed in performing it if I try (meaning that I may succeed by my ability, rather than merely by fluke).

Some valuable options may never be(come) available to an agent. It would be (intrinsically) good if I climbed the Matterhorn. Possibly the option to climb it will never come my way. But there is a difference between climbing the Matterhorn and acquiring the magic cure. Though having the cure is good, being altogether impossible its value provides no reasons for action. It falls foul of the possibility filter. The goodness of climbing the Matterhorn relates to what is 'in principle' possible and does give rise to reasons. I have a reason to climb the Matterhorn. That is true even if it turns out that the option is never available to me. As I can climb the mountain only if I am at its foot (or higher) the option to do so is not available to me now. But even now I have a reason to climb it, even though I do not have a reason to climb it now.[7]

---

[7] It would be a mistake to think that I have the reason only when I have an opportunity to climb the mountain. The reason has other implications, not least that I have reason to try to find or create opportunities to climb, and that explains why we think of it as a reason we have, and not merely have when the option of climbing is available.

Given a particular situation, a reason for an action that an agent has is adequate if undefeated by any of the reasons for any of the other available options. It can be defeated by conflicting reasons, reasons to omit the action for which it is a reason, but also by other considerations. For example, it may be cancelled (as when the promisee releases the promisor from his promise) or excluded by an exclusionary reason. Given a particular situation, a reason is conclusive if it is adequate and if there is no adequate reason for any alternative incompatible action. It is reasonable to assume that the agent's beliefs affect which reasons are conclusive if and only if they can affect which reasons are adequate. But can they affect the adequacy of reasons?

A negative answer would be easy if the only issues to which epistemic reasons may be relevant are questions such as: which one of the available options would, when successfully pursued, be the best, or realize most value?[8] Were this the case it would be reasonable to hold that the agent's belief is irrelevant to the adequacy of reasons. A reason is adequate if undefeated by the reasons for the other available options, a matter unaffected by the agent's beliefs about which one that is, though naturally agents may reasonably but mistakenly believe that a reason that is in fact defeated is undefeated.

But things are not that simple. We may, for example, know that A is better than B, that if we bring it about that A we will realize more value than if we bring it about that B, but we may also know (or have a warranted belief) that our chances of succeeding in bringing it about that B are better than the odds that we will succeed in making it the case that A. What are we to do in such cases? Call this the problem of the second best, for one, colloquial, way of putting it is: 'when is it best to do the second best?' implying, in this context, that given the risk of failure, our best reason may be to choose the second best option when the risk of failure with it is smaller.

In many situations, when we sensibly think that the better reason is to choose the so-called second best that is because it is in fact the best available option, or so we think. That is, we think that we are bound to fail in pursuing the option that would be best if realized. We do not believe that it is available to us. We choose the one that is, in our view, the best of the available options. If we are mistaken, then we chose an option backed by a defeated reason, though we were, perhaps blamelessly, unaware of the fact.

On many occasions, however, agents do not believe that they will succeed or that they will fail in pursuing this option or that. They believe that they are more likely to succeed with one rather than with the other. Sometimes, though not very frequently, agents can put their views of the chances of success not only in comparative terms (more likely to succeed with A than with B) but in stronger ordering relations. In these cases, the premises the agents rely on do not include belief that the option which if realized would be best is unavailable, but rather belief that it is unlikely to be realized,

---

[8] This would have been the only question had the value of an action been the only consideration bearing on the case for performing it. If as appears likely, there are additional considerations the question should be taken to be illustrative only.

and they choose against it on that ground. The reason for action, in such cases, is the fact that the probabilities are such and such, not that the agents believe that they are. No revision in our understanding of adequate reasons is necessary to account for such situations.

As you see, I am taking the reference to likelihood to be a reference to some objective notion of probabilities. It may be, depending on context, the physical probability in an indeterminist system, or it may be evidential probability, relative to some evidential base, or whatever kind is appropriate to the occasion.[9] The normative/explanatory *nexus* requires that they will be relative to what agents can know. Given that the probabilities that affect an agent's practical reasons are assessed relative to what that agent can know, the agent has (and can become aware of) adequate reasons to believe that these are the probabilities. Are facts about objective probabilities of events either epistemic or practical reasons? They are not epistemic reasons. The probability itself is not evidence for anything. The facts that are evidence for the likelihood that the agents will succeed in performing their actions are also the evidence for the probabilities that they will succeed. So probabilities may be relevant in epistemic deliberation without being epistemic reasons.

Is the fact that an option is, if pursued, likely to be realized a (practical) reason to choose to pursue it? Obviously not. The likelihood of successfully doing something, if we try, is no reason at all to do it, or to try to do it. But probability can be a so-called 'weight' or importance or force-influencing factor. In that way it may affect what we have adequate reason to do.

The easy way to illustrate the point is to draw an analogy between facilitative reasons to do A in order to secure B, and reasons for trying to do B (I will refer to the trying as T). There is a facilitative reason to do A because there is reason to secure B. The reason for doing A is that it facilitates securing B. The likelihood that it will facilitate the end affects the force of the reason to do A. If there are several possible ways to try to secure B then, other things being equal, the better (or stronger, or weightier) reason is for the action that is most likely actually to secure it. The observations about the second best presupposed that the same is true regarding choice of end. Given two worthwhile ends, other things being equal the reason to pursue the one more likely to be achieved is the better or stronger reason. And as we saw this may sometimes mean that the reason to pursue the end that would—if both were achieved—be second best is the stronger reason. It defeats the reason for the best end.

---

[9] What if the 'likelihood' is an indication of degree of belief? First, I am compelled rather dogmatically to reject the view that what is known as 'subjective' probability is a measure of degrees of belief. Our belief-related attitudes admit of degrees, though these tend to be rather rough and ready. I may be to various degrees inclined, tempted, and so on, to believe: states of mind indicating a variety of conditions: awareness of an irrational factor affecting or liable to affect one's judgement, readiness to examine the case for or against the proposition, etc. These states are irrelevant here. I may also strongly or weakly believe something, again meaning a variety of different attitudes in different contexts: recognition that there is a case for re-examining the belief, awareness that it will not take much to convince me that the belief is mistaken, etc. Such cases, in which my belief is qualified in some way, are the same as those canvassed in the text.

Just as we can bring about B by A-ing we can do B by T-ing, namely by trying to bring about B. Some even take the relationship of trying to Φ and Φ-ing to be a means-end relationship. I do not propose this view. I merely point to the analogy between them to explain how the probability that we will succeed in Φ-ing if we try affects the force of the reason to Φ.

A natural way to describe the choice one faces in such cases is this: I do not know whether I will successfully Φ if I try, and I do not know whether I will successfully ϕ if I try. But, as I know, if I try either, I am more likely to Φ than to Φ. Assuming that the two are of equal value I have better reason to Φ. If Φ-ing has the greater value, the reasons for trying either may be incommensurate, but sometimes there may be an argument showing that the reason to Φ defeats the reason to Φ, and as we may find it more natural to say, the reason to try to Φ defeats the reason to try to Φ.

While allowing for the analogy regarding the effect of probabilities on choice of ends and choice of means, some will object to the conclusion that probabilities affect the weight of reasons even for means. If they do affect them it would follow that, other things being equal, agents who follow the most likely means will have acted as they had a conclusive reason to act even if they did not achieve their ends. Consider an example:

Flood: Florence ought to deliver food to people marooned on high ground after a flood. Food stocks are limited, so she can have only one shot at getting the food to them. Various options are canvassed and the most likely to succeed is a helicopter drop. Florence would be sure to arrive at the flooded area, though the drop may misfire—the food may be damaged or fall into the water, etc. The second best is to carry the food on a donkey: if she arrived safely with the food it would be securely delivered, but she is likely to be swept away by the flood, or find the terrain impassable, or be robbed on the way. Florence tries the helicopter, and the food falls into the water. She did her best, but failed.

Is it not the case, those doubting my conclusion above would say, that Florence failed to do what she ought to have done? Her failure was blameless, for she had reason to believe that the means she chose were the most likely to succeed. But nevertheless she did not do what she ought to have done. But that, I reply, is ambiguous. Florence failed to deliver the food, and she ought to have delivered it, but she took the means that she ought to have taken.[10] Clearly, one may fail to do what one ought to do even if one tries one's best. So the fact that one tried and failed does not show that the option was not available. My claim is that one may fail to achieve the end that one ought to have achieved while succeeding in taking the means that one ought to have taken.

---

[10]   Furthermore, the example strengthens the case for the relevance of objective probabilities. It shows that any sensible definition of 'available options' (remembering that only an available option can be the one that we ought to pursue or realize) yields the result that options are available if they may be realized if diligently pursued, that is if there is some likelihood that they will be realized (obviously a vague criterion, as the degree of likelihood can be specified only broadly).

Florence had conclusive reason for a helicopter drop. The failure to deliver the food that way does not show that that was not the case. Imagine that, fully aware of the odds, Florence set out with the donkey and arrived safely. She did deliver the food that she ought to have done. But she also acted irrationally, for as she knew, it was not the best means. She acted akratically, against her better judgement. And that means that, as she knew, she had a conclusive reason to choose delivery by a helicopter drop.

One cannot reply that Florence was akratic only because she had a mistaken belief. She thought that the donkey was not the best means, and it turns out that it was the best (or at least an equal best). Florence made no mistake. Had she believed that the helicopter was sure to succeed and the donkey sure to fail, and chosen the donkey, she would have been akratic, but her mistaken belief would have blocked any inference from that to what was really the best option. But she did not believe that. She believed that the helicopter was best because she knew the probabilities. And the probabilities did indeed make the helicopter the best option. That was not a mistake, and the probabilities do not change because of her success with the donkey, or failure with the helicopter. So we are forced to admit that—given, as it were, the concept of reasons (and of ought) that we have[11]—probabilities affect the strength of reasons.

5. Implications of imperfect positions

The basic characteristic of reasons is that they are not just any feature of the world which makes a particular response appropriate. They are such features that can be recognized and responded to by or through the mediation of our rational powers. That is one route leading to the normative/explanatory *nexus* and it entails that what one has an adequate reason to do depends on how one is placed: one's options, what one has opportunity to do, and what one can know, affect it. Because one's situation is not ideal what one has adequate reason to do may not be what would be, in some sense, the ideal thing to do.

In applying the *nexus* I have assumed an analogy between limitations due to lack of ability or opportunity and those due to inability to know. That analogy extends beyond the strict or narrow conception of the *nexus*, and applies not only to the filters that block the existence of reasons, but also to the force of existing reasons. These applications can be regarded as a result of the *nexus* when understood in an extended sense, for they too result from the conception of reasons as relating to the ability of our rational powers to grasp how things are and respond appropriately. The extended

---

[11] Why this caveat? Because I am relying on the text's representing correctly Florence's reasoning: a helicopter drop is much more likely to succeed therefore it is the better way to deliver the food. Was it not: the helicopter drop is much more likely to succeed therefore it is much more likely to be the better way to deliver the food? Of course, Florence believed that too. But my argument relies on her believing the first statement as well, and given how common or typical such reasoning is there are no grounds for suspecting her of a conceptual mistake.

understanding of the *nexus* is manifest when dealing with facilitative reasons: Given where I am, the means needed for doing X are beyond me, and therefore the reasons to do X are defeated. For example, I have reason to treat the injured person, but I cannot reach him; therefore my reasons to pursue one of the options open to me (say go to work) defeat my reason to treat him. Similarly, inability to know may have a similar effect. For example, I have reason to treat the injured person, but I do not know and cannot find out what action to take which will not aggravate his situation. Therefore my reasons to pursue one of the other options open to me defeat my reason to treat him.

Both limitations are slippery in analogous ways. Suppose that option A is beyond my reach. But option B is not and once I take it I will be able to do A. Or suppose that I cannot obtain the information about M, but I can obtain information about N and once I do I will be able to obtain the information about M too. Are the options to do A or to obtain knowledge of M available to me or not? If we allow free rein to transitivity we lose grasp of the notion of limits on our ability, opportunity, and knowledge, which is reflected in our concepts and deliberations. Instead, we allow that the imperfections of our situation may provide us with reasons to change, to improve, our options and our epistemic situation. Our situation may, or may not, be such that the reasons to change it are the best reasons we have. Even when the reasons to change the situation are conclusive they rarely efface the consequences of the imperfect situation in which we found ourselves to start with. The change itself, even when imperative, has its own costs and drawbacks.

The fact that from inside the limitations of our situations we may have reasons and opportunities to improve them takes some of the pressure off the need for a precise demarcation of what is available and what is not given where we are, while at the same time it explains why our concepts provide no sharp answer to that question. It may make little difference whether an option was available or not, if, should the verdict be that it was not available, we had sufficient reasons and opportunities to make it available. Our concepts embody the distinction between cases in which the reasons for an option are defeated by the reasons for another, due to the inability to realize the first, and cases in which we make a blameless mistake in appreciating our options and the reasons for them. They also embody a distinction between the way the reasons we have can be relatively independent of our context when it does not depend on what other reasons we have, and the way the strength of those same reasons depends on context because it does depend on conflicting reasons for alternative options. But while the distinctions are basic to our understanding and deliberation, the boundaries between the different categories are rough and undetermined over a large swathe of cases, for we rarely have practical need to make them precise regarding those cases, among other things because on most occasions the difference between the reason not being there (or being overridden) and our mistakenly but blamelessly believing that it was not there is not worth bothering with.

Still, the very claim that the *nexus* applies to epistemic inability just as it does to lack of an option may be disputed. For example, one may say that deliberation is about what we have best reason to do, not about what we have best reason to do given what we can know. In itself this point does not carry much weight. One might just as well claim that we deliberate about what we have best reason to do and not about what we have best reason to do given what we can do. The reply to both claims is that we deliberate about what we have best reason to do in our situation, and it is affected by our skills and opportunities as well as our epistemic abilities and their limitations.

Yet, some people may think that there is an asymmetry in the way imperfect options and imperfect epistemic situations impact the relations between agent and bystander. But is this so? Imagine two people, Marilyn and Jane, witnessing an accident. The only help possible on the spot is to take the injured person to the hospital. Jane is able to do so while Marilyn cannot drive. Both have reason to help, but only Jane has adequate reason to drive the victim to the A&E. Had their options been the same they would have had the same reasons; given that they are not they have different reasons. Jane may regret that Marilyn cannot help, but there is no doubt that given how things are she does not have adequate reason to drive to the hospital.

Now change the example: The victim requires first aid on the spot. Jane is the only one who can reach him, but she has only a rudimentary idea of first aid. Marilyn is an expert. She knows that the victim should be given some medication, which she knows is to be found in his, the victim's, car. In the circumstances, however, she cannot administer it. She would naturally think that Jane ought to, has conclusive reason to, administer the right medication. The fact that Jane cannot know that would not, it is suggested, affect Marilyn's judgement. Hence, it may be argued, while what agents have adequate reason to do can depend on their options, it cannot depend on what they can know, at least not if other people can know better.

Is this argument sound? At the very least the conclusion runs the risk of over-generalizing. Imagine that (a) Marilyn lives long after Jane's death (or long before her birth), and (b) that her knowledge derives from scientific advances which took place years after the accident (or were completely obliterated from collective human memory long before it). In such cases the common judgement would probably be not that Jane ought to, had conclusive reason to, administer that drug, but that had she been able to know of its properties she would have had conclusive reason to use it.

Now, suppose that Jane's ignorance at the time is due to her inattentiveness during first aid classes that she attended, or to skipping those classes. In such cases while there is a test of ability by which she could not have known at the time of the accident that she should use the drug, it is far from clear that that is the test by which to judge what people could know for the purpose of determining which of their reasons is adequate. Though I am not going to propose a definition of the right test, a little more will be said on the issue below.

Some writers worry that in yet another possible situation, differing from the preceding one in that Marilyn can communicate with Jane, and advise her what to do, she will not be able to do so.[12] For given that Jane does not know of the drug it is false that she ought to use it, and Marilyn, who is aware of Jane's ignorance, cannot truthfully tell her that she ought to use it. Alternatively, if Marilyn does not know of Jane's ignorance she may believe that Jane ought to use the drug, but her belief, and therefore her advice, would be false. But that worry is based on the false assumption that agents' actual knowledge, rather than what they can know, affects what adequate reasons they have. Given that Marilyn can advise Jane, Jane can know of the drug (barring circumstances in which it is impossible for her to credit Marilyn's advice—in which case Marilyn cannot effectively advise her, and once she realizes that she will have, in all honesty, to view the situation as equivalent to one in which she cannot communicate with Jane at all). In conclusion, I do not think that the argument for an asymmetry between imperfect options and imperfect epistemic situations succeeds.

6. Jackson cases

What I will call Jackson cases present the toughest challenge to the simple account.

> **Drug**: Jill is a physician who has to decide on the correct treatment for her patient, John, who has a minor but not trivial skin complaint. She has three drugs to choose from:…Careful consideration of the literature has led her to the following opinions. Drug A is very likely to relieve the condition but will not completely cure it. One of drugs B and C will completely cure the skin condition; the other though will kill the patient, and there is no way that she can tell which of the two is the perfect cure and which the killer drug. What should Jill do?[13]

Let us assume that the situation is such that Jill would be justified if she gives John drug A, and that no other course of action would be justified. I will further assume that absent the option of A she would be justified only if she does nothing, and unjustified if she administers either B or C, unjustified even if the one she administers cures the skin condition. **Drug** led Zimmerman, who used to hold what he calls the objective view, namely that 'agents ought to perform an action if and only if it is the best option that he (or she) has',[14] to change his mind. I will turn to the question of what one ought to do in the next section. The example is clearly also relevant to what one has an adequate reason to do. Does it reveal a mistake in the simple account? Zimmerman explains that in cases in which agents believed that the action they took was supported by the best reason when in fact it was not, they can later say 'unfortunately, it turns out that what I did was wrong. However, since I was trying to do what was best…, and the evidence

---

[12] See e.g. Kolodny and MacFarlane, '"Ifs" and "Oughts"'.

[13] Based on an example from F. Jackson in 'Decision-theoretic Consequentialism and the Nearest and Dearest Objection', *Ethics* 101 (1991), 461–82, at 462–3.

[14] Zimmerman, *Living with Uncertainty*, 2. The simple account is also an objective account, but it is not identical to Zimmerman's.

at the time indicated that that was indeed what I was doing, I cannot be blamed for what I did' (*Living with Uncertainty*, 18). However someone in Jill's position 'would once again decide to act as Jill did and so give John [drug A]....he could not say "unfortunately, it turns out that what I did was wrong. However, since I was trying to do what was best for John, and all the evidence at the time indicated that was indeed what I was doing, I cannot be blamed for what I did." He could not say this precisely because he knew at the time that he was not doing what was best for John' (ibid.).

We should temporarily put aside the question of whether in either case the action is wrong. The next section will argue that whether an action is wrong is not purely a matter of whether one acted for an adequate reason. Here I discuss only the question whether Jill acted for adequate reasons. Suppose yourself to be in a non-Jackson case. Zimmerman says that you will acknowledge (putting it in my terms) that you acted for a defeated, and therefore an inadequate, reason (or for no reason at all, depending on the nature of your mistake). You made a mistake about which reason is adequate, and you will not do it again. In a Jackson case—according to him—you made no mistake and you will do the same thing again. But that is true of the non-Jackson case as well if you have no more information now than you had then. You will act on the mistaken but warranted belief that you had, and still have—barring new information. Similarly, should you be given new information in the Jackson case you will not do the same again. You will choose the drug that will completely cure John. However, Zimmerman points out, Jill knew that the drug she gave John was not the drug it was best for John to get. In Jackson cases agents know that they are going for the second best option.

We have already seen that there are many other cases in which agents know that they choose the second best (and for what it is worth, in Jill's case too the epistemic doubts are about actions that have facilitative value). Are we using 'second best' in the same sense as before? There is one clear difference between the cases: the ones examined before were cases in which there was doubt whether the agents would, if they tried to pursue the option which is the best one, succeed in doing so. No such doubt exists for Jill. She can as easily give John the drug that will completely cure him as any of the others. The problem is, and it did not exist in the other cases, that she does not know which one it is.

Jill knows that should she choose randomly between drugs B and C the probability of her choosing the best drug is .5. That is an objective probability, but it is relative to her state of knowledge (or ignorance). Does not that show that which reason is adequate depends on one's warranted beliefs or on one's knowledge? This is Zimmerman's conclusion. But it is premature. Consider two variants of **Drug**:

Drug 1: Like **Drug**, except that Jill would have known which is the best option if only she could have asked the chief pharmacologist of the hospital. She tried in vain to contact him. He is temporarily out of reach and she must act quickly.

Drug 2: Like **Drug** except that no one knows who will be cured and who killed by drugs B and C. It depends on unknown features of their DNA, and cannot therefore be established.

Drug 2 is a case in which the curing drug cannot be known. The impossibility being robust it affects which reasons Jill has. It was unknowable that, let us say, B was the curing drug. Therefore that it was, was not a reason for Jill. What was knowable and what she knew was that (when randomly selected) the probabilities that giving either B or C will achieve the desired end (ameliorating John's condition) were .5. These were the reasons for them and they were defeated by the reasons for A. Therefore Jill acted as she should have done. No mistake occurred. She had conclusive reason to administer A.

The case illustrates the lesson argued for above, namely that the simple account is subject to the normative/explanatory *nexus*, and that is the same as being subject to the guiding role of reasons. They are valuable features of actions, but only such as can guide actions, and therefore they must be knowable. As you will recall I did not identify the nature of the modality, the dimensions or robustness, involved. To determine it one needs to consider the full range of cases to which it is relevant. Jackson cases are one such type, and a detailed discussion of different variants of them may lead one to take one or another view about the strength of the modality. Furthermore, it is likely that over a broad range of possible cases there is no truth of the matter as to whether the impediment to knowledge affects or does not affect the reasons the agent has. Conceptual boundaries are as sharp as there is reason for them to be, and in normal deliberation and discourse the boundary between epistemic limitations that change one's reasons and those that, though they render one's decision and conduct blameless, do not change one's reasons is immaterial and unexplored, with the result that the concept of a normative reason does not have a determinate boundary regarding such matters.

Possibly, **Drug 1** is different. Jill was not at fault in not knowing which is the curing drug, and she worked out correctly the implications of her ignorance. But she did not choose the best option because she did not know which one it is. Her situation is like that of second best choosers in non-Jackson situations, with the difference that unlike them Jill knows that she does not know which is the best option. This, and this is the crux of Zimmerman's argument above, suggests that (given that her reasoning and conclusion are flawless) we cannot represent her reasoning about what she has best reason to do without allowing that her best reason is to administer Drug A, and by implication that her ignorance changes either the reasons she has or their force.

Two questions confront us:

First, is administering drug A the option supported by the best reason? Second, if the answer is affirmative, does her case refute the simple account? Does it show that her beliefs affect which of her reasons are adequate, in a way that is inconsistent with the simple account?

Three arguments support an affirmative reply to the first question. All of them reply in the negative to the second question.

First, her case is just like that of other second best choosers. Because in their case and in hers if the odds that they will successfully realize the (apparently) best option are inadequate (the considerations that make them inadequate differ in different cases) their second best is really their best choice, the one supported by the best reason.

Second, the normative/explanatory *nexus* tells us that Jill does not have reasons of whose existence she cannot know. In acknowledging that in **Drug 1** Jill's best reason is to give John drug A we can allow that B is a better drug, but she cannot know that. She tried to obtain the information and could not, therefore she cannot know about the advantages of drug B, and that is why the fact that it is the curing drug (unlike the fact that there is .5 chance that it is the curing drug) does not constitute a reason for her, with the result that the curative powers of A are her strongest reason.

Third, and this is the strongest argument, there are constraints on the possibility of representing Jill's deliberation. We need not assume that she asked herself 'what is the best reason I have?' She may have asked 'what should I do?', 'what may I do?', 'what must I do?', or some other question. However, if the answers to any of these questions point to giving A to John they presuppose that the best reason is to give A to John. Since Jill reasoned her way to give A to John she must have at least implicitly believed that that is what she has best reason to do. Therefore, either Jill's best reason is to give A to John, or she made a mistake in her reasoning. Since she made no mistake her best reason was to give A to John.

None of the arguments makes Jill's beliefs determinative of her reasons or their strength. What determines them is her epistemic situation: not what she knows or believes, but what, given her situation, she can know, or can have a warranted belief about. Had she killed John by giving him C, because she thought that that is what she has best reason to do, we would still say, if convinced by the three arguments, that her best reason was to give him A. Therefore, the arguments do not challenge the simple account. They are interesting and important in their own right.

But are they convincing? They all have some force, but the first two are not that difficult to deflect. The first can almost be accused of begging the question. The question (or one of them) is whether any ephemeral epistemic conditions agents find themselves in at the time of action can make a difference to the force of the reasons they face. While the analogy between Jackson cases and non-Jackson second best choosers is real they differ precisely on the point at issue: only Jackson cases depend on epistemic conditions. Is not that sufficient to undermine the force of the analogy? That is the question, and the argument ignores it.

Matters are more complex with the second argument. We do not normally attach theoretically significant kinds of impossibility to ephemeral conditions. The thought that a phone call could make a difference to what Jill could or could not know does not have immediate appeal. On the other hand, the rationale of the normative/explanatory *nexus* may be thought to apply to this kind of impossibility: Jill could not have been guided by facts she could not have knowledge of, however passing and temporary the impediment was. I remarked above that the strength of the modality is determined by all the factors on which the interpretation of the *nexus* has any bearing. This one militates in the direction indicated by the second argument. But are there no counter-vailing considerations? We will see later that there are.

The third argument is the most convincing, for the ability of the simple account or any alternative to it, to represent the structure of people's practical deliberations is among the most fundamental conditions for its success. Is not belief that an action is supported by an adequate reason a necessary implication of any conclusion that deliberation, other than stalled or abandoned deliberation,[15] can lead to?

But perhaps even the third argument can be resisted. Consider another example.

> **Debt**: Bill knows that it is time to repay Jane's loan. He can do so by wire transfer from his account. But he does not remember how much money he owes her, and she is out of reach and cannot be contacted. Knowing that Jane is not rich and is merely an ordinary friend, he pays £500 into her account, thinking that this is probably more than what he owes.

Does Bill believe that paying Jane £500 is what he has best reason to do? He clearly believes that given his ignorance paying £500 is a sensible thing to do, but he may well reasonably believe (i.e. the following description of his belief may be accurate, even if he would not be able to describe his belief in this way) that (1) he does not know what he has best reason to do, but that (2) (to the best of his knowledge) paying £500 is doing what is closest to what he has best reason to do.

Why not concede that that means that in the circumstances he has adequate reason to pay £500? Because Bill knows that it is highly unlikely that his best reason is to pay that sum. He merely thinks that it is a reasonable approximation of what he has best reason to do.[16] His epistemic condition cannot create reasons for him. It merely constrains his ability to know what he has reason to do.

Debt provides an alternative conclusion (or an alternative implication of the conclusion) of practical deliberation: not that the chosen action is the one the agent has an adequate or a conclusive reason to perform, but that (it is reasonable to think that) it is a good approximation of what he has adequate reason to do (and that he can know no better). Does that help with Jackson cases? Jill deliberates about the way to ameliorate John's health. Given what she knows she cannot say that giving him A is what she has best reason to do. Clearly, the best reason supports one of the other drugs. But she correctly concludes that giving A to John in **Drug 1** is the action that (it is reasonable for her to believe) is the best approximation to what she has best reason to do in the circumstances.[17] The third argument assumed that practical deliberation has no alter-

---

[15] Leaving aside the possibility of epistemic akrasia, as it does not affect our problem.

[16] He is also guided by the thought that he should err on the side of generosity, but that does not affect our concerns.

[17] How is it the best approximation? Why is it not simply a second best option? The two notions should not be confused. An option is second best if it is defeated by one other option only (this is obviously an inclusive understanding of 'second best'). It is the best approximation if epistemic limitations force one to the conclusion that it is the closest one can reasonably get to realizing the reasons one aims to approximate. Not

native but to have a conclusion that entails belief that the chosen action is supported by the best reason. **Debt** shows that there is an alternative, and it allows us to understand Jill's reasoning in **Drug 1** in a way that avoids allowing that temporary epistemic limitations affect the force of reasons.

Does this suggestion strike you as forced and artificial? I think that it is quite natural in **Debt**, but much less so in **Drug 1**. That does not mean that it is wrong. As was explained at the outset, the aim of any account is not to explain natural discourse. It is to provide a theoretical sound and systematic account of practical thought. If that is a possible representation of Jill's deliberation then this blunts the force of the third argument. **Debt** undermines the premise of the third argument, namely that practical reasoning can only be represented as implying belief that the action chosen is the one supported by an adequate reason. It is important in assessing the impact of **Debt** on the third argument that the argument proceeded not from independent considerations about what reasons Jill has, but from the alleged impossibility of representing her deliberations coherently without presupposing that temporary epistemic limitations affect the force of reasons. That makes **Debt** an appropriate rebuttal: it provides an alternative way of representing the conclusion, or the implication of the conclusion, of practical reasoning, thus undermining the third argument.

In Jill's case the decision affects only one person, John. Other Jackson type cases concern decisions that affect several people.

> **Miners:** Ten miners are trapped either in shaft A or in shaft B, but we do not know which. Floodwaters threaten to flood the shafts. We have enough sandbags to block one shaft, but not both. If we block one shaft, all the water will go into the other shaft, killing any miners inside it. If we block neither shaft, both shafts will fill halfway with water, and just one miner, the lowest in the shaft, will be killed.[18]

I assume that the agents will rightly block neither shaft. Assuming again that the epistemic limitation is superficial, here the agents ('We') decide to take not the action supported by what they believe to be the best reason, but the action that is the best approximation of what they have best reason for. They have most reason to save all of the miners, and the best approximation is to save all but one (see Chapter Ten below). Perhaps this representation of the conclusion of the agents' deliberation in **Miners** is more natural that in **Drug 1**, though this analysis of both cases calls for further defence.

---

every second best serves the same concerns. Therefore not every second best can be thought of as an approximation of the best. An option adopted as the best approximation may turn out to be exactly the one that one was aiming at, the one conforming to the reason one tried to approximate, or else it is an option that is as close to realizing the concern (or reason) one aims to approximate, as one has could have warrant to believe. In choosing what one knows to be a mere approximation, one also takes it to be a second best option. In Jill's case the choice of drug A is a second best, and also the best approximation of meeting the reason she is pursuing: saving the life of the patient.

[18] The quotation is from Kolodny and Macfarlane, '"Ifs" and "Oughts"'.

To resist the combined force of the three arguments there must be some independent motivation against the suggestion that superficial epistemic incapacity can affect the force of reasons. It is not far to seek. If we allow that role to all epistemic limitations in Jackson cases we have to allow it in all cases (given the absence of a way of drawing a line between them). Take the following example:

Promise: Max promised Jack to bring him supper to his hospital bed every night, (because Jack cannot stand the hospital-provided food). Yesterday Max heard that Jack died. He rang the hospital and it confirmed that Jack died. So he did not go to the hospital that evening. In fact Jack did not die, but given limited visiting hours there was no way that Max could have discovered the mistake in time.

Is it not clear that Max had an adequate reason to bring Jack his supper that night (i.e. his promise) and that his reasonable mistake about it does not affect matters? There are innumerable cases in which superficial or ephemeral epistemic limitations do not produce the slightest temptation to think that they affect the force of reasons. An account that ignores that does not seem to be an account of our concept of a practical reason.

I conclude that Jackson cases are particularly difficult because on the one hand they resemble other second best choices where the force of reasons is affected by the circumstances, but on the other hand they are cases in which one chooses the second best because of epistemic conditions that do not normally affect the force of reasons. Given their difficulty we are naturally torn both ways, but ultimately they neither undermine the simple account, nor show that temporary epistemic limitations affect the force of reasons.

The discussion of these cases brought out possibly an important weakness of my position. While relying on powerful considerations which establish a case for an epistemic filter, and for excluding cases of superficial ignorance from its scope, I offered no principles determining the limits of the filter. True, we should expect wide-ranging indeterminacy, but some principled guidelines are nevertheless desirable. Further investigation may discover them, but it may not. That is, while there is theoretical significance for the distinction, the factors which affect this boundary, which is the boundary of our concept of a normative reason, may not be theoretically significant. They may be largely determined by historical factors of no theoretical significance, or by the circumstances of communication, rather than by the concerns reflected in normative theory.

Finally, the fact that practical reasoning need not be aimed solely at what we have best reason to do, that it may be aimed at discovering the best approximation of what we have best reason to do, is of importance whether or not one agrees with the use to which this point was put in the discussion above.

7. What we ought to do: justification and wrong action

So far I avoided consideration of what action ought to be taken, what actions are wrong, or blameworthy. The discussion was focused exclusively on what reasons there are, and how they fare in conflict, or rather whether the agents' beliefs affect the reasons they have or how they fare in conflict. I suggested that neither what reason one has, nor which reason is adequate or conclusive, is affected by the agent's beliefs about what reasons he or she has, though they are affected by what is knowable.

So far as ought-propositions go, the answer follows from their explanation in Chapter Two. One ought to do or believe what one has reason to do or to believe, a reason which is sometimes conclusive. Therefore, just as discourse and deliberation about what to do combine reasons both for belief and for action, so they combine, often implicitly, both kinds of ought-propositions.

Just as in its application to reasons, so too with regarding 'ought', the distinction the Simple Thesis asserts is enshrined in our concepts and expressed in our thoughts and discourse. But as with reasons, so with 'ought': often in making statements about specific situations or even more general statements about types of situations commonly encountered, we do not bother to spell out whether we refer to epistemic or practical reasons, or to the 'ought' that is based on one or the other of these kinds of reasons, or to some mix of them. The Simple Thesis helps us separate the various ideas expressed in such statements.

Does it mean that agents' beliefs are not relevant to the evaluation of their actions? The mistake to avoid is to allow that there are two kinds of ought-propositions, often known as subjective and objective ought, the subjective one being a function of the agents' beliefs. Zimmerman explains the hopelessness of this suggestion:

You therefore reply, 'Well, Jill, objectively you ought to give John drug [B], subjectively you ought to give him [A]...'. This is of no help to Jill....She replies, '...Which of the "oughts" that you have mentioned is the one that really counts? Which "ought" ought I to act on?'.'[19]

It does not follow, however, that agents' beliefs are irrelevant to the evaluation of their actions. They do not affect what they have reason to do, but people's warranted beliefs, and the epistemic reasons they have, determine the justification of their actions.

Reasons are forward looking: the reasons that apply to agents must be capable of guiding their conduct and beliefs. When people deliberate about what to do (or believe) they aim to determine what practical reasons apply to them and which are adequate or conclusive. They do not deliberate which action (or which choice) would be justified. It would not help to do so. If an agent deliberates which action would be justified the answer is: it is the action that one takes following a correct deliberation about what to do, namely about what action one has a conclusive or at least adequate reason to do.

Even in this formulation 'justification', while referring to the reasons one has, has a more agent-focused character: from the perspective of deliberating agents an action is justified

---

[19] *Living with Uncertainty*, 7; I adjusted the names of the drugs to fit those used above.

because it is led to following a correct deliberation. That explains why deliberating agents do not normally ask what would be justified. And it explains why justification comes into its own, is most naturally considered, when one engages in assessing actions or choices. This can take place before the action, or hypothetically: would Jill be justified in leaving Jim (should she do so)? But in all such contexts justification relates to agents' subjective reactions to the situation in which they find themselves.

Sometimes justification amounts to claiming something like an excuse: Of course, he should not have driven Jill to suicide, but given that she sorely provoked him, he was justified in replying as he did, even though he knew of Jill's fragile mental state. His reaction was understandable; it would have taken more than normal self-control, or willingness to put up with being abused, etc. On other occasions it is understood that what is justified is beyond reproach. It may have been unfortunate, or had unfortunate results, but it itself is beyond reproach. According to the simple account actions are justified when their agents conduct themselves, meaning deliberate and follow through in action, as a responsible agent would. That condition divides into two: first, that one's deliberations were epistemically responsible, and second that one is not akratic, that one follows one's conclusions in one's actions. This issue will be re-examined in Part Three of the book.

Our actions can be justified and we can be justified in taking them even when we fail to do what we ought to do. This distinction is also firmly embedded in our concepts. This is not to deny that we sometimes say not 'you did all that could be expected of you' but 'yes, that was what you ought to have done' to express the view that the action was justified, that you were justified in taking it. But that is a concessive use of 'ought'. If we say 'you should not have done what you did' even though we are not saying that the action was unjustified, a criticism is conversationally implied. And saying: 'that was not what you should have done, but you were justified in doing what you did' the shadow of criticism remains. Hence the reassuring, concessive use of 'ought'.

But which actions are wrong? Are they actions that deviate from what one would have done had one followed the best reasons (i.e. regardless of what one believed, or could have believed about one's reasons)? Or are they unjustified actions? 'Wrong' could mean either, or neither. I may say about my own action yesterday 'I just now realize that that was the wrong thing to do', and I may say that without acknowledging any fault or blame. 'Given my situation my action was justified. But there was a conclusive reason against it, of which I was blamelessly unaware'. But often 'wrong' is used to assert or imply blame: 'You acted wrongly!' etc. When so used it at least implies that the action was unjustified. Sometimes it is used to imply that the action both flouted a conclusive reason and was unjustified. But 'wrong' has other uses or meanings as well. If any action that wrongs another is wrong then an action that I have a conclusive reason to do, which I ought to do, may be a wrong, wronging, or wrongful action. We were dealing with what one has reason to do, and what one ought to do, for these are among the simpler normative concepts. 'Wrong' belongs with a more complex range of concepts and its explanation needs to take account of issues not canvassed here.

7

Practical Reasoning

It is not uncommon among writers on practical thought to refer to *practical* rationality, *practical* reason, or *practical* reasoning. I do so when wishing to indicate that the subject is rationality as manifested in practical matters, the powers of reason when applied to practical matters, or reasoning about practical issues. Such uses of 'practical' do not imply that there is a difference between two kinds of Reason when addressing practical or theoretical matters. Nor do they presuppose that there is a special form of reasoning, unlike in important respects theoretical reasoning, to which 'practical reasoning' refers. So far as I am aware, Practical Reason is just Reason. There is no distinctive ability designated 'practical reason'. *Practical Reason* is *Reason* when dealing with *practical reasons*. As we saw practical reasons differ in important respects from other reasons. But the capacity reflectively to recognize and respond to them is the very capacity reflectively to recognize reasons generally. Empirical studies may expose a mistake in this view. It is certainly plausible to speculate that some of our rational powers may be more dominant in reflection about practical matters or in forming decisions and intentions than in reflection about theoretical matters or in forming beliefs. In the absence of comprehensive empirical findings I will assume that such differences are of secondary importance.

But is there a distinctive kind of reasoning: practical reasoning, distinctive as a form of reasoning, rather than in the premises employed in it? Again there is no doubt that practical reasoning often involves using concepts that rarely if ever figure in theoretical reasoning, and they come with their specific rules of inference. But are there more fundamental differences between these forms of reasoning? I am not aware of such differences. The defeasibility of practical reasoning was recognized perhaps before it was recognized that theoretical reasoning is also defeasible. But once the non-monotonic character of much theoretical reasoning is acknowledged that—once important—consideration supporting the distinctness of practical reasoning disappears. Writing of inferences rather than reasoning, Aristotle famously thought that practical syllogism differs from other forms of syllogism. I will briefly comment on the suggestion that he identified a form of inference that is central to practical reasoning, before turning to two other questions: Are there either special premises or special conclusions that can feature only in practical reasoning, and mark it not merely as reasoning about a special subject matter but as a special kind of reasoning?

1. Special practical inferences

Reasoning is one kind of norm-guided reflective activity, though of course not all instances of reasoning are successful, that is not all of them are correctly guided by the norms that govern the kind of reasoning of which they are an instance. If practical reasoning is a distinctive kind of reasoning then instances of practical reasoning are those activities that it is appropriate to evaluate, to criticize, by their conformity to the norms that govern practical reasoning. To identify practical reasoning one needs first to identify the norms governing it, and second to determine under what conditions it is appropriate to evaluate activities by their conformity to those norms. In examining the question whether practical reasoning constitutes a distinctive kind of reasoning we need be concerned only with the first of these questions.

Reasoning can involve the realization that some propositions entail another, but cannot be identified with inferences, or the realization that certain inferences are valid, the realization that certain inferential relations hold among sets of propositions. Nor is reasoning to be identified with the activity of inferring. Inferring is a more inclusive activity, and need not involve reasoning, as when I infer from her smile that she disbelieves me. Remembering the difference between rules of inference and the norms governing deliberation and reasoning, we start with a brief comment on practical syllogism. Aristotle thought that practical reasoning involves, or consists in syllogisms of a special kind. The question is: are Aristotelian practical syllogisms central to practical reasoning? Tony Kenny, endorsing Aristotle's account, provided a formalization of practical inferences that he informally explains as follows:

A piece of practical reasoning must contain a premise which sets out a goal to be obtained (such as 'Charles is to be kept warm'). The other premises commonly set out facts about the present situation, plus information about ways of reaching the goal from that situation. Indeed the commonest pattern of practical reasoning is: 'G is to be brought about. But if I do B then G; so I'll do B'.[1]

Noting that this is not a pattern of valid theoretical reasoning he explains:

Practical reasoning is the reasoning we use in planning how to achieve our goals. If there are rules of practical logic their function will be to see that we do not pass from a plan which is adequate to achieve our goals to one which is inadequate to achieve them....So in the sense in which rules of theoretical reasoning are truth-preserving, we can say that rules of practical logic are satisfactori-ness-preserving.[2]

Let us call a goal 'absolute' just in case it is (a) *independent*, that is it remains a goal whatever the circumstances, and (b) *overriding*, that is the reasons for it are conclusive whatever else is the case (as we say: 'whatever the consequences'). That I need a coat

---

[1] A. Kenny, *The Metaphysics of Mind* (Oxford: Clarendon Press, 1989), 43.   [2] Ibid. 44.

(which can be read as stating the goal of getting a coat) is not an independent goal since if it gets warm (and is likely to remain warm) I will not need a coat. Nor is it overriding: it should not be pursued if the only way to pursue it is to kill someone.

Aristotelian practical syllogism, while possibly helpful in identifying what we are to do given knowable absolute goals, cannot be taken to represent the general form of practical deliberation. Arguably, we are never warranted in assuming that any goal is absolute. In any case, much practical reasoning does not take any goal to be absolute. Aristotle's examples, a need for a coat, etc., are no exception. Much practical reasoning concerns identifying (a) what goals to have, and (b) what are we to do when goals conflict, as they regularly do, or when there are goal-independent considerations against pursuing some of our goals or against taking some of the means to their realization. Aristotelian practical syllogism is no help in either task. It does nothing to help with resolution of conflicts of reasons, and even in the absence of conflicting reasons the premises of Aristotelian practical syllogism do not warrant any conclusion, for they do not include a closure premise, like 'all other things are equal', without which no conclusion is warranted, but with which the inference is no longer distinct, being similar to probabilistic reasoning.[3]

2. Special kind of conclusion

A fairly common view identifies practical reasoning with reasoning whose conclusion is an intention. Some, starting with Aristotle, take the conclusion to be an action. Since presumably only intentional actions can be the conclusions of practical reasoning,[4] I will focus on the possibility that practical reasoning is reasoning having an intention as its conclusion.

John Broome writes:

Aristotle took practical reasoning to be reasoning that concludes in an action. But an action—at least a physical one—requires more than reasoning ability; it requires physical ability too.

---

[3] As R. Chisholm ('The Ethics of Requirement', *American Philosophical Quarterly*, 1 (1964), 147; 'Practical Reason and the Logic of Requirement', in S. Korner (ed.), *Practical Reason* (Oxford: Basil Blackwell, 1974), 1) and D. Davidson ('How is Weakness of the Will Possible?', in Davidson, *Essays on Actions and Events* (Oxford: OUP, 1980)) pointed out.

[4] Some object to the possibility of actions as conclusions of practical reasoning on the grounds that actions do not have propositional content. They are events, or perhaps they belong to a *sui generis* metaphysical category that shares some of the features of events, and therefore cannot be the conclusion of reasoning. The objection cannot be disposed of by pointing out that locutions like 'I thought about the matter long and hard and in conclusion did…' are perfectly natural. Individual actions, like other individuals, have a multitude of properties. They cannot be the conclusion of reasoning if this implies that one concluded to perform an action with precisely the properties that the action one did perform has. But that need not be the conclusion. Only intentional actions can possibly be claimed to be the conclusions of reasoning, in the required sense. Intentions do have propositional content. The suggestion is that the reasoning led one to an action with the properties in virtue of which it is intentional.

Intending to act is as close to acting as reasoning alone can get us, so we should take practical reasoning to be reasoning that concludes in an intention.[5]

The question is: does reasoning take us that far? Here are some doubts:

First, as Broome notices, his argument applies neither to mental acts nor to omissions. It may be that some acts can and others cannot be the conclusions of practical reasoning, but it makes one wonder whether the considerations that tell against physical acts being the conclusions of reasoning do not also tell against mental acts and omissions being such conclusions.

As Broome says, the question is how far can reasoning take us? One way of explaining why it cannot take us as far as to physical acts is that failure to perform the act need not be a failure of *reasoning*. Even when we reason with a view to acting the failure to act as a conclusion of the reasoning need not be a failure of reasoning. But if that is the argument then it applies to mental acts and omissions as well. In both these cases people may fail to act or to omit to act even when they reason correctly, and their reasoning instructs them to act or to omit. Reasoning cannot take us as far as action, for intentional action (which is the only kind of action reasoning can lead us to) depends on the will. The possibility of weakness of the will is precisely the possibility of failure to act that is not due to failure of reasoning, and we can fail to intentionally omit an action, or fail to perform a mental act through weakness of the will.

Things are different when we reason with a view to examining the case for modifying our beliefs. Here if, once the reasoning is done, we fail to have the belief that should be its conclusion, then our reasoning failed: we failed to reach the conclusion we should have reached. To reach a conclusion is to believe it. The failure may be due to the improper intrusion of the will: it may be due to irrational reluctance to come to disagreeable conclusions, and so on. But whereas the will is an essential contributor to intentions and intentional actions, it is an irrational intruder in theoretical reasoning. Hence its interference means that the reasoning was subverted, reaching an incorrect conclusion, or failing to reach any conclusion at all. The failure is a failure of reasoning.

But this argument shows that reasoning cannot take us as far as intentions either. Weakness of the will is paradigmatically failure to form intentions when our best judgement, possibly based on impeccable reasoning, tells us that we should. So understood,[6] Broome's argument refutes his own view that intentions can be conclusions of practical reasoning.

This argument does no more than remind us what we know. Suppose someone objects that the argument is guilty of *petitio principii*. Those who claim that an action or

---

[5] Broome, 'Practical Reasoning', in J. Bermúdez and A. Millar (eds.), *Reason and Nature: Essays in the Theory of Rationality* (Oxford: Clarendon Press, 2002).

[6] This qualification is important because Broome's reasons for his view are not made explicit. But even if this was not Broome's reason for his position it is a good reason, and the refutation of his position is not affected.

an intention is the conclusion of practical reasoning would simply reject my claim that the failure to act or to form an intention is not a failure of reasoning (and need not result from a failure of reasoning). They will claim simply that, given that an action or an intention is the conclusion of practical reasoning, it follows that failing to act or to intend is a failure of reasoning. I failed, the objection goes, to produce an argument against them. But that is to misconceive the nature of the argument. It merely, but crucially, reminds us that we know that the reasoning is over before the act is performed or the intention formed. We know that if someone fails to act or to intend as he should have and is challenged: 'why did you interrupt your reasoning midway? Why did you not complete it?' he will reply, truly, that he did. The problem was not with his reasoning but with his willpower.

Second, often when reflecting on what to do we find that there are several eligible options, in that while each is supported by various reasons, the reasons for each option neither defeat nor are defeated by the reasons against it. When we form intentions to take one of the eligible options our intentions are based on the reasons for the option we chose. But given that the existing reasons do not determine that we should choose any one of the various eligible options, there must be other factors influencing our choice. Among A and B we choose A, and we choose it for the reasons for A of which we are aware. But we also know (or have a warranted belief) that the reasons for A do not defeat the reasons for B (nor are they defeated by them). It follows that something besides the reasons for A determines our choice of A.

How far can reasoning take us in such cases? Does it lead to an intention to proceed with all the incompatible but eligible actions (an intention to do both A and B)? We can dismiss this option. Normally we do not have such incompatible intentions, and certainly not as a result of sound reasoning of the kind described. Admittedly, there are cases when it is rational to have several incompatible intentions, i.e. intentions that cannot all be realized.[7] But normally the mutual incompatibility of the different options would feed into the reasoning and would indicate that there is no need to form all the intentions, and perhaps even that it is best not to form all of them, or even that one should not.

A more reasonable possibility is that the conclusion is an intention to perform one of the eligible acts (in my schematic example: an intention to A). Generally speaking when aware of various eligible but incompatible options one *may* form an intention to perform at least one of them. So imagine the following situation:

Holiday: Mary needs a holiday. Her employer offers her an opportunity to take a holiday next week or the week after. Deliberating about the various considerations for and against either option Mary realizes that the reasons for neither of them defeat

---

[7] See N. Kolodny, 'The Myth of Practical Consistency', *Journal of European Philosophy* 16 (2008), 366. For example, when the intention is to perform the acts at some future time it may be reasonable to intend, and therefore prepare for, doing all of them in case one may become impossible, and but for the advance intention and preparation so would the alternative, or it may become more costly or difficult.

the reasons for the other. She concludes (perhaps an interim conclusion): 'I may take my holiday next week, but I also may take it the week after. I should not, however, defer it to a later date'. (Apologies for the strained formal way of putting the point.) She proceeds to choose to take the holiday the week after next.

Could that intention or its formation be the conclusion of her practical reasoning? It is certainly something that happens as a result of her reasoning. But not everything that is a result of her reasoning is also a conclusion of *that* reasoning. Another result is that she asks her mother to lend her some money in a week's time. But that surely is not the conclusion of that reasoning. What makes her intention to take the holiday the week after next a conclusion of her reasoning? It is not entailed by the reasoning, the reasoning did not require her to have that intention. She might have decided to take her holiday next week. Would that have been the conclusion of her reasoning? How can the same reasoning lead to two mutually exclusive (assuming that it would have been irrational to intend to take the holiday next week and also to intend to take it the week after next) conclusions? Mary deliberated in order to find out when to take her leave, next week or the week after. At some later point she has decided. If her decision or her intention is the conclusion of her reasoning it would follow that her reasoning solved her problem, the problem of when to take her holiday. But did it? If asked 'Did your reasoning solve the problem?' She would say 'No. It merely told me that there is nothing to it, that I may do either thing.' So, in what way was her intention a conclusion of that reasoning?

Possibly, some people think that if Mary forms an intention there was more to her reasoning than I allowed so far. They may think that had Buridan's ass been a person, he would indeed have died on the crossroads unless he found a reason to favour one bale of hay over the other. I have argued against this view elsewhere.[8] A more plausible response has it that reasoning leading to a permissive conclusion is theoretical and not practical. The difficulty with this response is that, all the way down to a stage near the end of the deliberation (if not at its end), reasoning to a permissive conclusion is similar in all relevant respects to reasoning to a (possibly intermediate) conclusion that there is a conclusive reason for one of the available options. Until we conclude whether the reasons for the action that we end up intending defeat all conflicting reasons there is no fact of the matter regarding whether our reasoning is practical or not. If at the last stage of the reasoning the conclusion emerges that the reasons for the action defeat all competing reasons then the ensuing intention renders the reasoning practical. If the last stage shows that the action is eligible but that the reasons for it do not defeat all the conflicting reasons then it turns out that the reasoning was theoretical, ending with that conclusion, whereas the intention to perform the action we intend to perform is not the conclusion of the reasoning. Though dependent on the reasoning it is separate from

---

[8] Cf. *The Morality of Freedom* (Oxford: OUP, 1986), ch. 11. See also S. Morgenbesser and E. Ullmann-Margalit, 'Picking and Choosing', *Social Research* 44 (1977), 757–85.

it. Is it plausible to distinguish between the two cases of reasoning just on the basis of a transition that happens right at the end?

One possible response[9] is that sometimes we reason directly to the intention, without pausing to draw the conclusion that the act is one we have conclusive reason to perform. That would suggest the possibility of parallel pieces of reasoning: theoretical reasoning ending with the belief that one must Φ, and practical reasoning ending with the intention to Φ, which differ only in their conclusion. Someone who has already engaged in the theoretical reasoning may rationally acquire the intention to Φ without any further reasoning. But at times one would be reasoning practically to the intention to Φ, without first engaging in the theoretical reasoning.

This suggestion seems attractive, provided there is a form of valid reasoning that leads to an intention to Φ via a reasoning route that does not include as an intermediate conclusion that one must Φ (or has a conclusive reason to Φ). If such an intermediate conclusion is required then we are back where we were before. But, I will argue, there is no such valid reasoning form. First, the premises of a reasoning that would yield an intention to Φ as its conclusion would also entail, or at any rate warrant, the conclusion that one must Φ. Second, unless one reasons to the conclusion that one must Φ one would not be justified in forming an intention to Φ *as a result of the reasoning*. That is, though the intention may be justified it cannot be regarded as a valid result of the reasoning. The existence of reasons to Φ is not sufficient to justify an intention to Φ. The intention is justified only if the reasons are not defeated. So if the intention is the conclusion of reasoning then the reasoning must include, as an intermediate conclusion, either that the reasons to Φ are not defeated by the conflicting reasons, or, that the reasons to Φ are conclusive. But if the intermediate step is permissive, that is, merely that the reasons to Φ are undefeated, then the intention is not warranted by the reasoning, as has been explained before. So if the intention is warranted by the reasoning the intermediate step must be that the reasons to Φ are conclusive. Hence we are back with the objection.

A *third* difficulty with the thought that practical reasoning is characterized by having intentions as its conclusion arises out of comparing reasoning of an agent about what to do with the reasoning of the same person about what he should have done. In the second case the reasoning concludes with a belief (I should have done A, A was the best option available to me, it was wrong (or would have been wrong) not to do A, etc.). But such non-practical reasoning is—or can be—identical with the reasoning of the agent who is wondering what to do at all the stages barring, so it is claimed, the last one, the one of forming the intention at the end.

Perhaps the most plausible response to all the objections has it that even when an intention is formed following a conclusion that there is a conclusive reason for the intended action, the reasoning down to that conclusion is theoretical, just as it would

---

[9] Suggested to me by a remark of Peter Railton, made in another context. It is endorsed by J. Dancy regarding practical reasoning.

have been had it led to a permissive conclusion. Practical reasoning is the reasoning from 'I must Φ' or 'there is a conclusive reason for me to Φ' to having or to forming the intention to Φ.

Yet that final stage is least likely to be part of any reasoning. There seems to be little here which can be characterized as reasoning. Of course, P entails P, but that is mere statement of an inferential relation between them. We do not deliberate from P to P. Do we deliberate from 'I ought to believe that P' to believing that P? According to the conclusions of Chapter Three in believing that I ought to believe that P I believe that P, and if I did not do so before the thought that I ought so to believe, I acquire the belief that P as I acquire the belief that I ought to believe that P. It is odd to talk here of reasoning, because there need not be a transition from one psychological state to another (from believing that I ought to believe that P to believing that P). If I believe that I ought to believe that P, I believe that P (though as always, exceptions due to pathological aberrations are possible). Existence of the first belief is a sufficient conceptual (non-inductive) criterion to attribute the second (assuming that the person concerned has the concepts possession of which is required to attribute such beliefs to him). This is clearly not the case with the relation between believing that I ought to Φ and intending to Φ. The two are distinct psychological states, and while the first ought to be accompanied by the second it may not be. That fact would have lent support to the view that one reasons one's way from the belief to the intention had the transition been a cognitive one. But it is not. What is required is the marshalling of one's will. Failure to form the intention one believes one ought to have is a failure of the will, and anyone who makes the distinction between cognitive and volitional powers would have to conclude that the transition is not one of reasoning.

The preceding case draws attention to yet another difference between ought to believe and ought to act. While it is possible to come to believe a proposition because one's attention is drawn to the fact that one ought to believe it (say by the advice of a credible expert) such cases are rather unusual. Typical reasoning bypasses that step, even though it is implied. I reason from all humans are mortal and Socrates is a man to Socrates is mortal. I do not interpose an intermediary conclusion: I ought to believe that Socrates is mortal. It is otherwise with reasoning about what is to be done. Whether or not reasoning processes conclude with an intention or an action, it is undisputed that they often include as an interim step beliefs about what one has adequate or conclusive reason to do. I argued above that such a step, interim or not, is essential to all reasoning about what to do. Why does reasoning about what to do (and I have in mind reasoning regarding action or omission on a specific occasion) include as a step that one has an adequate or a conclusive reason to perform an action, whereas reasoning leading to a belief, though it may, need not include a comparable step about reasons to believe? As has already been intimated, the difference is that beliefs track beliefs about the reasons for them more directly. Regarding action and intention once we know what reasons we have we need to marshal the will to follow them, a step missing in the case of coming to form beliefs. This again suggests that the reasoning stage ends with forming beliefs about what one has reasons to do, or other normative beliefs.

To be sure, often if one's theoretical deliberation soundly concludes with the belief that one must Φ and one does not form an intention to do so one may well be irrational. Some writers' inclination to take the intention, when formed, as a conclusion of the agent's reasoning derives from the correct view that the formation of intentions is an exercise of one's rational capacities. I argued to that view in Chapter Five, as well as for the concomitant conclusion that intentions can be rational or irrational. As was there established irrationality need not be the result of faulty reasoning, nor is the fact that an intention is rational necessarily the result of its being the conclusion of successful reasoning. Furthermore, while some intentions are formed following reasoning about what to do, others are not. Not all intentions, and not all actions with intentions follow any form of reasoning. As was also argued in Chapter Five, not all intentional actions are preceded by independent intentions. It has, however, been suggested that when they are future-directed independent intentions comprise or contain practical reasoning which keeps them on track, keeps them oriented towards the intended action. It is this reasoning aspect of the intention which enables us to avoid behaving in ways which will bar or impede the performance of that action when its time comes, and which alerts us that the time has arrived to act as intended. In themselves these observations show that having future-directed independent intentions, like having commitments, goals, being aware of duties (like the duty to drive carefully or to pay tax at the end of the year) may trigger one, in full awareness or below the level of awareness, to reason about the ways to proceed. They do not show that intentions either are or result from reasoning any more than showing that commitments, goals, or awareness of duties either are or result from reasoning.

None of these objections entails that the view that practical reasoning is a distinct form of reasoning characterized by having intention as its conclusion is false. Rather, they suggest that this way of classifying types of reasoning responds to no theoretical concerns and may mislead and confuse.

My view can be resisted in an additional way: one can claim that a fundamental difference between theoretical and practical reasoning lies first and foremost in their premises.

3. Special premises

At least two types of premises may be thought to be acceptable in practical reasoning, but not in theoretical reasoning: intentions and accepted, but not believed, propositions.

We regularly rely on propositions we accept, but do not believe, in forming intentions and in reaching decisions. An obvious example is the presumption of innocence. There are many common situations in which we should decide what to do on the basis of presumptions. Suppose that what is to be done depends on the truth of a proposition, whose truth is unknown to the agent. The situation may arise when, even though there is not enough evidence for the agent to form a belief about the truth of that proposition, there is a case for not prolonging deliberation, for concluding right there and then what is to be done. In such cases agents typically accept the proposition at issue or its negation, and form intentions on the basis of reasoning that accepts a proposition that the agent does not, and should not believe.[10]

It appears that while one may be warranted in accepting a proposition that one would not be warranted to believe, that acceptance cannot extend to accepting it as part of a course of reasoning leading to the formation of belief. How could a belief be warranted by considerations that themselves do not merit belief? Two qualifications are obvious: First, one can accept a proposition in order to refute it, as in *reductio ad absurdum* argumentation. Second, beliefs in normative propositions may be based on accepted propositions.[11] One may rightly conclude that one ought to offer someone a job because one accepts that he ought to be treated as innocent of any offence, given that he has not been convicted.

Even so, one is warranted in accepting a proposition (other than for the purpose of examining its implications and presuppositions) only if one would be warranted to believe that it is justified to act on the assumption that the accepted belief is true. So the fact that accepted propositions feature in different ways in practical and theoretical deliberations does not represent any deep difference between them. Both rely on believed propositions, or at least on considerations that would warrant belief.

Some readers may have felt for some time that at various points I have begged the question in arguing against some alternative views. In particular I have been assuming that practical reasoning proceeds from propositions that are either believed or assumed, hypothesized, etc. That made it natural, perhaps inevitable, to hold that evaluative propositions express the content of the conclusion of such reasoning, and that concluding is coming to believe. The alternative view identifies practical reasoning with reasoning that proceeds from intentions, or goals one set oneself, and that makes it natural to take intentions to be its conclusions. At the very least, it may be said, one has to agree that there are cases of reasoning from intentions to intentions, from goals to goals, and not only reasoning from normative or evaluative beliefs to other such beliefs.

Confining my considerations to intentions (goals follow the same road) it has to be admitted that observations such as, 'intending to A I reasoned my way to decide to B' are quite natural. But the question is whether the statement indicated not merely that

---

[10] As before I assume (a) that while there are degrees of belief, meaning degrees of confidence in one's beliefs, and also degrees of belief meaning degrees of willingness to give them up in face of conflicting evidence, believing that something is the case is an on/off condition. I also presuppose that people may withhold belief, and that in principle there are rational grounds for all these reactions; (b) sometimes in situations of this kind people form intentions ignoring the disputed propositions. My only point is that sometimes they do not, and are right to proceed on the basis of accepting a proposition that they do not believe.

[11] Though, arguably, this is true only of a conclusion about what is to be done in particular circumstances. That is, arguably, belief in, as against acceptance of, general propositions cannot be justified in that way.

the reasoning was motivated by awareness of one's intentions, but that intentions figured among its premises.

Intentions are subject to consistency and inferential relations with other intentions and beliefs. But, of course, statements of consistency and inferential relations between intentions or imperatives and actions, between goals and actions and the like, are not to be confused with rules of reasoning. Establishing that certain intentions are, given other assumptions, inconsistent can figure in reasoning leading to a belief in their inconsistency, or to other beliefs. The question is: Is there reasoning from intentions, goals and beliefs to intentions as conclusions? Possibly, but I suspect that when reasoning in order to establish what to do the intentions are not essential to the reasoning, that is that the reasoning will be essentially the same without them.

Suppose that I intend to read philosophy this evening, and that reading Kant's *Grundlegung* would constitute reading philosophy. Can I validly reason from these premises to the intention to read the *Grundlegung*? Of the many difficulties with this suggestion the one relevant here becomes evident if we substitute 'murder someone' for the first intention and 'murder my neighbour's child' for the second. It becomes clear that while there is a necessary relation between the two intentions (namely that realizing the second would realize the first) it is not the case that I would be warranted in forming the second because I have the first. It seems more appropriate to reason from the first intention to an intention to find a way to rid myself of murderous intentions.

For reasoning to warrant adopting or endorsing an intention it must include, at least as an interim conclusion, that the intention in the conclusion is one that one has an undefeated reason to have. Normally, that would depend on the intentions that figure among the premises being ones that one has undefeated reason to have. In all cases, one would have to include among the premises, or as an interim conclusion, some proposition about the character of the initial intention. But once the reasoning relies on the proposition that one has a certain intention that has some features (is unobjectionable, reasonable, etc.) the initiating intention is no longer an essential part of the reasoning. It is external to it, even if it motivates the agent to deliberate.

4. Does it matter?

Some, in spite of their interest in normativity, rationality, and reasons, cannot see the point of claims, like mine, that practical reasoning is (crudely speaking) but reasoning about a particular subject matter, that there is no distinctive form of reasoning called practical reasoning. Some of them suspect that the dispute may be merely terminological. At first blush this is a surprising response. After all the concepts of reasoning and of practical reasoning, have been a subject of philosophical reflection throughout much of its history. They are among a family of concepts that are uncontroversially the subjects of such reflection. But perhaps what motivates people's reactions is the thought that the arguments for and against the distinctive character of practical reasoning are so finely balanced that there is no truth of the matter on this issue. To be sustained that reaction cannot consist of merely saying that it does not matter who is right about these matters. It has to be supported by pointing to the flaws in the argument of this chapter, and indeed of the book more generally. For the thesis of this chapter while being supported most directly by the arguments advanced in it, follows from the general conclusions of Part One, which therefore support and are reinforced by the arguments here given. Part One showed how Reason, namely the rational power, includes more than the powers of reasoning—and did so on the basis of arguments that are quite independent of the debate concerning the nature of practical reasoning. Part One offered an explanation of the relations between Reason, rationality, and reasons, which—when applied to the examination of reasoning—leads to the conclusions that were here supported by arguments more narrowly focused on the nature of reasoning.

One way in which the conclusions of Part One support the view I argued for here is by providing an explanation of an error. Those who thought more deeply on the nature of practical reasoning—for example Anscombe and a number of more recent writers influenced by her work—argued (mostly implicitly) that actions or intentions must be the conclusions of practical reasoning because they are (or can be) Reason-guided, that they can be rational or irrational. Part One established that that argument is a non sequitur, and that it is important to grasp that Reason includes more than the power of reasoning, and manifests itself in other activities than reasoning. Once the confusion of this argument for taking actions or intentions to be the conclusions of reasoning is brought to light, there is little else to support the distinctiveness of practical reasoning, and the task of explaining reasoning is clarified and simplified.

8

The Myth of Instrumental Rationality[1]

Recent interest in the nature and presuppositions of instrumental rationality was inspired to a considerable degree by arguments designed to show that it presupposes other forms or kinds of rationality, or (to put it in the non-equivalent way in which the point is more commonly put) that claims that there are reasons to pursue the means to our ends presuppose that the ends themselves are worth pursuing, or that there are adequate reasons for pursuing them. The discussion of instrumental rationality is bound up with discussions of instrumental reasons and of instrumental reasoning that guides deliberation, and which, other things being equal, it is irrational knowingly to flout. The interest in understanding instrumental rationality was thus at least partly a result of an interest in—often hostility to—an ambitious claim, namely that all practical reasons are instrumental, that practical normativity is about the normativity of following the means to our ends.

I say little about this issue. My main aim is to explain the normative character of the phenomena that are commonly discussed when writers on practical reasons discuss instrumental rationality and instrumental reasons. The discussion will assume that there are forms of practical normativity, kinds of practical reasons, that are not instrumental in nature. The question central to the inquiry is what, if any, normative difference does adopting or having an end make? For example, are there instrumental reasons, and if there are, how do they relate to having ends? Are instrumental reasons a distinctive kind of reasons, whose normativity differs in its underlying rationale from that of, say, moral reasons, or of other kinds of reasons? Similarly, is instrumental rationality a distinct form of rationality?

Reflecting on these questions we are liable to be torn both ways. On the one hand we feel that the value of the means derives from the value of the ends. If there are reasons to take the means they must be none other than the reasons to pursue the ends, or at least they must derive from them. They cannot derive simply from the fact that we have these ends. On the other hand, we also feel that failure to take the means to

[1] The issues raised in this chapter are further discussed by R. J. Wallace, M. Schroeder, D. Sobel, and J. Broome, in a published symposium, which includes my response to their criticism, in *Journal for Ethics & Social Philosophy* 1/1 (2005) (http://www.jesp.org/).

one's ends is a distinct kind of failure, different from the failure to have proper ends, or to value them properly. This is the puzzle of instrumental rationality. The first response, that there are no distinctive instrumental reasons, no reasons to take the means to one's ends, is reinforced by the thought that, say, a would-be murderer cannot create for himself a reason for poisoning his intended victim just by making it his goal to kill him. If so then adopting an end does not necessarily generate a reason either to pursue it, or to take the means for its realization. The second response, however, is reinforced by the thought that a person with evil or worthless ends who fails to take the proper means to his ends is, perhaps luckily, irrational in a way that is indifferent to the character of his ends. He is irrational in the same way as someone whose ends are worthy, but who fails to take the means towards them.

My way with the puzzle is to embrace both reactions. In the first section I will suggest that (subject to some qualifications) we have reasons to facilitate the realization of anything of value whose realization is not deeply impossible, regardless of whether or not its realization is one of our ends. In other words I will offer a principle of the transmission of normativity, of the generation of reasons, whereby the generated reasons derive from the fact that they facilitate realization of the generating reasons, but which does not depend on the generating reasons being our ends. In Section 2 I agree with those who (a) deny that our ends (and intentions) are reasons to take the means for their realization, and (b) argue that nevertheless our ends affect what is rational for us to do. I do, however, contend that some attempts to square this circle failed, and offer a different solution. Sections 3 and 4 defend the proposed position by arguing (a) that the value of being an effective agent does not provide reasons to avoid instrumental irrationality, and (b) that we do not have reason to avoid contradictions as such. Section 5 complements the earlier discussion by pointing to additional practical implications of ends.

The conclusions of these sections, while following in the footsteps of a number of recent writers on the subject, do deviate from long-established ways of treating the phenomena philosophers discuss under titles such as instrumental reasons, normativity, or rationality. I allow that there are 'instrumental reasons', facilitative reasons as I call them, but deny that they have anything to do with our ends. I allow that ends while not providing reasons for the pursuit of the means, may render us irrational if we do not pursue the means. Because the accounts of facilitative reasons and of instrumental irrationality differ from many current accounts, the instances in which, according to these accounts, we have facilitative reasons or are instrumentally irrational, also differ from common views on these matters. Section 6 faces the oddity of my conclusions. It does so by challenging the thought, common to some writers who otherwise vary considerably, that instrumental rationality or instrumental reasons or both are a distinctive type of rationality or of reasons. In particular it reinforces the critique, implied in the preceding sections, of the view that 'instrumental reasons' or instrumental rationality are a basic, perhaps simpler, domain of reasons or rationality that, according to some, exhausts practical reasons and practical rationality, whereas according to others it constitutes their most elementary and theoretically least problematic part. The final appendix, about the many occasions on which it is rational not to have intentions to pursue the known means to our ends, exemplifies a central difference of approach between my account and many others: they ignore the significance of rational people's ability reliably to respond to reasons.

1. Instrumental reasons without ends

I start with informally reminding us of some of the terminology I use and the theses I presuppose. Imagine some good, valuable, worthwhile objects, states, or activities, whose value is not (or not exclusively) due to the value of their actual or probable consequences, or consequences their existence facilitates (e.g. by being preconditions for their existence, or tools that can be used to bring them about). Say a beautiful musical composition, canoeing down the Colorado River, the state of understanding Kant's philosophy in all its details. I will proceed on the assumption that (subject to the normative/explanatory *nexus* and some other exceptions that need not concern us) their value is a reason (which we call 'non-instrumental') for everyone to engage with and to respect what is of value, provided only that doing so is not deeply impossible.

There is no quick explanation of what it is to engage with something of value, or what constitutes respecting it. It all depends what kind of value it has. If it is a concert, engaging with it could be to listen to it, or play in it, or conduct it. If it is a dance or hill walking it may be joining in; if it is knowledge of Kant then it may be a matter of reflecting on Kant's views, comparing them with others, raising issues and responding to them, in short making one's knowledge active, making it play a part in one's life or work. Respect for what is valuable is expressed by avoiding harming it, protecting it from harm, and so on. For present purposes we can rely on examples such as these to guide us.[2]

The reason-negating character of deep impossibilities follows from the normative/explanatory *nexus*. It is not the case that I have reason to attend the symposium that was recorded by Plato in the dialogue of that name, nor is it the case that I have reason to travel outside the solar system, but I have reason to go to the concert conducted by Abbado tonight even though I cannot as it is sold out. I do not know how to distinguish in the abstract between reason-negating and other impossibilities. Perhaps it is just a matter of the likelihood that the impossibility will lift, or of the kind of conditions which would lift it.

The reasons that will be discussed here are, of course, normative reasons, and they are *pro tanto* reasons. Normative principles are propositions about normative phenomena (about reasons, values, virtues, responsibilities, rights, etc.). To avoid tedium I will

---

[2] See more generally my *Value, Respect and Attachment* (Cambridge: CUP, 2000), ch. 4.

refer informally to normative and rational principles, considerations, etc. assuming that in the contexts their interrelations are easy to discern.

Some things that we have reason to do we do simply by doing them. In doing so we may also be doing something else. Davidson's familiar example will serve: we may turn on the light by flicking the light switch.[3] I do not flick on the light switch by doing anything else.[4] I just flick it on. I do turn on the light by flicking the light switch, the second act being, in the circumstances, a constituent of the first, of my turning on the light (though not of the action-type of turning on the light). Often, however, things are different, and we can perform an action only by performing another action first, one that is not a constituent part of the main action that we can then proceed to perform. I can travel to Oxford only if I first stop writing this chapter, get out of my chair, and put on my shoes. None of them is an element of going to Oxford, but they are, in the circumstances, preconditions for doing so. Other actions may be means for doing so. For example, filling my car tank with petrol (if I intend to drive) or buying a ticket (if I intend to go by train). One can spend a happy time distinguishing means from preconditions from facilitating conditions and so on. I will avoid that, and will refer to all of them as facilitating steps or acts.

Facilitating steps can come in ordered sequences, each constituting one way of bringing us to the point where we can take the action the facilitating steps facilitated, the action we have reason to take. We could call each a (possible) plan[5] of how to get to a point at which we can take that action.[6]

An initial, approximate statement of a principle that I will call the **facilitative principle** has it that when there is an undefeated reason to perform an action there is also a reason to facilitate its performance. The principle states that one reason (call it the generating reason) can generate another (call it the generated reason). These generated reasons are reasons for taking facilitative actions, and can also be called facilitating reasons.

It seems plausible to assume that much of what people have in mind when they talk of *instrumental reasons* is captured by this principle. But if this is so then we have instrumental reasons independently of having any ends. The facilitative principle is indifferent to what our ends are, and asserts that we have instrumental reasons to

---

[3] Davidson, 'Actions, Reasons and Causes' (1963), repr. in *Actions and Events* (Oxford: OUP, 1980), 14. Needless to say my use of it is not Davidson's.

[4] Some would insist that only actions consisting in nothing more than bodily movements caused by the appropriate intention can be acts not done by doing others. It seems to me, however, that that is an artificial stipulation. The fact that normally we do not intend to move our fingers, but rather intend to flick the switch (as well as, of course, to turn on the light) is a good ground for taking flicking the switch not to be an action done by performing another action even though I do it by moving my fingers (which was intentional because I intended to flick the switch in that way).

[5] Needless to say plans can overlap: if the nearest bus stop to Oxford is at the train station then going to that location is part of both the plan to get to Oxford by bus and the plan to get there by train.

[6] On various senses of 'plans' see M. Bratman, *Intention, Plans and Practical Reason* (Cambridge, Mass.: Harvard UP, 1987), ch. 3. Here 'a plan' refers to an abstract structure in the nature of a recipe.

facilitate any worthy state or action, even those whose performance is not among our ends, even those that we cannot pursue if we pursue our ends.

The facilitative principle reflects a few considerations about the conditions for the generation of reasons for facilitating actions. First, that there is no reason to facilitate conformity with a defeated reason. Therefore only undefeated reasons generate facilitative reasons. Second, given that the principle is the only one governing the generation of facilitative reasons, it presupposes that there are non-facilitative (or 'non-instrumental') reasons. The remarks about the various relations between actions one of which facilitates performance of another show that facilitative reasons include more than those normally thought of as 'instrumental reasons'. This raises the difficult question of what kind of dependence of A on B does not render B valuable (if at all) merely because it facilitates A. For example, if A and B are constitutive parts of C which is intrinsically valuable (as I will call all value which is not merely facilitative), then (assuming that they have no other value) even though the value of A depends on B the value of B is not in facilitating realization of A, but in being a constituent element of C, which is intrinsically valuable. I do not offer an account of intrinsic value. It is not needed for the application of the facilitative principle, for while the principle pre-supposes that there are non-facilitative reasons they are not the only ones that generate facilitative reasons. Facilitative actions are themselves valuable and their value can generate reasons to facilitate their performance.

The third basic consideration underlying the principle (though not yet unambiguously expressed in its initial statement above) is that there is no point in taking a facilitating step if the generating reason will not be conformed with even if it is taken. If to get today to Oxford I need to get a bus ticket and to get to the bus stop before the last bus leaves, and I can get a ticket but cannot get to the bus stop in time then I have no reason at all to buy a bus ticket. Therefore, one has reason to take a facilitating action only if it is part of a feasible plan whose execution does, or is likely to generate, bring about, an opportunity to conform to the generating reasons. Chapter Six already examined the dependence of facilitative reasons on the probability of success. What was not discussed there is what constitutes success. I suggest that it is the generation of an opportunity—namely that no other prior conditions for performance of the act the originating reason is a reason for need obtain before the agent (who has the reason) can just perform that action. Having an opportunity to Φ does not mean that one will Φ. It does not even mean that one will Φ if one tries—there is many a slip between cup and lip. Yet, it is reasonable to take opportunities to conform to the originating reason as the goal of facilitative actions. Needless to say opportunities can exist under various conditions, some making success in conforming to the originating reason (should one try) more likely than others, and there are stronger facilitative reasons to generate those opportunities in which one is more likely to succeed in performing the generating action if one tries.

There is another factor which may make facilitative action pointless: it may be part of a plan which is, to coin a phrase, factually possible but normatively impossible because there is a conclusive reason against taking one of the steps in the plan. The point seems straightforwardly reasonable, and can easily be supported by examples. Going back to my travel to Oxford example, assume that while I can get to the bus stop in time for the last bus, I should not do so for the only way to get there in time is by appropriating without permission a friend's car. Even considering the case for getting to Oxford today I should not 'steal' my friend's car (or so I shall assume). That means that the plan (buying a bus ticket and going to the stop to catch the bus) fails, and therefore I have no reason at all to buy a ticket for the bus. Normative impossibility has the same effect as factual impossibility. Yet the point merits some further discussion as it involves one theoretical and one technical interesting issue.

The technical issue revolves around the relations between reasons for adopting facilitative plans and reasons for taking facilitative steps. Any plan consists of a series of sequential steps (each containing possibly more than one action) determined by the latest time each has to be initiated in order to be part of the plan (or the point at which once initiated it cannot be aborted). Some of these steps facilitate performance of later steps (I borrow my friend's car to get to the bus stop in time, to catch the bus to Oxford, etc.). As the facilitative principle makes clear, there is reason to take a facilitative step only if the reason for the action it facilitates is undefeated. That lesson is generalized above by observing that there is reason to take a facilitative action only if it is part of a feasible and undefeated plan leading to an opportunity to conform to the generating reason.

These remarks highlight the fact that the relation of a generating to a generated reason is non-transitive. While only undefeated reasons generate facilitative reasons, the generated reasons are not necessarily undefeated. An obvious explanation of the possible difference in force between the generating and the generated reasons is that the probability that a facilitating plan will succeed, is different from the probability that the action for performance of which the generated reasons provide an opportunity will be successfully performed, if tried. An obvious explanation for the fact that a generated reason can be defeated even though the generating reason is not is that it may conflict with different reasons. This point does, however, require further explanation: the question is—how can a generating reason remain undefeated even if all the reasons it generates are defeated, namely even if in order to have the opportunity to conform to it one has to take some facilitating action but all the available ways of creating an opportunity to conform are defeated? Should not that fact defeat the generating reason?

The answer lies with the fourth consideration presupposed by the principle, regarding the difference between intrinsic and facilitative reasons (so it does not apply to all generating reasons, but only to intrinsic generating reasons). The reasons for facilitative acts depend on the action they facilitate, which makes them more dependent on the circumstances of action. No occasion of possible realization is presupposed by true propositions of intrinsic reasons. I have a reason to see the film *The Seventh Seal* even though I do not know when, if ever, it will be possible for me to do so. The statement is true even if conformity is not possible, except, as was remarked above, that it excludes deep impossibility. Statements of facilitative reasons, that is of reasons to take facilitative actions, presuppose an occasion (or class of occasions) on which the facilitative actions will be possible, and will facilitate: if they could facilitate under different conditions but would not facilitate today then I do not have reason to take them today. So, for example, if I have reason to visit my grandmother who lives on Easter Island today I also have a reason to buy a flight ticket to go there today but only if she is there or will be there, and only if it is possible to get there by air today. If there is an air strike I have no reason to pursue the plan of flying there today, and therefore no reason to buy a flight ticket. Such actions will not facilitate my visiting her,[7] even though I still have a reason to visit her today, albeit one with which (let us assume) it is impossible for me to conform.

As we saw, another way in which facilitative reasons depend on circumstances is that we have facilitative reasons only in circumstances in which the generating reason is not defeated. Imagine that I have to choose which of three films, A, B, or C, to go to. I can see any, but no other option is available. Imagine further that all three are worth seeing. So I have reason to see each of them, but cannot see more than one today. Finally, let it be assumed that for some reason I should see A or B rather than C, but there is no better case for seeing A rather than B, nor the other way round. In this situation I have reason to facilitate seeing A as well as reason to facilitate seeing B, but no reason to facilitate seeing C. For example, I have reason to buy a ticket for A, and reason to buy a ticket for B, but no reason to buy a ticket for C.[8] Because it is a good film I still have reason to see C. But because in today's circumstances that reason is defeated I have no reason to facilitate action conforming to it. This is nothing to do with seeing C not being my end. I have no end, no decision what to do.

Suppose that I resolved my doubts and do intend to see film A. I have reason to facilitate doing this, but do I still also have reason to facilitate seeing film B? The answer depends on whether my intention means that now the reason to see A is stronger than the reason to see B. If it is, the reason to see B is defeated, and I do not have reason to facilitate seeing B. If, however, my intention does not affect the stringency of the reasons for either option I still have reason to facilitate each of them. You may ask: since I cannot see both why do I have reason to facilitate both? Given my intention I will not do so, rather I will buy a ticket for A. That will affect my reasons about which film to see. I will have a better reason to see the film I have a ticket for. This means, according to the facilitative principle, that I no longer have a reason to facilitate seeing B, as the reason to see B has been defeated. If, however, I buy a ticket for B, I have

---

[7] This appears to be a special case of the following: if it is certain that I will not do the source action, whether or not I can do it, there is no reason to take the facilitative action.

[8] It may be said that I have reason to do that too, as insurance in case I am wrong in thinking that I can see either A or B. Without denying this, I will continue in this chapter to ignore insurance-type reasons (cf. Chapter Six above). Also, note that because I can only see one film I have no reason to buy tickets for both A and B. The reasons are dependent, and conforming with one cancels the other.

reason to change my intention, as now the case for seeing B is stronger than the case for seeing A.

The preceding reflections suggest a somewhat more accurate statement of the **facilitative principle**:

> when there is an undefeated reason to perform an action (the source action) there is also a reason to take any action which facilitates its performance, provided that it is part of a feasible and undefeated plan whose pursuit by the agent is likely to generate an opportunity to perform the source action, where a plan is defeated if the reason for any of its indispensable steps is defeated.

The hard question is: Is the facilitative principle sound? The simplest argument is that it is good to facilitate worthwhile actions. This argument may appear too quick and question-begging. Another way to approach the issue is to imagine a situation where something clearly should be one's end, though it is not. Suppose Annabel has, in her care, a 2-year-old child, her child, and she should have been feeding it properly as one of her ends. As it happens Annabel cares for nothing but her career, and feeding her child means nothing to her (though she will feed it if its cries disturb her peace, or to avoid being prosecuted for child abuse or neglect). Thinking of such a case it seems difficult to deny that she has reason not only to feed the child but to buy food, which will facilitate feeding him. It seems to make no sense to think that she has a reason to feed the child, but no reason to make it possible for her to do so. That feeding the child is not an end of hers seems to be neither here nor there.

But if this is so regarding what should be her end, why is it not also true of valuable pursuits that she has reason to make her ends, but will not be wrong not to do so? Suppose that reading Conrad's *Lord Jim* is such a pursuit, but she could instead spend her free time reading Hardy's *Far from the Madding Crowd*, or watching the films of Orson Welles. That she may read Hardy rather than Conrad does not mean that she has no reason to read Conrad. Of course she does. If so does she not also have the reason to take steps to make it possible to do so? As explained, if she pursues a permissible alternative course of action there may be nothing wrong in her not taking such steps. If she intends to read Hardy and borrows his novel she need not (for now) also borrow Conrad's. But until and unless her intentions and her pursuit of means change her reasons she has reason to facilitate whatever ends she has undefeated reason to adopt.

Yet another approach to the facilitative principle is to think of the nature of reasons. One aspect of reasons for action is that they make choices, intentions, and actions intelligible both to the agent and to others. If Betty were to decide to live in L rather than B on the ground that L, being a metropolitan city, has many more cultural activities than B, her choice would be intelligible.[9] The fact that modern dance is the only

---

[9] Some mistakes are intelligible, i.e. we can understand how people come to make them: they were brainwashed since childhood, etc. The intelligibility I refer to has a different object: it is intelligible as a reason.

cultural activity she regularly takes an interest in (the only cultural pursuit that in some form is among her ends) is neither here nor there. It is intelligible that she would want to choose her town of residence in a way that facilitates pursuit of a wide range of cultural activities. If so then in making such a choice she would be acting for a reason, and that reason is of course one that is available to all, and would make any person's choice intelligible were they to make such a choice. Hence they all have the facilitative reason whether or not they decide to follow it, and whether or not they should conform to it.[10]

2. The difference ends make

I have argued that at least some instrumental reasons do not presuppose having ends, that we have instrumental reasons that are unrelated to ends that we do have. It does not follow that our ends do not make a difference to the reasons we have. They can constitute or generate additional reasons, or they can affect the character or stringency of reasons we have anyway. If they do either they may similarly affect instrumental reasons that we have.

What are people's ends? For a start they are not what they want or desire. There are many things that people want but achieving or getting them is not among their ends. This may be because their desire is to achieve or be given something without trying, or because they do not think they stand a chance of getting it, or because they want other things more, and think that they cannot get both, or they may be just too lazy or diffident to pursue it, to have it as their end, or they may believe that theirs are unworthy desires, or that the objects of their desires are unworthy, or that they are under a duty not to pursue them. There are many other ways and factors that stop people from pursuing many of their desires, or from having their satisfaction or the realization of their objects among their goals or ends.[11]

Several recent writers agree that it is not the case that our having ends, whatever their content, is a reason for us to pursue them, or that they are or generate reasons to take facilitative steps towards their realization.[12] I have already indicated the difficulty:

---

[10] Ulrike Heuer suggested to me that such cases are simply ones in which one has 'reason to make sure that means are available if one were to adopt new ends'. This seems to me close to the truth, and consistent with my contentions here. The point I am making is that such reasons do not presuppose a prior end that they facilitate, such as the end to find ends in the future. Note though that it is not so much that we have reasons to facilitate adopting new ends, as reasons to facilitate acting for adequate reasons. The adoption of ends or forming of intentions is merely the way we come so to act. Thus formulated we can more clearly see that those reasons do not depend on having an end to act for adequate reasons in the future, including actions that we are not yet resolved to take. Rational agents, in being rational, are open to reasons that they have not considered before, or to which they did not yet respond.

[11] A similar point is made by R. J. Wallace in 'Normativity, Commitment, and Instrumental Reason', *Philosophers' Imprint* 1/3 (2001), at 14 (repr. in his *Normativity and the Will* (Oxford: OUP, 2006)).

[12] See Bratman, *Intention, Plans and Practical Reason*; J. Broome, 'Normative Requirements', *Ratio* 12 (1999), 398, repr. in J. Dancy (ed.), *Normativity* (Oxford: Blackwell, 2000), 78–99, and 'Practical Reasoning', in J. Bermúdez and A. Millar (eds.), *Reason and Nature: Essays in the Theory of Rationality* (Oxford: OUP, 2002); C. Korsgaard, 'The Normativity of Instrumental Reason', in G. Cullity and B. Gaut (eds.), *Ethics And*

out of ignorance, weakness of the will, rashness or carelessness, or mistaken moral convictions, people may have ends that they should not have, ends that are worthless or even evil. Can they have reason to facilitate their realization just because they are their ends? It is no reply to this question that one's end is only a *pro tanto* reason. That one's end is to kill some innocent person is no reason at all to buy poison or take any facilitating measures towards killing him. The view I defend here is of this family. I will not argue directly that our intentions or ends are not reasons. Rather, given the above objection to the view that they do in and of themselves provide reasons for action I will try to show that the considerations that lead us to think that intentions and ends provide reasons can be, and should be, explained without that assumption.

For example, the fact that people who pursue their ends act intelligibly, even when there are no adequate reasons for them to have the ends they pursue, does not require us to assume that their ends are their reasons, and that that makes their pursuit of them intelligible. To have an end involves believing that it is worth having (at least other things being equal).[13] That belief explains why people pursue ends. They take what they believe to be reasons for the ends as reasons to pursue the ends, and, as explained by the facilitative principle, to take steps to facilitate them.[14]

Some may be inclined to think that ends provide reasons to pursue the means because they perceive an asymmetry between our attitude to our ends and to the means for their realization. When faced with people who have ends and do not pursue the means to realize them we do not think: they should abandon their ends. Perhaps sometimes we do, but the more natural inclination is to urge them to adopt the means, or condemn them for failure to do so. The asymmetry may not be absolute, but it is fairly pronounced, and is manifested by the widespread belief in the so-called instrumental principle: that one ought to pursue the means to one's ends. The asymmetry, such as it is, is readily explained without the assumption that ends are or provide reasons. Most of the time we do not settle on a goal until we consider at least some of the problems that its realization may give rise to. So that agents who have a goal already have a settled, though revisable view that it is worth pursuing, even though the means

---

Practical Reason (Oxford: OUP, 1997); Wallace, 'Normativity, Commitment'. My agreement with this view does not contradict the view that I defended elsewhere, namely that there are personal commitments or resolutions that are reasons; indeed what I called protected reasons. They are the personal analogues of institutional decisions that, in a sound institution acting within its jurisdiction, are protected reasons for carrying out the decisions. See *Practical Reason and Norms* (1975; current edn. Oxford: OUP, 1999), 65–72. Contrast e.g. J. L. Mackie: '"If you want X, do Y" (or "You ought to do Y") will be a hypothetical imperative if it is based on the supposed fact that Y is, in the circumstances, the only (or the best) available means to X....The reason for doing Y lies in its causal connection with the desired end, X; the oughtness is contingent upon the desire' *Ethics* (Harmondsworth: Penguin Books, 1977), 27–8, or J. Dreier: 'If you desire to A and believe that by phying you will A, then you ought to phy' in 'Humean Doubts about the Practical Justification of Morality', in *Ethics and Practical Reason*, 93.

[13]   The qualification allows for having ends against one's better judgement.

[14]   Though the reasons may change over time, and may come to include the fact that one is trapped with an end one would be better without, but cannot give up because its pursuit incurred obligations to others, or for some other reason.

are not without costs and difficulties. Therefore, barring occasions where there is a case for revising that judgement, agents have an asymmetric attitude to the ends and the means: they do not think that they should abandon their ends because of the difficulties or costs of pursuing the means. It is a result of what constitutes a rational adoption of ends. If, or where, agents adopt ends without any attention to the means no asymmetry exists. [15]

Even so, there appears to be a strong case for thinking that ends and intentions provide reasons. After all, people who fail to pursue the means to their ends display, or at least appear to display, a distinctive form of irrationality. 'Have you not resolved to buy this car?' (we are hardly likely to ask: 'isn't buying it an end of yours?', but it comes to the same thing). 'Yes,' she says. 'Do you realize that you cannot buy it without making an offer to buy it?' 'Of course', she says, 'I am no fool'. 'So, when will you make an offer?' 'Oh,' she replies, 'I have no intention of ever making an offer.' Something has gone wrong, and that is so whatever the merit or demerit of her buying the car. It appears that just by failing to intend to pursue the means to her end she is behaving irrationally. [16] But if her end is no reason for her to facilitate its realization how can that be?

One approach to the relevance of ends has been advanced and explored by J. Broome, and by R. J. Wallace, who explains:

The principle [that he, following Korsgaard, calls the instrumental principle] imposes rational constraints on the attitudes of agents without entailing either that they have reason to take the means necessary relative to their ends, or that they are rationally required to believe that they should adopt the necessary means. ('Normativity, Commitment', 16)

Perhaps those who think that our ends or intentions create reasons for taking the means towards their realization believe that all rational constraints consist in reasons that constrain what we may rationally do or believe. That is their mistake.

But how does rationality constrain agents' attitudes? By 'governing combinations of attitudes' ('Normativity, Commitment', 17). Broome has explored this idea in detail (and in summarizing his position I adapt it to apply to the way the issues have been presented here). He points out that some conditional ought-propositions do not allow for detachment. Even if one ought (to do A if P) and P, it does not follow that one

---

[15] R. J. Wallace thinks that my explanation of the asymmetry, namely of the normative pressure we are subject to, and that we feel, to adopt instrumental intentions is inadequate, because the pressure applies to akratic agents as well. However, the facilitative principle applies to akratic agents, for they too act for a reason—the akratic guzzler of chocolate eats chocolate because he enjoys its taste, or whatever. In as much as he believes that he has a reason for the end, he also believes that he has a reason for the means that facilitate it. True, the explanation of the asymmetry in the previous paragraph does not apply to some akratic agents, those who know that the reasons against the means should make them abandon the end, yet they do not. More generally, as the akratic sees matters, he has an adequate reason neither for having the end nor for pursuing the means, but at some point rationalizing explanation cannot explain irrational conduct.

[16] Ignoring this point seems to vitiate Korsgaard's account ('Normativity of Instrumental Reason') of 'the instrumental principle'.

ought to do A. To conclude that one ought to do A is to detach where detachment is not warranted. For example, if P entails Q then, according to Broome, one ought (to believe that Q if one believes that P). But it does not follow that if one believes that P one ought to believe that Q. P may be false (or, if you think this makes a difference, obviously false), in which case the fact that it entails Q and that one believes that P is no reason at all to believe that Q.

Therefore, from

(1A) One ought (to do M if one intends to do E and M is a means to E), and
(2A) One intends to do E and M is a means to E, it does not follow that
(3A) One ought to do M

Following Broome one may be tempted to claim, though he himself does not consider this matter, that the same is true regarding some conditional reasons. It does not follow from one has reason (to do A if P) and P that one has reason to do A. Similarly, it does not follow from:

(1B) One has reason (to do M if one intends to do E and M is the means to E); and
(2B) One intends to do E and M is the means to E; that
(3B) One has reason to do M

Adapting to Broome's reasoning we can say that either (1A) or (1B) expresses the rational constraint imposed by the instrumental principle, and since they do not entail (3A) or (3B) one's ends are not and do not generate reasons for action.

The problem is that (3B) is entailed by both sets of premises.[17] Forget about ends. Reasons are reasons to do what will constitute conformity with the reason. (1B) does state that one has a reason. What is it a reason for? A roundabout way to identify the reason is to say that it is a reason to avoid being in a situation in which one would be in breach of that reason. And one would be in breach of it if one both intends E and fails to do M. There are two ways to avoid being in that situation. One is to abandon the intention to do E. The other is to do M. So one has both a reason to do M and a reason to abandon one's intention to do E (though no reason to do both because once one does one of them the reason to do the other lapses). That means that, so long as M is the means to E and one intends to do E, one has reason to do M. By doing M, when it is

---

[17] In fact the conclusion follows even from weaker premises. As Simon Ripon observed to me: (1B) One has reason (to do M if one intends to do E and M is the means to E) and (2Bvariant) M is a necessary means to E; entails that One has reason (not to intend E or to do M), and therefore that (3) One has reason to do M.

I formulated (1B) following Broome. Ripon pointed out that it leads to various puzzling consequences, and I believe that it is not the correct rendering of: one has reason not to be in a situation where one intends an end and does not intend the means. (1B') seems better: (1B') if one intends E then one has reason to (not intend E without intending the necessary means M). Needless to say (1B') will serve to support my conclusions in the text.

the means to E, one acts in a way that puts one on the right side of reason. By doing M one conforms to the reason stated in (1B). It follows that one has reason to do M.[18]

Can one argue that Broome is right and *the reason* (to take the means) is not one's intention, or one's having an end? This seems like hair splitting given that even if one does not have a reason to do E, once one intends to do it one has a reason to M (which is the means to doing it). This suggests that it is not only natural, but also true and not misleading to say that the intention gives one a reason to pursue the means to its fulfilment.

In sum, (1B) in effect states that given that M is the means to E, one has a reason (either not to intend E or to do M). If one does M one (either does not intend E or does M) and thereby one conforms to the reason stated in (1B) and to the ought-fact (Broome's term) stated in (1A). So both undetachable conditional ought-propositions, and their corresponding propositions about conditional reasons, entail that one has a reason to take an action just because it is the means to one's end.

Broome is right to say that (1A) and (2A) do not justify the conclusion that one ought to do M. But the explanation of that has nothing to do with the relations between means and ends. Ought-propositions state something like undefeated reasons.[19] (1A) and (2A) do not yield the conclusion that one has an undefeated reason to do M. Even if M is the only means to E, doing M is not the only way of conforming to (1A) and to (2A). One could do so by not intending to do E. While (1A) and (2A) state (all the time assuming that M is the means to E) reasons of equal stringency for doing M and for not intending E, there may be other factors that discriminate between the two ways of conforming with (1A) and (2A), and that may show that even though one has a reason to M, one ought not to do so. The inference will be valid only if one adds to it a closure premise (e.g., that there is nothing else that bears on whether one ought to do M).

Hence the fact that (3A) does not follow from (1A) and (2A) does not support Broome's view (about the normative significance of having ends), whereas the fact that (3B) follows from both sets of premises shows his failure to achieve the goal explained by Wallace, that of explaining the normative constraints of instrumental rationality while denying that having an end is or provides a reason to pursue the means to its realization.[20]

---

[18] My argument here is incompatible with accepting a rule of inference allowing introducing a disjunction within the scope of a modal operator, i.e. if 'M' is a modal sentence-forming operator it licenses inferring M(P or Q) from M(P). I believe this rule to be unintuitive and unjustified. The inference from M(P) to M(P) or Q is fine, because the reverse would be invalid, i.e. M(P) does not follow from M(P) or Q.

[19] Cf. Chapter Two. The analysis of Broome's mistake in his treatment of instrumental rationality is due to and illustrates his failure to grasp the nature of reasons and their relations to what one ought to do or believe, which was explained in Chapter Two.

[20] In all these regards this case parallels the considerations that apply to facilitative reasons. I may have a duty to be in Oxford by noon, and buying a train ticket will facilitate getting there. But it does not follow from these facts alone that I have a duty to buy a train ticket, only that I have a reason to do so. The fact that there may be alternative plans facilitating fulfilment of my duty, that others may be preferable, etc., may

As mentioned above, Broome points out that so-called theoretical reasoning is affected by an analogous problem: If P entails Q it does not follow that if I believe that P I ought to, or have reason to, believe that Q. Among other reasons this is to avoid the absurdity that since any proposition entails itself if I believe a proposition then I have reason to believe it (or ought to believe it). Here too we are looking for a way of explaining what is the fault with a person who believes the premises and the negation of the conclusion of a valid argument, without taking his belief in the premises as a reason to believe the conclusion.

Here too Broome's solution is to use undetachable conditional ought-propositions to dissolve the difficulty: One ought (if one believes the premises to believe the conclusion). Once again, however, it follows from this conditional that one has a reason to believe the conclusion, just as one has a reason to suspend belief in the premises. Either would constitute conformity with the conditional ought-fact. Again, until further features are drawn into the explanation, this is tantamount to taking the very fact of believing the premises as providing a reason to believe the conclusion, which is what we wanted to avoid.

Wallace adopts Broome's view on the matter:

I submit that we do well to interpret the instrumental principle along similar lines, as a constraint on combinations of attitudes that does not license detached normative judgements to the effect that we have reason to take the necessary means to our ends. Thus if you intend to do x, and believe that you can do x only if you do y, then the instrumental principle imposes a normative constraint on your attitudes. You can comply with this constraint either by giving up the intention to do x, or by forming the intention to do y. But it does not follow from the constraint, together with the fact that you intend to do x and believe that you can do x only if you do y, that you ought to intend to do y. ('Normativity, Commitment', 17)

Unfortunately, while (for the reasons explained above) it does not follow that you *ought* to intend to do y, Wallace does not explain what blocks the conclusion that you have *reason* to form the intention. Wallace himself notes that you can comply with the constraint by forming the intention. Other things being equal, that is enough to show that you have reason to form the intention. But that, as Wallace says, is unacceptable.

An alternative approach has been offered by Bratman. He too argued that one's ends and intentions in themselves are not, and do not provide, reasons for action. He was therefore faced with the same problem, namely, how to understand and justify the view that under some conditions failure to follow one's ends is some sort of a fault, sometimes amounting to irrational conduct, or to having irrational attitudes. His reply is that the fault is in the process.

---

explain this diminution in stringency. But my objection (in the text) to Broome's position does not rely on the facilitative principle. That deals with the relations between facilitative actions and the source action, whereas the objection to Broome concerns the relations between the source action and actions that constitute performing it (i.e. the fact that making true one disjunct makes true the disjunction).

In assessing the rationality of an agent for some intention or intentional action our concern is to determine the extent to which the agent has come up to relevant standards of rational agency. A failure on the agent's part to come up to such standards makes this agent guilty of a form of criticisable irrationality. In reaching such assessment our concern is with the actual processes that led to the intention and action and with the underlying habits, dispositions and patterns of thinking and reasoning [that] are manifested in those processes. Our concern is with the extent to which these processes—and the underlying habits, dispositions, and patterns they manifest— come up to appropriate standards of rationality.[21]

The fallacy to avoid is the thought that irrationality in thought or action occurs only if one fails to conform to a reason (or a valid principle). It can consist in *faulty functioning*, that is in ways of thinking and of forming beliefs or intentions and so on, which do not conform to standards of rationality.[22] People's ends may be relevant because they are the starting or initiating points of the processes whose rationality is in question. Failure to take advantage of opportunities to pursue one's ends can be *evidence* of irrationality in the agent, in the mental processes that failed at least on this occasion to conform to rational standards of deliberation, of belief or intention formation, of coherence of belief and intention or others.[23]

I will refer to such standards as standards of deliberative rationality. They include much more than standards governing the capacity to discern inferential relations, or their absence. They involve, for example, standards by which we judge the proper functioning of abilities to end deliberation when appropriate (and avoid the vices of dithering and indecision), abilities to stick with a conclusion (and avoid the vices of continually changing one's mind, feeling that the grass is always greener on the other side, etc.), as well as the ability to re-examine one's conclusions and intentions when appropriate (and avoid dogmatism, pig-headedness, etc.).

Much, though—as noted in the previous section—not all, of the discussion of instrumental reasons and of instrumental rationality aims to explain the very same phenomena that I identify here as a certain aspect of our rational functioning. I will here confine the term 'instrumental irrationality' to the malfunctioning of our capacity to react properly to perceived reasons that manifests itself in failure to pursue available means to our ends. A person may be irrational in this way only on a single occasion, but even then his failure manifests a malfunctioning capacity, though one that may function properly most of the time.

Nothing has been said so far to explain why having ends affects the way we should think and form intentions, but without such explanation it is not clear how having ends

---

[21] *Intention, Plans and Practical Reason*, 51. Other differences in their views notwithstanding, a broadly similar attitude on this aspect of the nature of rationality is taken, among others, by R. Nozick in *The Nature of Rationality* (Princeton: Princeton UP, 1993) and by P. Railton in various papers, e.g. 'How to Engage Reason: The Problem of Regress' in R. J. Wallace et al. (eds.), *Reason and Value* (Oxford: OUP, 2004), 176.

[22] See my remarks on the subject in *Engaging Reason*, ch. 4, and in Chapter Five above.

[23] Not all such failures will be relevant to assessment of how rational people are. See a brief comment on the issue in Section 4 below.

is relevant to the well-functioning of our deliberative processes. One explanation is offered by Wallace. He is one of those who trace the normative force of 'the instrumental principle' to the incoherence of the beliefs that its violation involves. He argues that (1) if we have ends and do not intend to take what we believe to be the necessary means towards their realization we have contradictory beliefs, and that (2) that is the rationale of the normative constraint to which we are subject once we have ends.

Wallace's defence of the first contention assumes that one can intend to perform an action only if one believes that its performance is possible. Hence, if you believe that doing Y is necessary to doing X, which you intend to do, and you believe that you will do Y only if you intend to do Y, and all the same you do not intend to do Y then

You will be left in effect with the following incoherent set of beliefs (assuming you are minimally self-aware): the belief that it is possible that you do x, the belief that it is possible that you do x only if you also intend to do y, and the belief that you do not intend to do y. The incoherence of these beliefs is a straightforward function of the logical relations among their contents, suggesting that the normative force of the instrumental principle can be traced to independent rational constraints on your beliefs—in particular, to constraints on certain combinations of beliefs. ('Normativity, Commitment', 21)

He follows up with a complex defence and elaboration of this argument to meet various objections, and to apply the argument to a wider range of cases, but I will not consider those. I will assume that the above is broadly sound and that instrumental irrationality involves agents in some form of conflicting beliefs or beliefs and intentions that establishes or makes it likely that some of their beliefs are false or that their intentions are not well supported.

The question remains whether the explanation of instrumental irrationality is where Wallace locates it, namely in the fact that instrumental irrationality leads to holding this incoherent set of beliefs. It is natural to expect that instrumental irrationality involves violation of some constraint and therefore leads us into trouble. But did Wallace identify the source of the trouble or one of its consequences or symptoms? In Section 4 I will say something about the kind of defect contradictory beliefs involve. To anticipate: the fact that a person has contradictory beliefs shows that at least one of that person's beliefs is false. The information is often of little value as often it does not help identify which belief is false. In the present case we know which belief is false: According to Wallace the instrumentally irrational believe that an action that they intend and that in the circumstances cannot occur can occur. What is wrong with that? Well, it is the having of a false belief, and that is a fault. Let us accept with Wallace that the instrumentally irrational are always guilty of that falsity, and assume that they are guilty of no other. The question is, is it this fault that explains why the so-called principle of instrumental rationality is one of the standards that determine well-functioning deliberative processes?

The answer is not obvious. When people who are not instrumentally irrational intend to perform an action that in fact they cannot perform they may be led to spend much effort trying to bring about what is impossible. But the instrumentally irrational has no intention to take steps to facilitate the impossible action. That is supposed to be his problem. Now it appears to be his saving grace. These reflections make me suspect that, whatever the merits of his argument, Wallace did not identify what makes instrumental irrationality irrational. Being in the grip of the static conception of rationality (explained in Chapter Five) he felt forced to identify irrationality with having conflicting attitudes, missing the point that Irrationality generally consists in a malfunctioning of our rational faculties, and instrumental irrationality is an instance of irrationality.[24]

We see now why even if Wallace is right and when one is instrumentally irrational one has a false belief, which is no doubt regrettable, that is not the explanation of instrumental irrationality. The source of our sense that something there is irrational is not that the irrational agent's beliefs or actions are undesirable. It is that he is not functioning properly. His irrationality is in his failure to conform to the standard of adequate agency. Possibly in the circumstances of the case the outcome is better than had he functioned well. But his failure of rationality is nevertheless a blemish. This is no consequentialist reasoning: it is not that it shows that he is likely to act badly some other time, though it may show that. Rather there is an ideal of rational agency which that agent failed to reach on that occasion. If the results were beneficial that was lucky. It was not due to him.[25]

3. But is not instrumental irrationality bad?

Still, something is surely missing from my account so far. Chapter Five explained that it is not the case that there is a reason to avoid every instance of irrationality. The fault of the process does not necessarily make its product undesirable. But is this true of instrumental rationality? Is there no value in being instrumentally rational?

One part of the missing story seems fairly obvious: if you are prone to instrumental irrationality you are less likely to achieve your ends, whatever they are. That is what is

---

[24] For detailed and incisive criticism of Wallace's position on other grounds see J. Brunero's 'Two Approaches to Instrumental Rationality and Belief Consistency', *Journal of Ethics & Social Philosophy* 1/1 (2005) (http://www.jesp.org/).

[25] Nomy Arpaly in her *Unprincipled Virtue* (Oxford: OUP, 2004) points out that failure to pursue the means to one's end may be due to realization, below the level of consciousness, that one should not. This may indeed be so. Sometimes such realization may warrant saying that the person concerned has abandoned his end, even though he may not be aware of the fact, or at least not fully aware of it. If so then no irrationality is involved. On other occasions the situation is different and the person is torn two ways. He is neither fully willing to abandon his end nor to pursue it, a conflict that may be psychologically understandable. In such cases, however sympathetic we are, the case is still one of irrationality manifested in this paralysis, or unresolved state. I will return to these observations below. Here I am merely pointing out that my discussion does not imply that one acts for a reason only if the action is preceded by or is caused by reasoning.

hinted at by calling instrumental rationality a form of skill (as Wallace, following Aristotle, does). The term is not altogether appropriate here, as skills are more specific. Abilities to see, speak, or think are not normally thought of as skills. Our reliance on them is too pervasive, unlike our skills as drivers, or carpenters, or computer programmers. Still, the point is well taken: these capacities are valuable primarily, or at any rate in large part for the uses they can be put to. They are valued for making us more effective as agents.

If so, is there no reason to be an effective agent and therefore no reason to pursue the means to our ends as such? Instrumental irrationality reveals an executive defect in the agent, a limitation on his ability to be an effective agent, and it locates the fault in the functioning of his Reason, of his rational capacities. Agents may, on occasion, hope that they will fail, but while they may merely pretend to intend or to try, when they actually do intend or try they intend or try to succeed. Being an effective agent is not a good separate from that of being an agent. To be an effective agent is to be successfully an agent, and for creatures like us it generally (though not always) means functioning rationally. As to the value of rational agency, it is, as is the value of capacities generally, in the value of the option to use it, and in the value of its actual use. Its effective use does not guarantee that value, but is a condition for it. Hence if the power of rational agency is valuable so is its effective exercise.

I claim that the value of a properly functioning rational capacity does not provide a reason for taking the means to our ends. But, where failure to take the means to one's end would be irrational, is there not a reason to take the means (as well as a reason to abandon the end) in order to avoid the irrationality? Does that not follow from the fact that the capacity of rational agency, and therefore its proper functioning, are valuable? If so, then the standards of rational functioning are simply reason-stating principles, like any other normative principle.

In commenting on my views in the preceding paragraphs Schroeder quite sensibly wondered (I express his objection in my own terms) how I can both maintain that possessing (well-functioning) rational powers is valuable, and yet deny that we have a reason to avoid their malfunctioning on each occasion. Put in a rough and ready way, Schroeder's argument is:

(1) Having rational capacities is valuable; therefore
(2) being irrational is, as such, bad (on each occasion); therefore
(3) we have a reason to avoid being irrational (on each occasion); therefore
(4) (by the facilitative principle) we have reason to take the means to that end.

Each one of these transitions is unwarranted. The value of a capacity does not entail that every case of its proper, or successful, use has value. This is very plain in the case of those capacities we exercise at will. It may be valuable to be able to swim, or to play chess, or to drive, but we do not have reason to swim, drive, or play chess whenever we can, nor whenever we could do so well—and not every time we do, not even every time we do so well, is our action of value at all. Sometimes there is nothing to be said for the use of the capacity, and sometimes it is better to do it badly, sometimes there is no reason at all to do it well, and some reason to do it badly. The explanation is that the value of the capacity is partly in the freedom it gives us, the choice whether to use it and when, and partly in the fact that sometimes its use is valuable. The two are interconnected, and the freedom would not be valuable if its use could not be valuable. But it does not follow that every use is valuable, or that we always have reason to use the capacity.

Rationality is not a capacity we use at will. Therefore a freedom to use it or not cannot be where its value resides. But the same structure applies to other capacities we use automatically, e.g. our perceptual capacities. So long as I am conscious I hear sounds, if, that is, I am not deaf. I can manipulate myself by blocking my ears, or trying to divert my attention, but these are very different from the decision to do something one has the capacity to do at will, like raise one's arm, or turn one's head. Hence, the value of perceptual capacities does not relate to freedom, but to their epistemic, aesthetic, sexual, and social advantages. Still, while their value depends on the fact that some occasions when the capacity is used are valuable, it does not follow that all such occasions are, not even to the slightest degree.

Rationality is like perceptual capacities in being engaged willy-nilly, in not being a matter of choice (though being subject to manipulation via the use of alcohol, etc.), but it differs from them in reaching deeper into who we are. However much loss of sight, hearing, or tactile sensations would affect me, it does not touch me in the way that complete loss of rational powers, as in advanced dementia, does. Such loss means that I am no longer a person. The value of rational capacities is therefore different again. It lies in the value of personhood, of which it is a constitutive part. But yet again, while its value depends on its exercise being sometimes valuable, it does not imply at all that all its instances have value, not even to the slightest degree. Hence if, for example, one has murder as one's goal, there is no value at all in being rational about the pursuit of the means to that goal, and no reason to take them, not even to avoid the irrationality of not taking them (while not abandoning the goal).[26]

The transition to the third proposition above is undermined by the fact that the use of our rational capacities does not require a decision or intention. Regarding such capacities, the question whether there is a reason (or motivation) to use them does not arise. We may have reasons to listen, but we cannot have reasons to hear. The case of our rational capacities is essentially similar, only more complex, as was explained in Chapter Five.

Examining the fault in the transition to the fourth proposition helps in bringing out the point that while rationality is a capacity to appreciate and respond to reasons, its exercise is not to be understood exclusively in terms of following or of failing to follow reasons. Rather, the exercise of rationality is a process, a functioning, which goes well

---

[26] We may still admire the skill of the murderer. But that is a point about a different object of evaluation.

or badly. We judge it by its success or failure to conform to standards that govern it. How does this affect the issue at hand? Schroeder's challenge depends on agents having reason to take the means to their ends, the reason being that that is one way of avoiding being irrational, or, if you like, one way of being rational. Suppose John intends (it is one of his ends) to get a bottle of milk (because his baby needs feeding). John knows that he will get one if and only if he goes to the shop. He has a reason to go to the shop, but it would be funny to think that he has a reason to go to the shop as a way of not being irrational on this occasion. Clearly the only reason he should recognize is that it is a way of getting the milk, which he has reason to do. It is true that, in the circumstances, if he does not, he will be irrational, and this is a case in which it is bad to be irrational. The point is that the rationality is the process that leads you to the reasons, and to the correct reaction to reasons; it is not itself a reason, it is not what the process is about.[27]

4. What price contradictions?

Rationality consists in part in proper functioning. People who fail to pursue the means to their ends display or manifest a form of malfunctioning criticizable as a form of irrationality. There are further doubts about the success of the well-functioning approach in avoiding what Broome sought unsuccessfully to avoid, namely the conclusion that having ends provides reasons for taking the means to their achievement. Let it be agreed that the primary locus of the sort of rationality (or its failure) that the so-called instrumental principle is about is in the functioning of mental processes, initiated (or failing to be initiated) by the having of ends, and leading (or failing to lead) to consequential beliefs and intentions regarding facilitative actions. Is it not nevertheless the case that those processes have end-products, and that those may be faulty if they result from a faulty process?

When people's mental processes fail to function properly with the result that they fail to take appropriate actions to facilitate realization of their ends they are left with inconsistent or at any rate incoherent sets of beliefs, or beliefs and intentions. The simplest case is when people believe in the premises and in the negation of the conclusion of a valid deductive inference. They then hold inconsistent beliefs. If the inference is non-deductive, but valid, the beliefs may not be inconsistent but suffer from some form of incoherence.

The challenge facing anyone who believes that one's ends are not in themselves reasons, and do not provide reasons, is to explain how the well-functioning approach avoids the conclusion that when the process is faulty and its result is, therefore, faulty,

---

[27] While rationality is exercised automatically, one may have reasons to remain rational or to end one's life or one's life as a rational being, and one may have reasons to manipulate one's exercise of rationality on occasion, or in general, just as one may have reason to improve one's hearing or reduce it, generally or on occasion.

one has reason to repair that result. Or in plain language: how does this approach avoid the conclusion that if I do not have the intention to take an action necessary to achieve my end then I have reason to abandon my end, and also a reason to form the missing intention (though once I do one of these things the reason for the other lapses)?[28]

The answer is that there is no reason to avoid a contradiction as such. In extreme and rare circumstances people who profess simultaneous belief in propositions that are straightforwardly contradictory or contradict each other have no belief at all (if now I profess to believe that John is alive and that John is dead then I have no belief on the matter). More familiar are the occasions when the fact that people profess belief in fairly obviously contradictory propositions indicates that they do not have a stable belief, that they vacillate one way and another, etc. Most occasions when we hold contradictory beliefs are not like that. We can have stable contradictory beliefs either without being aware of the fact, or while being aware of it.

When we learn that there is a contradiction among our beliefs we learn (1) that some of our beliefs are false, and (2) that we hold some beliefs which if used together as premises in an argument may lead us astray in a special way. Big deal! We hope that we all know that some of our beliefs are false anyway. And the risk that we will actually be led astray not by the logical implications of our false beliefs, but by their contradictory features is, for all practical purposes, negligible.[29]

If we know not only that some of our beliefs are contradictory, but also that a specific subset of all our beliefs contains contradictory beliefs, our knowledge may be somewhat more useful. The general knowledge that some of our beliefs are false is so useless because it does not help us locate them. Knowing that a relatively small set of our beliefs contains contradictory beliefs may be helpful in locating the false one. Even if we do not know which belief is false, circumstances may indicate that we should suspend belief in all the propositions in the contradiction-infected set. But nothing follows about what we ought to do or believe and when we should suspend belief from the mere knowledge that a set of beliefs contains a contradiction. In particular the mere fact that, say, three propositions form a contradictory set does not mean that we should suspend belief in all of them until we find the false one. The logical paradoxes, for example the sorites paradox, teach us at least that.

---

[28] The problem is most clearly recognized by Scanlon. He too appears to hope to avoid the conclusion that agents' goals are reasons for them to take the means to their realization. But he thinks that (at least in certain circumstances) agents should take their goals as reasons. The escape appears to be that that does not mean that they really are reasons, only that the agents are irrational if they do not take them to be reasons. But he also thinks that they have a second order reason to take their goals as reasons in order to avoid irrationality. See Scanlon, 'Reasons: A Puzzling Duality', in Wallace et al. (eds.), Reason and Value, 231ff., at 236–7. I will argue that agents' goals are neither reasons nor (with the exceptions explained in the next section) should they be taken as reasons. Agents do not have a reason so to take them.

[29] These remarks merely reiterate the importance of the difference between inferential relations among propositions or a person's beliefs and the dynamic process of belief adjustment and revision which is pointed out in G. Harman, Change in View (Cambridge, Mass: MIT Press/Bradford Books, 1986), and by others.

Hence while the irrationality of the ways in which we do or fail to reason from ends to means and to other facilitating actions may land us in a contradiction it does not follow that we have any reason to do anything as a result. In particular we have no reason to form intentions to follow the means to our ends, nor to believe the conclusions of valid inferences in whose premises we believe, to avoid the relevant contradictions in these cases. Wallace, who argues for the existence of such a contradiction, does not suggest which of the contradictory beliefs that he alleges that the instrumentally irrational is landed with should be abandoned. And in fact there is no general reason to abandon any of them, or any combination of them.[30]

To conclude: There is nothing wrong with holding contradictory beliefs as such, and the fact that one does is no reason to change one's beliefs. At most we could say that we should abandon our false beliefs. But that is so not because of the contradiction. Knowing that a set of propositions is contradictory has epistemic relevance: it tells us that the contradictory set contains a falsehood. It may be part of a case for believing that one particular proposition is false. But it is no such case by itself. Without such a case we have no reason to abandon any of them. For all we know we may then abandon a true belief and remain with false ones. Nor do we have reason to suspend belief in all the propositions in the contradictory set. The cost, epistemic and otherwise, of doing so may be too great.[31] That is why the logical paradoxes are rightly not generally taken as a reason to suspend our acceptance of the principles that generate them.

If principles of logic apply not only to propositions but also to intentions, then the preceding remarks apply to intentions too, as they do to other conflicts that cast doubt on the truth of the conflicting propositions, but fall short of contradiction. That is why the well-functioning approach does not yield the conclusion that our ends generate or provide reasons after all.

5. The difference ends make—another round

I have tried to do justice to the view that ends affect whether those who have them act rationally without taking them to provide reasons, and to do justice to the view that there are facilitative reasons without connecting them to ends, or to a specific form of rationality. Yet, I believe, there is another way in which ends affect our reasons, and thereby the rational constraints we are subject to.

---

[30] It may be tempting to think that as the intention to pursue the end is formed first the intention to pursue the means, and the beliefs attending its formation, should be the ones to be adjusted, or abandoned. But Arpaly's argument shows this not to be so. In some cases the reluctance to intend the means is evidence that there is good reason to abandon the end.

[31] I realize that these remarks raise many questions that I cannot but avoid here: why not say that knowing (through the discovery of a contradiction or otherwise) that at least one of our beliefs is false is a reason to suspend all of them, though not an adequate one? Do I assume that we can decide, at least in some circumstances, whether to suspend belief or not? These and others cannot be dealt with here. However, I believe that the substance of my remarks applies whatever position we take on these additional issues.

Start with the obvious: we lead our life by considering our options and choosing. Often we have a number of options the case for any of which is neither better nor worse than that for some of the others. We choose in a way that manifests tastes and other dispositions that are not themselves reasons for one or the other of the options. Many, and typically the more important, of our choices are pervasive (affecting many aspects of our life) and long range (meant to be pursued over long periods of time). If we assume that having such ends makes no difference to the reasons we have then even if we choose one and set out to pursue it (say, that we choose a hobby, such as stamp collecting, or playing all of Beethoven's piano sonatas) the reasons we have to engage in some activity that contributes to our pursuit (say adding some rare stamps to our collection) are, other things being equal, neither better nor worse than reasons we have to engage in a different activity that belongs with another pursuit, one of those we did not choose.[32]

We may think that given our initial choice we will be disposed to engage in activities belonging with it, and will not frustrate its pursuit by choosing activities that do not, regardless of the fact that they are no less attractive. Moreover, sometimes the actions we took in the past incurred costs of various kinds that make deviation from our previously chosen path no longer rational. The alternatives have become less attractive. We may have actually spent money on equipment, say golf clubs, etc., whereas were we now to start on tennis we would need further expenses, a fact that makes it less rational to do so. Or we may just have delayed starting on the alternative activity, which means that we are less able to reach as high a level of accomplishment in it as in the option on which we did already make a start, and so on. These factors, and the fact that there is nothing inherently wrong with changing course and abandoning our initial choices, may be thought to show that the account so far given needs no supplementation.

I think, however, that we still miss something. One additional aspect of the situation is already covered by the earlier discussion of instrumental rationality. While there is nothing inherently wrong in changing course, a tendency to do so every other day shows indecisiveness, dissipation, lack of purpose, or other mental dispositions that make one a less effective agent, and, since they relate to one's response to perceived reasons, reflect on one's rationality.[33] This, however, does not account for an important feature of our experience: We rely on the goals we have as contributing to the reasons to choose activities that belong with them, rather than those no less attractive activities that do not. How are we to understand this phenomenon? First, it does not involve changing our goals. I have in mind choices when this is not on the horizon: we feel no temptation or inclination to do so, and have no conclusive reason to do so.

---

[32] This applies to facilitative activities as well, but it is more helpful here to focus on activities that constitute pursuit of one or another possible ends.

[33] That is, very roughly, where Bratman leaves matters. I believe that in doing so he ignores the points made below.

We choose among alternatives, and we notice that one of them belongs naturally with one of our goals (e.g. being an opportunity to improve, display, or contemplate our stamp collection) whereas the others do not. Some actions that belong within a goal have no point (unless they happen to facilitate something worth doing) if one does not have it. Buying collectable stamps is probably an example. Other actions may have value in themselves, but their meaning to agents who have the goal is different than to those who do not.

This suggests that our goals play a role in determining our reasons and their force. How can that be? That one has an intention or a goal is just a non-evaluative fact like any other. How can one's intention or attitude, or an expression of such intention, or its communication, create reasons? This applies even when the intention is to create a reason (as in promising, or commanding). In general form, the answer is familiar: facts provide reasons when general evaluative or normative considerations determine that they do: that I am driving a car imposes on me a duty, which derives from the implications (for driving cars) of general considerations about our responsibilities towards others. Similarly our intentions, goals, and their expression and communication impose duties when background considerations determine so. I have written extensively about how authorities can impose duties and confer rights just by their say so, and how promising can impose duties. I have also argued[34] that certain ways of forming intentions, broadly speaking by reaching decisions following deliberation on the merits, provide exclusionary reasons. Decisions, I argued, are (among other things) reasons not to unsettle one's intentions. In each of these cases, the considerations that determine that such intentions or their expression provide reasons also set limits to the circumstances in which they do. And, in each of these cases, different considerations are at play.

Perhaps the best way to represent the way our goals affect our reasons is to take them to activate conditional reasons that we have anyway, though sometimes the condition affects not the application of the reason but its strength or stringency. Actions whose point depends on (or is affected by) being taken as part of the pursuit of some goal are ones that not everyone has reason to take. There is reason to do so only for those who pursue the goal. If the goal affects only the significance of the action, then the strength or stringency of the reason for the action is conditional on pursuit of the goal. For someone intent on running a marathon every day during August, running a marathon today, the 20th of August, is crucial to the realization of his ambition. For me it is just an opportunity to know what running a marathon feels like—a matter of much less moment. On other occasions the option may be more valuable when it is a stand-alone option than when it is part of a goal, being a unique opportunity of some interest to those who do not share the goal, while rather a routine one for those who pursue it.

---

[34] *Practical Reason and Norms*, 65–71, though I would have argued the case somewhat differently, and would have somewhat modified the conclusion there expressed had I revisited the issue today.

Crucially, the way goals acquire their normative relevance is by being conditions on the applicability or stringency of reasons. Therefore, they can have that effect only if the goals are worth pursuing in the first place. On this point my account is close to Korsgaard's.[35] It combines two elements: the normative impact of a potential goal depends (a) on its being worthwhile, that is on there being reasons to adopt the goal, and (b) on the contingent fact that it is actually the agent's goal. If either is missing then the conditional reason does not apply.

These points do not affect the view of facilitative reasons and instrumental rationality proposed in this chapter, but the rational impact that our goals have had to be mentioned to avoid the misleading impression that the previous discussion of ends would have left had it been taken to imply that they have no other rational relevance.

6. The myth of instrumental rationality

I can no longer ignore the strangeness of the view I am defending. Professing to explain instrumental reason and instrumental rationality, I have drawn a distinction between facilitative reasons that are, I suggested, the reasons that people have in mind in those areas of thought that philosophers analyse as having to do with instrumental reasons, and the form of rationality that philosophers normally call instrumental rationality. Indeed, I drove a wedge between them. Instrumental rationality, it turns out, is not a matter of conforming to facilitative reasons. I followed Bratman in claiming that instrumental rationality consists in the proper functioning of some of the mental processes leading to formation of beliefs and intentions. And I followed those, like Bratman, Broome, and Wallace, who deny that ends or intentions as such constitute or provide reasons. At the same time, facilitative reasons, which explain our view that there are instrumental reasons, have nothing to do with the ends that people actually have. What explains this divide between facilitative reasons and instrumental rationality?

The answer is that there is no *distinctive* form of rationality or of normativity that merits the name instrumental rationality or normativity. In particular there is no specific form of rationality or of normativity that concerns the relations between means and ends. Philosophers fostered a myth of instrumental rationality, sometimes taking it to be the only, sometimes the simplest and clearest, type of practical rationality or of normativity. In doing so they created a hybrid that lacks unity as much as it lacks distinctness. The discussion so far explained the lack of unity, the absence of any special relations between facilitative reasons and so-called instrumental rationality. It is time to turn to the question of the distinctness of each of these subtypes of instrumental normativity.

---

[35] 'Normativity of Instrumental Reason'. It does not of course endorse her anti-realist way of thinking. Interestingly, however, much of what I suggest here can be readily adapted to non-realist frameworks.

While facilitative reasons depend on source reasons, in that they are the source reasons plus the facilitative relationship (which is typically a non-normative relationship) between the facilitative action and the source action, reasoning about whether we should take a facilitative action is ordinary practical reasoning. It depends on what other reasons (facilitative or other) there are for that facilitative action, and what reasons (facilitative or other) there are against it, a reasoning that includes considering available alternative actions and the case for and against them. I do not think that there is any distinctive form of reasoning concerning facilitative reasons that can be called instrumental reasoning and underpin a form of rationality that can be called instrumental rationality. The facilitative character of some reasons is important since it may affect the case for the actions they are reasons for. Facilitative reasons obey the implications of the facilitative principle, which means that they have some properties that distinguish them from other reasons. But there are many other kinds of reasons, all with some distinctive features, as well as many common ones. Whenever reasons both (a) can bear on the case for and against one and the same action or attitude, and (b) can conflict, they can feature inseparably in the same arguments, and in the same deliberative processes, and therefore share the same form of practical rationality.

That form of rationality is the one that directs us in determining what we have most or undefeated reason to do, or which attitude is supported by the best or by undefeated reasons. Irrationality is manifested in failing to realize what those reasons are or to conform with them, under certain conditions (when the agent could have known what they are, etc.). There is nothing that can be called instrumental rationality there, not even where facilitative reasons are involved.

Are things any different when we turn to the way that having ends affects our mental processes? The cases normally identified as manifesting instrumental irrationality are failures to conform to certain deliberative standards. This raises a major worry: is there anything distinctive to instrumental rationality or irrationality, so understood? If it is just a matter of proper functioning of some of our executive abilities and skills, a matter of effective agency, is it a form of normativity failure that can be regarded as failure of rationality? Clearly, not every failure that makes us likely to fail to realize our ends is a failure of rationality. For example, some people tend to fumble, drop things, mix them up, mix up left and right, etc. None of these makes them instrumentally irrational however much they affect their abilities to realize their ends. What distinguishes instrumental irrationality from those other failures?

Broadly speaking the answer is obvious: instrumental irrationality is failure of rational capacities that has a specific effect on the ability to realize one's ends. But what are one's rational capacities? Again there is a ready broad answer: they are those capacities that are involved in discerning which features in the world merit a response, and how to respond to them, including both intellectual and motivational capacities. Even if these observations are along the right lines in explaining why so-called 'instrumental rationality' relates to the degree to which our deliberative processes conform with normative standards, deviations from which manifest failures of rationality, they leave unresolved the worry about the distinctness of so-called instrumental rationality. Is it not the case that the rational standards that should govern our deliberative processes, which are or should be initiated by the adoption or the having of ends, are simply the same standards that should govern all our deliberative processes?

Take one example to illustrate the point: sometimes the explanation for failure to take the means to our ends is weakness of the will. We know (or believe we do) what we ought to do, but are affected by various forms of self-indulgence that overcome our better judgement, and we act against it. Now, weakness of the will is not confined to cases where we fail to take the means to our ends (say fail to engage in the vigorous exercises that are essential to our health, whose fate is dear to our heart). Weakness of the will can make us fail to adopt ends that we know (or believe we do) that we should adopt. If I believe that I ought to care about how well I teach my students, but I do not, I display weakness in adopting ends. If I do care about how well I teach my students, but I fail to give them detailed comments on their essays, in spite of my belief that commenting on their essays is essential to teaching them well, I again display weakness which this time is a manifestation of instrumental irrationality. It seems plausible, however, that the standards by which I fail are the same in both cases.

Not all cases of so-called instrumental irrationality are cases of weakness of the will. They may involve other failures of rationality. To give but one other example, chronic dithering and indecision may make me fail to take the means to my ends. My dithering may make me miss the opportunity to realize my ends. But clearly chronic dithering and indecision may also make me fail to adopt ends that I am in a position to know that I should adopt. I cannot bring myself to conclude what is obvious: that this is an end to adopt. That too is a form of irrationality, this time about ends, not about the choice of means to existing ends. Again, the source of the failure is the same, regardless of whether it affects choice of ends or of means.

It appears that there is no such thing as instrumental irrationality. That is, there is no distinctive set of deliberative standards that are involved in getting us to reason correctly from ends we have to means, and that are different from those that are involved in reasoning about which ends to have. Of course, there is a difference between facilitative reasons and others. Facilitative reasons have a special kind of dependence on source reasons. But that is a difference in the content of our deliberation, not in the standards that should govern the deliberative processes. They are the same when we try to determine our will to adopt, or maintain, or abandon some ends, as when we try to determine what facilitative steps to take in pursuit of goods we take ourselves to be pursuing as our ends.

If so, why the widespread view that instrumental rationality is a distinctive and particularly unproblematic form of rationality? The answer is well known. Those who find it difficult to find a place for normativity (for values and reasons) in the world in which, they think, everything can be explained by the physical sciences, are tempted to focus on so-called instrumental rationality for at least one of the following three reasons. Some think that normativity can and should be explained away in favour of accounts relying on motivations, subjective preferences, coherence relations among one's attitudes or the like.[36] Others, conceding the 'objectivity' of normative relations and properties, think that instrumental rationality can be reconciled with their world view because it is all there is to practical normativity, and instrumental rationality itself can be reduced to some analytic truths about the relations between having means and having ends, perhaps with the additional admission that reasons for belief are also involved, they being less suspect than reasons for action. Finally, there is the common view that animals of some other species do have goals and direct their behaviour towards them, that is that they have the capacity for instrumental rationality, even though they do not adopt their ends for reasons, and they lack the capacity to deliberate about their ends. This seems to imply that instrumental rationality is a separable and more basic type of rationality.

Ends are, or can be, psychologically complex. At one extreme to have something as one's end is nothing but intending to do or achieve it, immediately or in the near future. But the notion is most at home with more remote and complex states, which consist in and manifest themselves in a range of attitudes, dispositions, beliefs, and actions, over a period of time. This complexity allows for various forms of mismatch between the dispositions, intentions, attitudes and beliefs. Some mismatches will simply show that the person, or other animal, no longer has the end. Others will establish the existence of some deviations from the normal for those who have ends, which fall short of abandoning the ends. They can be attributed to stupidity, incompetence, or, sometimes, irrationality.

The fact that the pursuit of the means is part of what makes one have the ends misled some into thinking that instrumental irrationality is impossible. If one does not pursue what one believes to be the necessary and available means then one does not have the end. With a simple end this may be close to the truth. If I do not reach for the glass on my desk, to sip from it, then can it be my end to drink its contents now? However, even in such cases, it is not failure to pursue the means alone, but also the absence of feelings of conflict (I should really reach out for the glass. Why don't I do so?, etc.), guilt, and remorse that establish that I do not have the end. Most ends are not that simple, and their attribution depends on various criteria. Conflict among these criteria does not always establish that the person does not have the end. Hence the possibility that some mismatches are due to failure of rationality.

Since ends range from simple to complex it is not surprising that the criteria determining their existence, the criteria for the attribution of ends, vary between animal species. Since the mental abilities of some species do not enable them to engage in complex hypothetical thinking, or to have any grasp of distant future prospects, their members can only have relatively simple ends. With many species reasoning about

---

[36] Among those who challenged such views is J. Hampton, *The Authority of Reason* (Cambridge: CUP, 1998), chs. 4 and 5.

alternative ends is impossible. Hence they cannot adopt ends for reasons. But they may still have ends and direct their conduct and attitudes in light of those ends, set themselves to achieve those ends, consider alternatives, try, fail, and try again, and so on.

The existence of behaviour in pursuit of ends in creatures that cannot adopt ends for reasons encourages the thought that the same is true of humans. The refutation of that view is not a matter for this chapter. What is relevant here is that some of those who accept that there are reasons for ends, and that humans are capable of adopting and changing ends for reasons, take the existence of ends and the pursuit of means by creatures who cannot reason about ends as evidence that there are radically two different forms of rationality involved. It is, however, a mistake to think that animals of species with more extensive mental capacities simply have what the others have and more. Rather, the existence of more extensive mental capacities transforms the functioning of many of the more basic ones. Even the most biologically rooted needs, such as eating, defecating, having sex, and finding shelter from extremes of temperature, are, with humans, subject to deliberation leading to their endorsement, rejection, channelling, and control in a variety of ways. Hence with creatures capable of reasoning about ends, reasoning about means is not distinctive and special, but part and parcel of their general rational functioning. The thought that with humans instrumental rationality is a distinctive and more readily established form of rationality is a myth.

Appendix: When is it irrational not to intend the means to one's ends?

Some regard it as a firm principle that he who wills the end must will the means, often with the implication that failure to do so is irrational. It is obvious that the principle is false if 'wills' means 'wants'. It is all too common for people to force themselves to take means that they very much do not want to take. Here I want to contest the view that takes it to mean: must, on pain of irrationality, intend the means. Refuting this view illustrates one central case in which the account of irrationality in this book differs in its applications from some views of instrumental irrationality.

At a minimum one must allow for a time gap between adopting a goal and forming an intention to pursue any particular action or plan to bring about or to facilitate its realization. This is particularly obvious when there are various plans by which it may be realized, and one has to choose among them. In such circumstances some delay would be reasonable. I decided two weeks ago to visit a friend in Covent Garden tonight. I could go there by underground, by bus, by taxi, or on foot, yet I have no instrumental intention, no intention which way to get there. The visit is still some two hours away, and as whichever way I go I do not need more than an hour, I need not think about the way to get there yet. This is not a trivial or minor point. We all have ends without any intentions regarding any means for their realization, and the time gap need not be brief.

I may intend to buy a new house in five years' time, have no relevant instrumental intentions, and yet be perfectly rational. Moreover, I may abandon such a goal after three years, never having had any instrumental intentions and having been innocent of any irrationality as a result.

It could be that all the feasible plans for some goal have a common step, which is therefore a necessary step for the realization of the goal. One may form an intention to take that necessary step, before any decision about which plan to pursue. But on the other hand, one may not, and, other things being equal, in circumstances in which it is not irrational not to have decided on the plan, it is not irrational not to have an intention to take that necessary step either. There is no reason to adopt that part of a plan before adopting the plan, even if it is known or believed that eventually one will be irrational if one fails to adopt it. Similarly, while one can, and philosophers do, regard the disjunction of the alternative plans as itself a plan (which, moreover, is or is believed to be necessary for the realization of one's goal), there is no reason to adopt that plan before adopting one of the more specific plans which would facilitate one's goal. Hence, in the circumstances illustrated in the examples, failure to intend the disjunctive plan, or some less specific variant of it (such as the intention to do something about one's goal), is not irrational.

A delay in forming instrumental intentions may be reasonable for other reasons as well. Imagine: One of my goals is to give up smoking. My various attempts have so far failed. Once I decided to smoke one fewer cigarette each day. Having failed to do so, I adopted a different plan: first to limit the occasions I smoke (after meals, etc.), then gradually, week by week, reduce the number of permitted occasions. I failed in that too. I have not abandoned my goal, but I am yet to adopt a new plan for achieving it. At the moment I have no relevant instrumental intention. I think that I know what plan to adopt. I believe that I should simply stop smoking altogether, and that I should do so immediately upon adopting this plan. I should have a glass of water whenever the desire to smoke swells inside me. But I am still smoking. I have not yet formed the intention to follow that plan. I am still nerving myself up to do so. In such cases, and no doubt others too, I have a goal and do not intend any of the means to it, yet I am not—not yet—irrational.

This example shows that even if I believe that a particular plan will not only facilitate the goal, but also is the only way to achieve it, even if I believe that it is the necessary and sufficient means to the end, I may still not be irrational if I have not formed the intention to pursue it. My delay in forming an intention to try what I believe to be the only plan to achieve my goal may not be irrational. 'Building up' one's resolve before taking the plunge can be useful, or even essential.

It may be thought that in examples like these, while no facilitative plan is yet adopted, the agent is not irrational, because he has an intention when and how to adopt a facilitative plan. Alternatively, it may be thought that in cases where there are alternative possible plans, the agent is not irrational because he intends to pursue the disjunctive plan—that is, he intends to pursue one or the other of the sufficient plans.

Sometimes this is indeed the case. I may intend to adopt the plan once I feel strong enough to do so, or I may intend to wait till the weekend and decide whether to adopt it then. I may intend to decide which way to get to my friend an hour before our meeting, and so on. But, on the other hand, I may not. The situations I described are ones in which even if it may be rational to have instrumental intentions, it is not yet irrational not to have them. Rational agents form instrumental intentions some time during such intervals. They do not need a prior intention in order to do so.

All the sketched examples illustrate situations in which it is not irrational to lack instrumental intentions. In cases like these it may be both rational to form such intentions, and rational not to do so. However, this need not always be so. It may actually be irrational to have instrumental intentions to pursue any particular means to one's ends (even when it is not irrational to have the ends). Obviously, not all instrumental intentions are rational. One can be irrational not only through failing to have instrumental intentions, but also by having such intentions that one is in a position to know one should not have. The kinds of examples I gave make it plausible to think that in some circumstances it would be premature to form any instrumental intention regarding one's (rational) ends. And if so, there will no doubt be circumstances in which it will be irrational for a person not to know that that is the case, and therefore also irrational to form instrumental intentions of any kind regarding one or another of his rational ends.

It would be good to subsume the preceding remarks, supported by examples, within a more abstract explanatory framework. I am able to offer only a partial analysis. I am relying on two general propositions. First, it is possible to believe that an action is best, or that one has conclusive reason to perform it, without intending to perform it. Second, while we sometimes have intentions to form intentions they are not necessary to be able to form intentions (on pain of regress). We form intentions in response to reasons that, as we see it, make them intelligible or necessary. This is true not only of intentions to pursue ends, but also of intentions to pursue means. The thought that adopting an end involves forming an instrumental intention, if only an intention to take some means towards its realization, is prompted by belief that one can only account for the way having an intention sets one towards action by assuming the adoption of another—instrumental—intention. In fact it can also be accounted for by the fact that a rational being will form instrumental intentions when, as he sees things, it is appropriate or necessary.

Next, consider a possible objection to the facilitative principle. That principle indicates that we have many more instrumental reasons than is sometimes assumed. A mistaken chain of reasoning can lead one to think that, if we have all those facilitative reasons, then (assuming that a reason for an action is a reason to intend that action) we also have reasons to intend to take those facilitative actions. From this it is tempting to conclude that, when we have reasonable beliefs about worthwhile ends and about facilitative steps towards their realization, we are irrational if we fail to have such intentions. If this chain of reasoning were sound, it would refute the facilitative principle, for it would entail that we are irrational on many occasions when we are not.

There is, however, much wrong in this chain of reasoning. Relevant to our purpose is the misperception of the relations between reasons, including reasons to have intentions, and motivations, including intentions. I have discussed elsewhere,[37] and cannot revisit here, a variety of ways in which too close a relationship between reasons, or belief in their existence, and motivation is often postulated. An example will have to do. Regarding each of the following three ends I have, and know I have, an undefeated reason to pursue it: have a holiday next spring on a Greek island; have a holiday next spring in the American Southwest; spend the time at home catching up on some writing. I should not realize more than one of these ends. At the moment I have no intention regarding any of them. I assume that it will be agreed that the circumstances may be such that I am not irrational or at fault in any other way as a result. Nor do I have instrumental intentions regarding any of these undefeated ends. Note that by the facilitative principle it may be rational to form an instrumental intention before forming an intention regarding the goal that it will facilitate: It may be rational to intend to take an option on a cottage in the Greek island in order to keep that option cheaper than it would otherwise be, even though I do not yet intend to have that holiday. But, equally, it is often rational (i.e. not irrational) not to form any instrumental intentions even while one has a reason to have such intentions, though possibly a time may come when such failure would be irrational. In general, just as having (a reasonably believed or known) undefeated reason to have an end does not make failure to intend it irrational, so having (a reasonably believed or known) undefeated reason to have an instrumental intention does not make failure to have it irrational.

---

[37] *Engaging Reason*, ch. 5.

9

Reasons in Conflict

Neither in social order, nor in the experience of an individual, is a state of conflict the sign of a vice, or a defect, or a malfunctioning.

S. Hampshire, *Justice is Conflict*

This chapter can be seen as an introduction to the two that follow. For the most part it is a preliminary reflection about the nature of practical conflicts confronting single agents (though as always clarification of significant matters is involved; in the present case various issues regarding the nature and role of conditional reasons are explored). It explains what conflicts are, and what questions they raise. We have two distinct notions of single-agent conflicts reflecting two distinct theoretical questions. The first concerns the possibility of there being a right action in conflicts. It is the question whether, and if so how, reasons deriving from different concerns or affecting different people can be of comparable strengths. The second concerns a sense that there is something unfortunate about conflicts, and that when facing conflicting options just taking the best or the right one is not sufficient. I will offer (in outline) an answer to the second question, which indirectly helps with the first question as well, in the form of **the conformity principle**, which asserts that if one cannot conform to reason completely one should come as close to complete conformity as possible. I will show that this innocent-sounding principle has far-reaching consequences, and they will be further explored in the next chapter.

1. Practical conflicts: initial characterization

What are practical conflicts? A fairly common way of characterizing them has it that

(Initial 1st Definition): agents face a practical conflict when they are in a situation in which they have reasons to perform two acts (or more) such that they can perform either but not both.

A second, closely related characterization says that

(Initial 2nd Definition): agents face a practical conflict when in a situation where they have several reasons for action such that complying better with one makes it impossible to comply fully with another.[1]

The two definitions seem to be formally equivalent,[2] the first emphasizing the inability to perform all the actions for which one has reason, the second the inability to comply with all the reasons one has. One problem with the definitions is their vagueness. For example, the nature of impossibility remains obscure. And there are many other points to explore. The following clarifications will help, but will not eliminate the vagueness.

(1) Conflict is relative to how things stand: i.e. same reasons may apply to an agent in situations where they do not conflict, but as things are they do.

(2) It does not matter whether the agent is aware of the reasons. (As we saw, reasons apply to agents only if it is possible for them to find out what they are. This will not matter to our discussion.)

(3) The inability may be due to the limitations of the agents, their weakness of body, lack of skills, lack of imagination or knowledge, but not to absence of will, or weakness of will or resolve.

(4) We should understand the definitions to allow for conflict where one can comply partially with all the reasons that apply to one, so long as complying to a higher degree with one makes it impossible to comply with another to the degree that would have been possible had the first not applied to the agent.

I rely on our pretheoretical understanding of this idea. Yet, a word of explanation may point towards a possible analysis: the proximate reasons for actions are evaluative properties of those actions, and they often 'derive' from the relation of the action to some other evaluative fact, which is the 'root reason'. Thus that an action is buying needed clothes for one's children or repaying a loan is a reason for it, and that is so because of one's duties towards one's children and their needs, or one's promise to repay the loan. Where reasons for different actions derive from the same root reason one of the actions may satisfy the root reason better than others, depending on the character of the root reason.[3]

Not intending to deal with all the technical emendations of these characterizations let me mention but two of the more far-reaching objections to them. The first regrets their exclusive orientation towards action. Surely, we can be confronted, for example, with emotional conflicts, which themselves may be the product of reasons for different emotions such that one cannot have all of them in the purest and most appropriate (appropriate to the reasons, that is) form. As this remark shows, it is possible to extend

---

[1] The conflicts here discussed are complete conflicts, to be distinguished from partial conflicts, in which some, but not all, ways of conforming to one reason are inconsistent with conformity with another reason.

[2] A conclusion depending on the characterization of reasons given below.

[3] Neither this remark nor anything else in this chapter denies that the individuation of reasons is often underdetermined.

the two definitions to the emotions, and beyond. Conflicting emotions can be irrational, in not being adequately reason-sensitive. Fear displays lack of sensitivity to reasons when we are afraid of a forthcoming journey or (different emotional colour) of a job interview even while we know that the fear is without foundation. There could be more extreme cases, belonging to the pathology of the emotions. However, such pathological cases apart, even irrational emotions, like 'normal' irrational beliefs, are reason-related. They merely fail to be adequately sensitive to reasons. Hence, emotional conflicts have similarities to the conflicts as defined above.

In confining my attention to conflicts among reasons for action I do not mean to suggest that they are more important or more fundamental. The limitation is made necessary by the differences between conflicts in different domains. For example, we can be subject to conflicting emotions, and having conflicting emotions need not be regrettable. It may be an essential part of a constructive experience, e.g., experiencing conflicting emotions may be an appropriate reaction to a development in one's relationship with a friend. In contrast, one cannot perform both actions for which one has conflicting reasons. It is therefore necessary to confine the present discussion to conflicts regarding reasons for action.

The second objection is more troublesome. It can take various forms. One way of expressing its main point is this: practical conflicts are conflicts between reason and the passions, desires, or inclinations. Conflicts internal to reason can occur, but far from being the essence of practical conflicts they are a special, and a less important, case of conflict. In overlooking this fact I succumb to an inappropriately rationalistic view of people.

The objection raises two issues: the role of reason in our life, and the relation between practical conflict and personhood, especially its relation to the unity of the person. I say nothing of the second here. But consider for a moment the first: There are two familiar metaphors for the role of reason. It is sometimes regarded as a protagonist in (potential) conflicts, and sometimes as an adjudicator in conflicts among others. Both metaphors mislead, though that of reason as adjudicator less so than the other.

It was the burden of Chapter Five that the facts that constitute reasons, the facts on which the so-called verdict of reason is based, are not themselves 'facts of reason', whatever that may mean. They are not produced or generated by reason. They are merely recognized by it for what they are, that is considerations favouring an action, or against an action. Reasons for action are facts such as that some action will cause distress or that an action will be fun, and so on. They are evaluative facts, that is, facts consisting in the possession of an evaluative property.[4] While facts that the action in question possesses an evaluative property are the primary reasons for or against that action, other facts, those in virtue of which the action has the reason-making evaluative property, are also reasons for and against it. These are facts such as that one has an illness that will be

---

[4] We take both the fact that a particular action has an appropriate evaluative property, and the fact that actions of a type have such a property as reasons.

cured by a particular medicine, which is a reason for taking the medicine, for it shows that that action will restore one's health (the primary reason).

The facts that constitute reasons can be, and often are, facts about our emotions, feelings, passions, and desires, and about what arouses them, or assuages them; alternatively reasons often presuppose such facts. They may include facts such as that it is best to give vent to one's emotions, rather than bottle them up; or, that humility in the existing circumstances marks lack of self-respect, that defiance is the appropriate reaction to the behaviour one encountered, or that jealousy can be destructive of a healthy relationship. None of these facts (those constituting primary reasons, or others, including facts about our emotions) is in any sense 'a fact of reason'. Some of them can be recognized only by rational creatures. But recognition is one thing, authorship is another. There are no conflicts between reason and the passions if that implies that reason is the source of, the author of reasons, rather than merely the power to recognize their existence.

Pascal's famous 'Le cœur a ses raisons que la raison ne connaît point'[5] is different. This resonant statement is not amenable to obvious philosophical analysis. I think that three points are relevant in this context. The first two are about two ways, one modest, one more radical, in which our responsiveness to reasons does not always involve the power of reason. The heart responds directly to reasons, to some reasons, reasons to do with our emotions, or with other psychological conditions, and more. Its response need not always be mediated by reason. The first, modest, point is that some reasons we can learn to detect and come to respond to, spontaneously, in a flash, or at any rate without deliberation. Typically, in these cases reason is present, but behind the scenes. Our responses are immediate and 'intuitive', but they are typically monitored by our reason. That is we are, typically, in a condition such that if our spontaneous response appears to us unreasonable it will be checked. We start reflecting about it, and deliberate its pros and cons.

We are often in such a state: we drive automatically without paying attention to what we do, but if something irregular happens we as it were step in and take over from the autopilot. In all such cases our actions are not a result of deliberation, but our reason is in the background monitoring what is going on, and triggering our attention when things appear irregular. I described this condition metaphorically, personalizing reason, comparing it to an independent agent acting within us. Needless to say that is not literally the case. It is just a handy way of saying that the process within us that triggers our attention when things appear irregular is to be regarded as an expression of our rational powers.

---

[5] *Pensées* (1670), sect. 4, no. 277. The full remark reads: 'The heart has its reasons, which reason does not know. We feel it in a thousand things. I say that the heart naturally loves the Universal Being, and also itself naturally, according as it gives itself to them; and it hardens itself against one or the other at its will. You have rejected the one and kept the other. Is it by reason that you love yourself?', trs. W. F. Trotter (London and New York: Dents/Dutton, 1943).

Pascal's statement if it is to be understood in the most general way embeds this point. It affirms the ability to know the right thing spontaneously and without deliberation. But it implies much more than that. It implies, secondly, a capacity to respond to reasons that altogether bypasses reason. It is a capacity to respond to facts that are reasons, in the way appropriate to their being reasons, without recognizing them or thinking of them as reasons (nor in analogous concepts).

That may be a more troubling thought for anyone who believes that reason is the capacity to recognize reasons. Would not that imply that any responsiveness to reasons is a manifestation of our rational powers? I do not think that it does. The power of reason is the power to identify reasons as reasons, that is to identify both that some condition does, or would, or may, obtain and that that is a reason for a particular action (and thereby, the disposition to be motivated to act for reasons, or at least to be open to such motivation[6]). But our responsiveness to reasons need not depend, and does not always depend on recognizing them as reasons. Most notably, we may be, as they say, hard-wired to respond to reasons of some kinds, and culturally conditioned to respond to others. If something in the environment causes pain we retreat from it. We need not think of the pain-causing feature, nor of the fact that the action will avoid the pain, as reasons for the action in order to respond to them as to a reason. Creatures who lack the power of reason, or have it to a limited degree only, can respond to such reasons. Moreover, given that the response is hard-wired it is not accidental. It is fairly reliable and regular.

Finally, this second point combines with the third,[7] namely that various psychological states, especially the feeling of various emotions, are themselves reasons, that is they are either welcome, desirable or unwelcome, undesirable ones. To that extent, that some emotional states, or other psychological facts, obtain or that they will obtain if some action is performed, are reason-constituting facts, and they may conflict with other reasons.

That emotional states we do or may have can be reasons for us helps, of course, to explain how we can respond to some reasons (to such reasons) directly, without realizing their standing as reasons (though it is not the only case where we can do that: we are also 'hard-wired' to respond to sudden movements, etc.). It also helps explain how the popular image of the conflict between reason and the emotions developed. It is natural that both on the personal level and on the cultural one, there will be people who respond more readily to reasons involving emotions than to others, and there are cultural periods when they are in tune with the dominant

---

[6] See Chapter Five above, and on the relation between reason and motivation *Engaging Reason* (Oxford: OUP, 1999), ch. 5.

[7] The interrelation of the two points misleads Pascal in no. 276: 'M. de Roannez said: "Reasons come to me afterwards, but at first a thing pleases or shocks me without my knowing the reason, and yet it shocks me for that reason which I only discover afterwards." But I believe, not that it shocked him for the reasons which were found afterwards, but that these reasons were only found because it shocked him.' Pascal's remark does not conflict with M. de Roannez's. My points two and three above echo M. de Roannez's view.

mood of the time.[8] It is also natural that when we are inclined, individually or culturally, to respond more to emotion-relating reasons we will more often be impatient with people who tend to rely, as we see it, 'excessively' on reason in identifying the considerations to respond to and in deciding what to do.

The so-called conflict between reason and the passions is no such thing, at least not if it means that reason and the passions (or the emotions) are two sources of reasons that may conflict. Rather, talk of such conflict refers to the degree to which one is inclined to respond to emotion-related reasons, and to the degree to which one relies on one's reason in deciding what to do, rather than responding to one's emotions directly.

2. Practical conflicts and pluralistic choice

Is it not clear that the definitions are too broad? They identify conflict with apparent choice. Whenever we have more than one option supported, as it appears to us, by reasons we have to choose which one to take. That is the nature of choice. Some people omit the 'supported by reasons' from their characterization of choice. This suggests that as I write I have a choice not only between carrying on with this chapter or taking a break to listen to the news, but also between either of these options and cutting off my finger or my ear, or taking my shoes out of the cupboard and putting them back in again, etc. All these are options available to me, though I have not the slightest reason for any of them. But this is silly. Choice implies not a plurality of options but a plurality of options that are, as we believe,[9] supported by reasons.

Conflicts exist if things are a certain way, not if they appear to be that way. That marks a major difference between facing a conflict and facing a choice. But the relations between the two, according to the definitions, are too close. The definitions identify apparent conflict with choice. But not all choice implies apparent conflict. Suppose a good friend makes me two mutually exclusive gift offers (on an occasion when it would be proper to give friends such gifts): either he will give me £10 or he will give me £15. I have to choose. There is no downside to either offer, and no other normatively relevant circumstance. It would be silly to say that I face a conflict. Of course I should choose the £15, and no conflict is involved. Or, suppose that I go shopping for shoes. I find one pair that looks fine, and though not a perfect fit, it will be fine after the first painful week. Then I find another pair that looks even better and fits my feet perfectly. I have to choose. There are reasons for the first pair, but clearly the reasons for the second are better, and I should choose it. Equally clearly I did not face a conflict.

---

[8] In saying this I am assuming that commonly we are confronted with many incommensurate reasons. Which ones we respond to is a matter of personal inclination, since responding to any of them would be rational.

[9] Though sometimes this qualification is out of place. There is a use of 'choice' where if I had no reasons for an alternative course of action then I had no choice, however matters appeared to me.

Why not? Perhaps because the choice was so easy. Does not 'conflict' imply a difficulty in making up one's mind? Does it not imply a difficult choice? Perhaps it does, or rather, perhaps we would not describe a situation as one of conflict unless we were conflicted, unless we were torn both ways, finding it difficult to see which option is the better one, or finding it difficult to decide for the option we take to be the better one. But I will disregard this psychological dimension of conflict, or of the use of 'conflict'. There is at least in the philosophical tradition but beyond it as well, a familiar notion of conflict as a normative property of choice situations, rather than as a psychological property of the response to them. I will concentrate exclusively on this normative, rather than psychological, notion of conflict.

Besides, even if we modify the shoes example so that the choice is no longer easy the situation will still not be one of conflict. Imagine, e.g., that one criterion for the suitability of the shoes is whether I could wear them to work, and I am not sure what is the dress code in my new place of employment. Or imagine that though one pair is a much better fit, when I try it on that is not evident to me, and I hesitate. The case turns into one of difficulty and uncertainty, but not one of conflict. The difficulty is epistemic. The normative nature of the situation has not changed. It is still a case where one pair of shoes trumps the other by all the relevant criteria.

'(Practical) normative conflict', in one central understanding of the term, imports pluralism, that is a plurality of irreducibly distinct concerns supporting various options, such that in a pair-wise comparison none of the options scores higher than all the others in each and every one of the concerns affecting the situation. Thus in having to choose between £10 and £15 we do not face a conflict, for only one concern is relevant to the choice, and the choice between the shoes is not a conflict because even though several concerns bear on it (suitability to wear for work, attractiveness, fitting one's feet) one option is superior to the other in every single one of them. Conflict exists where there is choice between different options supported by distinct concerns such that one option is better supported by some of them and another is better supported by the others. A choice between two jobs, say, involves conflict when one of them is a better job, while the other will enable one to live in a more interesting or agreeable city. To accommodate this point the definitions can be revised as follows:

Conflict as pluralistic choice, 1st Definition: agents face a practical conflict when they are in a situation in which they have reasons deriving from distinct values to perform two acts (or more) such that they can perform either but not both, and where each option is better supported by reasons deriving from a value different from those supporting some rival option.

The second definition can be more smoothly adapted:

Conflict as pluralistic choice, 2nd Definition: agents face a practical conflict when in a situation where they have several reasons for action deriving from distinct values such that complying better with one makes it impossible to comply fully with another.

3. Conflict and imperfect conformity with reason

So understood conflict is tied up with value pluralism, and the interest in conflicts is in the possibility that reasons deriving from different distinct values may be compared in strength, weight, or stringency. But there is another strand to our thinking about conflict. There is something unfortunate about conflicts. It is better not to have them. When in conflict we cannot do everything that it would be best for us to do. All these ideas are often associated with conflicts. They are not always clearly distinguished from the thought that conflict is an expression of pluralism. It is often, usually implicitly, assumed that the two strands of thought go hand in hand. It is assumed that the 'unfortunate' aspect of conflict is an inevitable result of pluralism.

That assumption is mistaken. The 'unfortunate' aspect of conflict is a common, but not an inevitable, result of pluralism. Nor is it always absent in single-value conflicts (though this depends on how we identify what is unfortunate in such situations). In the £15 versus £10 case it is unfortunate that I cannot have both. So having to choose is unfortunate, even though it is a single-value case. Similarly, imagine that I am interested in Dreier's films and that I have a chance to see two of them tonight (and am unlikely to have another chance to see either for the next year or so). I should clearly see one of them, which is one of his most important, rather than the other, which is one of the short documentaries he did during the lull years. Yet, even though the decision is clear and easy, and only one concern is involved,[10] it is a case of conflict, for it is unfortunate that I have to choose between the two. The result of the choice leaves me with a reason to see the other, when I can.

The most striking examples of single-value choices that are cases of conflict, and are so because it is unfortunate that one has to choose, are cases affecting more than one person. If I have to choose between two courses of action, one that will benefit me and my oldest child but harm my youngest, and the other that will be beneficial to the youngest child, but will mean a loss of opportunity to me, I have a conflict on my hands. This is so regardless of degrees of benefit and harm, and regardless of whether there is one or more value, or type of consideration involved. As in the Dreier example, I am left with an unrequited reason to do at some future time what I could not do (=should not have done) now. Many-person conflicts give rise to troubling special questions that will be considered in the next chapter.

Just as choice can be unfortunate, in a yet to be explained sense, in cases of single-value choices, so it can lack that aspect when multiple values are present. The shoes example is one where various distinct considerations bear on the choice: aesthetic considerations, convenience, and possibly others. Assuming that I have no reason to

---

[10] To be sure the example can be developed in a different direction, pointing out that the different films will have different valuable features, manifesting different values. My example assumes one concern only: becoming familiar with all of Dreier's films, where the importance of each film is in its significance among his films.

have a spare pair of shoes, once I have bought the better pair I have no reason left to have the other pair,[11] and being offered a choice has no downside.

Here and elsewhere, I disregard the possibility of the very need to make up one's mind (collect information needed to do so intelligently, etc.) being unfortunate. Since we are looking for conflict as a normative property of choice situations I will again disregard its psychological aspects, that is I will not take difficulty or reluctance to choose, make up one's mind, or gather information necessary for decision as a mark of conflict.

Another example of a multiple-value choice not involving conflict is slightly more complicated. Suppose I have a reason to do something for another person, but not to do too much. Doing too much will send the wrong signal, will put him in my debt and in these and other ways will spoil things between us. If so then I have reason to do this for that person and reason to do that, but if I do one of them the reason to do the other is cancelled. The choice between the different possible options may be a multi-value one, but once I make my choice I no longer have any reason to pursue the other option.[12] In such cases being faced with a multi-value choice does not seem unfortunate. Even though we have yet to identify the sense in which conflicts can be unfortunate we have no reason to associate it with multi-value choices.

The examples just given suggest a way of understanding why conflicts are often thought to be unfortunate. They are when whatever the agents do there will be an unsatisfied reason left behind. This suggests the following notion of conflicting reasons:

Conflict as the impossibility of perfect conformity, 1st Definition: agents face a practical conflict when they are in a situation in which they have reasons to perform two (or more) acts such that they can perform either but not both, and where performing one does not cancel the reasons to perform the other nor make them inapplicable.[13]

Conflict as the impossibility of perfect conformity, 2nd Definition: agents face a practical conflict when in a situation where they have several reasons for action such that complying better with one makes it impossible to comply as fully with another as would be otherwise possible,[14] and where compliance with one does not cancel the other nor make it inapplicable.

---

[11] And having chosen the better pair I have no reason to have the other unless I fear that I will not be able to get my chosen pair. I will disregard such complications.

[12] I am assuming that my sole reason for giving him e.g. the book and the CD is that these will be ways of 'doing something for him', which is the only thing I have reason to do (i.e. I assume that I do not have an independent reason to give them to him. I only have a reason to do something for him).

[13] To be more accurate the definition should meet an additional complexity. Sometimes an action cancels a reason or makes it inapplicable by being the wrong action whose performance makes the right course of action no longer possible, thereby making certain reasons inapplicable. The definition should therefore read: '...does not cancel those reasons nor make them inapplicable, and where if they are cancelled or rendered inapplicable this is not due to the fact that the wrong action was chosen or taken'. For the sake of brevity I will not include this qualification when repeating the definitions, or modifying them.

[14] I rely on this condition, rather than on the simpler 'makes it impossible to comply fully with another' so that we need not worry that there are cases where the underlying reason does not admit of complete and

The impossibility of perfect conformity, naturally negating any thought that the agents are at fault, is what is unfortunate. However the agents choose there will still be reasons that apply to them that they cannot follow or conform to. That does not mean that it is unfortunate for the agents to find themselves in such a situation, or that it is against their interests. The conflict can be a moral conflict such that whichever way they choose their choice will not bear at all on their self-interest, or, alternatively, will be equally adverse to their self-interest. As noted, not all conflicts as imperfect conformity are conflicts as pluralistic choices, nor the other way round, though the two categories overlap.

4. Conditional and independent reasons

Arguably this definition does not exhaust the sense in which conflict is understood to be an unfortunate situation. Think of all the things that I have reason to do tonight. I could go to a jazz concert, or to a rock concert, or to a good silent film from the 1920s. Or, I could go for a walk along the river, or hear the Emersons live playing the Razumovsky Quartets. Do I face a conflict of reasons? One doubt about a positive answer is that I am fortunate in having so much to choose from, and yet the case falls under the definition of conflict as the impossibility of complete conformity.

One reaction to this objection is to doubt that I really have a reason to do all those things. I am assuming that they are not, as I put it, 'integrated' into my goals, aspirations, etc., that is that I am not a music lover, nor a walker, nor a film buff, and so on. All the options I mentioned are attractive ones, all have their value, but as none is part of any goal or habit, etc. of mine, so this response to the objection goes, I do not have a reason to pursue any of them. This response overlooks the fact that if I chose one of these options I would be doing so for a reason, and the reason would be (unless when choosing the option I act out of some mistaken belief) that the option is attractive in the way the response concedes them to be attractive. It follows that I have reason to follow each of them.

Another response claims that to succeed the objection must show that the reasons we face in *embarras de richesse* cases are independent of each other. Otherwise, given our definition, the reasons do not conflict at all. Perhaps while I have a reason to follow any of the options, once I do follow one of them I no longer have a reason to follow any of the others. Following one cancels the reason to follow the others. At first blush this is unconvincing (I will return to a variant of this response below). If I do one of them I still have reason to do the others, only I cannot. If I have reason to see each of two films now, seeing one does not cancel the reason to see the other. It only makes it impossible to do so.

exhaustive compliance, for there is always something more one can do for that reason (say the reason parents have to look after their children).

Yet another response points out that I have only a conditional reason to do any of these things. I have reason to do them only if I want to do them. Some people think that desires are reasons, or that reasons consist in appropriate combinations of desires and beliefs. I do not share this view,[15] and the thought that such reasons are conditional on the will is not meant to reintroduce it. Rather, desires are part of the factual background that conditions the application of reasons. Sometimes there is no point in taking an action unless one does it in a spirit of willing engagement, or at least the point is much reduced. Notice that the desires that condition reasons in this way could be those of people other than the agent: there can be no point in going to a party with X if X does not want to go there, or will do so unwillingly, and so on.

Reasons that are conditional on the will, the reply goes, do not conflict. In general, conditional reasons do not conflict. Perhaps they can conflict conditionally, that is they can conflict once their condition is met, but not before. This response is helpful in drawing attention to conditional reasons generally, and to will-dependent and goal-dependent reasons in particular. Will-dependent reasons are a special case of conditional reasons, when that last concept is broadly understood. They are reasons whose application, or whose strength or stringency are conditional on people's inclination, desire, or willingness, at the time of action, to engage in that particular action.[16] Another interesting case of conditional reasons is goal-dependent reasons, which are those whose application or strength depends on the agents having a particular goal. In as much as people's goals were willingly assumed by them, or at least are willingly pursued by them (even though not all the time, nor on all occasions) then goal-dependent reasons are reasons that depend on a desire. They depend on a desire to persevere with the goal, but not necessarily on a desire to perform the particular act for which the goal-dependent reason is a reason.[17] For example, Judith, a dancer, has a reason to rehearse today, a reason that is goal-dependent, because she would not have it unless she were a dancer, though it is not will-dependent, as she has it irrespective of whether she wants to rehearse today, and independently of whether she would be doing it willingly.

Traditionally, categorical reasons, though said to be contrasted with conditional ones, are contrasted not with them but with will-dependent and with goal-dependent reasons. Categorical reasons are—as often defined—reasons whose application and stringency do not depend on the agent's desires, inclinations, or goals, at the time of action. Some reasons, we could call them 'purely categorical' reasons, are independent

---

[15] See *Engaging Reason*, ch. 4.

[16] I will use 'will-dependent' to refer only to reasons where the dependence is positive, i.e. where one has the reason or it is stronger if one desires the act, or would do it willingly. Sometimes the connection is reversed: you have reason, or more reason to do something if you do not want to do it. These are not will-dependent in the sense here meant.

[17] The matter was considered in the previous chapter. Sometimes one is caught up in a goal, which one may have assumed willingly in the past, but has to carry on with now even though one no longer wants to at all. Reasons one has because one has such a (currently) unwilled goal are not goal-dependent in the sense here defined.

of any desire of the agent at any time. Typical purely categorical reasons are reasons of respect. We have reason to respect other people, to respect works of art, etc., regardless of our own goals, tastes, or preferences. Other categorical reasons depend on one's past will, as, for example, one's reason to keep one's promise depends on the voluntary making of a promise, but is irrespective of a desire to perform the promised act.

With these points in mind let us return to the objection. One response to it, I pointed out, was to agree that the examples it relies on, i.e. cases in which we have many attractive options to choose from, are not cases of conflict as impossible complete conformity, but to deny that that is an objection. Because the reasons we face in them are will-dependent, and therefore conditional, they do not conflict even by the definitions given at the outset.

In general it is true that conditional reasons do not conflict just because were their conditions to be met they would conflict. (Though where it is known that the conditions will be met, that is that they will conflict at some future time, they can be treated as conflicting ahead of time.) But the same cannot be said of will-dependent reasons. Whatever we have reason to do if we want to, we do also have reason to want (other things being equal). Our will as well as our actions are subject to reasons and in general these are the same reasons, that is, with some exceptions, reasons for an action are also reasons for wanting to perform it, and the other way round. Hence will-dependent reasons that would conflict if the will were there already do conflict, for they are also conflicting reasons for wanting to perform those actions. So the objection is still with us.

To repeat, the objection says that situations in which one faces plenty of attractive options should be distinguished from cases of conflict for there is nothing unfortunate in them as there is about being in a conflict situation. We must distinguish, it says, between conflict and an *embarras de richesse*.

I am, of course, exaggerating. The options may not be so many and so luxurious as to deserve that appellation. But the point is clear enough. Possibly, however, the notion of will-dependent reasons allows us to modify the definition of conflict to avoid the objection. Perhaps we should simply add to the definition the proviso that a conflict does not exist if one of the allegedly conflicting reasons is will-dependent.

Would that modification meet the objection? The thought behind the objection was that there is something unfortunate in being in a conflict, which is not captured by the original definition. Does the fact that some of the putatively conflicting reasons are will-dependent show that there is nothing unfortunate in the situation? Are there no other cases where the situation is not unfortunate? I think that the modification proves inadequate on both counts.

First, a distinction must be drawn between those cases in which we have a duty to meet the condition of a will-dependent reason, and to have a positive, willing attitude towards the action, and those where no such duty exists. The example of a teacher who has a reason to pay special attention to one of his students may illustrate the point. True, he should not attend to the student if he is reluctant and unwilling to do so. Or, at least, he has less reason to do so reluctantly for his attention will be less effective. However, he may well have a duty to have a willing attitude to spending more time with his students when his attention is needed.

In such cases the fact that the reason, or its stringency, depends on our will does not matter to the way we should think of conflict. Conflict is a conflict of reasons that apply to us, not of those we are minded to conform to. Extending this thought suggests that reasons that should apply to us, or should have certain weight (because we should be willing to perform the actions for which they are reasons) are, so far as identifying conflicts is concerned, to count as reasons which do apply to us. If conformity with them is incompatible with conformity with other reasons we are in a conflict situation (assuming the other conditions for conflict are met).

Different considerations apply to will-dependent reasons where we have no independent reason to want to perform the act for which they are reasons (i.e. no reason other than the will-dependent reasons themselves).[18] In such cases, if we do not desire the action, the reason either does not apply or has lesser weight. If it does not apply it does not conflict with reasons that do. Does it follow that we can dissolve the objection by modifying the definitions in a more complicated way to exclude will-dependent reasons except when we have a special reason to make true their condition? I do not think that that gets to the root of the difficulty. It does not explain in what ways there is something unfortunate about facing a conflict.

What is the source of the problem? The definitions assume that the unfortunate aspect is the impossibility of complying with all the independent reasons that apply to the agent. The objection suggests that that is not necessarily true. According to it inability to comply with all the reasons applying to the agent need not be unfortunate. When is it? Perhaps only when it means that the agent's compliance with reason on this occasion falls short of a required standard. To meet the objection by augmenting the definitions we need to specify the relevant standard. That is not a straightforward task. Obviously it is not the standard of blame, or of doing one's best. Conflicts exist only where doing one's best is not good enough, and where the agent is not to blame. What standard does one fall short of in cases of conflict?

Perhaps we should define it as follows: For all agents, two reasons conflict only if each of them is a reason such that, had the conflict not occurred and had the agents failed to conform with it, they would have been at fault. This will not do as it stands. The agents may be excusably unaware (that is, their ignorance cannot count against them) of the existence of these reasons.[19] To meet the point we may refer to a reason

---

[18] As noted above, in general reasons for action are also reasons to want to do the act for which they are reasons. The fact that with (some) will-dependent reasons the stringency of the reason depends on one's willingness to perform the action makes them no exception. Assume, however, that the very applicability of the reason is conditional on the will. In such cases the reason can be said to be an invitation to want to perform the action. It shows that should we want it the action would have merits, that it is desirable if wanted.

[19] According to some views of 'acting wrongly' agents act wrongly, though they are not blameworthy, even when their action is due to excusable ignorance. If that is so then the emendation built into the modified definition to meet the point can be dispensed with.

for the flouting of which they would be responsible, if the conditions of responsibility were met. The revised definitions may be:

Conflict as the impossibility of complete conformity, possible revision of 1st Definition: agents face a practical conflict when they are in a situation in which they have reasons to perform two acts (or more) such that they can perform either but not both, and where performing one does not cancel the reasons to perform the other nor make them inapplicable, and where, had the conditions of responsibility obtained, they would have been at fault should they have failed to take either action, had the reason for the other not applied.

Conflict as the impossibility of complete conformity, possible revision of 2nd Definition: agents face a practical conflict when in a situation where they have several reasons for action such that complying better with one makes it impossible to comply as fully with another as would be otherwise possible, and where compliance with one does not cancel the other nor make it inapplicable, and where had the conditions of responsibility obtained, they would have been at fault should they have failed to act for either reason, had the other reason not applied.

Do the revised definitions improve on the original ones? Three questions remain: If the definitions are good ones, do they vindicate the suggestion we started from, namely that situations of *embarras de richesse* are not situations of conflict? After all, the revised definitions in order to determine whether there is conflict where the options are plentiful look at what things would be like were all but one of them to be removed. Would it not follow that if we were at fault then we are facing conflict even when there are plenty of options? Second, arguably the revised definitions are extensionally equivalent to the original ones, for possibly failure to comply with any undefeated reasons is, if the conditions of responsibility obtain, a fault. Needless to say this is not the place to settle this matter. Finally, and most important, even if the revised definitions are extensionally correct they fail to explain what is unfortunate about being in a conflict situation. After all, that we would have been at fault had the situation been different does not show that there is anything unfortunate in the situation as it is. Perhaps it is rather the contrary. After all it is a situation where we are not at fault, at least not for that reason.

Let me, therefore, return for the final time to the type of situation I used to raise the objection: they are situations relatively isolated from one's major concerns, or from possible major consequences to the world in general. Questions like 'What shall I do tonight?' or 'How shall I spend the weekend?' asked on an ordinary day. What characterizes the sort of reasons that apply (to play chess, go for a walk, see a film, etc.) is not that in the context there would be no fault in not choosing (had the other reasons not applied). There may be such fault (the failure may be irrational, show one to be lazy, etc). Rather, it is that they are what I will call opportunity-reasons: reasons one has because one's background reason is to do something worth doing on a relatively isolated occasion. The reasons for each of the specific options are dependent on their background reason. Once one course of action, no worse than its alternatives, is undertaken the background reason is satisfied, and one has no uncomplied-with reason. Hence the case is not one of conflict given the (unrevised) definition above.

This makes the identification of conflict sensitive to background reasons. Take, for example, a choice of career. We may say that the core reason is to have a worthwhile career, and again the existence of multiple worthy options fails to establish a conflict. But this time the situation is different, since there may be background reasons to have a career with various aspects, satisfying various needs, etc., such that none satisfies all of them. A choice of any career leaves some of them unsatisfied, and that makes the situation one of conflict.

5. Conflict and compliance

The distinctive feature of conflicts is the impossibility of complete conformity with reason, or, to be precise, the fact that conflict makes it impossible to conform to reason as well as, but for it, one would have been able to do. In conflict situations our best efforts still leave us short. Even when we do our best, even when we act effectively and without fail, the conflict either makes it impossible to conform completely to reason, or it reduces the possible degree of conformity. Whatever we do some of the reasons remain unmet (that is, they are fault-establishing reasons and are not cancelled, nor made inapplicable by our actions). This is why conflict situations are unfortunate, or rather this is what is unfortunate about them. This is the standard we fall short of; not a standard of knowledge, will, or competence (for one may be in an unfortunate situation even when faultless so far as these factors go), but of reason: Conflicts generate ways in which one is unable to conform to reason in full.

How unique are conflicts in this regard? There are cases in which it is impossible for us to follow all the reasons that apply to us (or to follow them to the highest degree) due to our blameless ignorance of what they are. The point reminds us that the boundary between failure due to our shortcomings (incompetence, weak will, ignorance, carelessness, etc.) and impossibility of full conformity with reason due to the way the world is, is not a sharp one. The inability of the blind due to their blindness counts, normally, as an aspect of the world constraining their options, while inability due to forgetfulness is put down to us. When we fail fully to comply with reason due to forgetfulness it is we who fall short of the mark. And there are many other cases in which the distinction is vague, and the rationale for applying it one way or the other is not all that firm.

Leaving ignorance aside, there are many other factors that reduce the possible degree of conformity with reasons. One typical case is where the impossibility of complete conformity results from a past failure. Assume that, modifying the shoes example, I choose the wrong pair. I still have a reason to buy the better pair, since the one I did buy is not entirely satisfactory. But I can no longer do so. It has gone, or I lack the money, etc. I made a bad decision and bought the wrong shoes. As a result the reason I failed to act for is not cancelled. But I can no longer follow it. Now I face no conflict, but just as in the case of conflicts I cannot fully conform to reason.

Needless to say that latter situation where I have reason to get a pair of shoes, or to take any other action, but am unable to do so, can arise not only through a previous bad decision, but in a whole range of other circumstances, which will often, but need not, involve conflict. Such cases resemble conflict in being situations where awareness of our inability to conform to reason may burden us. They lack the feature that makes conflict distinctive, namely that we can choose which reason to conform to, and which to neglect. The 'burden of choice' when without conflict (or when the conflict is that of pluralistic choice only) has a different aspect: it is the burden of having to choose what is the right thing to do. In situations of conflict we have that burden, but also the burden of choosing which good to sacrifice. When the reason for one option is taken to be better than the reason for the other that burden merges with the burden of establishing which is the better reason. Often enough, however, there are several incommensurable best options (i.e. ones better than which there are none in the situation). In such cases the burden of deciding which reason to let go unfulfilled, or, as is sometimes the case, the interests of which person to sacrifice, where the sacrificing is justified, but regrettable, is distinct and particularly irksome. It forces us to be involved in certain events in ways in which we may well not wish to be involved. This is an important difference between such conflicts, and other cases of inescapable incomplete conformity with reason. But it is not one affecting practical reasons, or practical rationality. Given that in such conflict situations reason gives us no guidance in the choice, the fact of the burden of choice has no bearing on the rest of this discussion, which revolves on the consequences of conflicts to the reasons that apply to agents facing them.

6. Consequences of conflict and of incomplete conformity

My claim is that conflicts of incomplete conformity are not normatively distinctive. There are, as we saw, other cases where incomplete conformity is inevitable. Besides, cases of (not necessarily inevitable) incomplete conformity are very common. They include all occasions on which agents fail to conform to reasons that they could conform to, through their mistakes, irrational motivations, weakness, incompetence, bad luck, or other factors. In discussing many of these cases the question of whether agents are to blame often occupies centre stage. Agents who face conflicts are clearly not to blame (except where they are to blame for being in the conflict situation[20]).

---

[20]   This point is important to the argument of Ruth Marcus in 'Moral Dilemmas and Consistency', *Journal of Philosophy* 77 (1980), 121–36.

Incomplete conformity, however, whether or not in situations of conflict, has consequences important in practice and challenging in theory.

In principle these results are simple and straightforward:

The conformity principle: One should conform to reason completely. If one cannot one should come as close to complete conformity as possible. The first part of the principle is tautological. The interest in the principle is in its second part.

The two most common and important implications are:[21]

(1) There may be 'a next best possibility': I should (meaning I have reason to) send my child to the best school, but I cannot. So I should (i.e. have reason to) send him to the next best school.

(2) Not being able to conform with reason completely is a matter of regret, which it may be appropriate to share with another if the reason is a relational reason addressed towards that person.

The conformity principle is not 'an independent' principle. It is not as if one has a reason to do something, and because of the conformity principle one should conform to that reason. Rather that one should conform to it is what we say when we say that it is a reason. And if we have two reasons, which do not cancel each other, then we should conform to both. That too is what we say when we say of each of them that it is a reason. The conformity principle merely repeats this. Nor does the second part of the principle, about coming as close as possible to complete conformity, state anything other than is stated by a statement of reasons for action. If I have reason to give you £10 and I can only give you £8 then that same reason is a reason to give you the £8.

The second part of the conformity principle is spelt out in the first implication above. The second implication is merely an expression of the fact that reasons can be known and appreciated. Knowing that they require conformity means that inability to conform is a source of regret. I will not elaborate on the tail end of that implication here. It applies to relational reasons, that is reasons we have towards some people. Reasons are relational in that way if they arise out of a relationship (e.g. reasons that are constitutive of friendship or of parent–child relationships), or are justified out of concern for the other (e.g. reasons not to assault a person). In most cases it is appropriate to regard relational reasons as owed to the person to whom they relate. It is part of what makes relational reasons what they are that (other things being equal) it is appropriate to make the regret known to those to whom the reason is owed. Elaborating that aspect of the principle will have to involve an account of relational reasons, and thus of the character of certain relationships and transactions. Conformity with such reasons is, by the nature

---

[21] It may be worth mentioning that partial conflicts (see footnote 1 above) allow complete conformity, and that agents facing them should perfectly conform by avoiding the ways of conforming with one reason that would constitute or lead to nonconformity with the conflicting one.

of these reasons, a matter of concern for those others too. But elaborating on the nature of such relational reasons will take us too far from the concerns of this chapter.

I hope that the conclusions so far seem uncontroversial, for they have far-reaching and often-neglected consequences. They show that both some reasons to compensate and some reasons to apologize are implications of incomplete conformity. This means that

(a) They do not require independent principles of compensation.
(b) They do not presuppose fault.
(c) Finally, they do not presuppose conflict. Some reasons of compensation and apology are consequences of incomplete conformity, of which conflict situations are but one special case. When I cannot send my child to the best school does it matter whether this is because I do not have the money for it, or because though I have the money I have a conflicting reason to feed my child? Probably not. Either way I should simply look for the next best school.

In one of its senses compensation is a reaction to failure fully to conform to reason, when the failure compromised the rights or interests of another person, a reaction aimed at mitigating the consequences of that failure. But one can compensate oneself as well, as when I go to the cinema today to compensate myself for missing an opportunity to have an enjoyable evening yesterday.[22] The principle of conformity points out that when we fail to conform fully to a reason we have reason to come as close to full compliance as we can, call it reason to do the next best act. It is the very same reason that we did not conform to which is, or becomes, reason for the next best thing. The first point above claims that in some cases compensation to others for harm inflicted or for rights violated is just a special case of the conformity principle, or a natural extension of the reason to take the second best course of action, having failed fully to conform to reason. So if I have reason not to damage your property, and I do damage your fence, I have reason to compensate you, that is to mitigate the consequences of failure, and this reason is the very same reason I had initially (the reason not to trespass or not to disturb your peace). There is no need for an independent principle of compensation to establish the case for it.

Determining to which cases of compensation the conformity principle applies, and establishing that it does is not a task for this chapter. Perhaps the reason for its application can be partly surmised by listing some of the implications it does not have. Most important, it does not claim that one has a conclusive reason to compensate whenever one fails to conform to reason. The strength of the reason is its original strength. It may be defeated by conflicting reasons when it comes to the second best just as it was defeated, assuming that compensation is a result of acting correctly in a case of conflict, when the question was whether to take the action needed for full conformity with that reason. Of course, by the same token if it is so defeated it does not

---

[22] Most generally compensation is just rendering an equivalence, or as near an equivalence as can be, or is thought appropriate. For example, a salary is compensation for work done.

disappear. It merely becomes a reason for the third best course of action. This qualification has important practical consequences. For example, many reasons to refrain from certain actions are, in normal circumstances, easy to comply with, as conformity does not reduce one's options, and has virtually no cost. Compensating for violation of the reason to refrain will typically be a much more burdensome and costly action, which may therefore be more frequently defeated in normal circumstances.

Furthermore, the claim is not that compensation should be required by law, or obtainable through some other enforcement mechanism. Normally there are numerous adverse effects to any legal intervention and that would undercut the argument for legal enforcement in many cases. However, it has to be borne in mind that the claim is a relevant consideration in the argument for legal enforcement.

Third, either by law or by custom different societies can accept regimes in which compensation is subject to conditions inconsistent with the conformity principle and which constitute societal norms locating rights and duties, increasing (let us say) people's liberty of action (by releasing them from the need to bear the cost of their nonconformity in some circumstances), in exchange for increasing their security in some respects. Many such regimes are sensible and can override and displace the reasons that obtain in their absence.

Finally, while the conformity principle itself points to the existence of reasons to compensate that do not derive from independent moral duty to compensate, or from independent duty of compensation, it does not negate the possibility that such independent duties may exist to supplement it in certain circumstances. Indeed, if common legal duties of compensation reflect moral duties then there are such additional moral duties to compensate. Not only can punitive and exemplary damages not be justified by the conformity principle, nor can, for example, many cases of damages for suffering. If we define 'compensable harm' to mean harm that can be remedied at least in part, then we can say that the conformity principle explains compensation for compensable harms only, and only to the extent that they mitigate the harm.

Many cases of legal liability for damages as well as common beliefs about what compensation is morally required are unjustified by the principle of conformity. To give but one example: suppose I undertook to make it possible for you to get to Australia for your mother's wedding (I may be your employer, and I promised timely leave and the cost of the ticket). Having failed to do that, I offer you a week's holiday in Brighton as compensation. This may be a sensible way to mollify hurt feelings, but it does nothing to bring you closer to sharing in your mother's great day, and therefore nothing to get me closer to fulfilling my undertaking. It may be justified, and something like it may be required, but it is not required or justified by the conformity principle.

Probably the most controversial implication of the conformity principle is that the reason to compensate that it points to does not depend on the agent being at fault, for the failure to achieve full conformity with reason. If compensation is nothing but acting to get as close as possible to complete compliance then the reason one has to compensate is the reason one had in the first place. That reason does not (special cases apart) presuppose fault, and nor does the reason to compensate. I ought to send my child to the best school, to avoid damaging my neighbour's tree, to avoid polluting the river, to acquire full command of Brandom's theory, and none of them arises out of any fault of mine. Therefore, if I cannot achieve them I should come as near as possible, which may involve sending my child to the next best school, paying to cure the damage to my neighbour's tree, and to clean up the river, and for any interim damage caused until the harm is undone, and learning as much as I can of Brandom's theory (say reading *Articulating Reasons* because I cannot manage in time to read *Making Explicit*). This suggests there is strict liability to compensate, liability regardless of the fact that the harm we caused was not our fault.

The strict liability implication is avoided where the reason, failure to conform with which is the ground of liability, is a reason intentionally (or with knowledge) to refrain from some action. If I do not have a reason not to kill others, but only a reason not to murder them then I do not fail to conform with reason if I kill others, so long as I do not do so intentionally. Hence the principle of conformity does not lead to strict liability in such cases.[23] There are cases where the reasons we have are reasons for intentional omissions. But most common cases are not like that. This is clear in the case of reasons for positive action: I have reason to repay my debt, not to repay it intentionally. If it were the latter I would not be failing to comply with reason so long as I merely forgot to pay my debt. Hence, no one could reproach me for being forgetful or for failing to repay my debt. There is nothing I have reason to do that I failed to do. Similarly I have reason not to humiliate other people, not merely a reason not to do so intentionally.

In some ways this implication appeals. It confirms the view that what matters is what we do, how we live, whether we respond to reason, and not what we intend or want as various Kantians would have it. But it may be premature to claim the conformity principle in support of this way of thinking. There is more work to be done before we get there. The conclusion argued for so far is merely that we think of conflicts either as cases of pluralistic choices, or as a special class of cases of inevitable failure of complete conformity, and that as such conflicts are not normatively distinct, but are subject to the very general conformity principle.

---

[23] This conclusion does not apply where I have a reason to act, rather than to refrain from action. I have a reason to feed my child. Suppose it is a reason to feed intentionally. My unintentional failure intentionally to feed my child does give rise, by the conformity principle, to the strict liability standard.

10

Numbers: With and Without Contractualism

Perhaps the most discussed problem regarding conflict resolution is the problem of the relevance of numbers, sometimes called the problem of aggregation. I will reintroduce the **conformity principle**, discussed in the last chapter, and examine the case for it in more detail. It will be further examined and applied in Chapter Eleven. We can start the discussion focusing on a simple case.

Perhaps it is even too simple. Most people find it irritatingly childish to wonder whether there is anything wrong if a lifeguard who can save several people drowning to his right lets them drown in order to save one person drowning on his left, even though saving the several would have been as easy as, and no more risky than saving the one, and he knew that, and knew that he could not save them all, and that he has no special obligation to any of them. Surely, we say, numbers matter. Surely the lifeguard would be wrong not to attempt to save as many as he can.

However, in exploring the general features of practical reason such cases are challenging. The more obvious the answer the more difficult it is to find non-question-begging reasons for it. Besides not everyone shares the common certitude. Some feel that it is up to the lifeguard, or at least would be up to him if his employment does not impose any special obligations, for example an obligation to save as many people as he can. We will ignore such complications, assuming only that the rescuer has a moral reason to save at least one of the drowning, and that there is no reason to favour or disfavour any of them.

I will consider only reasons for action failure to conform or to try to conform with which is, other things being equal, a flaw, a fault, rendering one's conduct wrong, imprudent, unwise, foolish, or marred by some other defect. My discussion is neutral on whether all reasons are of this kind. Failure to conform with some reasons is, other things being equal, a moral fault, or it renders the action morally wrong (whether or not the agent is blameworthy for it). Some reasons amount to, or establish duties. My discussion will include, but will not be confined to such reasons.

The problem to be discussed here should not be confused with another: if one is morally entitled to refrain from doing some good, but chooses to do it, is one then at fault if one does not do as much good (of that kind) as one can on that occasion? At least sometimes the answer seems to be that if one ventures to do some good, one has to do the best one can. Imagine a situation where though it would have been perfectly all right to stay on shore, you set out in your boat to save a drowning person. Your action may even be foolhardy. But you venture out, and given that you do, can you really pass by and leave another drowning person in the water, if picking him up will not increase the risk to yourself or to the other person you save, and there are no other reasons against saving him? You are already running the risk, or incurring the costs avoidance of which would have justified your forbearing from any rescue attempt. They can no longer justify not saving all those you can with no extra risk and cost. Needless to say this argument presupposes, among much else, the answer to the question to be here considered, namely that if you have a 'fault-making' reason to save some, you have a 'fault-making' reason to save the many rather than the few, other things being equal.

One difficulty with that answer is that it seems to conflict with other views that many find equally obvious. One may not kill a person to use his kidneys to save two who would otherwise die, even though, arguably, it is permissible for a person to choose death in order to donate his kidneys. One need not have two children rather than stop at one, even though, arguably, one may have two for the reason that having a second child will likely bring into being a person who will have a fulfilling life. If so why not save the few, even if one may save the many? The question why do numbers count among the drowning is important to an understanding of why, when, and how they do in general.

An obvious line to explore is that there are reasons of various kinds, and that numbers count within kinds but not across kinds (i.e. not when the reasons involved are of different kinds). That is, e.g., the view taken by Scanlon. I will examine his Contractualist argument for it below. I consider two questions regarding Scanlon's theory. First, what is it a theory of and what kind of theory is it? Clarifying our view on that is needed for a consideration of the second question: How successful is Scanlon's theory in dealing with the question of numbers? But first, do numbers count at all?

1. Defending the conformity principle

If numbers count it must be for reasons independent of Scanlon's Contractualism.[1] His Contractualism is not a general theory of practical reason, but an account of a special category of reasons, those arising out of what we owe each other. Scanlon identifies them with wrong-making reasons. The cogency of his argument does not depend on this identification, and I will not comment on it. It suggests, however, that Scanlon's Contractualism presupposes not only a general theory of reasons, but also an account of how numbers matter, for if there are non-contractualist reasons there are questions about the relevance of numbers within them.

---

[1] 'Contractualism' here refers to Scanlon's version of it, as set out in *What We Owe to Each Other* (Cambridge, Mass.: Harvard University Press, 1998).

The conformity principle explains a basic way, perhaps the basic way in which number counts. Its first part: one should conform to reasons completely, is tautological and trivial. The interest is in the sequel, in the implication for situations in which complete conformity to reasons is impossible.[2] Conforming to reason is potentially a matter of degree. Apart from the two extremes of full or no compliance there are usually possibilities of partial compliance. If I owe you £100 and I give you £60 I do less than I ought to have done, but more than nothing. It would have been better had I given you £100, but worse had I given you nothing. Why? Because had I given you £100 I would have completely complied with reason (that reason), whereas I did not. And had I given you nothing I would have been further away from complete compliance than I am. Having reasons means that one should comply with them, that is comply perfectly. It also means that it is better to comply partially than not at all, and the closer one is to complete compliance the better. In saying that, one is not adding anything to the idea of a reason for action. It is essential to the concept of reason that complete compliance is what it calls for, and that the closer one gets to it the better. That is what was argued for in the last chapter, and stated by the conformity principle.[3]

That much is implied by nothing more than the possibility of incomplete compliance, and the possibility of different degrees of compliance. If we deny that then, if I owe you £100 and do not have it, and therefore cannot do what I have reason to do I have no reason to give you the £60 that I do have. Of course, I would admit, I should give you £100, but why—given that I cannot—should I give you the £60? It is not what I have reason to do. But I do have a reason to do so. The reason to give you £100 is also a reason to give you £60, given the circumstances.

The difficulty is not in accepting the point but in applying it. Money is, other things being equal, an easy case. But is giving one shoe to a person to whom we owe a pair better than giving him none? It all depends, it may be better, it may be worse, or at any rate not better. Moreover, what appears like partial compliance may be doing something good of a different kind, which cannot count as partial compliance with the original reason at all. Suppose you promised a friend a ticket from London to his brother's wedding in Australia (to vary an example from the last chapter), and instead you give him a bus ticket to Dover. Dover is closer to Australia and a pleasant town. But getting there will not help him in getting to the wedding at all, and the pleasantness of spending time there has nothing to do with the original promise, and cannot count

---

[2] I will use 'conformity' and 'compliance' interchangeably. That is, I will not assume that 'complying' with reasons requires knowledge of the reasons, nor being motivated by them. Following a reason, on the other hand, is action for the reason (e.g. the love of another may be a reason for people who do not have the concept of a reason). See Chapter Four above.

[3] Being so close to a tautology it is difficult to speak of the conformity principle without circularity. In describing it in terms of how good degrees of conformity are I refer of course to acts being good because of their conformity (and not because of their reason-independent value that provides or constitutes reason to perform them). That does not avoid circularity, but makes the meaning more graspable.

as partial compliance with it.[4] Such cases far from undermining the general point that partial compliance is better than none reinforce it. They show how what constitutes partial compliance is sensitive to an understanding of the reason, and is partial compliance only if it is required by that reason.

Sometimes incomplete compliance results from complying fully with one reason while failing to comply with another. A parent of two children who looks after one, but neglects the other is failing to comply completely with reason, but his failure would have been greater had he neglected both (other things being equal, as for current purposes we put aside envy, possible hurt to the self-esteem of the neglected child, etc.) More generally, if one has two independent[5] reasons then complying with only one of them is not complete compliance with reason, for the other is not complied with (if the other were the only reason applying one would not be in complete compliance without complying with it, and how could the fact that one complied with another, independent, reason change that?). Yet, compliance with one is partial compliance, as can be seen by the fact that if the other no longer exists or no longer applies, having complied with the one will constitute complete compliance, whereas had one not complied with it one would not be in complete compliance. The same goes for any number of reasons. This too seems to me to be part of what is built into the notion of a reason for action.

The concept of complete compliance is vague. I use it as meaning that during the relevant period the agent completely conformed with each of the reasons that then applied to him. As I use it, it does not refer to how perfect were the agent's motives or intentions, nor to perfection in the manner of complying with reason (swiftly, etc.) so long as they do not mean that what was done was less than what there was reason to do. I do use it to apply to reasons to refrain from action (not to kill, etc.) These clarifications leave it vague. Some doubts about the concept are reflected in the parental example. I may prefer to have parents who, if they neglect their children at all, neglect all of them, rather than pick and choose. It may speak worse of their character that they pick and choose. However, in discussing complete compliance, this is irrelevant. A parent who neglects only one of his children would be neither a better person, nor a better parent, nor come closer to complete compliance with reason if, having grasped the point just made, he started neglecting his other children as well.

The principles of counting reasons are indeterminate over a vast range of cases. Often, of course, the individuation of reasons is important. It matters, e.g. in order to establish whether one reason derives from another, whether they are independent of each other, in order to understand their rationale, and sometimes in order to judge their stringency. However, often the way we individuate reasons is unimportant. What

---

[4] Some people regard any specific promise, e.g. to give you Kant's First Critique, as a promise to give something of that value, something which costs as much as Kant's book. They have similar ways of understanding non-voluntary duties. Believing these to be mistaken I disregard them here.

[5] Meaning that compliance with one does not affect the existence, application, or stringency of the other.

matters is that we comply with reason. It matters little whether we have a single reason or several. Do I have one reason to look after my children, or several, a separate reason to look after each one of them? Who cares? But then complying with each of the reasons for looking after this child or that brings me closer to complying with the one general reason of looking after my children, thus confirming the general principle that *for any reason applying, one is closer to complete compliance with reason if one complies with it than if one does not.*[6]

These observations show that the notion of degrees of compliance does not depend on the possibility of perfect compliance. Perfect compliance may be possible when debt repayment is considered, but—as was observed in the previous chapter—if perfect compliance means that nothing can be done that will improve compliance then perhaps there is no perfect compliance with the reasons parents have to care for their children. It may always be possible to do more for one's children. The notion that we require for our discussion is that of **degree of compliance**. That degree depends on three factors. When the reasons applying are independent and of equal importance the more reasons we comply with the closer we come to complete compliance. Our understanding of degree of compliance suggests, however, that it depends on the importance, as well as the number of reason we comply with, and the degree of compliance with each of them.

These observations also suggest, though it requires further argument to establish the point, that there is one overarching concept at work, namely what we have reason to do, and that separate independent reasons are by their nature contributory factors towards that, constituting what we have reason to do. For example, sometimes it is best, when we are unable to comply perfectly with all the reasons, to comply partially with all of them rather than completely with one and not at all with the others. If I cannot meet all my children's needs it is better to meet all their most essential needs, and leave some less essential needs unmet, rather than meet all the needs of one and none of the needs of the others, suggesting the presence of a general notion of conformity with reason to which conformity with each reason contributes. In all, degrees of compliance with reason depend on degrees of compliance with any single applying reason, the number of independently applying reasons one complies with, and their importance. As both the determination of degrees of compliance with single reasons and the ranking of the importance of reasons are very partial, degrees of compliance are often incommensurate.

How could it be otherwise? Assume independent reasons of equal stringency. Assume, to start with, that one has two reasons. Can it be other than that one would conform with reason if one conformed with each of them and will only partly conform if one conforms only with one? To deny that is in effect to claim that conforming with one reason rescinds the others, so that one is in complete conformity with reason

---

[6] It is no exception to this principle that if complying with it makes impossible complying with a more important reason one should comply with the latter.

having conformed with one only. But that means that the reasons are not independent of each other. Complying with one of the two reasons applying is complete compliance only if there are no independent reasons, a very implausible view.

This argument shows that complete conformity requires conforming with all the independent reasons that apply to one. A similar argument shows that, given our assumption of independence and equal stringency, complying with more brings one closer to complete compliance than complying with fewer: Assume that one has only two reasons. In that case conforming with two is closer to complete compliance than conforming with only one (because it is complete compliance). How can the appearance of another reason change that? Clearly once a third reason appears conforming with the previously existing two is no longer complete compliance with reason. But how can that change the relationship between complying with the one and with the two? How can it change the fact that complying with two is closer to complete compliance than complying with one? We know that for any number of reasons N, if there are no other reasons to comply with on this occasion then (1) complying with N is closer to complete compliance than complying with N minus 1, and (2) complying with N is complete compliance. Suppose that there are further reasons applying to the agent. That would invalidate (2), but how can it invalidate (1)? It does not seem to make sense that it does. These considerations do not show that degrees of compliance also depend on the relative importance of the applying reasons. If need be this dependence can be established via examples.

2. The core argument

That, then, is why the lifeguard would be at fault were he to save only one if he could save many. For the sake of the argument it is assumed that he has, for each drowning person, a reason to save him. Saving all is what he has reason to do. Saving one is only partial compliance with it. If he can comply fully he is at fault if he does not try. The more he saves the closer he is to complete compliance. If he cannot comply fully he should save as many as he can, and he is at fault if he does not try.

Is there no mistake? Surely he has reason to save only those he can save. If he saves the few he cannot save the many. Therefore, he has no reason to save them. This explains the difference between his saving one on the side where there is only one, and saving one only, where there are two near each other that he can save. In that last case if he saves one and stops he is at fault, for he could have saved the other as well. In the two directions case he can save only those in one direction. Once he sets out to save them he cannot save the others, and therefore has no reason to save them. Therefore, he is at fault only if he is at fault to set out in one direction rather than the other. But that, the argument goes, he is not, for either way he will save as many as he can.

This argument fails for two reasons. First, we sometimes have reason to do what we cannot. Finer discrimination is needed to show when inability negates reasons. Second, even if we waive this point the guard would be at fault were he to save the one rather than the many, for he would be at fault not to choose the direction of the many. Regarding any of the drowning people the guard has reason to save them. It is true that he cannot save all. So if there are three drowning people, his reason to save each of three, and at the outset he can save each of them, sums up as a reason to save two, never mind who. He can save two, has a reason to save them, and, as a result will have completely complied with reason (assuming he has no reason to do more than he can) were he to save two. Therefore, he ought to choose the direction of the many, and he is at fault if he does not. His voluntarily and knowingly rendering himself, by choosing the direction of the one, unable to save more than one is no excuse for failing to comply fully with reason (for a further discussion see Chapter Twelve).

So much for my core argument that numbers count. It is, of course, an argument that compliance with reason counts, and that means that for any independent reason that applies to agents they come closer to complete compliance if they conform with it than if they do not. As we saw this is sufficient to establish that numbers count in a very restricted class of cases. It does not follow that they do not count in any other way. I do not know of any general argument to establish this negative conclusion. It is not, however, implausible.

Contrast, e.g., reasons to perpetuate the Nation with reasons to save people. Presumably the only way to save the Nation is to save or protect people who do or will belong to it. However, it does not follow that the more people saved or protected the better. Possibly once a certain number of people are saved, or their life secured, there is no further point in saving or protecting more. That would no longer affect the survival of the Nation. It may even be that its survival will be safer with a smaller number of nationals dedicated to its perpetuation, than with a larger number who are more or less indifferent to it, and it may be that, once the threshold of adequacy has been achieved, dedication to the perpetuation of the Nation is in reverse proportion to the number of nationals. On these assumptions the single reason to perpetuate the Nation, if there is such a reason, will not necessarily show the linear sensitivity to numbers that the basic argument establishes regarding the number of equally important and independent reasons, and no alternative route to making numbers count appears on the horizon regarding this case.

Other examples may be more controversial. For example, does the reason we have to respect persons mean that we should strive to extend people's lives as far as possible? I do not believe that it does. Here the more the better does not follow from the argument offered above, nor is it a sensible conclusion to reach. You may disagree with this remark, but the lesson that what matters is what would be a greater degree of respect (the reason relevant in this case) is unaffected by such doubts. It all depends on the nature of the reasons involved. In this example it depends on how far the reasons of respect extend. If so then it is not implausible to think that numbers count only where that brings a higher degree of conformity with reason.

One reaction to the argument above is that it accomplishes nothing. It says, the objection runs, that numbers count if reasons say that they do. We know that. The question whether numbers count is the question whether reasons establish that they count, and the argument above does nothing to answer that question. Up to a point this is of course true. But there is something more to the argument than that. It establishes that to the degree that reasons can be individuated and counted numbers must count, for the number of reasons matters to achieve full conformity with reason.

Just as some may suspect that the argument above does not go far enough so others will fear that it goes too far. Does it not yield the conclusion that we should have two children rather than one? Does it not entail that we should kill one person to use his kidneys to save two? These are natural concerns. But they do not necessarily show that there is anything wrong with the argument I outlined. They may dissolve once we understand correctly the reasons which seem to give rise to them. Alternatively, they may be resolved by the presence of additional factors and principles, ones we have not considered. Scanlon draws on such additional principles.

3. The aims of Contractualism

To examine his way with aggregation, with the ways numbers count, we need to consider briefly the aims of Contractualism. As he sees it Contractualism contributes in several, interrelated ways. It establishes a connection between wrong-making reasons[7] and a special kind of motivation, the motivation to act on principles that similarly motivated people cannot reasonably reject. It explains what unifies a central area of morality, that of wrong-making reasons. It provides a common focus for thought, and a framework for arguments on these matters. But Contractualist arguments do more than explain independently existing reasons. They constitute wrong-making reasons. Contractualist arguments are the reasons why certain actions are owed to others, and other actions are wrong.[8] This makes Contractualism a constructivist theory.

This, it is sometimes thought, marks clear water between Contractualist and other accounts of reasons. But the difference is easily exaggerated. Some, myself included, believe that reasons (and values) are inherently intelligible, that it is possible to explain

---

[7] Scanlon identifies his subject in two ways: an account of what we owe to each other and an account of moral wrong-making reasons. I debate its standing as an account of wrong-making reasons. The appendix to this chapter explains why it is not a successful account of what we owe to each other.

[8] Replying to Thomson, Scanlon writes: 'the contractualist formula…is intended as an account of what it is for an act to be wrong. What *makes* an act wrong are the properties that would make any principle that allow [sic] it one that it would be reasonable to reject' (*What We Owe*, 391 n. 21). Naturally, he is not saying that 'wrong' means 'ruled out by a principle that no one can reasonably reject'. But neither is he saying that the formula merely theoretically classifies actions we should not do into wrong ones and, say, merely ill-advised ones. For Scanlon, a wrong-making reason defeats reasons of all other kinds. There are, therefore, specific wrong-making reasons. His way of establishing such reasons is by arguments using the Contractualist formula. Hence the most abstract wrong-making-reason is that the action is prohibited by a principle to which no one can reasonably object, and 'this is torture', e.g., instantiates it in particular circumstances. They relate in the way that, e.g., if the only moral principle is to promote the interests of the state, promoting the interests of the state, the most abstract moral reason, relates to not-spying, a concrete reason instantiating it in particular circumstances.

why any specific reason is a reason. When the thesis about the intelligibility of reasons is taken to imply that explanations are always available, it too asserts a constitutive relationship between explanations and reasons, for according to it there are no reasons that cannot be explained. The difference is that constructivists alone hold that there is a master argument that establishes the validity of all moral reasons (or whichever class of reasons one is constructivist about). It alone, or its exemplifications, are reasons of that kind. The thesis about the intelligibility of reasons does not privilege any form of explanation, and is acceptable to those who doubt that one master argument is either available, or necessary to show of any moral reason that it is a reason.

Scanlon may accept the intelligibility of reasons generally. But he thinks that one form of argument has a privileged position in establishing what we owe each other. It is not obvious what is the special privilege. Is it that no other argument can explain what is wrong with rape, or cruelty, or deceit, and so on? That implies either that no one understood what is wrong with such acts until *What We Owe to Each Other*, or at least until Kant, the first constructivist, or that those who did understand were constructivists *manqués*.[9] If there are other explanations for moral reasons then Contractualism does not establish the existence of reasons that cannot be established some other way. Rather, it provides additional arguments for them, arguments that are perhaps the only ones to explain why those reasons are ones we owe each other, and are the only ones that provide a full, or 'deep' understanding of why we owe each other what we do. If I am right then Contractualism claims not so much to improve our knowledge of moral wrongs as to deepen our understanding.

This modesty may mislead. While it allows for knowledge of moral right and wrong even by people who reject Contractualism, their views are sound only if there are Contractualist arguments that vindicate them. Contractualist arguments are the ultimate arbiter of what we owe each other. This means that Contractualism is successful only if it has the resources to establish moral conclusions, and to do so independently of non-contractualist arguments or reasons. Even before *What We Owe to Each Other* was published critics alleged that it does not. In the book Scanlon squarely faces the objection:

Deciding whether an action is right or wrong requires a substantive judgment…about whether certain objections to possible moral principles would be reasonable….a judgment about the suitability of certain principles to serve as the basis of mutual recognition and accommodation…. (T)he idea of what would be reasonable…is an idea with moral content. This moral content…invites the charge of circularity. By basing itself on reasonableness, it may be charged, a theory builds in moral elements at the start….[E]verything we are to get out of it at the end we must put in at the beginning as part of the moral content of reasonableness. (ibid. 194)[10]

---

[9] A third option, that they understood through some intuition that they could not articulate, is ruled out by Scanlon's belief that moral views always come with beliefs in reasons for them: *What We Owe*, 198.

[10] For an early version of the objection see Pettit, *The Common Mind* (Oxford: OUP, 1993), 297–302. Pogge's 'What We Can Reasonably Reject' (in Sosa and Villanueva (eds.), *Philosophical Issues* 11 (2001),

We see how serious this difficulty is when considering how the Contractualist test works: A principle is proposed, which either permits or prohibits behaving in a certain way, say doing A. It is valid if and only if it passes the Contractualist test which pits it against all possible objections. It does not matter whether these objections are actually advanced by anyone. The principle is valid if and only if no one *can* reasonably object to it, that is only if none of the possible objections is reasonable. Whether the possible objections are reasonable, and justify rejecting the proposed principle, depends on the ways in which people would be burdened by forbidding or permitting an action. Suppose that, compared to the objections to a permissive principle, the objections to the prohibition that its denial entails are not significant. That would establish that it is reasonable to reject the permissive principle, and that the prohibitive principle is valid (*What We Owe*, 195). This test makes the theory Contractualist: any principle is vetoed if there is a reasonable objection someone can raise. The suspicion that the test renders the theory vacuous, or 'circular', is that what is reasonable is, as Scanlon is aware, a moral matter.

Scanlon is clear that broad areas of morality lie beyond the boundaries of Contractualism.[11] The suspect feature of Contractualism is not that. It is that its test yields results only by presupposing moral views that can only be established independently of it. Is it not the case that those results can be derived from these premises independently of the Contractualist test? Consider Scanlon's discussion of the relevance of the likelihood of burdens and benefits (*What We Owe*, 206–9). He rejects the suggestion that in determining the reasonableness of possible objections to a principle the probability that any particular individual will benefit or be burdened should be ignored (to avoid bias favouring or against that person), but that the percentage of the population likely to benefit or be burdened should be taken into account. He rejects the suggestion because it 'leads to unacceptable results', for 'a contractualist would want to keep open the possibility that [a principle imposing severe hardship on a few for the benefit of many] could be reasonably rejected' (ibid. 208–9). In brief, you determine the moral outcome in some non-contractualist way, and shape the test to yield the right conclusion, the one you started from, except that now it receives the imprimatur of having been established by the Contractualist test.[12]

118–47) shows the difficulties Contractualism encounters should one try to use it to establish concrete moral conclusions, without importing moral premises independently established.

[11] *What We Owe*, 171–87. Scanlon's observation that 'contractualism...is not meant to characterise everything that can be called "moral" but only that part of the moral sphere that is marked out by certain specific ideas of right and wrong' is meant to address three different cases: (1) false beliefs about what is moral or immoral, e.g., that masturbation is immoral; (2) cases falling outside Contractualism proper, but that can be covered by certain extensions of it (the 'trusteeship' idea, p. 183); (3) cases of moral concern lying outside the scope of the Contractualist test.

[12] Does not the reference to 'a contractualist' in the quote suggest that there are Contractualist arguments to that conclusion? None is provided. Scanlon's subtle discussion shows that the principle that yields the outcomes that he, for reasons not given, believes are right, is consistent with Contractualism, not that the alternatives are inconsistent with it. They simply do not deliver the wished-for results.

Whatever we think of his treatment of this example, it does not establish that relying on pre-established moral claims renders Contractualism vacuous. It is vacuous if what you get out of it is what you put in as premises, without Contractualism itself making a difference to our moral conclusions. Michael Ridge argued that Contractualism is not merely an 'unhelpful epicycle' because it makes a difference by barring certain considerations from affecting the outcome of the Contractualist test. Scanlon, he claims, does not allow all moral considerations to bear on what objections are reasonable, only agent-relative objections do.[13]

Ridge's suggestion misinterprets Scanlon's observation that 'impersonal reasons do not, themselves, provide grounds for reasonably rejecting a principle' (*What We Owe*, 220). Scanlon's point is that right and wrong are determined by considerations affecting people (and not mountains, or the American condor). He does not, nor should he mean that right and wrong are determined by agent-relative considerations only. People are affected by the impact on them of agent-neutral considerations, and there is no justification to deny the reasonableness of objections based on such facts. To be sure every person can rely only on the effect a principle would have on him. If some principle will, e.g. reduce my educational opportunities, which is a harm because of the agent-neutral value of education, my objection must relate only to my interest in education, and has the weight due to my interest alone, and not to other people's interest in education. But would this save Contractualism from the charge of vacuousness? As we saw, Contractualism does not deem every setback to a person's interests or concerns as grounding a reasonable objection. Whether they ground reasonable objections depends on a comparison of the burdens a principle imposes compared with the burdens imposed by its rejection (ibid. 195). Hence there is no reason to think that the limitation of the grounds for reasonable objection to personal reasons would affect the outcome, *unless the Contractualist treatment of aggregation affects the outcome.* The success of Contractualism depends on the success of its treatment of aggregation.

4. Contractualist aggregation—the positive argument

That seems to be Scanlon's own view. His reply to the charge that his theory 'builds in moral elements at the start....[E]verything we are to get out of it [the theory] at the end we must put in at the beginning as part of the moral content of reasonableness' lies in the way all Contractualism privileges the reasons of individuals. Contractualism insists

that the justifiability of a moral principle depends only on various *individuals'* reasons for objecting to that principle and alternatives to it. This feature is central to the guiding idea of contractualism and is also what enables it to provide a clear alternative to utilitarianism and other forms of consequentialism. (*What We Owe*, 229)

---

[13] 'Saving Scanlon: Contractualism and Agent-Relativity', *Journal of Political Philosophy* 9 (2001), 472.

Of course, non-contractualists too take account of the concerns of individuals. Does Scanlon privilege each person's reason in a way non-contractualists do not? He does not rely on any claim that a person has special authority regarding how things are normatively from his point of view. His general view suggests that people have no such authority regarding at least some of their own reasons; e.g., they may reasonably object to principles that exempt some people from general duties arbitrarily, and therefore unfairly, even when the exemption does not disadvantage them. In such cases any person, including the people favoured by the principle, can know that the principle is open to that objection, and that it is open to the objection from the point of view of other people as well. No one has special authority in the matter.

Moreover, as this example shows, Scanlon, unlike some Contractualists, does not wish to derive moral reasons from considerations of individuals' well-being. Nor does he give individuals who have sound reasons against a principle a veto over it, as Contractualists generally do. The reasons they have must be considered against reasons for the principle that they and others may also have. Whether anyone has a reasonable objection to a principle depends not only on his or her reasons against it, but on some comparison between their reasons against and the reasons for the principle, given the available alternatives.

In what way, then, does Scanlon privilege individuals' reasons? The answer lies in his treatment of aggregation. Contractualism is not so much an account of moral reasons, as an account of moral aggregation. It is a thesis about the ways in which numbers do and do not determine the outcome of moral conflicts. This is the implication of the fact that Scanlon's treatment of aggregation is his one reply to the charge of vacuity. Scanlon's interest in aggregation was the motive for his initial interest in Contractualism.[14] His success in accounting for aggregation is the key to the success or failure of *What We Owe to Each Other*.

Scanlon aims to establish that Contractualism would allow for aggregation in some cases and not in others. Here is his argument that 'in cases in which one has a duty of [rescue]…and one has to choose between preventing a certain level of injury to either a larger or a smaller number' (*What We Owe*, 232) one must prevent the harm to the larger number. Imagine that the matter is saving life, and the choice is between a group of two and a single person. A principle permitting the rescuer to save the single person ignores the value of saving the life of some people:

{1} Either member of the larger group might complain that this principle did not take account of the value of saving his life, since it permits the agent to decide what to do in the very same way that it would have permitted had he not been present at all, and there was only one person in each group. {2} The fate of the single person is obviously being given positive weight, he might argue, since if that person were not threatened then the agent would have been required to save the two. And the fact that there is one other person who can be saved if and only if the first

---

[14] See Scanlon, 'Preference and Urgency', *Journal of Philosophy* 72 (1975), 655; 'Contractualism and Utilitarianism', in A. Sen and B. Williams (eds.), *Utilitarianism and Beyond* (Cambridge: CUP, 1982), 103.

person is not saved is being given positive weight to balance the value of saving the one. {3} The presence of the additional person, however, makes no difference to what the agent is required to do or to how she is required to go about deciding what to do. {4} This is unacceptable, the person might argue, since his life should be given the same moral significance as anyone else's in this situation (which is, by stipulation, a situation in which no one has a special moral claim). [*Endnote omitted*]

{5}…The conclusion…is that any principle dealing with cases of this kind would be reasonably rejected if it did not require agents to treat the claims of each person who could be saved as having the same moral force. Since there is, we are supposing, a positive duty to save in cases in which only one person is present, this means that any nonrejectable principle must direct an agent to recognise a positive reason for saving each person. Since a second reason of this kind can balance the first—turning a situation in which one must save one into one in which it is permissible to save either of two people—the reason presented by the needs of a second person in one of these two groups must at least have the power to break this tie. (ibid.—numbers between { } added)

Needless to say the conclusion (point {5}) is similar to my conclusions in Section 2. Its gist, denuded of its Contractualist cladding, is that we have separate reasons to save each person. Where we part company is in the reasons for this conclusion, and from it to the next step, namely that one must save the two rather than the one.

Scanlon is clearly right in {4}, special status or relationships having been excluded by stipulation it follows that the moral significance of each person's life is the same. Scanlon takes this to imply that the value of each person's life must make a 'difference to what the agent is required to do or to how she is required to go about deciding what to do' on every occasion affecting people ({3}, and also {1}). This amounts to denying that a reason is a reason unless it should make a difference to the outcome of deliberation or to the manner of decision (whatever that may mean) on each occasion to which it applies.

But if so how can Scanlon advance {2}? If I am one of the two, he says, I can complain that my life is not given any value by the permissive principle, while maintaining that the life of the single person is given value. How? His presence turns the agent's duty to save the two into a permission to save either the single person or the two. But in objecting to the permissive principle I deny that the single person's life is entitled to have that effect. I claim that his presence makes no difference, and there is a duty to save the two rather than him, as there would be if he were not there. His situation under the correct principle is exactly like mine under the permissive principle.[15]

---

[15] Even more so: Scanlon's {1} runs into the following apparent paradox: According to him both I and the other person in the group of two have a valid complaint that our lives were not taken to be of value. But if neither of our lives is valuable it follows that only the single person's life is taken to be valuable and the resulting principle should be a duty to save him. No such apparent paradox affects the argument that under the correct principle the single person's life makes no difference to either outcome or mode of deliberation.

There is no reason to expect a reason to affect either outcome or manner of decision in every case. If a house is on fire, with people inside who can be saved only by putting out the fire, it matters not how many there are. If I save one I save all. One cannot object that I did not take the life of each person to be of value, simply because I knew that it makes no difference to the outcome.

Another problem with the argument turns on the requirement to take each person's life to be of equal value. It is valid, but it does not imply that the value of people's life yields a reason to save them. This is evident once we realize that the permissive principle complies with the requirement. It is consistent with every person's life being such that if it is threatened it should be rescued unless doing so would mean not saving at least one other, in which case respect for each of the endangered lives requires saving at least one. Here every person's life is given a positive and an equal value, but not enough to yield an outright reason to save him or her. Without such reason it is not possible to explain why the correct principle is correct. This, as we saw, is Scanlon's own view.

This point is of some moment, for it rebuts one reason for preferring Scanlon's argument for the principle to mine. I built my argument on the assumption that there is value to human life, and a reason to save lives. I did not argue for these assumptions.[16] Does not Scanlon plug the omission with a Contractualist argument? Unfortunately not. He gives no argument to show that there is a reason to save. That is assumed. His argument is for the equality of the value of people's life. And that equality is established simply by *the assumption* that the people involved have no special moral claims.

I conclude that this argument (*What We Owe*, 231–4) fails to establish that the correct principle is required by Contractualism. In any case there is nothing Contractualist about the argument, except its terminology (one person or another objecting). The whole passage can be recast in non-contractualist terms without losing any of its content or force. This may show that Scanlon's views and mine are closer than may otherwise appear, except that I do not rely on the unhelpful equality argument.

My comments so far do not challenge the Contractualist enterprise. As mentioned already, Contractualism must presuppose ways of dealing with aggregation independent of it. It is natural to assume that they apply to Contractualist reasons as well, unless blocked by Contractualist arguments. Scanlon's argument criticized above aims to show that Contractualism does not go too far in blocking aggregation. To do this Scanlon need not establish Contractualist reasons for aggregation (as he aims to do). It is enough for him to show that Contractualism does not block sensible aggregative moves sanctioned independently of it. I agree that it does not. The question is, does it block any aggregative moves? Does it succeed in ruling out aggregation where aggregation should be ruled out?

---

[16] I offered some arguments in *Value, Respect and Attachment* (Cambridge: CUP, 2001), ch. 4.

5. Contractualism against aggregation

Scanlon's guiding principle regarding aggregation is:

In situations in which aid is required and in which one must choose between aiding a larger or a smaller number of people all of whom face harms of comparable moral importance, one must aid the larger number. (*What We Owe*, 238)

It is this principle that requires the rescue of the two rather than the one, and it is this principle that, I claimed, is not established by Scanlon through a Contractualist argument, an argument not available to non-contractualists. The principle itself is, I believe, sound, but it does not block any form of aggregation. To block all other forms of aggregation the most sensible **anti-aggregation principle** would be:

> In situations in which aid is required and in which one must choose between aiding a larger or a smaller number of people who face harms that are not of comparable moral importance numbers do not matter, and one must aid those facing the harm of greater moral importance, even if this means not aiding a larger number of people facing harms of a smaller moral importance.

I am not sure whether this principle is sound, nor is Scanlon.[17] But my interest is not in its merits, but only in the question whether Contractualist arguments can establish it, and can do so without begging the crucial questions. To explain my doubts I need do no more than follow Scanlon's own discussion.

The principle relies on a classification of the moral importance of different harms, and Scanlon implicitly acknowledges that Contractualism, while presupposing such a classification, contributes nothing to establish it. The very important moral question of what matters and how much, morally speaking, is one to which Contractualism itself has no answer. Contractualism does, however, aim to help with aggregation. One objection to the anti-aggregation principle which Scanlon considers is:

It may seem that there are harms such that, although it would not be permissible to save one person from this harm rather than to save someone from drowning, nonetheless an agent would be permitted, perhaps even required, to prevent a very large number of people from suffering it, even if that meant that she would be unable to save a drowning person....perhaps blindness and total paralysis are examples of such harms. (*What We Owe*, 239)

Scanlon does not feel able to reject the view that in a choice between saving many from paralysis or one from death it is permitted, or even required to save the many. To accommodate this with Contractualism he feels that he has to reject the **anti-aggregation principle** in favour of weaker principles barring impermissible aggregation. He considers a distinction between harms by their relevance to each other:

---

[17] The nearest he comes to this is in a less explicit and apparently narrower formulation: 'Contractualism does not...permit one to save a larger number of people from minor harms rather than a smaller number who face much more serious injuries' (*What We Owe*, 238).

If one harm, though not as serious as another, is nonetheless serious enough to be morally 'relevant' to it, then it is appropriate, in deciding whether to prevent more serious harms at the cost of not being able to prevent a greater number of less serious ones, to take into account the number of harms involved on each side. But if one harm is not only less serious than, but not even 'relevant to', some greater one, then we do not need to take the number of people who would suffer these two harms into account. (ibid. 239–40)

Can this suggestion be justified on Contractualist grounds? Perhaps, he says, the person facing paralysis could reasonably reject a principle requiring saving a single life rather than a large number of people from paralysis on the ground that

it did not give proper consideration to his admittedly less serious, but still morally relevant, loss. One might then argue that such an individual's claim to have his or her harm taken into account can be met only by a principle that is sensitive to the numbers of people involved on each side. I am not certain how such an argument would go, but it does not seem to me to be excluded in advance by the general idea of contractualism. (ibid. 240–1)

And that is the problem. The problem is that Scanlon's Contractualism does not exclude arguments of that form. It means that a person can object to a principle if, by disallowing aggregation where it is required, the principle does not give that person's harm the weight or role that it merits. And that means that the problem of aggregation has to be solved first, and Contractualist arguments far from contributing to its solution cannot be deployed until it is solved.

Scanlon's conclusion (*What We Owe*, 241) is plausible. All he claims is that the Contractualist position on aggregation maintains that only the legitimate concern of individuals can count in deciding the soundness of moral principles. If that is meant to rule out the thought that 'morality is most fundamentally concerned with producing the greatest possible benefit' (ibid.) one should agree, but wonder whether Contractualism helps in establishing the claim.

It may be that Scanlon's line of thought, based on distinguishing broad categories of moral importance of harms and benefits, and between harms that are relevant and those that are irrelevant to other harms points in the right (non-contractualist) direction. It may set relevant questions when considering whether to help the few or the many. Contractualism, however, offers no help in answering them.

Appendix: On what we owe to each other

Scanlon denies not only that his Contractualism is an account of morality, but also that it is an account of what is morally right and wrong. He says that he 'offers an argument for establishing that an action is wrong in one particular way (a violation of what we owe to each other)'.[18] In saying this he shows that he takes the category of what we

---

[18] Scanlon's reply to various comments on his work, including mine, in P. Stratton-Lake (ed.), *On What We Owe to Each Other* (Oxford: Blackwell, 2004), 123 at 127.

owe to each other to be important in itself, and his Contractualist theory to be (among other things) an account of that category. In this he fails for reasons I will briefly outline.

Is the question 'what do we owe to each other?' the same as 'what do we owe others?' Perhaps not. Perhaps it applies only to a class of reciprocal duties, such that if I owe you something you owe me something reciprocally. While there is interest in this narrow class of reciprocal duties, for example in duties to act in ways favouring some people the existence of which is conditional on those people having the same duties towards us, or on those people complying with their duties towards us, Scanlon's interest was not confined to duties that are reciprocal in any narrow sense.

So what, typically, do we owe to others?[19] Several writers think that we owe a duty to someone if the duty is the one correlated to a right held by that person. Briefly, and perhaps rather crudely put, the thought is that rights, at least some rights, are the grounds of duties, duties to comply with the right. So, I have a duty not to kill you because you have a right to life, I have a duty to pay your wages on time because as my employee you have a right that I do so, etc. Duties that are grounded in rights are called 'directed duties': I have them towards the right-holder, and that is what is meant when saying that they are owed to the right-holder.

If that is so then what we owe to each other is far from capturing that part of morality that deals with the way the existence, conduct, interests of some people, or the possibility of their existence, affects what duties people have. Here are some such duties that do not correspond to a right: a duty not to litter the streets, a duty to give to charity, a duty not to destroy works of art, and indeed not wantonly to destroy (wantonly meaning other than by way of consuming it—as when we eat food—or using it) anything that can be of value to others. Furthermore some duties against discrimination belong here. An employer's duty not to turn down a job candidate on grounds of race corresponds to that candidate's right not to be excluded on such grounds. But the employer's duty not to draft job advertisements in ways which de facto disadvantage members of some race (indirect discrimination) does not correspond to anyone's right against that employer.

These duties neither correspond to rights nor are they duties that we owe to others. But there are duties that we owe others even though they do not correspond to rights.[20] Surprisingly they are not the kind of duties Contractualism focuses on. One category of duties owed to others are duties of gratitude, but they do not correspond to a right of the people to whom they are owed. I may have a duty to offer to compensate

---

[19] If we owe things (books, money) or attitudes (friendliness, respect) or emotions (love) and the like then we have duties to give them to or to have them towards those to whom they are owed. And in such cases the duties we have are also duties we owe to those others.

[20] Arguably, there are also duties that correspond to rights but where it is odd to think of them as owed to the right-holder. For example: assume that a big corporation, or a billionaire residing in London owns a million acres of land in Mongolia. I have a duty neither to trespass on the land (say, to shorten my way home from the shops) nor to pick an apple growing on it. But it is odd to think that I owe that duty to the owner, be it a corporation, the state, or an individual. That a duty is owed to someone indicates a more direct, and most often a personal connection.

someone who helped me out, but that person does not have a right to the compensation (and under some circumstances it would be unseemly of him to accept it). Another class of duties owed to others includes many duties among family members. I may have a duty to inquire after the health of my aunt, or to offer to do her shopping when she is unwell, without her having a right that I do so.

It would seem that duties we owe others arise in three (overlapping) ways: they may be the result of commitments or undertakings, the product of relationships, or debts of gratitude. They presuppose some kind of a personal relationship. But it is not for me to offer an account of what we owe each other. My purpose was merely to point out that Scanlon's Contractualism, as expressed in his writings, clearly aims to apply also to duties other than those we owe each other, and it is doubtful that it aims to apply to all the duties we owe each other, properly understood.

11

Promoting Value?

The last two chapters argued that there is a clear (though not uncontroversial) way in which numbers count. According to the conformity principle they count when more gets us closer to perfectly conforming to reasons that apply to us. Add to that the view that underlies so much of the discussion at least from Chapter Four on, namely that the reasons for an action are the valuable aspects of that action (the reasons against it being its bad features, including its opportunity cost) and it may appear that there is no escape from the very controversial view that can be formulated as:

The only thing we have reason to do is to promote value.[1]

I will call it **the promotion of value** thesis (or principle), **PV** for short.

Variants of the principle are widespread. In recent times something like **PV** was regarded by many as obviously true. Even those who rejected it often acknowledged its power and appeal.[2] Opposition to the thesis triggered some influential developments in the writings on practical reason over the last forty years or so. Contemporary Con-tractualism,[3] for example, arose as a way of rebutting it.

This chapter argues against **PV**, or more accurately, against the thought that it follows from the fact that ultimately reasons are provided by the value of actions. Furthermore, it will be argued that no version of **PV** that I can think of is consistent with various reasons for action whose existence is known to us.

1. Background

I have been assuming that

Reasons for action are such reasons by being facts that establish that the action has some value.[4]

---

[1] I take the natural reading of this to say more than that one should do only what is good, but rather that one should do what is most good, or something like that, as will be explained below.

[2] See Scanlon, 'Utilitarianism and Contractualism', in B. Williams and J. J. C. Smart (eds.), *Utilitarianism: For and Against* (Cambridge: CUP, 1973).

[3] In the hands of both J. Rawls (*A Theory of Justice* (Cambridge, Mass.: Harvard UP, 1971)) and T. Scanlon (*What We Owe to Each Other* (Cambridge: Harvard UP, 1998)). The same is true of contractarians of other ilks, e.g. D. Gauthier's *Morals by Agreement* (Oxford: OUP, 1986).

[4] Cf. Chapter Four, above.

Call this the **reason/value** *nexus*.

Actions have value in virtue of value properties that they possess. Some actions are good because they have some deontic properties: It is good to pay your debts because doing so is doing what one has a duty to do. Are deontic properties of actions non-derivative, or do they in turn derive from some other values? For example, the duty to pay one's debt may derive from the value of reliably following rules that impose such duties, that value being that compliance tends to enhance people's powers by increasing their resources.[5] Needless to say, it will not be possible to examine here the forms derivations can take, nor to discuss whether values are ultimately the only underived sources of reasons. I will proceed on the assumption (**the constitutive assumption**) that

(a) deontic properties ultimately derive from value, but that
(b) there are cases in which deontic properties are irreducible constituent parts of some values.

For example, I assume that friendship is in part constituted by duties friends owe each other, and that those duties are valid (binding) because friendship is a valuable relationship (though not all its instances are). Some may support versions of **PV** that are inconsistent with that view, and for them what follows begs the question. But not all promoters of value would object to the constitutive assumption.[6]

Some writers on practical reason assume that an adequate account must entail that whenever reasons conflict, one (or one set of non-conflicting reasons) prevails, defeating all the others. This view is sometimes known as the one right answer thesis. Adding it to **PV** suggests that in every choice among actions one and only one is supported by an undefeated reason, and that action promotes value to a greater degree than any of its alternatives. The one right answer thesis appears natural to those who think of reasons as constructed to serve some practical goal, but does not fit well with any form of 'realism' about reasons, namely with any view that takes the reasons we have to be a feature of the world we live in. 'Realist' views do not have the resources to assure one that unresolved conflicts do not obtain. It all depends on how things turn out in the world. Rejecting the right answer thesis means that if conflicts regularly remain unresolved, in the sense that the reasons for more than one of the incompatible but available options are undefeated, it is often less natural to describe actions that conform to undefeated reasons as promoting value. They do not promote it more than their undefeated alternatives, and there are—according to this view—many such alternatives in most choice situations.

---

[5] I will assume that both the underived value and the duties etc. derived from it are reasons for action. For an analysis of the way rules issued by legitimate authority function see *Between Authority and Interpretation* (Oxford: OUP, 2009), ch. 8.

[6] e.g., A. Sen seems to support a form of Consequentialism that allows for ultimate and non-derivative instances of deontic properties: 'Rights and Agency', *Philosophy & Public Affairs* 11 (1982), 3.

In previous writings[7] I emphasized the prevalence of unresolved conflicts, and of choices not determined by reasons. In particular I tried to show how most ordinary decisions are taken in the face of incommensurable reasons. My discussion this time will not rely on these factors, though it reinforces the conclusions reached there.

The view examined in the rest of the chapter is a version of the promotion of value principle that is consistent with the constitutive assumption and with widespread incommensurabilities, a view that understands **PV** to entail maximization:

> **The maximization thesis:** A reason for action is undefeated only if and because, in the circumstances, the action for which it is a reason is the action that, of all available alternatives, will best promote value, where that is measured by a balance of value gained or likely to be gained by it against the value lost or likely to be lost because of it.

The views commonly identified as upholding maximization can be, and often are, expressed in different terms. Indeed in the course of the chapter I will explore alternative ways of understanding maximization. There are others. I claim nothing more than that the theses here discussed are sometimes endorsed, and are plausible enough to merit consideration.

A basic principle, embedded in our concept of reason, says that one should in one's actions conform to the better reason. That is

> **PR1:** It is irrational knowingly to act or try to act so that one's action (if successful) conforms to a less good reason, being aware of one's ability to act so as to conform to a better one.

Related is the principle saying:

> **PR2:** When facing a conflict of reasons Reason requires that action that conforms to the better reason.

These principles have nothing to do with the promotion or maximization of value. They do not even presuppose any relationship between value and reasons. Yet they may appear to compel maximization in a few easy steps. For example it may be thought that the following are derivable if one adds a few indisputable premises:

> *First*, when there are several reasons for the same action their combined weight is greater than the weight of either.
> *Second*, the stringency of any reason for any action is proportionate to the value that the feature the presence of which constitutes the reason confers on the action for which it is a reason.
> *Conclusion*: Practical Reason requires promoting value, namely only acts that promote value conform to the reasons that agents have.

---

[7] See in particular *The Morality of Freedom* (Oxford: OUP, 1986), ch. 13, and *Engaging Reason* (Oxford: OUP, 1999), chs. 3 and 4.

Assuming the reason/value *nexus* it is plausible to accept a modified version of the second premise. First, to be true, 'proportionate to the value' must mean 'proportionate to the importance of the value'. It is far from clear whether importance can be understood quantitatively. Let us assume that the twins' love for each other is the most valuable aspect of their life, but 'how much value does it have?' is not a meaningful question. Second, factors other than the importance of the value may affect the force of the reason it provides. For example, Chapter Six argued that the probabilities of valuable outcomes also affect the force of reasons.

The first premise, which means that the combined weight of two reasons for the same action is greater than the weight of either of them, is false, and those who accept the promotion of value thesis are almost always careful to reject it. The reasons for its rejection show that the better reason principle is neither itself a principle of aggregation, nor does it entail aggregation, at least not if the entailment relies on the first premise. Had the premise been true, maximization would have been not a moral or evaluative belief, but a requirement of reason, a condition of rationality. The rejection of the first premise denies maximizers one argument for that conclusion.

Imagine that I have reason to go to Paddington station to catch a train to Birmingham where I am due to lecture later today, and that I also have another reason to go to Paddington, to catch a train to Oxford where a friend is arriving from abroad for the day. However, I cannot both meet my friend and get to Birmingham for my lecture.[8] The two reasons to go to Paddington derive from two conflicting source reasons. Hence the force (strength, stringency, weight, etc.) of my overall reason to go to Paddington is no greater than the force of the weightier of the two reasons to go there. It appears, therefore, that the first premise applies only to reasons that do not derive from conflicting reasons.[9] But does it apply to them without further restriction?

Imagine that I have a headache and I have reason to go to the pharmacy, buy aspirin and take it. I also have reason to take an Advil tablet, and therefore I have another reason to go to the pharmacy, i.e. to get Advil. The reason to take Advil and the reason to take aspirin do not conflict: I can take both. But I have no reason to do so. I will assume that taking one of them will yield all the benefits that can be expected. Therefore there is no advantage in taking both. The situation is typical of cases where there are various ways, not necessarily equally satisfactory, of conforming to a reason. We then have reason to adopt each one of them, though some of them may be better than the others. Once we successfully conform, one way or another, with the root reason the reasons to pursue it in other ways lapse. The various reasons to pursue the means for satisfying the root reason are dependent reasons. Conforming to one makes the others lapse. Dependent reasons provide another exception to the first

---

[8] And the trains will depart shortly so no further information can become available in time to affect the case.

[9] I ignore the impact of the possibility, where it exists, that due to change in circumstances the conflict may disappear.

premise. For our purposes we can take one reason to be dependent on another if conformity with the second cancels the first. If one has several reasons for taking the same action then the overall force of one's reasons to take that action is a positive function of them only if they are independent reasons, which do not derive from conflicting reasons.

The interesting lesson from these examples is that, since whether or not reasons are independent of each other in the sense explained depends on moral or other evaluative considerations, the first premise cannot be amended to yield an informative formal principle applying to all reasons for action. Here is an example that illustrates the point. Think of a small community, say a family, and of reasons applying only to its members. Both of us are members. I have reason to help you and also a conflicting reason to buy myself a CD. Are they independent? They appear to be. But suppose that given that I have the conflicting reason to buy a CD, which is a reason of a kind that I am known within the community to have, if I buy myself a CD someone else will help you, and because this is so, once I buy the CD I no longer have a reason to help you. Does that undermine their independence? Does my reason to help you depend on my reason for buying a CD because if I buy myself a CD I no longer have a reason to help?

Of course, the characterization of dependence among reasons that I gave is too vague and needs tightening. We can make it more precise so that the two reasons in the example will turn out to be dependent if and only if the fact that, given that I have a reason to buy a CD, someone else will help you if I do not is sufficient to establish that I am not at fault for not helping you myself. Otherwise they are independent. If the reasons in the example are dependent, the first premise does not apply to them, and the principle of maximization does not apply.

Once the characterization of dependence is made precise the resulting revised first premise may turn out to be a principle of practical rationality. But it will not be a principle that applies to all reasons for action. It turns out to apply only to some such reasons, and whether it applies to any pair of reasons is a matter of substantive moral or evaluative judgement. Possibly regarding reasons to which the principle applies maximization reigns (I will question that later), but whether any kinds of reasons are subject to maximization is a moral or evaluative question.

In fact, even when revised as suggested, the first premise is subject to additional exceptions. I will give but one example: We have reasons not to kill people, and not to rape them, deriving, I will assume, from a duty of respect for people, which is rooted in the fact that people are valuable in themselves.[10] We also have reasons not to kill and not to rape deriving from the fact that the law of our countries, and I will assume it to be a legitimate, morally binding law, forbids murder and rape (as well as an additional reason deriving from the penalties specified for murder and for rape). But the existence

[10] See my account of duties of respect in ch. 4 of *Value, Respect and Attachment* (Cambridge: CUP, 2000).

of legal reasons against murder or against rape does not make my reason not to murder or not to rape more stringent than it would have been without it.

The same applies to some promises. If I promise not to murder or not to rape someone I have no greater reason not to do so than I had before. To make the case more vivid imagine a country where the law permits killing or raping retirees. When I visit that country (and am not subject to the law of my country) I have as much reason to refrain from killing or raping retirees as I have when at home. The absence of a legal reason not to kill retirees makes no difference to the overall stringency of the reasons not to kill and not to rape. Yet the legal system (in the country imagined) and the promise do constitute reasons.[11]

Note that I am not claiming that the law or promises, when morally binding, do not make a normative difference, or that they never affect the stringency. On the contrary, it is a condition on the adequacy of explanations of the nature of law or of promises that they show how they do, and when they do, when binding, affect the stringency of the reasons applying to us. The point I am making is that we rely on substantive accounts of the nature of various values and reasons in reaching conclusions about their interaction, and not on a formal principle of maximization. That, if valid at all, applies only when the substantive considerations indicate that it does.[12] All this is well understood by maximizers who do not rely on the first premise. I spent some time explaining why, to show that an apparently quick route from the fact that we ought to act for the better reason to the promotion of value is a dead end.

2. Is 'promoting value' the one practical reason?

PV is about what reasons for action we have. It says that the only reason is to promote value, that is to perform that action that will (or is likely to) promote value more than any of the available alternatives. The normative/explanatory *nexus* taught us that only what could be followed in action as a reason, only what can be taken to be a reason for action can be a reason for action. Could any faultless action be taken to promote value (as is the case if **PV** is true)?

Most of the time when people consider their reasons the promotion of value is not one of them. Advancing education, expanding job opportunities, designing ways to relieve the tedium of boring tasks at home or at work, are among the reasons we have for various activities. Promoting or maximizing value is hardly ever a reason we consider. But can we do so in all cases where we have a good reason for action? If

---

[11] This is the assumption, i.e. that that legal system is morally legitimate.

[12] Some people think that what is special about murder and rape is that the reasons to refrain from them are maximally strong, and therefore cannot be enhanced by the law or by promises. This is a supposition that cannot be accepted without other theoretical claims. Otherwise, it will turn out to assume not only that the reasons against rape and murder are of equal stringency, but also that that the reason to avoid killing one person is as strong as the reasons not to kill a million. These conclusions or the additional assumptions needed to avoid them may well be true, but are unlikely to give any support to the promotion of value thesis.

we can then perhaps the reasons that we normally follow can be seen as instances of that reason, as specific ways of promoting value on this occasion. We would then be able to argue, for example, that when we take an action because it advances job opportunities our reason is really (though implicitly) that opening up new job opportunities is, in the circumstances, the way to promote value. Given that promotion of value is, on this view, the only reason there is, it is not surprising that it remains implicit, in the background, and that in thought and argument we concentrate on the ways it is instantiated on the various occasions for action.

A common objection has it that some reasons of importance cannot be seen as instances of the promotion of value, even when they are conclusive. For example, I sit at home with nothing special to do, and a friend calls and offers to come over for conversation and a glass of wine. In the circumstances, there was nothing wrong with my being at home with nothing special to do. I like my friend and will enjoy spending the evening chatting with him. Moreover, he will be somewhat disappointed if I decline his offer. It seems to me that I have an undefeated reason to invite him over. Is it my way of maximizing value in the circumstances? My reason is the pleasure of my friend's company, and the appropriateness of inviting him (the inappropriateness of declining in the absence of a sufficient reason) given our friendship. It is not the case that I regard these reasons as a way of promoting value in the world. If I do I fail to act in friendship.[13] And if I am a thoroughgoing maximizer I have no friends, unless they are deceived about my reasons.

How successful is the objection? It is easy to underestimate it. One familiar reply, for example, has it that it is successful against those who take friendships to be instrumentally valuable, that it shows that one cannot be a friend without taking friendship to be intrinsically valuable. But, the thought is, acknowledging that friendship is intrinsically valuable is compatible with the promotion of value thesis, for the value of a successful friendship is a constituent part of the goodness of the state in which the friendship features. The promotion of value thesis tells us to choose the action that would result in a state most likely to be better than the available alternatives, and in assessing value we take account of the value of constituent states that are intrinsically good, as well as of instrumentally good states.

The reply does not succeed. There are two types of constituent goods. One contributes to the good it constitutes by being valuable independently of that contribution (call them: value-dependent constituents of value),[14] the other is not independently valuable; its sole value consists in contributing to the good of which it is a

---

[13] When acting in (or out of) friendship the friendship is a (part of the) reason for the action, but the reason is not necessarily for the sake of the friendship, understood as aiming to protect it from erosion, or other dangers. When acting out of friendship, friendship may be in the background to one's deliberation: it may be merely part of the conditions that shaped one's inclinations, and affected what reasons one recognizes, and the force one assigns them.

[14] I am assuming that generally the value of the whole is not the sum of the value of its parts, but there is no need to explore variations on that theme here.

constituent. The most familiar examples of the distinction come from works of art. A part of a painting can be beautiful in itself (a view of Delft seen through a doorway, for example), and it contributes to the beauty of the painting (at least partly) by being beautiful in itself. But other elements in the painting may contribute to its beauty independently of any other value that they may or may not have. To simplify the discussion I will refer to elements that have no value other than their contribution to the beauty of the painting as a whole (a patch of green near the top left corner, for example) as value-independent constituent values (and apply the term to all similar cases). If friendship is a constituent part of the value of some state without being of value in itself then one cannot act in friendship or for the sake of the friendship. One can only act for the sake of the value of which friendship is a constituent. In fact one can act out of friendship (without holding mistaken beliefs), and otherwise friendships would not be what they are. Therefore, the reply to the objection must take friendships to be a value-dependent constituent of value. But if friendship is valuable in itself then there is a reason to act in friendship, and the promotion of value is not the only reason there is.

A second objection to **PV** rests on the fact that acting out of friendship is only contingently related to promoting value (if at all). If on balance acting out of friendship will not promote value (because there is another action that will produce more value) then, so far as the promotion of value principle goes, we have no reason to act out of friendship. In other words, the promotion of value principle can acknowledge only that acting out of friendship can be a conditional reason. We have reason to act out of friendship only if it promotes value. The objection need not deny that when acting out of friendship will not promote value we should not so act, that in those circumstances we should take the action that will promote value. The objection can allow that in such circumstances reasons of friendship are defeated by competing reasons. But it insists that defeated reasons are reasons. **PV** does not admit that. According to it the reason to act out of friendship is merely a conditional reason. We have it only if it promotes value. It follows that if we have reasons to act out of friendship pure and simple, rather than out of friendship as a way of doing something else, then the promotion of value principle is mistaken, for there is at least one reason, or really one kind of reason, besides promoting value.

3. Maximization without promoting value

The significance of the objections so far should not be exaggerated. In a way value promoters know all of these points. Their views, as they interpret them, are not open to these objections. My aim so far has been to consider how promotion of value can be incorporated in an account of practical thought that takes 'reasons' to be the key notion. The interim conclusion is that one cannot hold that promoting value is the sole reason for action there is. Once that is conceded, however, the case for going further mounts. Observing that people hardly ever refer to the promotion of value as their reason, I replied that if it is the only reason one has one would not expect people to refer to it. It will not be informative to do so. But now, having allowed that there are other reasons, the puzzle returns. Moreover, there is an alternative way of understanding the views of promoters of value, or a view close to theirs, that is free from this difficulty. It denies that promotion of value is a reason for action.

Perhaps it is possible to jettison the promotion of value principle, but hang on to the maximization thesis. The maximization principle says nothing about what reasons we have. It is a principle of conflict resolution directing that when there are conflicting reasons the better reasons are those conformity with which will lead to a state of the world likely to have in it more value than conformity with any of the reasons for available alternative options. If the promotion of value principle is mistaken, while the maximization principle is true, people are able to act out of friendship and nothing more, but when the reasons for acting out of friendship conflict with reasons for another, incompatible act, that reason is the better one that will lead to higher expected value.

However, abandoning **PV** leaves us with a puzzle: why are conflicts to be resolved in accord with the maximization thesis? If promoting value is not what we are after why in conflict between reasons is the better reason the one conformity with which leads to more value? I see no way of answering this question, and therefore will continue on the basis that maximization presupposes the promotion of value, but that the promotion of value cannot, because of the objection we considered, be a principle about what reasons we have.

4. Can 'the promotion of value' be the ultimate principle of action?

The reinterpreted principle of the promotion of value says nothing directly about what reasons there are. Rather, it is a principle about the justifiability of actions, whatever reasons there are for them, and whatever the reasons for which they were taken (when they were taken):

> an action is justified (i.e. faultless) only if and because it is the most value-promoting action of those available to the agent at the time.

If maximization is a requirement of rationality it is so not because of the nature of reasons but because of the nature of values, in as much as it relates to the justification of actions (or of whatever else is subject to justification). But is it? First, even if the promotion of value is interpreted along the lines suggested, the problems raised above do not disappear. Any account of practical rationality has to do more than characterize a test under which action is defensible or justified. It has also to explain the relation between reasons and the principle of justifiability of actions. It is a condition of the validity both of the revised promotion of value principle and of the doctrine of reasons for action that they mesh, that is that valid reasons are such that acting for them would lead one to comply with the promotion of value principle, or at least to do so better than one would acting for any alternative considerations.

This point will return to haunt us, but let it be put on one side for the moment. I will avoid the complex question of whether we should maximize facilitative (or instrumental) value. There are difficult questions there, though one thing is clear: by definition an object's facilitative value is due to the value of its likely effects, or the effects it can be used to achieve, or creates opportunities to achieve, etc. In the last resort facilitative value depends on and derives from non-facilitative value (and that is so even if there are agents—for example governments—who must pursue or maximize what is of facilitative value and ignore other kinds of value). Therefore, if the promotion of value and maximization principles do not apply to all intrinsic values they cannot without reservation apply to all facilitative values.

So finally we face the central question about the promotion of value: what is to be promoted or maximized? What does it mean to maximize (non-facilitative) value, given that value is a property of objects, events, actions, institutions, people, and much else? An answer that no one believes is that we should maximize the number of valuable things. But why not? One reply is that different things of value vary in how valuable they are. Therefore, a small selection of well-chosen things may, taken as a totality, be more valuable than a larger number of individually less valuable things. We should, the maximizers will remind us, promote not things of value, but value.

This explanation leaves intact the suggestion that other things being equal we promote value by adding another valuable object to the world. But should we, other things being equal, amass as many good paintings as possible? That is not what promoting value means to maximizers, and for good reason. There is little point in a storehouse full of paintings that no one will ever see, however beautiful they are. We are not considering the value of the activity of creating them. That activity is consistent with destroying them once created. What is at issue now is the value there is in maximizing the number of good paintings in existence as a way of maximizing value. Why does promoting value not entail maximizing the number of good paintings in order to maximize value in the world, other things being equal? I suspect that there is a temptation to say that good paintings are only instrumentally good. What is good non-instrumentally is painting them, looking at them, or contemplating them, or living with them, or being inspired by them, and so on, or doing all that with understanding, or with pleasure, and so on. According to this line of thought objects of beauty, or those possessing other aesthetic values, are only instrumentally valuable.

It is best to resist the temptation. Yielding to it leads to the conclusion that having the experience of listening to Schubert or of looking at a painting by Cézanne is as good as actually listening to Schubert, or looking at a Cézanne.[15] I will take for granted

---

[15] See e.g. Nozick's famous experience machine in *Anarchy, State and Utopia* (New York: Basic Books, 1974).

what you may call a reality principle, which while not denying that illusory experiences may be instrumentally valuable (e.g. in calming one down, or taking one's mind off undesirable thoughts), says that they are not intrinsically valuable (except as ways of realizing certain special kinds of valuable ends, like experimenting with illusions).

However, it is possible to try to explain in a more plausible way, consistently with the promotion of value principle, why it is pointless to maximize the number of good paintings. For the promotion of value principle good paintings, and other intrinsically good objects, do not matter in themselves. They are constituents of complex states of making them, appreciating them, or whatever, that are intrinsically good not merely as constituents of more complex intrinsic goods. We can grant that they are constituents of such complex values only because they are intrinsically valuable. But their intrinsic value matters (for the principle) only because they are constituents of larger complex value-states. Only such goods, that is those that are of value in themselves and not merely as a constituent of other valuable objects, activities or states, are the object of the promotion of value principle. It does not apply to good paintings, novels, etc., which though intrinsically good, ultimately matter merely as constituents of good activities, objects, and states.

There is nothing here that should be taken as an objection to the normal usage of 'intrinsic value', according to which good works of art are intrinsically valuable, as well as, often, valuable instrumentally, e.g. having a market value. It merely means that we should limit the kind of intrinsic value to which the promotion of value principle applies to those that are not valuable only as constituent components of valuable objects, activities, experiences, etc.

5. Types of values and their promotion

How convincing is this narrowed promotion of value principle? To answer we need to consider different kinds of values, and since this is not a book on normative ethics the following are merely examples. The lesson to draw from them does not require agreement with the views they express. Two kinds of values can be roughly distinguished, and used in illustration. One consists of experiences and activities of people and other creatures or objects that 'count in themselves'.[16] To simplify I will refer only to people. The other consists in the instantiations in conduct, attitudes, institutions, and so on of many moral values, especially those relating to social institutions and to conduct among people (even) in the absence of personal relations among them, e.g. fairness, justice, tolerance, respect. I will call the second kind enabling values, and the first meaning of life values. The reason is that while striving to rectify injustice, improve tolerance, etc. can give meaning to the life of those who so do, merely living in a society that is just and not suffering from intolerance, unfairness, etc. does not give

---

[16] See my discussion of things that are valuable in themselves in *Value, Respect and Attachment*, ch. 4.

meaning to the life of those who do so. Living in environments that conform to those values does, however, generate conditions that help people successfully to conduct a rewarding life. Friendships, and valuable social activities (dances, parties, food, sex, conversation, and the rest), sporting activities, leisure pursuits and hobbies, an interest in literature and the arts, and suchlike can make life meaningful.

Enabling values come closest to conformity with the promotion of value principle. The realization of these values is a matter of degree, in as much as a society or people can be more or less just, more or less tolerant, and so on. It is best to achieve the highest possible degree, but in practice this is commonly impossible. In fact quite often people and governments face choices between options, each favouring some of those values at the expense of the others. We thus engage in trade-offs which, when the options are not incommensurable, may be subject to the maximization principle. I will say little about them except by way of gesture. Some enabling values are what I call satiable values, that is they can, in principle, be satisfied to a maximal degree. This is particularly so with values such as fairness and toleration whose satisfaction means that the corresponding vice is avoided. We are fair when we are not acting unfairly. We are tolerant when we do not manifest intolerance. Since it is possible, in principle, to avoid the offensive conduct it is possible, in principle, to be in a situation where fairness is maximally realized, and nothing can be done to make the world fairer or more tolerant. Such values are good candidates for maximization. Other enabling values are not like that. They allow for indefinite improvement. Generosity and mercy are examples of those. One can always be more generous and merciful than one is. I believe that the promotion of values does not apply to those values, for reasons similar to those that make it inapplicable to meaning of life values. But I will say no more about this and turn to those meaning of life values. Are they to be promoted?

There are two obvious objections. The first addresses the applicability of the promotion of value principle. The second addresses directly the maximization principle. First, suppose that I can listen many times to the Schubert Octet with attention and appreciation. Even if I do so twice a day for many months I still get a lot out of doing so. Will doing so increase value in the world? Will the world be a better place, other things being equal, if I listen to the Octet twice daily? I have to admit that I find no meaning in the supposition that doing so will, other things being equal, increase value in the world. I suspect that those who are inclined to affirm that this will increase value do so because they think that (a) given that I will appreciate and enjoy the Octet I have reason to do so; (b) unless I have a reason that is no worse than the reason to listen to the Octet the reason to listen is the better reason. They are fortified by the belief that whenever the situation is as in the example one would have other reasons that will not be defeated by the reason to listen to the Octet, and the absurdity of supposing that one must on pain of irrationality listen to it all the time will not arise in practice. I agree with this judgement. But see no comfort in it for the promoter of value. The argument rests on the relations between reasons. Namely, on taking reasons to be presumptively sufficient, and as entailing that knowingly and voluntarily failing to conform with a reason that is better than all conflicting reasons is irrational. This argument, whatever we think of its merits, does not rely on the thought that we ought to maximize or promote value, a thought that remains without content when applied to cases of this kind.

We can return to friendship to illustrate the second objection, the one applying directly to the maximization thesis as a thesis about trade-offs in conflict. If the maximization principle reigns supreme then it would seem that, when I move to a new town and am looking to forge new friendships I should, other things being equal, make friends with a person whose neighbours will benefit from this new friendship rather than with someone who has no such neighbours. Assume that the benefit to the neighbours of my friendship with the first person is real and visible, but that forgoing the benefit will not condemn them to great misery. It is incompatible with relations between friends that one chooses who to be friends with not because of a liking for the friend, concern for him and for oneself, but out of concern for his neighbours. If maximization dictates that our choice is wrong when we do not choose the person whose neighbours would benefit, then maximization cannot be coordinated with a correct theory of reasons, and is to be rejected.[17]

There seems to be an obvious reply to these objections. Listening to Schubert, or making friends, are good only in context. Listening to Schubert is not, for example, good if it is the only thing that person does. It is good only if it makes his or her day good, and that depends on listening to Schubert having a proper place within that day, alongside food, work, and much else. But then, why care about how good his or her day is? What makes a day a more worthy unit than an hour? 'Nothing', I think, is the right answer. Pointing to the day is just a step to what is, ultimately, the relevant context, namely the life of that person as a whole. So finally we arrive where some readers may well have wanted to start: what counts is the well-being of people (and of other beings that count).

Some maximizers take well-being to be the only intrinsic value (other than values that are mere constituent components of value), and therefore well-being is what we ought to promote and maximize. For the purposes of the present discussion we need not endorse this view. We can allow that enabling values are intrinsically valuable in their own right. The question we need to examine is whether so far as our choices depend only on the reasons that meaning of life values provide, the contribution of options to the agent's well-being is the measure of their importance, the measure that determines which options are supported by undefeated or even conclusive reasons. I have argued elsewhere that it is not. Many of our options have no impact on our

[17] Notice that having reinterpreted maximization as well as the promotion of value as principles justifying actions, without being principles about what reasons we have, I am not claiming that they are right only if we can act in order to conform with them. The objection is based on the weaker assumption, namely that the principles that justify actions must be coordinated with the doctrine of reasons for action, i.e. that acting for sufficient reasons will not turn out to be unjustified, and that whether or not it is justified will not be a matter of chance.

well-being even when some are better than others. Given that I am tired after a day thinking about well-being I should (I have a better reason to) play tennis with friends rather than go to a philosophy lecture. But whatever I do will have no impact on my well-being. There are endless examples of this kind. Susan has many friends. Friendship is important for her well-being. But will her well-being improve if she strikes up another friendship? It will make no difference to the overall quality of her life, or to her happiness or well-being. Yet, given her situation, and current relations with Rachel, the better reason may well be for her to develop a friendship with Rachel. Furthermore, some choices that adversely affect well-being may not be against a better reason. Friendships provide easy examples, but so does any pursuit people set their heart on. Sometimes pursuing friendships constrains people's opportunities in life, restricts them to the pursuit of interests that they share with their friends, and that may lead to a less rich and rewarding life. Yet, while in such situations people may distance themselves from their friendships, they may also keep their attachment at a cost to the quality of their life; both options may well be supported by undefeated reasons.

The examples given in this section are just examples. They conform to my views about the values involved, but their role here is different. Their purpose is to make the case against taking the promotion of value thesis as either a conceptual truth or a principle of rationality. As we saw in the last chapter, there are areas of practical thought where the force of reasons depends on which of them realizes outcomes with greater value, but that is so because of the nature of the values that bear on those choices, and the way they constitute reasons. There is no case for taking maximizing or promoting value to be the general rule for the resolution of practical conflicts.

PART THREE

On Responsibility

Introduction

Normativity has forward and backward looking implications. The reasons that apply on any one occasion determine what is to be done or believed, etc. They also provide the basis for evaluating and judging what was done or believed, etc. Part One focused on what it is for there to be reasons. Part Two looked at some of the problems that arise when people are guided by reasons. Part Three considers the conditions under which people are responsible for actions, omissions, their consequences, or for other states or events, thus raising some of the problems concerned with evaluating and judging (past) actions, beliefs, etc. Chapter Six may be thought to have solved these problems. It explained the distinction between what agents have reason, or adequate reason, to do on any occasion, and what they are, or would be justified in doing on those same occasions. The distinction is of course relevant to questions of evaluating actions and beliefs, but it leads nowhere unless the agents were responsible for their actions, or for having those beliefs, etc.

Explaining the conditions of responsibility is the task undertaken in the following chapters. They assume understanding of the concept of responsibility, though as there are several concepts the word is used to express, they identify several of them, and point to the relations between the concept investigated here and some of the others. Furthermore, in pointing to some other connections between responsibility and other concepts, e.g. blameworthiness and praiseworthiness, these chapters provide a partial explanation of the concept. But their primary role is to establish when we are responsible and (to a degree) for what. As with other topics the productive way to discuss responsibility is in the context of some real philosophical puzzles. One common focus of discussion is the relations between responsibility and free will. But this book has nothing to say on that issue. It takes its cue from the puzzle about the possibility or impossibility of moral luck. That problem was put centre stage by Williams in his 1969 article on moral luck, and it forms the starting point for the reflections in Chapter Twelve. While the views I defend differ from Williams's I believe that they are not only inspired by his writings, but also faithful to their spirit. The key idea is that the conditions of responsibility reflected in common beliefs about responsibility are connected to the way we feel about Being in the World, for example, to spheres in which we feel confident, and others in which we are at risk, subject to luck and so on. Elucidating these ideas enables us to provide an account of the conditions of responsibility, which allows for what is often considered to be moral luck. It turns out that common views about responsibility are inconsistent with common views about blame. I take the first to be well founded, whereas the latter, the views about blame, to be confused. But establishing that would take us beyond the scope of this book. Instead I merely point to the fact that the conditions of responsibility here explained and defended presuppose a somewhat different understanding of the conditions of responsibility and its role.

In arguing for the account of responsibility in Chapter Twelve I rely on the fact that we are responsible for negligent conduct. The nature of negligence is explored in some detail in the final chapter. Given that the concept is discussed mostly by legal theorists, the chapter, while dealing with negligence generally, is informed by its role in the law, and its discussion is meant to connect with the concerns of legal theorists. So the book ranges widely from discussions often called meta-ethical to more substantive normative concerns in Part Three (and the three last chapters of Part Two). This is no accident. It reflects a belief that the various domains of inquiry are strongly interconnected, with conclusions in one supporting or undermining views in the others.

12

Being in the World

We actively engage with the world through our actions. Among them those for which we are responsible hold a special place. They constitute our engagement with the world as rational agents, for we are responsible for actions in virtue of their relationship to our capacities of rational agency. The question of responsibility is largely the question: what is that relationship, and how does the criterion for responsibility for action extend to account for responsibility for whatever else we are responsible for (e.g. for omissions or for consequences of our actions)?

Following some clarification of the sense of responsibility this part of the book is about, Section 1 briefly criticizes three principles of responsibility: one takes us to be responsible only for our intentional actions, and for their intended or foreseen consequences, the other takes us to be responsible only for actions and outcomes that are under our control. The third, combining aspects of both, takes us to be responsible for actions that are guided by our powers of rational agency. I will then take a first step towards an alternative. It aims to show how our way of Being in the World accounts for the conditions of responsibility.

1. Responsibility, guidance, control, and intentions

For our purposes three uses of 'responsible' are of interest:[1]

(1) People are responsible₁ if and only if they have the capacity for rational action (as when we say 'he is not in his right mind and therefore not responsible for his actions'). The powers of rational action are more extensive than just our rational capacities (powers of reasoning, of decision, etc.)[2] including also perception, memory, and control of the body without which one cannot act effectively. While mental actions require relatively limited abilities, when dealing with responsibility for other kinds of actions one has to take account of the abilities that make them possible.

---

[1] Naturally we are not interested in the use of 'responsibility' to indicate causality (as in 'the earthquake is responsible for the power failure'). Similarly, neither the use of 'is responsible' as a commendation (as in 'you can trust him. He is a responsible fellow'), nor its reverse, namely its use as equivalent to blameworthy (as 'the doctor is responsible for his death' would normally be understood) are of interest.

[2] Cf. Chapter Five.

(2) People who are responsible$_1$ are not necessarily responsible$_2$ for everything they do.[3] In some cases they are not responsible$_2$ because their powers of rational agency are temporarily suspended or blocked: they may, e.g., act while sleep-walking, or under hypnosis. But they may also not be responsible$_2$ while their powers are unimpaired if their actions or omissions fail to be appropriately related to their capacities of rational agency. Otherwise it is mysterious why only those with capacities of rational agency can be responsible$_2$.

(3) In a different sense having a responsibility$_3$ is like having a duty (as in 'it was your responsibility to secure the building').[4]

My aim is to contribute towards an answer to the question: what relationship between our capacities for rational agency and an action makes us responsible$_2$ for the latter?

The core question is about a non-mediated relationship between action (say) and the capacity for rational agency that renders one responsible$_2$ for the action. There is widespread agreement on several derivative principles of responsibility$_2$. I will mention only one: *intentional disabling does not disable*: if a person Φs, having generated (in ways he is responsible$_2$ for) conditions that would otherwise make him not responsible$_2$ for Φ-ing in order to avoid being responsible$_2$ for Φ-ing then he is responsible$_2$ for Φ-ing. This is barely an extension of direct responsibility$_2$. For the most part when discussing examples I will assume that derivative responsibility$_2$ does not apply to them. Principles of responsibility$_2$ will be implicitly qualified to allow for the application of derivative responsibility$_2$.

The thought that among our actions we are responsible$_2$ for our intentional actions and only them[5] appears natural to those who think that intentional actions are performed for what their agents take to be reasons for those actions. For then we are responsible$_2$ for actions that are guided by our rational capacities. This inclines some to think that we are responsible$_2$ for actions that are under our control: we control actions by guiding them in light of what we take to be reasons for those actions.

The Control Principle, namely that we are responsible$_2$ for X if and only if X is under our rational control, or only because, and to the extent that X has aspects that are under our rational control,

appears to coincide with

---

[3] Responsibility$_2$ for a state or an event presupposes that one brought it about, preserved it, or contributed to its coming about or being preserved, or that one allowed it to continue. Most of the time I will inquire about responsibility$_2$ for actions, assuming that if one is responsible$_2$ for a state or an event, etc. that is in virtue of responsibility$_2$ for an action that brought it about, caused it, preserved it, or allowed it to stay in existence, etc. This greatly simplifies exposition, and whatever distortion it introduces can be readily corrected. Responsibility$_2$ is a matter of degree. Or rather, responsibility$_2$ can be used either as an on/off concept, or as admitting various degrees. To simplify I will treat it as an on/off concept.

[4] Responsibility$_1$ is also a matter of degree, but at its minimum it is presupposed by responsibility$_2$ and responsibility$_3$. Only those with rational capacities can be subject to duties, and only they can be responsible$_2$.

[5] Here I disregard the question of responsibility other than for actions.

The Intention Principle, namely that we are responsible$_2$ for X if and only if X is an intentional action and for the foreseen or intended consequences of such an action.

This appearance is, however, misleading. Not all intentional actions are under our control. 'Control' is used in a context-sensitive way, and there is no need here to explore the notion, except as it is used in the Control Principle. Roughly it means: being moved and guided by reasons as one sees them.[6] A simple example helps in establishing that not all intentional actions are 'under our control'. A drunk who decided to leave the bar, wobbles his way out, but on his way he bumps into a table, breaking a wine glass. Breaking the glass was unintentional and uncontrolled. But his walking out was intentional, and yet not properly controlled. Control is a matter of degree. The drunk controlled his walking sufficiently to get out of the bar, but not well enough to avoid bumping into the furniture.

Examples suggest that *one controls an action if and only if*

(1) either one performs it because one intends to do so, or one performs it, aware that one does so, by performing another action that one intends to perform
(2) the performance is guided by one's intention and one's beliefs, so that to the extent that one's factual beliefs are true one does not, in performing the action, do anything else that one believes one should not (on balance) do
(3) in so far as realization of the previous conditions depends on control of one's body they are securely realized.

The thought is that for actions to be controlled it is not enough that they are motivated and guided by agents' intentions. Control requires that the guidance reflect agents' views of all the reasons that apply to the occasion, and ways of pursuing them.[7] And it requires reliable muscular control. This third condition recognizes the distance between cases in which though one is doing what one intends to do because one intends to do it one is not doing it intentionally, because the intention does not play its proper guiding role in directing the action, and cases in which the action is intentional even though the guidance by the intention is wobbly. These latter cases are those where the action is intentional and yet not controlled. But there are other cases of intentionality without good control, including expressive actions and marginal intentional actions, like doodling, etc.[8]

A principle that unites several aspects of the Control and Intention Principles, and is more clearly successful in establishing a relationship between actions for which we are responsible$_2$ and our rational capacities is **the Guidance Principle**, as I will call it. According to it we are responsible$_2$ for Φ-ing if only if our Φ-ing was guided and controlled by our powers of rational agency. An action is so guided and controlled if

---

[6] See *Engaging Reason* (Oxford: OUP, 1999), 11–12.
[7] If the drunk believes that bumping into the furniture should be avoided, and fails to do so, then his walking is not adequately controlled by him.
[8] See Chapter Four and *Engaging Reason*, 36–44.

and only if, first, it is either done for (what the agent takes to be) a sufficient reason, or is done, knowing what one is doing (thus implicitly accepting that if there is a case against it, it does not defeat the case for it),[9] by doing another action for (what the agent takes to be) a sufficient reason, and, second, in doing it one is not doing anything else which one believes that it would be better not to do.

The thinking behind this principle is readily explained. When we initiate an action because we see, as we believe, a reason for it, and whatever consequences we believe it will or probably will have are, if not desirable in themselves, at least not sufficient to make the action undesirable to us, and when in performing it we do not also perform other actions we would rather not perform, like stumbling and injuring other people, then our powers of rational agency are in charge, and we initiate and guide the action by their use. In such cases the action manifests our powers of rational agency and we are responsible$_2$ for it.

The Guidance Principle does not take people to be responsible$_2$ for all their intentional actions, for some intentional actions are neither done for a reason, nor by performing another action for a reason. Nor does it take people to be responsible$_2$ for all the actions they do for what they take to be a reason, for the performance of some of these actions is not controlled by their agents. The principle never holds one responsible$_2$ for accidental actions whose performance or consequences were not foreseen, nor for any omissions, other than those that were either decided upon or foreseen (intentional omissions), nor for any weak-willed actions, because though they may be intentional and well controlled, they are not properly guided by our rational powers.

The appeal of the Guidance Principle is in relating what we are responsible$_2$ for to our powers of rational agency in the right way: we are responsible$_2$ for actions taken and guided by our powers of rational agency. By mixing two components: acting for what one takes to be a reason, and control, the principle identifies actions regarding which we are maximally responsible$_2$, in that where it applies we are responsible$_2$ for all aspects of the action of which we were aware.

The Guidance Principle makes responsibility$_2$ turn on successful guidance. The success referred to is not that of doing what we have adequate reason to do, and avoiding what we have conclusive reasons to avoid—or something like that. It is not success consisting in following right reason. It is the successful functioning of our capacities of rational agency. People often do what they should not do without their powers of rational agency malfunctioning. This, for example, can be the case when they have false, but rational, beliefs about what they ought to do. We are used to distinguishing between failure in the functioning of our powers, be they powers to control our limbs, or mental powers called upon in forming and executing intentions,

---

[9] That agents take it that there is no sufficient case against the action is not so much an implication of the fact that they know what they are doing as a clarification of what level of knowledge is required: such as to imply that if they perform the action they believe that the case against it does not defeat the reasons for it.

and failure in 'getting it right', in taking the right action. The way the distinction applies is controversial, and most likely partly depends on normative considerations. But the existence of the distinction is generally (often implicitly) recognized and underlies, or so I claim, responsibility$_2$.

It seems reasonable to take both the Guidance and the Intention Principles to state sufficient grounds for responsibility$_2$. But their satisfaction is not necessary for responsibility$_2$. The problem is that the Guidance Principle makes responsibility$_2$ depend on too tight a connection between our powers of rational agency and our actions. For us to be responsible$_2$ for an action it must, according to the principle, be successfully guided by our powers of rational agency. In fact we are responsible$_2$ for actions where the guidance fails: in common situations the drunk (of our example) is responsible$_2$ for the walking in spite of lack of control, and we are normally responsible$_2$ for accidentally bumping into people in the street. Some exceptions apart, we are responsible$_2$ for our intentional actions even when we do not adequately control them. Hence, responsibility$_2$ is sometimes independent of control, and does not depend on the relations between action and capacities that control manifests. The Guidance Principle presupposes control, and is thus inadequate. Besides it fails to explain why we are responsible for weak-willed actions. But neither is the Intention Principle true. We are responsible$_2$ for some non-intentional omissions, and for some of their consequences, as in many circumstances when we forget to do something we ought to do. Similarly, we are responsible$_2$ for negligent actions, and for negligently produced harm. (One standard way of refuting a charge of negligence is to show that one is not responsible$_2$ for the allegedly negligent conduct). So the Intention Principle too fails to identify a necessary condition for responsibility$_2$. Furthermore, so far we saw no account of how the fact that an action is intentional relates it to capacity responsibility (as—following Hart—I will occasionally refer to responsibility$_1$) to make us responsible$_2$ for it.

To anticipate: The account of responsibility$_2$ that will be defended here can be expressed as the

Rational Functioning Principle: Conduct for which we are (non-derivatively) responsible$_2$ is conduct that is the result of the functioning, successful or failed, of our powers of rational agency, provided those powers were not suspended in a way affecting the action.

A word of explanation regarding the proviso: Only creatures with capacity responsibility can be responsible$_2$ for their actions. But even people or other creatures that have the capacity for rational action may find it blocked or suspended temporarily, as by sleep, hypnosis, temporary paralysis, or other conditions. When such conditions affect an action (as when we act while sleepwalking) they negate the proper connection between the action and the powers of rational agency, thus negating responsibility$_2$ for that action.

This account is to be judged by two tests. First, whether it really does apply to clear examples of conduct for which we are responsible$_2$ and to no other. Second, whether the relations between powers of rational agency and action that it insists on are the right ones.

If the **Rational Functioning Principle** is sound we can expect the first test to be inconclusive. That is because the standing of the examples depends on several kinds of judgements whose soundness is independent of this conception of responsibility. First, there is the question whether one's powers of rational agency were temporarily disabled so that one is not responsible for any conduct performed during that period. Second, there is the question whether one's powers malfunctioned. For example, the fact that one does not rely in deliberation or action on all the propositions entailed by one's beliefs does not establish that one's rational powers malfunctioned. On the other hand, failure to realize and rely on some implications of one's beliefs does point to a malfunction of rational capacities. There is no determinate boundary between the two classes of case. This makes it all the more important that there be a sound rationale behind this conception of responsibility$_2$, and that is not at all obvious. We can understand why we are responsible$_2$ for conduct successfully guided by our rational powers, but why are we responsible$_2$ for conduct that is the result of a malfunctioning of those powers?

2. Agent-regret

We need a fresh start, and I turn to Williams for a nudge in the right direction. Williams, who gave the question of moral luck its name,[10] did not focus on responsibility. He identified one attitude people may have to their actions and their consequences that we know by the name he gave it: agent-regret. Commentators observed that he hardly addressed the question he raised, the question of moral luck. True, but he signalled that the way we are attached to our actions and their consequences is key to an understanding of responsibility, resulting in acknowledging that responsibility is subject to moral luck.[11] Agent-regret is, according to Williams, one special attitude people may have to their actions and their consequences.

The constitutive thought of regret in general is something like 'how much better if it had been otherwise', and the feeling can in principle apply to anything of which one can form some conception of how it might have been otherwise, together with consciousness of how things would then have been better. In this general sense of regret, what are regretted are states of affairs, and they can be regretted, in principle, by anyone who knows of them. But there is a particularly important species of regret, which I shall call 'agent-regret', which a person can feel only towards

[10] B. Williams 'Moral Luck', in *Moral Luck* (Cambridge: CUP, 1982), 20–39.

[11] This section is heavily influenced by B. Williams. However, my purpose is not exegetical. I aim to use his views and develop some aspects of them. I therefore took the liberty when describing Williams's views of paraphrasing in a way that is not altogether faithful to Williams's views. Some of my formulations are cognitivist renderings of Williams's views. Williams's own understanding of responsibility (which I do not share) is explained in *Shame and Necessity* (Cambridge: CUP, 1993).

his own past actions (or, at most, actions in which he regards himself as a participant). In this case, the supposed possible difference is that one might have acted otherwise. ('Moral Luck', 123)

This passage identifies agent-regret by its object: it is regret for having acted in some way. The regret is essentially self-referential. My regret that JR has done something is not agent-regret. My regret that I have so acted may be. Williams is clear that that is not the only difference:

There can be cases directed towards one's own past action which are not cases of agent-regret, because the past action is regarded purely externally, as one might regard anyone else's action. (ibid. 123)

Agent-regret has, he explains, a specific expression, to do with a desire that one had not done what one did, and a desire to repair, to undo what one did or come as close to that as possible.

Arguably Williams's account of the feeling is incomplete, for it does not fully identify the difference between regretting one's own action that is agent-regret and regretting one's own action that is not.[12] I will suggest that an additional aspect of agent-regret accounts for that difference. But, as Williams does not mention this feature, I am not sure that the emotion that I am describing is the one he had in mind, though it seems to me consonant with his thought, and to mark an important distinction between two kinds of self-directed regret. The additional element, I suggest, is that agent-regret relates to one's sense of who one is. When I agent-regret an action of mine I feel bad or sorry about being or having become a person who acted in that way.[13]

According to my suggestion agent-regret is a feeling that can be associated with a number of distinct attitudes to oneself, united by being attitudes to who one is. Here is one imaginary example: I admire Dustin Hoffman, and would like to see him in the flesh. Being at home with a friend (who shares my attitude to Dustin Hoffman) I learn that he is nearby visiting someone in Montague Square, and that a few people are there waiting to see him come out. However, I do not go there and miss that chance to see him. Later I regret (a) missing the opportunity, and (b) not taking the very little trouble

---

[12] See 'Moral Luck', 125, 126. Williams points out that some desires to compensate do not involve agent-regret. That is the case when insuring against any harm done by the regretted action would have been taken to be sufficient to put an end to the regret. Nor does the desire to undo itself explain the essential self-referential character of agent-regret. I can regret your action, and desire to undo what you did, or to come as close to that as is possible. Similarly I can wish that some other people did not act as they did. The self-referential element is in the difference between wishing that JR did not act as he did and wishing that I did not act as I did. But what is the significance of that distinction (its meaning, not only its logical features)? I do not think that Williams explains that.

[13] Meir Dan-Cohen's discussion ('Luck & Identity', *Theoretical Inquiries in Law* 9/1 (2008)) in explaining Williams's *Gauguin* example as turning on Gauguin's decision being self-constituting, in that it relates to a pursuit central to his life from then on, lends some support both to my 'additional element', on which I rely in identifying the emotion, and to my contention below that Williams's explanation of the conditions under which the emotion is justified do not extend to simple cases of agent-regret.

to go there to see him. Reflecting on my feelings I conclude that my regret about my failure is of the same kind as my regret that my friend did not go to see Hoffman. She and I are unlikely to have another opportunity to see him, and I regret that we missed the opportunity we had.

Given what Williams says about agent-regret, this is not agent-regret. It is a regret that I have had or did not have a certain experience, or that my biography does or does not include performing a certain action. It is not first-personal or self-referential in the right way. Why not? Suppose we vary the example by adding that I failed to go out to see Hoffman because I was ashamed of being seen to engage in star-gazing. In fact I find nothing wrong in moderate star-gazing, and my regret now includes feeling bad about myself for having succumbed to a feeling of shame which I regard as misguided and snobbish. If that is how I regret not going out then it is agent-regret. In this case I regret being a person who failed to go out.

But do I not also regret in the same way that my friend succumbed to an inhibition that she regards as unjustified (and let us assume that that is so)? I may well, but that regret is not self-referential in the way that my regret about myself is. I may hear a story—like the Hoffman story (and I mean just what was done on the occasion and the explanation, excluding the later regrets about it)—about someone, let's call him JR, and having forgotten that I behaved in that way myself I may or may not regret that JR succumbed to such an inhibition (there is nothing wrong in not caring enough about an unknown stranger not to regret that, indeed not to care whether, he is a person with this or that disposition). When I realize that I am JR I *cannot avoid* the regret, and it is a different kind of regret from the one I had before (if I had one before) about JR. It is regret that *I* am such a person. The essentially self-referential character of regret is particularly poignant due to its being, in part, about the person one is or was, as manifested on that occasion. It is poignant in being not regret that there is such a person, but that *I* am such a person. More specifically this instance of self-regret, though not all, involves something of a self-reproach, and self-reproach is essentially self-referential.

The Hoffman example is of a case where the regret is motivated by the realization, or the confirmation, of a known weakness. Other cases of agent-regret are different. In particular in some of them the agent regrets having become, through the action, someone he would rather not be. The person who runs over a child, through no fault of his own, and kills him becomes a killer, someone who killed a child, and he regrets that. Having killed is something that may haunt him, and affect his attitudes to himself and to the rest of the world. (I mention these possible consequences of having killed a child to indicate the significance that being a person who killed has for some people. I do not mean that one agent-regrets the killing because one would rather not suffer these consequences.) Guilt and fault are not the only factors that can have such an effect on our sense of who we are. There is a genuine difference between agent-regret in which one's regret is directed at who one is, or who one has become through one's action, and other kinds of regrets about one's actions. And the difference is significant in that only in the one case does the agent regret being a person who so acts.

In drawing our attention to the prevalence of agent-regret Williams reminds us that we are attached to, care about, our involvement in the world, including aspects of it that are beyond our control. It will be evident by now that I do not think that agent-regret is unique in displaying the way our sense of 'who we are' is connected to our perception of what we do. Similar connections are displayed when we are proud, or ashamed, or feel guilty that *we* did this or that. Moreover, while agent-regret is, by Williams's definition, directed at one's action, it is not significantly different from the regret a teenage girl may feel at having become who she is by having experienced being abused by her father. In that case too, having become a certain person looms large.[14] Feelings of agent-regret serve as a good example which brings out the point, but other emotions will do as well.[15]

However, to vindicate this attachment Williams has to show that feelings of agent-regret can be justified, and to explain their significance in our lives. Williams provides a beginning of a reply to the first of these two questions:

...it would be a kind of insanity never to experience sentiments of this kind...and it would be an insane concept of rationality which insisted that a rational person never would. To insist on such a conception of rationality, moreover, would, apart from other kinds of absurdity, suggest a large falsehood: that we might, if we conducted ourselves clear-headedly enough, entirely detach ourselves from the unintentional aspects of our actions. ('Moral Luck', 125)

So long as we are the kind of creatures we are, he observes, we cannot detach ourselves from the unintentional aspects of our actions, a detachment necessary for the elimination of agent-regret. Therefore, it would be wrong ('insane') to think that such attachment is always irrational.

As explained in Chapter Five, I use 'irrational' of an action or an attitude to indicate that it is a product of a malfunction of our rational capacities. I assume that Williams is using it more broadly, to indicate that the attitude or feeling is against reason, that it cannot be supported by reason, meaning something close to saying that if it is not irrational then it is alright, not defective, and in that sense justified. He is saying that while sometimes a person's feeling of agent-regret is unjustified, there are no grounds for thinking that agent-regret cannot ever be justified, for that would leave us with the puzzle of why we cannot avoid a feeling that is necessarily unjustified, not even when we believe that it is unjustified.

This is not a conclusive argument. To supplement it we need to answer the second question I mentioned, we need to understand the significance of agent-regret in our

---

[14] I am grateful to Ulrike Heuer for the suggestion and the example.
[15] Nor is there any reason to think that Williams would disagree here. He focuses on agent-regret because he finds in it a clear example of retroactive justification. It is less puzzling that our pride in an action depends on outcomes beyond our control than that the very justification of an action depends on them.

life. If it is not only inescapable but also plays a significant role in our life then some instances of it can be justified. When is agent-regret justified? When its occurrence is appropriately related to the significance the feeling has for us. Here I part company with Williams, because his explanation applies only to regretting important, life-changing decisions. He expressed the hope that his discussion will illuminate more mundane occurrences, but I do not see how the rationale he offers for it can do that. Here are examples of reasonable but minor cases of feeling agent-regret: I say something uncomplimentary to a friend hoping that it will spur him to confront his current difficulties. It may achieve its goal, and he may be grateful for my rudeness. But it may misfire, give offence and nothing more. In that case both of us may forget the incident before long. But before I do I may well regret my remarks, and that may be an appropriate case of agent-regret, at least it will be agent-regret by all the criteria that Williams mentions, as well as by mine. It will not, however, relate to a failure in a project that contributes to the meaning of my life. My project, to prod my friend a bit, was purely altruistic, and its presence in my life was never meant to involve anything more than doing what I did. Williams fails to explain why agent-regret is here appropriate.

Other cases, while apparently cases of appropriate agent-regret, stray even further from the type of case he has in mind. Suppose that when I am on edge I express myself indelicately, in a way that could understandably and reasonably offend the friend whom I am addressing. I did not intend to offend, and do not feel that what I said accurately represents how I feel or what I believe. I regret having said what I said. I do not merely regret that JR said it; I regret that I said it. My regret is agent-regret. So far I said nothing about the consequences of what I said.[16] We can schematically distinguish three possibilities:

(1) my friend does not take offence (perhaps his attention is on something else);
(2) he is mildly offended, but quickly forgets the whole episode;
(3) he is deeply offended and our relationship is diminished for a significant period, or declines altogether.

To simplify let me assume that whatever his reaction it is not unreasonable or inapt. Only the third of these possibilities would warrant agent-regret on Williams's understanding of its justification. But it seems to me that I may well regret what I have done in all three cases (though possibly my regret may be greater in the third). Can such regret be justified? 'My' kind of agent-regret, regret about who one is, is becoming, or has become, comes with a ready explanation: we can reasonably wish or aspire to be like this and not like that, and so long as our regret at having become different is attached to such reasonable aspiration and is proportionate to its importance it is

---

[16] Of course, my success in saying it is due, in part, to elements beyond my control. But they are not related (in the relevant way) to my regret.

reasonable. Given how fundamental such emotions are to the kind of animals we are no other vindication is needed, and probably no other is possible.[17]

Williams discusses agent-regret to impress on us how deeply connected we are to some aspects of the world which are beyond our control. Is his discussion irrelevant to questions of moral luck as many have alleged? No, and yet—Yes. No, for agent-regret is neither a necessary nor a sufficient condition for responsibility$_2$. We are responsible$_2$ for what we need not regret, and we properly regret actions and consequences for which we are not responsible$_2$. Yes—but very indirectly, for to understand responsibility$_2$ we need to understand our attachment to consequences of our actions which are beyond our control. The key, my explanation of agent-regret suggests, lies in the way our actions are related to our sense of who we are. In spelling out this thought we go beyond Williams's writings. For the rest of the chapter we leave agent-regret behind, and find the relevance of our attachment to aspects of our actions that escape our control in the basic modes of our active engagement with the world.

3. Engaging with the world

Our sense of who we are is partly shaped through our actions and experiences. To clarify this commonplace observation we must challenge the identity, often assumed, between matters beyond our exclusive control and matters of luck.

The success of our actions depends on factors beyond our control, but typically they are not matters of luck. People develop skills that enable them to do many things with confidence that they will succeed, barring some extraordinary events like an earthquake or a seizure. Of course, those who accepted Williams's terminology[18] warned that they use 'luck' stipulatively. But the choice of terminology betrays a willingness to imagine our Being in the World as being in an alien environment, tossed about on the waves of fortune whenever we venture beyond our thoughts and intentions. An understanding of our engagement with the world should distinguish between the ways we gamble, deliberately taking risks, and the ways our actions, while depending on matters over which we have little influence, are not gambles, and make plain the roles of these different forms of engagement in the constitution of our sense of ourselves.

The distinction between risk-taking and other actions and activities is inevitably a soft one. But it is important in demarcating two distinct attitudes, with many

---

[17] It is sometimes assumed that if an action or attitude is justified then not taking the action or not having the attitude is unjustified. But that is not generally true, and I will assume no such implication. Justification is permissive, as we might say. The justification of regret does not imply anything about the justification of its absence.

[18] which he introduced tongue in cheek, intending it to be self-undermining, thus leading to the rejection of the 'morality system' (see his 'Postscript', in D. Statman (ed.), *Moral Luck* (Albany, N.Y. (State University of New York Press, 1993), 251).

intermediate ones. At one extreme are gambling[19] and other actions over whose outcome we have hardly any influence, and where we do not have warranted beliefs about their outcome (except, sometimes, about the chances of different outcomes). Here belong, along with playing roulette, also more ordinary enterprises, such as hitch-hiking (assuming, perhaps unrealistically, that little skill is involved in hiking).

Other activities are very different. We expect their outcome to depend on our skill and effort. We are aware that they too depend on factors over which we have little influence, but take our skills in using and navigating around such factors to justify confidence that we will succeed. Many activities (cooking, eating, shopping, visiting friends, studying for a degree, etc.) fall into this category. Others are mixed cases. In opening a grocery store I rely on my skill for success, but am aware that an economic downturn, etc., is not unlikely. One is both taking a gamble and relying on resolution and skill to navigate to success.

These two ways in which our activities depend on risk are important in our lives in different ways. The case in which one relies on nature to play along (even though aware that it may not) is crucial to one's ability to act (with a modicum of success) at all. To do so one must learn to assess what is likely or unlikely to happen in the normal course of events, to judge whether one's situation is normal, and to develop skills that assure one of success in the normal case, by testing one's skills to their limits. That is how we learn when we can trust our skills, and depend on nature (including other agents) cooperating, and when we are placing ourselves at the mercy of luck. Unless I can trust the chair to carry my weight, the ground not to give way when I walk, the plate to maintain rigidity when I hold it, etc., I cannot perform even the simplest act. More complex acts require similar understanding of one's environment, though to a higher degree.

Learning how to perform actions mostly involves developing and honing the needed skills by trying to perform them, testing the limits of one's abilities and skills as one expands them. Failure is an essential part of the learning process, a process that for the most part is not separate from normal acting. For the most part, the learning is concurrent with the acting. The pianist improves as he practices, gives recitals, makes recordings, etc. Failure remains, throughout one's life, part of learning, solidifying, and reassuring one about one's skills and their limits.

That is in large part how we make ourselves. Who we are, in the relevant sense, is partly determined by dispositions and attitudes that incline us to pursue some goals and keep clear of others. And these dispositions are shaped in part by our skills, and our

---

[19]   One gambles when taking the risk is an end in itself or a means to the end of gaining whatever is the prize for winning. In other cases in this category, the risk is not the means to the end, but merely a feature of the situation one puts up with. Gambling does not pose the problem for the Control Principle that other risk-dependent outcomes do. Either one is not responsible for the outcome at all, or in cases one is, one knowingly undertook the risk of that outcome, and in so doing as it were consented to the outcome.

awareness of them, by our self-image as people who, aware of their abilities, are willing or unwilling to challenge their limitations, to run or to avoid certain risks, etc.

To summarize: *First*, our life, its successes, failures, and meaning, are bound up with our interaction with the world, our impact on it, and its impact on us. *Second*, while in some of our activities we put ourselves at the mercy of luck, and sometimes that may be the point, the thrill, of it, in others we rely on our skills, confident, to various degrees, that we know how to succeed given normal conditions. *Third*, our sense of who we are while in part determined independently of our activities (say by gender or ethnicity and their social meanings) is in part determined by our sense of our abilities and their limitations (against the background of the natural and social environment of our life), which (in ways dependent on our temperament and dispositions) fixes the limits of our ambitions and aspirations. *Fourth*, that sense of who we are is continuously being moulded through our understanding of our actions, which reinforces, extends or undermines our confidence in our abilities and skills.[20] *Fifth*, the process of shaping who we are is normatively driven, that is we form views of who or what we want to be in light of views of what people like us should be. *Sixth*, our actions and their success both reveal who we are and make us who we are, in ways that are often difficult to disentangle.

The connection between our actions and who we are explains why emotions like agent-regret which express our feelings about who we are, who we are becoming, or have become (or may become), apply to our actions, including aspects of them which exceed our control. Regarding any instance of such a feeling the question of its justification is a question about the appropriateness of taking that view of the significance of the action to who we are.

4. Responsibility$_2$: the reach of the Guidance Principle

I began by outlining a conception of responsibility$_2$, expressed in the Rational Functioning Principle, which was only partly explained. The preceding reflections on our connectedness to the world provide the material for the missing explanation. It comes in two parts. In the present section I will explain that the Rational Guidance Principle reaches further than is often appreciated. In the next section I will explain why responsibility$_2$ extends to certain cases of failed guidance.

The Guidance Principle holds people responsible both for their independent intentions and for completed intentional and controlled actions. Both are guided by us through the use of our powers of rational agency, but differently: independent intentions are formed in light of our view of our situation, and of the proper response to it, the case for planning for the future, etc., all manifestations of our powers of rational agency. Intentional actions are typically governed by embedded intentions through

---

[20] Though some actions affect us not gradually, but dramatically.

which we guide and control them. But note, that it is the action itself, not merely the intention, which is guided by us through our powers of agency.[21]

Some writers on moral luck miss the point. They think that even though we can be said to be responsible$_2$ for completed intentional actions this is so merely because we are responsible$_2$ for the intention that produced the action. Hence according to them the consequences of responsibility, the attitudes and responses sanctioned by our responsibility for the action, are the same as the attitudes and responses sanctioned by the intention (i.e. the independent intention) to perform it. This seems to be a mistake due to a misguided notion of control.[22] Even aspects of intentional conduct that depend on matters beyond agents' exclusive control are typically guided and controlled by them as I have explained earlier.

Some writers believe that people are responsible$_2$ for their actions simply because they are responsible$_2$ for attempting those actions. The completion of the action, i.e. those parts of it beyond the attempt to perform it, are—they maintain—not controlled by the agents who are therefore not responsible$_2$ for the actions beyond the attempt stage. And, to be sure, in many cases the embedded intention in an attempt to Φ is the same as in Φ-ing. For example, when one attempts to kill someone by poisoning him, and does kill him by that poisoning. Therefore to the extent that responsibility$_2$ depends on being guided by the embedded intention it would appear that the agent is responsible$_2$ for the action because he is responsible$_2$ for the attempt. Talk of responsibility$_2$ for the action is mere *façon de parler*.

But the argument is flawed. In typical intentional actions we guide and control not merely the intention but the act, including its result. To be sure, sometimes people intentionally succeed due to sheer luck. A hopeless shot can intentionally hit the bull's-eye. But such cases are atypical. Typically, we control intentional acts, including their aspects that depend on factors beyond our control, through the embedded intentions, which guide our movements, adjust them to the circumstances in a way calculated to secure the intended result.

That is also why we are responsible$_2$ for most attempts. For the most part an attempt to perform one action is the performance of another action. For example, a failed attempt to murder someone may consist in firing a gun and missing the intended victim. So for the most part responsibility$_2$ for attempts presupposes responsibility$_2$ for completed actions because most attempts are completed actions.[23] When assessing an

---

[21] See Chapter Four.

[22] There can be no denying that one can stipulatively define 'control' to make it true by definition that one can control one's intentions and nothing else. But stipulations do not generate philosophical puzzles. The puzzle of moral luck arises only if we are to blame for actions or consequences that are beyond our control (given the meaning of 'control' when used in these contexts). Hence my claim that some writers misunderstood it.

[23] The exceptions are those special circumstances in which one can try to do something (normally a basic action) without performing any action, as when one regains consciousness after an accident and tries unsuccessfully to move one's arm (such tryings are, like some other doings, not themselves actions). Normally, we cannot try to move our arm, though we can move it. These controversial claims have been

intentional action (e.g. a murder) we assess something quite distinct from what is assessed when assessing an independent intention (e.g. an intention to murder someone). This makes it possible to maintain that the responses and attitudes appropriate to intentional actions differ from those appropriate to an independent intention, consistent with the denial of moral luck.

What of cases in which we are subject to risk, and to luck, as when we bet on the horses, or make speculative investments? It is easy to misperceive the role of intention in such actions. To be sure I intentionally go to the casino, and I intentionally place a bet. But I do not intentionally win the bet, rather, luckily I win. I intentionally make the speculative investment, and I may even intend to make my fortune by making such investment. But I do not intentionally make a fortune through that risky investment. It just happens to turn up trumps, as I hoped that it would. To be sure the divide is anything but sharp. The more skill and foresight go into the action the more appropriate it is to say that I intended its result.

Given that conforming to the Guidance Principle is not necessary for responsibility$_2$, the absence of anything like a sharp boundary does not matter. At the present stage of the argument all I am claiming is that quite often when acting intentionally we are in control of the result. Those tempted to reject this conclusion have to deny that we are responsible$_2$ for most attempts as well, for they too are actions. What could motivate such rejection? One thought is that the action successfully completed on this occasion might have failed had factors beyond our control intervened. But that can only establish that had we failed because of such factors our failure would have been beyond our control, and we are not—if the Guidance Principle sets a necessary condition for responsibility$_2$—responsible$_2$ for the failure. That does not establish that in the circumstances that actually existed at the time of action we were not in control of the action and its result.

Another thought is that successfully performing the action depended not only on our intention or attempt but also on other factors (we succeeded in getting from street to kitchen because the lock functioned well, the floor supported our weight, etc.). These factors, the thought is, are not under our exclusive control, and therefore the action is not under our exclusive guidance and control. But that last step is a non sequitur. The action is under our guidance and control because we could and did adjust our action to the prevailing circumstances, took advantage of them, avoided difficulties they presented, etc. That is the way control is exercised when we engage with the world.[24]

---

much discussed. I do not rely on them in any way. When we do attempt a basic action, we are responsible$_2$ for the attempt, and sometimes we are responsible$_2$ for not attempting. My only claim relevant to the purpose of this chapter is that we are also responsible$_2$ for other attempts, like attempted murder, which are completed acts.

[24] M. Zimmerman ('Luck & Moral Responsibility', in Statman (ed.), *Moral Luck*) rightly warned against understanding 'control' in the Control Principle as some kind of exclusive control on all the conditions for the occurrence of what is supposed to be under control.

In his 'Involuntary Sins'[25] Robert Adams reminds us, putting his point in the terms of the present discussion, that people are often held responsible for their emotions (e.g. for excessive, irrational anger, or for jealousy), for their beliefs (e.g. that some races are inferior to others), and for other attitudes (e.g. self-righteousness) and are thought to be blameworthy (for beliefs, emotions, and attitudes like the above) or praiseworthy for them.

Adams explains why we are responsible for some of our psychological states:

> The deepest reason for accepting this responsibility…is that it is rightly ours. It is important for a correct ethical appreciation of one's own life. To refuse to take responsibility for one's emotions and motives is to be inappropriately alienated from one's own emotional and appetitive faculties. ('Involuntary Sins', 16)

That is true, but—as Adams recognizes—if unqualified it goes too far. We also feel cold when temperatures drop, disoriented when our blood pressure drops, but we are not responsible for these psychological phenomena (though sometimes we are responsible for their causes or their consequences). Therefore Adams qualifies the explanation, restricting it to a limited class of psychological phenomena:

> My suggestion is that among states of mind that have intentional objects, the ones for which we are directly responsible are those in which we are responding, consciously or unconsciously, to data that are rich enough to permit a fairly adequate ethical appreciation of the state's intentional object…(ibid. 26)

I think that in that explanation he is right. I have argued before for the fundamental importance of the distinction between the active and the passive aspects of people's lives, with the active being those aspects of our life in which we respond to reasons (practical or adaptive) as we see them. We control our beliefs, I suggested, and are in control of our emotions, desires, intentions, and actions in so far as we respond to reasons as we see them, and have those beliefs, emotions, desires, and intentions that we take to be in accord with reason. We are not in control; we are tossed hither and thither, when in the grip of urges, passions, moods, or emotions that we take to be out of line with reason. So up to a point, Adams's view is consistent with the Guidance and Control Principles. We control our beliefs and are in control of our emotions, desires, intentions, and actions in so far as we respond to reasons as we see them, and have those beliefs, emotions, desires, and intentions that we take to accord with reason.[26] In fact

---

[25] R. M. Adams, 'Involuntary Sins', *Philosophical Review* 94 (1985), 3–31. I believe that most of the sins Adams deals with are neither voluntary nor involuntary. They are psychological phenomena to which the distinction does not happily apply. See for more detailed discrimination *Engaging Reason*, 11–12. Adams identifies the voluntary with what is chosen or meant. That seems to me inaccurate.

[26] *Engaging Reason*, ch. 1; see also D. Owens, 'Rationalism About Obligation', *European Journal of Philosophy* 16/3 (2008), 403; S. Hurley, *Natural Reasons* (Oxford: OUP, 1989).

Adams rejects the Control Principle altogether.[27] So do I. The next sections examine my reasons.

5. Responsibility$_2$ and the domain of secure competence

To remind ourselves: I am looking to explain why conduct for which we are non-derivatively responsible$_2$ is related to powers of rational agency in accord with the **Rational Functioning Principle**, namely that we are non-derivatively responsible$_2$ for conduct that is the result of the functioning, successful or failed, of our powers of rational agency. As we saw, even the **Guidance Principle**, the relatively uncontroversial element of the Rational Functioning Principle, establishes responsiblity$_2$ for some aspects of conduct over which we do not have exclusive control. I will assume that its connection to our powers of agency requires little more than further elaboration of its details and implications. What is needed here is an explanation of those aspects of the Rational Functioning Principle that reach beyond the Guidance Principle, namely those that assert responsibility for acts and omissions due to the malfunctioning of our powers of rational agency. It is here that we find the examples of 'moral luck', which many found troubling.

The Rational Functioning Principle applies only to people who have powers of rational agency, and only when these powers are not blocked or suspended. It asserts that people are responsible$_2$ for conduct that is due to their powers of rational agency. People vary in the extent of their powers. Their abilities to absorb information, to use it in deliberation, to reach conclusions and be moved to conduct accordingly, as well as their ability to control their bodies, the range of actions they can perform with

---

[27] I am not clear what his view is. He writes: 'whereas the traditional theories are concerned with *conscious* recognition of the badness of the act, my criterion demands only that the data to which we are responding be rich enough to *permit* recognition of the relevant values....it would not be plausible to limit our responsibility for states of mind to cases in which we are or should have been conscious (so as to be able to say) that we are responding to those data' (Adams, 'Involuntary Sins', 26–7). As responsiveness to reason involves some degree of self-awareness the passage suggests a rejection of the Control Principle, at least if control is understood as responsiveness to reason. He also rejects a negligence standard in rejecting that the limit is at what we should have been aware of, and also in his earlier remarks about Alan Donagan who 'maintains... [that] "Ignorance...is culpable if and only if it springs from negligence- from want of due care"...Negligence, in this context, is a voluntary omission of actions that one ought to have performed and that would have cured or prevented the ignorance' (ibid. 19). But as Adams misinterprets here the nature of negligence, this is consistent with his view coinciding with setting a (properly understood) negligence limit to responsibility. Indeed later on he remarks 'I take it the imaginary Hitler Jugend alumnus...has rich enough data in his evidence of the humanity of the non-combatants in question, even if he is never told that they have rights. This will normally be true even if he has never met a member of the race or ethnic group to which the non-combatants belong; it is enough to know that they are human beings. On the other hand, I am prepared to grant, for example, that some conception of a preferable, workable alternative system may be part of the data needed for a fairly adequate appreciation of the injustice of a social or economic system, and that one's experience and education may leave one innocently unable to imagine such an alternative' (ibid. 27) which suggests endorsing a negligence principle.

confidence, and the circumstances in which they can do so—vary considerably. The principle takes this into account. It asserts responsibility$_2$ for conduct due to the powers of rational agency that the person in question has—the range of conduct one is responsible$_2$ for may therefore vary according to the range of one's powers of rational agency at the time.

Thus the principle connects with the earlier observations regarding our engagement with the world. We are non-derivatively responsible$_2$ for unintentional actions only if they are the results of a failed intentional action that falls within our domain of secure competence. Only then is the action due to a failure of our powers of rational agency, in the meaning of the principle. The second way in which the Rational Functioning Principle goes beyond the Guidance Principle is in affirming our responsibility$_2$ for unintentional omissions due to failure of our powers of agency, though in these cases the failure is mostly of our mental powers. Failures of both kinds are normally classified as negligence.[28]

The first of these two kinds of conduct involves cases in which people are responsible$_2$ for intentional actions that they do not control adequately, and because of that they are also responsible$_2$ for another, accidental action. The person who picks up a vase, which slips from his fingers and breaks, and the driver whose foot 'accidentally' slips off the brake, causing an accident, are examples. There was nothing wrong in the person who broke the vase picking it up, and the driver driving. But they did not control these actions adequately, and the common judgement, and it is correct, is that they are responsible$_2$. But why?

Two principles are involved. If they are responsible$_2$ for handling the vase and for driving even though they do not control these actions then they are responsible$_2$ for breaking the vase and for the accident. This responsibility$_2$ arises because of another principle of derivative responsibility$_2$, whereby one is responsible$_2$ for some of the consequences of actions for which one is responsible$_2$. I will return to this principle in the next chapter. The question I wish to explore here is why are they responsible$_2$ for actions they do not control in the first place? Because of the special standing of a domain of secure competence.[29] I have argued that central to our way of Being in the World is a permanently evolving sense of our own mastery and its limitations. Our sense of ourselves includes awareness of a domain within which we are confident that, barring competence-defeating events (a seizure, a biased teacher, etc.), if we set

---

[28] Negligence includes a normative element: failure of performance of a certain kind that *should not have occurred*. Given that the cases I am concerned with are ones in which one failed in doing what one intended to do, that one ought not have failed follows from the assumption that one's intentions were reasonable. It would follow, by the facilitative principle, that one had reason to execute them successfully. Where the assumption fails the cases are not necessarily cases of negligence.

[29] Cf. P. Railton's discussion, different in scope and purpose, but supplementing my observations about the domain of secure competence in 'Practical Competence and Fluent Agency', in D. Sobel and S. Wall (eds.), *Reasons for Action* (Cambridge: CUP, 2009), 81.

ourselves to do something we will. I call it the **domain of secure competence**.[30] A crucial feature of that domain is that acts within it are ones that we are entitled to undertake without reflecting on the prospects of successfully performing them (though the exemption does not extend to the case for their performance). Agency presupposes the availability of such actions. I have suggested that they are central to our sense of who we are, our sense of our own identity. The important point is that we hold ourselves and others responsible[2] for conduct within our respective domains of secure competence, and we do so even when actions within the domain fail, if the failure is not due to a competence-defeating event. In acknowledging responsibility[2] for actions due to our rational powers we are simply affirming that they are our secure rational powers. Our sense of who we are, which underpins our self-esteem, as well as our inclination to take or avoid risks and therefore our aspirations and ambitions, is tied up with our success in establishing a domain within which our powers of rational agency are securely reliable. In holding ourselves competent within that domain we hold ourselves responsible[2] for actions that fall within it. To disavow responsibility[2] for such actions is to be false to who we are.[31]

This is an observation about how we judge matters: When the glass we put on the table tumbles off it, when while taking a step towards the door we bump into the table, etc., we tend to feel annoyance, and to blame ourselves. In these and other reactions we show that we take ourselves to be responsible[2] for these actions. Moreover, these reactions are accepted as appropriate, so long as they are not based on mistakes about our domain of secure competence, do not ignore the occurrence of competence-defeating events, and are not disproportionate.

Failure to control conduct within our domain of secure competence threatens to undermine our self-esteem and our sense of who we are, what we are capable of, etc. We must react to it. We may conclude that we are no longer able securely to perform that kind of action. We have grown frail, our competence is diminishing. We come to recognize our limitations. Commonly that is not the case, and we do not allow it to be. We assert our competence by holding ourselves responsible[2] for it. To disavow responsibility[2] is to be false to who we are.

I am both drawing attention to the practice of holding ourselves responsible[2] for actions within our respective spheres of secure competence and justifying it, by pointing to its role in maintaining our sense of who we are, and of our relations to the world. So it misses the point to counter-argue that my observations are guilty of *petitio principii*, that we are false to ourselves if we deny responsibility[2] for failed actions within our sphere of secure competence only if I am right, which remains to be

---

[30] The principle of rational functioning is of course vague in various respects, and this paragraph provides one crucial part of its interpretation.

[31] Adams's observation quoted earlier though confined to our emotions applies to actions as well: 'to refuse to take responsibility for one's emotions and motives is to be inappropriately alienated from one's own emotional and appetitive faculties'.

established. My argument, such as it is, simply points to our practice of ascribing and acknowledging responsibility$_2$, in a way that enables us to understand its significance in our life. We should, however, expect an additional vindicating explanation of the practice, one that relates it to our capacities of rational agency.

Before giving my explanation, I will discuss two alternatives. The first regards responsibility$_2$ for intentional but uncontrolled action as derivative from responsibility$_2$ for the intention or from the attempt to act on it. It is unsatisfactory partly because such actions need neither be attempted in a controlled way, before we lose control of them, nor performed with an independent intention. They may be expressive actions or other acts whose intentionality is embedded, not arising out of an independent intention. Besides, there is the difficulty of justifying the principle of derivative responsibility$_2$ relied on. An explanation that is a variant of mine (below) for under-ivative responsibility$_2$ would not explain why the responsibility$_2$ is merely derivative.[32]

The second, more radical, alternative is that we ought to control actions that lie within the domain of secure competence. According to it while other duties, other practical reasons, do not establish responsibility$_2$, duties of control are special and do just that. It is true that duties to control our actions differ radically from other duties. Moreover, in many of the relevant cases we ought to have controlled our actions. But these duties do not explain why we are responsible$_2$ for the actions we should have controlled. They are, or are analogous to, instrumental duties. I ought not to break the vase. If I control my actions it will not break. Therefore I ought to control my actions. Note that where there is no sound end to which control is a means or a prerequisite, there is no duty to control. But responsibility$_2$ for these actions is not conditional on having a duty to control them. We are responsible$_2$ for them, so long as they belong within our sphere of secure competence. As with other duties, failure to comply with duties to control counts against us only if (on independent grounds) we are responsible$_2$ for the actions that constitute such failure.

The explanation lies elsewhere: the sphere of our secure competence demarcates the basic domain in which we are competent rational agents, capable not only of planning and intending, but of acting. It is the domain in which our capacities of rational agency are available to us, where (as I stated above) we do not need to assess our chances of success before we take the action. And that is the connection we were looking for: we are responsible$_2$ because we are rational agents, but only for those actions (we can extend the conditions to consequences later) regarding which our capacities of rational agency were available to us to guide and control our actions.

Their availability does not mean that we did control the action, or would have controlled it had we tried harder. We are always liable to fail to control actions within our sphere of secure competence, even when no competence-defeating condition obtains. The conditions establishing that the action is within the sphere of secure

---

[32] Importantly, the relation of an intention to the action it guides is not that of a means to an end.

competence apply to action-types. It does not follow that in an individual case where we did not control the action we could not. 'Can' and 'could not', having to sustain counterfactuals, must be generic rather than specific to the occasion. When applied to a specific act 'you can do it now', when it does not mean 'you have the opportunity to do it now' (conditions are right for successful performance) means you will succeed if you try. It need not presuppose the 'can' of ability.

Before further examining this principle of responsibility$_2$ consider complications in its application to the area of secure competence. The process by which people develop their sense of their secure competence is complex, and influenced by the fact that among various social subgroups certain views about what everyone could be expected to be able securely to do (walk, climb stairs, hold objects, etc.) prevail, and people tend to develop those competences. Beyond that basic domain of common competence various individuals develop further more advanced competences, following their inclinations and capacities.

Some people are disabled, and disability is (by a stipulative definition) the inability to control a range of conduct that is commonly taken to be conduct that could be expected to be within people's domain of secure competence. There are well-known disadvantages in being identified publicly as disabled. Therefore, people on the borderline of disability often prefer to avoid seeing themselves and being seen by others as disabled. They do so by holding themselves responsible$_2$ for conduct that they believe they could be expected to control (usually because of a common view that everyone could be expected to have it within their secure competence), even when their control of it is not fully secure. Needless to say, often others accept them at their word, i.e. as responsible$_2$ for conduct of that kind.

Furthermore, when people fail to do what they could be expected to have been competent to do, should have done, and tried to do, the question whether the failure was due to the fact that they were not as competent as they could have been expected to be, or whether they did not try hard enough, or whether their action just failed as some do, does not always have an answer. The boundaries between 'one's competence is not up to the required level', 'one did not try hard enough', and 'one just failed', are indeterminate. Often there is no fact of the matter as to which category an individual case belongs to, and where there is, it is rarely possible to be sure about it. Hence, absent manifestation of disability, the practice of holding people responsible$_2$ for actions which, by a reasonable social standard, they are expected to have within their domain of secure confidence, is justified.

This may seem harsh on individuals who cannot help the situation. But that is not so. Responsibility$_2$ applies only to people who could have been expected to have that competence and control, and that means that they could have had it. It does not apply in the same way to young children, people with disabilities, etc. I conclude that the practices I have described are, unless pushed to extremes, reasonable given their role in human life.

6. The case of omissions

Sometimes we are responsible₂ for not doing something. In the absence of a better word I will refer to not-Φing as omitting to Φ. As noticed earlier it seems impossible to explain responsibility₂ for omissions by reference to either Intention or Control Principles. As we are responsible₂ for many unintentional omissions the Intention Principle fails, and the very notion of control of omission is obscure. Suppose an omission is controlled if the agent would not perform the action unintentionally, and that condition is secure. Given this understanding, control is not necessary for responsibility₂. People who, due to some medical condition (e.g. Parkinson's disease, Tourette's syndrome), cannot control some of their omissions may well be responsible₂ for some of them. Besides, this version of the Control Principle does not establish any relationship between controlled omissions and the capacities of rational agency (and cannot therefore be sufficient for responsibility₂ either).

As we omit an indefinite number of actions at any given time, and never have occasion to think of almost all of them, it seems plausible to expect that there is no clear demarcation between those omissions we are responsible₂ for and others we are not, except where there is reason to refer to those omissions, for example, because they were wrong, or advisable. The demarcation that I propose below is suggested by general theoretical considerations, and is by and large consistent with other concerns.

Consider unintended omissions. They are unintended because the question whether or not to perform the omitted action was not fully resolved in the agent's mind. To simplify assume that it was not resolved because it did not arise. I will assume that in-between cases (ambivalence, etc.) could be explained once responsibility₂ for intended omissions and for omissions that never surfaced in the agent's mind is understood. Distinguish two kinds of cases in which at the time it did not occur to the agent to consider whether to perform the action or omit it. One is due to a failure in the functioning of the agent's powers of rational agency (he intended to set the alarm, but it slipped his mind and he did not). In the other kind of case so far as the agent's beliefs, resolutions, intentions, or other attitudes are concerned there is nothing to make him even consider whether to perform the action. For example, I did not call the person whose name is first in the Munich telephone directory today.

We are responsible₂ for clear cases of the first kind, and not responsible₂ for clear cases of the second. Had I functioned properly as a rational agent then given the person I am, that is given my beliefs, intentions, and attitudes, I would have set the alarm. My failure to do so was a failure to connect my various beliefs, intentions, etc. My omission is due to failing to function adequately as a rational agent, even though my capacities of rational agency were available to me (I was not drugged, do not suffer from amnesia, etc.). It was an occasional lapse of functioning just like the case in which I drop the vase. Omitting to call that person in Munich was not due to failure to function as a rational agent, because there was no fault in my functioning as a rational agent in not thinking about the question at all, in not noticing it as a possibility.

How far does the 'failure to connect', in ways that render us responsible$_2$ for omissions, go? It certainly extends well beyond the example of accidentally failing to act on a prior intention. In particular it includes cases in which one 'should have known better', that is some cases in which one failed to consider the case for an action because there was nothing in one's beliefs to suggest such a case, provided that a fairly minimal degree of reflectiveness would have made one change one's beliefs even without any new information. Had he been reflective he would have easily realized that an additional belief is implied by his existing beliefs, and that belief in combination with his other beliefs and attitudes would have indicated a case for considering that action. This too is a case of failing to connect: a case in which had he connected he would have modified his existing beliefs and attitudes.

Needless to say there are other examples of failing to consider an action due to 'failing to connect'. Obviously, the boundary is anything but determinate. If I am right that indeterminacy is a feature of our concept of responsibility$_2$ then a good account would preserve it. One confession of a possible drawback in the account: it may well lead to classifying some cases often taken as excuses for wrongful omissions due to ignorance as cases in which one was not responsible$_2$ for the wrongful omissions.

7. The emerging conception of responsibility$_2$

I focused on three types of case: (1) responsibility$_2$ for normal (intentional and) controlled action, where the qualification 'normal' excludes responsibility$_2$ for intentional and controlled action under hypnosis or other conditions that suspend one's ability to function as a competent rational agent; (2) responsibility$_2$ for uncontrolled action within one's sphere of secure competence;[33] (3) responsibility$_2$ for omissions due to failure to integrate one's beliefs, intentions, etc. What I said about them is a bare outline of an account, summarized by the Principle of Rational Functioning, leaving much to be fleshed out. Arguably, all cases of responsibility$_2$ are instances of the Principle of Rational Functioning plus principles of derivative responsibility$_2$. For example, the drunk wobbling his way out of the bar and accidentally breaking a wine glass is responsible$_2$ for breaking the glass derivatively, because he is responsible$_2$ for walking. And he is responsible$_2$ for walking derivatively because he is responsible$_2$ for setting out to leave the bar unaided. Why then is he responsible$_2$ for the latter? It is tempting to reply that he should not have started walking as he did. He should have stayed at the bar, or asked the bartender to help him. Perhaps so. But doing what one should not does not establish responsibility$_2$ for that action. Central to the notion of responsibility$_2$ is that actions, good, bad, and indifferent, are neither to one's credit nor discredit unless one is responsible$_2$ for their performance. The drunk is responsible$_2$ for setting out to walk because it was an action within his sphere of secure competence. So

---

[33] As the examples show responsibility$_2$ for actions within the sphere of secure competence exists only when they are intentionally initiated.

is walking, but not when he is drunk. But deciding not to walk **is**, even when ordinarily drunk. To be sure, there is a degree of inebriation that would suspend his capacity to function as a rational agent altogether. The example is of a case where this is not so.

It is no coincidence that all cases of responsibility$_2$ belong to one or more of the three categories I discussed. The order of presentation above started in the conventional way: with normal intended and controlled actions. The force of examples (negligence, unintended omissions, etc.) made us revise the Rational Guidance Principle. Yet the impression that normal intended and controlled actions form the central case remains. In a way they do: they are the paradigmatic cases of rational agents successfully deploying their powers of rational agency. But there is another way of looking at matters, which shows responsibility$_2$ for unintended omissions and actions within one's secure competence to be the core of responsibility$_2$.

They mark the most basic domain in which agents' rational powers are available and functioning (as they automatically are when available), even though not always perfectly.[34]

In remarks about what makes people persons, or rational agents, it is common to emphasize the ability to distance oneself from one's beliefs, commitments, and intentions, to review them and revise them. Equally essential, presupposed even by the ability to review and revise, is the ability to act with confidence, without the need to review, double-check, or reassure oneself. That competence—applying to forming beliefs, intentions, etc., and to actions alike—is essential if we are not to be stuck in loops of indecision. Moreover, we need to be aware (at least to a degree) of that competence. That awareness, which need not reach the level of explicit articulation, constitutes part of our understanding of who we are, and plays a major role in forming our dispositions to engage with or distance ourselves from various possibilities, prospects or risks. Being responsible$_2$ for actions that manifest, successfully or otherwise, that competence is part of the way (in our existing practices) that boundary of the self, and that sense of who we are, is acknowledged.

I discussed these matters when defining the notion of a domain of secure competence. It was defined in relation to secure skills in performing various actions, but it extends to competence in reasoning, mental arithmetic, kinds of memory, resoluteness, and other mental phenomena. The same rationale applies to the type of unintentional omissions for which we are responsible$_2$. It applies to those omissions where a moderate degree of successful functioning of our secure rational capacities would have alerted us to the need to consider the case for certain actions. In other words, it applies to our domain of secure competence in rational functioning.

---

[34] But the failure is not normative. It does not mean that we behaved in ways that we should not have. It means merely that had our faculties of rational agency functioned properly then, given our existing beliefs, intentions, etc. we would have considered whether to act or to omit (whether or not there was reason to do so, or it was best to do so).

As I explained, part of the case for not excluding these cases of unsuccessful functioning of our capacities for rational action from responsibility$_2$ is that the inevitable occasional lapse in their functioning is not a result of the capacities and skills being degraded, or of their contracting. Similarly, acknowledging others to be the people they take themselves to be includes accepting their responsibility$_2$ in such cases. I did not claim that we would not be rational agents if we did not have the concept of responsibility$_2$ that we have, merely that we do have that notion, and that it plays a significant role in our understanding of the way we act in the world.

8. But is it blame?

My account of responsibility$_2$ shows it to mean more than being worthy of blame or praise. There is a whole variety of responses and attitudes mandated by responsibility$_2$, other than blaming or praising. At the practical end of the range stands the duty to make amends when one wronged someone by conduct for which one is responsible$_2$. The availability of excuses, those that do not negate responsibility$_2$, does not exempt one from that (even though they exempt one from blame).

Still, responsibility$_2$ is also a condition of blameworthiness. Agents are to blame for conduct for which they are responsible$_2$ unless they are excused. It follows that the **Rational Functioning Principle** allows that people are to blame for conduct that they do not control, i.e. that they are subject to 'moral luck'. This consequence of the account is in line with common beliefs, as with the tendency to judge the negligent killer more blameworthy than the negligent driver whose good luck it was not to harm anyone. But it is out of line with a popular understanding of responsibility$_2$. As Nagel put it: 'one cannot be more culpable or estimable for anything than one is for that fraction of it which is under one's control'.[35]

Williams was indifferent to that worry. Undermining 'the morality system', or at least bringing out its limitations, was one of his goals. By and large my reaction is similar: I find that common understanding of blame indefensible, though I am unable to explore it here. One thing is clear: to undermine the misguided account of blame it is essential that the correct account of the notion, or, if you like, the alternative concept of blame, the one that is relied upon when holding people blameworthy for acts or omissions, is a familiar and important one. I will not say much in support of this contention, for I see little reason to doubt it. Blameworthiness is a broad category. It ranges from the trivial to the serious. Furthermore, various invocations of blame carry different pragmatic implications, and these accommodate all the distinctions that are called for.

Some will agree to the above, but insist that they have in mind a particular kind of blame only: moral blame. I do not see a case for assuming that there is here, any more

---

[35] T. Nagel, 'Moral Luck', in *Mortal Questions* (Cambridge: CUP, 1979) 28.

than elsewhere, a systematic and theoretically significant distinction between the moral and the rest.[36] More importantly, blaming can, and often has, a very specific object: I can blame Jones for the attitude, the intention, and the belief that his action expresses, and yet not blame him for his action. Or I can blame him both for his action and for his attitude, and so on. There is no case for maintaining that there are here different concepts of blaming. There are simply different objects of blame.[37]

What we needed, and this chapter aimed to supply, is an understanding of how it could be that we are responsible₂ and therefore may be to blame for aspects of conduct which exceed our exclusive control, and may be differentially to blame for intentions, attempts, and actions which share their mental component. I will summarize briefly how the argument of the chapter helps with this.

Consider intentional actions first, and accidental ones second. Some writers hold that the degree of blameworthiness or praiseworthiness of an intentional action is identical with that of an intention to perform it. Given the understanding of control I suggested earlier this would not be the consequence of Nagel's dictum. When acting intentionally we normally control the results and the foreseen consequences of our actions. But do we deserve praise or blame for them to a degree different from the praise or blame their intentions merit?

Intentions, like emotions such as fear, anger, pride, gratitude, jealousy, which also express ways of psychologically relating to and reacting to the world, are subject to judgements of responsibility, blameworthiness, etc. But as they are part of our interior lives, and merely aim at action, there is a good case for judging them on their own, and for not applying to them automatically the judgements that would be appropriate to apply to the actions or omissions they led to. That is the lesson of the discussion of the meaning actions and their consequences have for us. The lesson has to be applied with attention to different cases, but I will leave this matter here without exploring these implications.

Perhaps, while actions may merit blame and praise in ways that differ from the independent intentions to perform them, attempts to Φ necessarily merit the same praise or blame as Φing. That would tend to suggest not, as most writers do, that we are too lenient in our views of the degree of blame attached to failed attempts, but that we are too severe in the degree of blame we think that successful wrongdoers deserve. After all, we judge successful wrongdoers more severely because they succeeded, but their success—according to this argument—does not add to the blameworthiness.

Of course, the fact that intentional actions as a whole, and not only their intentionality, are under our control only means that the Rational Functioning Principle does not rule out the possibility that the degree of blame or praise their performance earns is

---

[36] See on the problem of distinguishing the moral from the non-moral *Engaging Reason*, ch. 11.

[37] There is a case for thinking that blaming the wind, just like believing that the wind is responsible, for the damage is blaming in a different sense from blaming a person for an unexcused wrongful action for which he or she is responsible.

affected by their results. Is there any reason to think that they actually have such an effect? We are told that most people believe that they do, for it is a widespread view that one is to blame more for a wrong done than for a wrong attempted. Williams's discussion, and my elaboration on his theme, explained why that belief makes sense. They explained why we care about the results of our actions, and often judge ourselves by our success or failure to achieve them. They explain the significance of the attachment to our actions, results included, and of the fact that we judge ourselves by our ability to achieve them in our life. This is consistent with the fact that agents who completed an intentional action may be to blame both for the action and for intending it, whereas if they tried and failed they are not to blame for the action (which did not take place) but may be to blame for the intention, and that blameworthiness is the same as the blameworthiness of those who complete the action for their intention to perform it (assuming that the circumstances are the same).

In one respect matters appear different when we deal with accidental actions. Think of an action (the bringing about of a result) which one regrets. If it was intentional the agent embraced that regretted result, either accepting it as a foreseen consequence or aiming to achieve it. This 'accepting' connects the agent to the regretted action and its consequences. That is why the agent may be to blame for them. If the action was merely negligent, and therefore accidental, the agent may not have foreseen the result. He regrets it now. But that regret is set aside from his responsibility$_2$ for the action. Think of the driver who negligently kills. Of course he regrets the killing. But he would regret it also had he not been negligent, and the killing were a mere accident. His regret is different because he was negligent. Crudely perhaps we will allow that it is greater in that case. But that may be because there are two things he regrets: his negligence and his killing. But they are unconnected. His regret for the killing is the same regret he would have felt had he killed without being negligent. Therefore, some would say, the agent cannot be more to blame for the negligent killing than for the negligent driving.

What I suspect we actually do, and certainly what we should do, is to refuse to judge all negligent agents with the same brush, one coloured by the facts that make them negligent and nothing more. Quite apart from the significance of their conduct and its consequences, their mental states differ a good deal, both on the occasion and as reflecting a habit of mind and action. In some cases of negligence agents actually foresee the accident they bring about. In some others they foresee the probability, or the likelihood, or the possibility, of the accident, with a greater or lesser degree of clarity and of determinacy. And sometimes they welcome it, at others they are indifferent to it, at others still they hope to avoid it, and again these appear in various degrees of clarity and determinacy. To claim that because they would have regretted the outcome even had they not been responsible for it, and because their responsibility is for negligence only they have failed to 'accept' the outcome, and their regret is independent of their responsibility, is to be fixated on a thin distinction among mental attitudes which bears little relation to people's experience, and to their normative understanding of themselves and others.

Those who think so could allow that many other reactions may be warranted by negligent killing and not by negligent driving which harms no one. But, they insist, when it comes to blame (or praise) evaluation is determined by the agent's attitude (or the part of his conduct that he controlled).

The previous analysis helps expose the artificiality of this conception of blame. There is no reason to deny that it is possible to form an attitude to negligent agents (and to others) that conforms to that artificial conception. Nor is there a need to deny that such an attitude has a reasonable role to play in people's attitudes to themselves and to others. But to assume that it has some unique moral standing, even though it ignores everything else, including the importance of the object of the agents' intentions and beliefs, the significance of their actions, and all more nuanced distinctions regarding their mental states, anything other than what they intended or knew, is the mark of living in a blinkered, impoverished, and distorted world.

13

Responsibility and the Negligence Standard

1. Preliminaries

The last chapter took responsibility for negligence to be a test case for an explanation of responsibility. But while cases of negligence were used as examples no analysis of the conditions of responsibility for negligence was offered. This is the task of the present chapter. It will recap some of the key points of the last chapter and apply them to an explanation of the Negligence Standard, as I will refer to the doctrine that agents are responsible for their negligent conduct, and for negligently caused harm.

The law is not my topic. But as most detailed discussions of negligence set out to explain its treatment in the law we may learn from them, and from the legal ways of understanding negligence. The law holds people responsible for various acts, conditions, or events. Put differently: people are legally responsible for various acts, conditions, or events; they are responsible according to law. Expressions to that effect are to be found in authoritative legal texts, such as court decisions, and in scholarly expositions of the law. This means that the law uses the concepts of responsibility and of negligence and assigns certain consequences to being responsible. Legal responsibility renders one legally liable in certain ways.

Hohfeld,[1] as we all remember, identifies liability with being subject to someone's (normative) power. Most commonly we refer to liability to indicate being subject to the power of another to impose on one some disadvantage. Typically, unlawfully causing harm places one under a legal obligation to compensate the harmed people. But again, typically, the law makes enforcement of that duty dependent on an enforcement process, often including a judicial decision, and the liability one incurs by so harming another is liability to be subject to those enforcement measures, for example, being liable to be sued for the damages one now owes. In some cases the very existence of a (legal) duty to compensate or to take some other remedial action, and not only its enforcement, is dependent on a court decision. In such cases unlawfully harming another makes one liable to be subjected to such remedial duties. I labour

---

[1] W. N. Hohfeld, *Fundamental Legal Conceptions* (New Haven: Yale UP, 1919), 5ff., esp. 58–9.

the point to emphasize that responsibility should not be identified with liability. Rather liability is—sometimes—a consequence of responsibility.[2]

Among the various senses of 'responsibility', the one basic for normative thought is that which Hart identifies as 'capacity-responsibility' (as in the last chapter I refer to it as responsibility$_1$):

'he is responsible for his actions' is used to assert that a person has certain normal capacities.... [namely] those of understanding, reasoning, and control of conduct.[3]

These, and the list can be extended, are our capacities for rational agency. The powers of reasoning and understanding are among our rational capacities, whereas the capacity to control our conduct enables us to express our rational capacities in action.[4] We are responsible for our conduct because we are rational agents, and as rational agents. We are not responsible in that way if we lack capacity-responsibility or if the powers of rational agency constituting it are temporarily suspended or blocked, as they are when we are asleep, or under deep hypnosis, or when sensory deprivation denies us the use of our rational capacities.

Now, in this remark 'responsibility' did not mean capacity-responsibility. The very point was to draw attention to the fact that we are not always responsible, in the relevant sense, for actions performed even while we possess the capacities possession of which constitutes capacity-responsibility. As before I refer to this second sense of responsibility as 'responsibility$_2$'. 'John was responsible$_2$ for Φ-ing' only if John's Φ-ing was related to his capacities of rational agency in an appropriate way.

Being responsible$_2$ for some act or state (such as the damage the act caused) is part of only one kind of liability-generating condition. For example, one can be liable for jury service; one can incur liability for tax in ways that do not depend on responsibility for any action. Responsibility$_2$ is a condition of liability that is triggered by what the law takes to be[5] failure to conform to a non-derivative reason.[6] It is a condition of liability

---

[2] Hart was right (*Punishment and Responsibility* (Oxford: OUP, 1968), 215–16) to correct his earlier (see ibid., ch. 8) mistake in thinking that in one of its senses responsibility is virtually identical with liability, and also right in criticizing other legal writers for taking this view. It is a pity that some writers still attribute to him the view that liability is one 'type' of responsibility. See e.g. P. Cane, *Responsibility in Law and Morality* (Oxford: Hart Publishing, 2002), 29.

[3] Hart, *Punishment and Responsibility*, 227.

[4] 'Control of conduct' is not strictly part of our rational capacities. It is however, as will be explained below, necessary for these capacities to be manifested in action in all but mental acts. See generally Chapter Four. Capacity-responsibility, as well as the concept of responsibility that I will discuss here, allows of degrees. To simplify I will not consider the implications of that fact. I will assume that below a certain level (probably to be only vaguely identified) one simply lacks capacity-responsibility, and as a result is not responsible for one's actions. Those who possess (that minimum degree of) capacity-responsibility are responsible for an action if and only if the conditions of responsibility discussed here apply to them, i.e. if their responsibility for the actions passes a threshold condition.

[5] For an explanation of my personalization of the law see *Between Authority and Interpretation* (Oxford: OUP, 2009).

[6] Derivative reasons are, typically, instrumental or constitutive reasons. For example, I may have a reason to take the train to Oxford, and also a reason to take the bus there, both deriving from my reason to be there

that arises in situations in which an action or a state of affairs is one that one should not have performed or allowed to exist and one is responsible$_2$ for the failure to conduct oneself as one should have done. Liability to punishment or to pay damages, etc. arising in such cases is responsibility-based.

In the last chapter I defended **the Rational Functioning Principle** as the correct account of the relationship between people's capacities of rational agency and their conduct or its consequences that makes them responsible$_2$ for them. Here I will again introduce it by arguing against an plausible alternative, the **Guidance** (by reason) **Principle** of responsibility according to which we are responsible$_2$ for actions that are guided by our powers of rational agency, and for none other. As was explained actions are guided by the agents' powers of rational agency when they are performed for, what the agents believe to be, an adequate reason, and their performance is controlled and guided by the agents' beliefs about what reasons they have and what conditions obtain, so that the intended actions, and no action they judge to be on balance undesirable, are performed. Regarding actions, but not omissions, and given an appropriate understanding of control, it coincides in application with the more familiar Control Principle.[7]

The Guidance Principle states a sufficient condition for responsibility$_2$; it does not set its limits. The **Negligence Standard** alerts us to clear cases of conduct for which we are responsible$_2$, even though the Guidance Principle would suggest otherwise. We need supplementary principles of responsibility.

That is why much of what is to follow is about negligence. But not necessarily about negligence law. Negligence is not a legal concept; it is merely borrowed and used by the law. Responsibility$_2$ for negligent actions is generally recognized in contexts where legal liability is off the horizon. Besides, the law of negligence, as commonly demarcated, deals with matters other than liability for negligent conduct, such as vicarious liability, standards for the assessment of damages, the impact of contributory or comparative negligence, issues to do with joint tortfeasors and much else. From time to time new grounds for liability emerge out of negligence law, as happened or is happening with product liability, and the boundary between them can remain obscure for a while. Furthermore, sometimes the courts might mistakenly identify liability as arising out of responsibility for negligent acts, when in fact it is based on some other

---

(say because I promised to give a lecture). If I take the bus I no longer have a reason to take the train. Taking the bus was a way of getting there, taking the train an alternative way to the same end. Failing to follow a derivative reason has no consequences, provided one took an alternative (adequate) route to the same goal. But if one fails to get to Oxford then one ought to do something in mitigation or compensation for this failure.

[7] The Control Principle says that *we are morally responsible for X only if X is under our rational control, or if we are responsible only because, and to the extent that X has aspects that are under our rational control.* It is often identified implicitly with the Intention Principle namely that one is responsible for one's intentional actions, and for their intended or foreseen consequences. I should add that advocates of the Control Principle often assume an understanding of control that differs from the one incorporated in the Guidance Principle, and that differs (though I will not argue the point here) from the common understanding of control.

ground. Such developments can confuse and sometimes distort the legal analysis of negligence.

Finally, much of the law of negligence concerns the identification of the standard of care people have to observe in their dealings with one another. An appropriate duty of care is essential to the Negligence Standard. As will be explained later, an inappropriately high level of care required by law may invalidate the claim that the liability due to its breach is liability for negligence. Allowing for this point, it is still the case that the law has latitude in determining the standard of care failure to comply with which renders one legally liable to compensate people injured through one's negligence. People may act negligently without being legally liable for harm caused by their negligence. In such cases we say that they are not negligent, meaning not negligent in law. If we were fussy we would say that they are negligent but not liable in law.

In saying that the law has some latitude in determining the standard of care I do not, of course, mean that its determination need not be guided by cogent reasons. I am merely saying that these reasons do not determine whether the action is negligent. They determine when one should be *legally liable* for harm caused by one's negligence. I will have nothing to say about such reasons. Similarly, the fact that negligent conduct is, other things being equal, wrong does not in itself establish the case for legal liability for negligence, and I will say nothing about the desirability of such liability compared with dealing with accidents through some insurance mechanism or in some other way.[8]

These observations make it clear how I avoid one of the dilemmas encountered in explaining common law doctrines. Given the impossibility of reductive non-normative explanations of normative doctrines, like negligence, sound explanations inevitably establish the conditions under which the doctrines would be justified. As a result all too often theorists of negligence law or of other legal doctrines offer justifications of existing law, manifesting the belief that used to be widespread in the legal profession, that the common law is the best of all possible laws. Such heresy cannot be further from my thoughts. In the first place, while I will attempt to vindicate responsibility for negligence, that is not a foregone conclusion. Second, even though people are responsible$_2$ for their negligence, it is an open question, and not one addressed here, whether the law should make such responsibility a basis for legal liability. Finally, if it is to be a ground of liability, the law has to comply with additional considerations in determining standards of care, and remedies for their violation. So, vindication of responsibility$_2$ for negligence is far removed from vindication of the law of negligence as we, or some other countries, have it.

---

[8] For example, New Zealand has abolished tort liability for personal injury, but negligently injuring someone is certainly still a moral wrong. There could also be cases of piecemeal rejection of such liability, by raising the standard of care required by law above the moral standard, or by implementing a different regime of liability for some harms (as in the law of strict liability and of product liability).

2. Negligence

Given that negligence law allocates risk of liability for damages, much writing about negligence law is concerned with the efficiency or fairness of the distribution. But negligence law allocates risk of liability in a special way: by holding people responsible for negligently bringing about certain harms. Other parts of the law distribute risk of liability without attributing responsibility, in the sense I am discussing, to those liable for the harm.

Strict liability, a term I will confine to doctrines that share their basic structure with the rule in *Rylands v. Fletcher*,[9] is a case in point. It imposes an independent duty to compensate for certain harms, 'independent' in not being incurred by violating another duty, in particular not being derived from a duty not to harm.[10] The duty to compensate is justified, to the extent that it is, as a form of compulsory insurance (with special damage-assessment rules) for damage or harm caused, for example, by dangerous things one possesses.

Not everyone takes this view of strict liability. John Gardner, for example, argues that in strict liability the duty to compensate derives from failure to comply with a duty not to harm.[11] This view has its appeal. After all it is not as if the agent may harm others so long as he compensates them later. It seems natural to say that he owes damages because he wronged them by harming them. Yet an argument along these lines is at best inconclusive. Insurance schemes, think for example of state unemployment insurance, are not normally indifferent between the compensable harm not occurring and its occurrence followed by compensation. Typically payment of compensation is the inferior option. The hoped-for result is that the harm does not occur. The trouble with the thought that strict liability to compensate depends on violation of some duty is that we lack an explanation for the duty. My doubt is not that there is no duty to do with avoiding the harm (the one that triggers the strict liability). It seems plausible to think that there is such a moral duty.[12] But what exactly is its content? Gardner argues persuasively that there can be duties to succeed, not only duties to try.[13] I would go

---

[9] (1868) LR 3 HL 330.

[10] See for example the explanation that part of the basis for strict liability is 'the ultimate idea of rectifying a wrong and putting the burden where it should belong as a matter of abstract justice, that is, upon the one of the *two innocent parties* whose acts instigated or made the harm possible' *Siegler v Kuhlman* 81 Wash 2d 448 (1972) 455–6 (emphasis added).

[11] J. Gardner: 'The truth is that when the law imposes strict liability on D for actions of D's that injured P, it asserts that D had (and failed to perform) a straightforward obligation *not to injure P*.' 'Obligations and Outcomes in the Law of Torts', in P. Cane and J. Gardner (eds.), *Relating to Responsibility: Essays for Tony Honoré on His Eightieth Birthday* (Oxford: Hart Publishing, 2001), 113. Alan Brudner also thinks that strict liability to compensate derives from a prior duty: *The Unity of the Common Law* (Berkeley and Los Angeles: University of California Press, 1995), 190. His variant is effectively criticized by Gardner.

[12] Honoré, in *Making Law Bind* (Oxford: Clarendon Press, 1987), 71, doubts that there is in such cases a legal duty of care, and it is natural to think that if he is right there is no legal duty to prevent harm either.

[13] Gardner, 'Obligations and Outcomes', esp. at 134–41.

further: even duties to try are duties to succeed, to succeed in trying.[14] We do not always try, and we may not succeed in trying to do something even when we set out to try to do it (I may set out to try to assassinate the president but on my way I may badly twist my ankle, spending the rest of the day in hospital, never actually trying to assassinate him).[15]

It is still an open question whether strict liability is a result of failure to comply with a duty to prevent harm (e.g. from dangerous objects in one's possession).[16] To show that that is the source of the liability we need a reason for the law to impose such a duty regarding dangerous objects, even though it does not impose a similar duty regarding harms covered by liability for negligence. The danger posed by dangerous objects can explain strict *liability* to compensate for harm they cause. It is less obvious that it can also explain why there should be a duty not to harm other than that covered by negligence law. The standard of care required by the negligence doctrine varies with the risk posed. If this is adequate in the generality of cases why not for cases covered by strict liability? In the absence of an answer, and there may be one that evades me, it seems that strict liability is independent of breach of a duty not to harm. One final, and crucial point: even on Gardner's view, just as on mine, the function of damages under strict liability is analogous to compulsory insurance because damages are not dependent on responsibility. They do not depend on establishing that the defendant is responsible$_2$ for the harm.

Negligence is different.[17] Negligent conduct is not careless conduct; it is careless conduct for which one is responsible$_2$, and where care was due. It is a conceptual truth that negligent conduct is a prima facie wrong for which one is responsible$_2$. One can rebut allegations of negligence by establishing that one is not responsible$_2$ for the conduct, or by establishing that even though the conduct was careless, one had no reason to be careful. Is it possible that one cannot ever be responsible$_2$ for careless conduct? It would follow that the concept of negligence has no application (in the

---

[14] Gardner would perhaps take issue with this characterization of the obligation to try: according to Gardner, it is not correct to think of an obligation to try as another kind of obligation to succeed: 'If some people do not perform their obligation to take care however hard they try, this does not go to show that it is not an obligation to try. It only goes to show that it is an obligation to try harder (more assiduously) than they are capable of trying.' See ibid. 118.

[15] Though in some cases the difference between trying to ϕ and failing to ϕ and trying to ϕ and failing to try to ϕ disappears, just as on occasion failure to try reduces to 'not trying hard enough', which concedes that one is trying.

[16] One cannot short-cut the argument by claiming that one has a right not to be harmed, or that one's property not be damaged, and therefore there is a duty not to harm or not to damage other people's property. Had there been a general right of that kind it would have made sense to think that strict liability arises when people invade the right but are not responsible for invading it. However, there is no general right not to be harmed. Establishing which rights we have goes hand in hand with establishing what duties we owe. That is the way I consider the matter in the text above.

[17] It appears that Cane (*Responsibility in Law and Morality*, at 3) really regards liability in negligence as similar in the respects analysed above, to strict liability, though his analysis of responsibility (which neither isolates nor focuses on the sense of responsibility I am investigating) may disguise the fact.

world—it may have applications in fiction, etc.). My aim is to use the conclusions of the last chapter to vindicate responsibility$_2$ for negligent conduct.

Not all writers on negligence agree that in attaching liability to negligently caused harm the law holds people responsible$_2$ for such harm.[18] Moreover, I have already mentioned that some parts of negligence law developed into independent doctrines of strict liability. It is possible for negligence law as a whole to undergo such transformation. My brief remarks about strict liability show that, given the legal focus on remedies, it can be difficult to identify the legal reasons for liability for damages. We rely on the structure of legal rules, on reasons stated or implied in legislation or the common law, but also on the presumption that the law remains faithful to non-legal reasons that are recognized in the society.

By such indications liability for harmful negligence in English Law is based on defendants being responsible$_2$ for the violation of some duty. But what duty? The most promising options are: *First*, there is **a duty not to harm**, but agents who caused harm are **excused** if they behaved with due care. *Second*, **there is a duty of care** which makes one liable to damages when its violation causes harm. *Third*, there are two duties, both a duty of care, and a duty not to harm through carelessness (i.e. through violation of the duty of care).

We can exclude the first option, for it misconceives the role of excuses. Some excuses negate responsibility$_2$. Others don't, and in referring to excuses I will have only the latter in mind. When a duty to compensate derives from breach of a primary duty it is typically not subject to excuses. Duties are practical reasons. Practical reasons generally admit the possibility of partial compliance. If I owe you £100, giving you £30 is paying part of my debt. I do not need a special reason to pay the £30. The reason to pay the £100 is also a reason to pay the £30. Similarly having paid £30 by the time payment was due I should still pay the rest (possibly with compensation for the delay), and that again does not depend on there being a special reason. The original debt is still all the reason required. Agents who are responsible$_2$ for failure to do what they had reason to do should, when possible, do the next best thing, in order to come as close as possible to doing what they had to do. So, if I should have cleaned your car yesterday and did not I should clean it today. The original reason is the reason for partial or second best compliance; no new reason is required.[19]

---

[18] It can be difficult to establish what writers on the subject think about this question. Many writers argue that individuals are responsible for negligently caused harm, but do not use 'responsible' in the sense I use it. Some writers use it to mean roughly the same thing as 'liable', with no implications for the characterization of the conduct outside the law. For example, Stephen Perry argues that responsibility in tort law hinges on the individual's ability to avoid causing harm. The obligation to compensate is normally triggered by fault (except in cases of strict liability), but responsibility itself is a stricter concept, and we are not always responsible only for harm we could have avoided. See Perry, 'Responsibility for Outcomes, Risk, and the Law of Torts', in Gerald J. Postema (ed.), *Philosophy and the Law of Torts* (Cambridge: CUP, 2001), 91.

[19] See Chapters Nine and Ten, where I argued that outside the law the duty to compensate for a wrong one did is nothing more than the duty not to do the wrong. Institutional legal considerations generally make

If the derivative duty to compensate is the duty not to harm transformed by failure to comply into a duty to do the next best thing (restore the victims to where they should have been, or as close as possible), then it is not subject to excuses. Excuses excuse from punishment and more, but are not relevant to compensation.

Therefore the second option I mentioned: that liability for negligent harming arises out of failure to comply with duties of care, is more promising. Whatever the doubts about their precise content, there seems little doubt that we have duties of care, which are recognized in law. Moreover, exposing people to risks they know of has real and mostly undesirable consequences,[20] and so does people's knowledge that the conduct of others may expose them to risks. It affects people's sense of security. Breach of duties whose purpose is to reduce the risk of harm by taking due care would justify liability to damages, and the law may be right to attach liability to damages only when the breach causes actual harm. Yet, it seems that we do not merely have a duty of care, with the purpose of reducing the risk of harm. We also have a duty to avoid harm to the extent that that can be done by acting with due care. Morally speaking we have two (kinds of) duties: a duty of care and a duty not to harm by negligent breach of duties of care. In other words, there is a moral duty whose point, and therefore whose content, is to protect people from negligent harm. This combination of duties (duty of care, and a duty not to harm through negligent carelessness) constitutes the Negligence Standard. In the absence of legal indicators to the contrary it would seem that at its core legal liability for negligence manifests the Negligence Standard. A more formal characterization goes as follows:

Principle of Responsibility in Negligence (PRNeg):
Part One: Given any two actions, Φ' and Φ'', if (a) an agent Φ's, (b) is responsible$_2$ for Φ'-ing, (c) has a duty to Φ' only if he conforms to some conditions, (d) the rationale of the duty is to avoid performing Φ-type actions by Φ-ing, (e) the agent failed to conform to that duty, (e) as a result the agent Φ''ed by Φ'-ing, then that agent is responsible$_2$ for Φ''.
Part Two: Given any omission Ω, and a state or event E, if (a) an agent Ωs, (b) is responsible$_2$ for Ωing, (c) has a duty not to Ω, (d) the rationale for the duty is to avoid states or events like E, (e) had the agent not Ωed E would not have happened, (f) E has happened, then the agent is responsible$_2$ for E.
Principle of the Duty of Care (PDC): Conditions (c) and (d) in both parts of **PRNeg** can normally be met without exceptional exertions by the people who are subject to them.
Principle of Duty in Negligence (PDN): Agents have a duty not to bring about harms of certain kinds, for which they are responsible$_2$ in virtue of **PRNeg**.

---

enforcement of such duties subject to judicial decision, and sometimes make the very recognition of their existence as legally binding duties subject to such decisions.

[20] Though sometimes it has desirable consequences as well, and sometimes they predominate.

3. Responsibility$_2$ for negligence—the problem

Negligence entails responsibility$_2$: if X's ϕ-ing was negligent then X is responsible for ϕ-ing. Since, as I suggested earlier, that is a conceptual truth, to deny responsibility$_2$ for negligent conduct is to deny that people's conduct can be negligent. That is an unlikely conclusion. Our belief that negligence is possible and common seems firm. So a correct account of responsibility$_2$ must be able to explain responsibility$_2$ for negligence.

That way of stating matters would, however, appear biased to some. It presupposes that belief that we are responsible$_2$ for negligence is sound. That is not a foregone conclusion. Given how well entrenched it is we can assume that it is likely to be sound. Yet it is possible that it is based on a corrupt or indefensible understanding of responsibility$_2$. After all, the Negligence Standard entails that responsibility$_2$ for negligence is inconsistent with the Guidance (as well as with the Control) Principle. First, failure to comply with the first duty, the duty of care, need not be under the agent's control. It may be due to forgetfulness, momentary loss of control (as when during driving one's foot slips off the brake), or to inexperience. Second, for every occasion on which the second duty is violated and one negligently causes harm it is possible that one would have performed the same action in an equally negligent way without causing harm. When one harmed another by negligent driving one *might* have been driving in an equally negligent way though the victim would not have been there to be harmed. The difference between the case in which negligence causes harm and the case in which it does not is due to factors beyond the agent's control.[21]

Faced with this challenge some have tried to explain negligence in ways that make it consistent with the Guidance Principle. In particular it has been suggested that any negligent act is the outcome of an intentional wrongful act at an earlier time. These views have been refuted by Honoré and others, and I will not consider them.[22] It is also possible to reject the very idea of responsibility for negligence. To defend it we need an explanation of responsibility$_2$ that not only explains responsibility$_2$ for negligence, but can be defended by additional reasons. In other words, given that responsibility$_2$ for negligence and for negligent harming is so central to our thought and to our attitudes to ourselves and others there is a strong presumption that the Negligence Standard is sound. But we need an account of why we are responsible$_2$ for negligence that will explain why and how the Guidance Principle falls short. Not only does the Guidance Principle appear reasonable, it does, as I indicated, provide a sufficient condition of

---

[21] The phenomenon adverted to here exists regarding intentional actions as well. I refer here to its application to negligence merely because I am discussing negligence, and not to imply that it is special to negligence.

[22] Honoré, *Responsibility and Fault* (Oxford: Hart Publishing, 1999). They have been refuted as explanations of negligence as we understand it. They can be advanced as alternatives to our concept of negligence. But the case for that depends on the failure of explanations of responsibility$_2$ to deny that the Guidance Principle constitutes a necessary condition for responsibility, a question to be discussed in the rest of this chapter.

responsibility$_2$. We are looking to a conception of responsibility$_2$ that generalizes and incorporates it, thus doing justice to its good sense, as well as explaining its limitations.

Not all theorists writing on negligence so much as attempt to explain how it is that people are responsible$_2$ for negligent harm.[23] The hard law and economics practitioners allow their preoccupation with the misnamed efficiency to mask all problems. Others affirm that liability for negligence is just, because it implements a fair distribution of the risks of being liable.[24] The justice of the distribution of legal liability is indeed crucial for the justification of the negligence law. After all, that I am responsible$_2$ for an action that harmed you does not in itself establish that I ought to compensate you. Suppose, for example, that I harmed you by employing an applicant who until then was working for you and without whom your business suffers.

Responsibility$_2$ is not sufficient for liability. But nor does the fact that a scheme of co-operation is fair establish either that people have a duty to participate in it, or that if they do their liabilities under it are based on responsibility$_2$ for harmful conduct. That there is no duty to participate in a scheme of cooperation merely because it is fair, was a matter much discussed by those who tried, to my mind unsuccessfully, to fix the flaws in Rawls's argument claiming that people have such an obligation, and that it may be enforced against them.

However, even if we are bound by a scheme of distributing liability analogous to that implemented in negligence law, it would not establish that the liability so justified is responsibility$_2$-based. As I have already mentioned there is liability deriving from fair schemes of social cooperation which does not depend on responsibility$_2$, such as liability to jury service, and to most common taxes. The Negligence Standard establishes responsibility$_2$-based liability, and we need an explanation of how it is that people are responsible$_2$ for negligent harm.

Honoré is one of the few squarely to confront the issue of responsibility$_2$. But his solution is essentially that liability for negligence is fair, being a species of people's responsibility$_2$ for the outcome of their actions, which is fair, because they normally win, i.e. when the outcomes are favourable, as well as occasionally lose. Even if this

---

[23] Notable exceptions are Enoch and Marmor, who argue that responsibility for negligence is consistent with the Control Principle, mainly on the ground that liability for negligent harm does not presuppose responsibility for the harm. In their view it only presupposes responsibility for the conduct that caused it. See D. Enoch and A. Marmor, 'The Case Against Moral Luck', *Law and Philosophy* 26/4 (2007), 405–13. John Goldberg and Benjamin Zipursky also see negligence law's apparent insensitivity to luck as an issue that a comprehensive theory of negligence should address, although their primary concern is different from Enoch and Marmor's. For Goldberg and Zipursky, the most troubling area of luck in tort law concerns 'actors who seem not to have behaved wrongfully in a full-blooded sense but nevertheless face liability for injuries they have caused. Often enough, an actor causes harm despite diligent efforts to comply with a standard of conduct.' see J. C. P. Goldberg and B. C. Zipursky, 'Tort Law and Moral Luck' (2007) 92 *Cornell Law Review* 1123, 1143.

[24] This seems to be the view of Cane, *Responsibility in Law and Morality*, and also A. Ripstein 'Equality, Luck, and Responsibility', *Philosophy and Public Affairs* 23/1 (1994), 3, 13 (though his particular argument that liability in negligence is required if the law is to treat people as equal 'protecting them each from the activities of the others, and leaving each with room to pursue his or her own purposes' is fallacious).

argument is successful (which is by no means clear) it fails, for the reasons just explained, to establish the outcome-responsibility[25] that he aims to establish.

To understand the nature of responsibility$_2$-based liability we need to understand the role of responsibility$_2$ (in the relevant sense of the term) in our life and in our practical thought. Responsibility$_2$ opens agents and their conduct to a variety of assessments, making various attitudes people may have to themselves and to others appropriate. An account of responsibility$_2$ would explain both for what kinds of assessment and attitudes is being responsible$_2$ a condition, and why. Much discussion focuses on responsibility$_2$ being a condition for moral praise or moral blame. But the preoccupation with praise and blame, natural in our blame society, misses the central role of responsibility. We need to bear in mind the full range of evaluations for which responsibility$_2$ is a condition. I will not be able to do so. But reflection on liability for negligent harm, being responsibility$_2$-based and not being subject to excuses, applies also to cases which do not warrant blame, thus helping to break the mesmerizing fascination with responsibility as a condition of nothing but praise and blame.[26]

A comprehensive account of responsibility$_2$ distinguishes between basic and derivative responsibility, the latter being responsibility for one thing deriving from responsibility for another. Negligence involves derivative responsibility: People are responsible for negligent harming because they are responsible for breach of a duty of care. For example, having failed to check the condition of my brakes, as was my duty, I accidentally rear-end the car ahead. The accident was due to the omission. I am in breach of my duty of care, and because of that also in breach of the duty not to harm negligently. But, as we know, my liability depends not only on wrongful action, but on wrongful action for which I am responsible$_2$. Rear-ending the car ahead was accidental. So why am I responsible for it? This is where a derivative principle comes in. It has the form: If one is responsible$_2$ for action A, and if by doing A one does B (which is the bringing about of some consequence), then one is responsible for B provided the actions meet a certain condition. This derivative principle extends responsibility beyond the reach of the Guidance Principle. Can that be justified? It all depends on the condition that extends agents' responsibility for the first action to the second one.

The condition is that avoiding that consequence was the rationale of the duty not to perform A (which is therefore 'a duty of care').[27] Moreover, the rationale of the duty of care was obvious to those subject to the duty. I do not mean that they either knew or

---

[25] Honoré does not indicate whether there are any limits to the outcomes for which one is responsible. J. Gardner remarked that Honoré does not distinguish between outcomes that are constitutive of the action, being the state it is defined as bringing about, and outcomes that are the consequences of the constitutive outcomes. See Gardner, 'Obligations and Outcomes', at 130. von Wright usefully draws this distinction using 'results' and 'consequences' to mark it. See G. H. von Wright, 'On the Logic of Norms and Actions' in von Wright, *Philosophical Papers*, vol. 1 (Oxford: Basil Blackwell, 1983), 107. Presumably Honoré means results, including the results of actions that are the bringing about of the outcomes.

[26] I consider some aspects of blameworthiness in Chapter Twelve.

[27] A couple of points to note: (1) If this principle is sound then principles of derivative responsibility can make responsibility depend on a duty or other normative condition, while basic principles cannot. (2) The

could readily know its precise content, or that they accepted it as sound. I mean that given the circumstances they could have easily known that they were subject to a duty of care, i.e. one designed to protect against some outcomes. I will shortly explain why in such circumstances if agents are responsible$_2$ when they know of the duty they are also responsible$_2$ if they could easily know about it.

This principle, which is relied upon by the Negligence Standard, is a moderate extension of the Guidance Principle by which people are responsible for the foreseen consequences of their actions. Here the foreseen consequence is the breach of duty not to negligently harm. The principle is extended to cover responsibility for the breach even if it was not foreseen (because the agent was not aware of the duty) provided it could easily have been foreseen, and to consequences of that breach that the duty was meant to prevent. There is much to say about the justification of this extension, but I will leave matters here. For an unresolved question awaits us: by the derivative principle I am responsible$_2$ for the accident only if I am responsible$_2$ for the breach of duty of care. My breach consisted in an omission, in the failure to check the brakes. Why am I responsible$_2$ for that? The derivative principle does not help us here.

Nor, as there is no common understanding of what it is to control one's omissions, can the Control Principle help. The last chapter suggested a couple of ways of understanding such control, but neither helps with our problem. Finally, the Guidance Principle too fails us. It establishes responsibility$_2$ for intentional omissions, for they are guided by our powers of rational agency. But assume that the omission was unintentional. Assume that I just forgot. Are we responsible$_2$ for all our unintentional omissions? That seems implausible. Think, for example, of a parent whose baby, unbeknown to him, becomes sick during the night, and dies, though he would have been saved had the parent attended to him. The parent did not, and is not responsible$_2$ for the omission because he did not know, and had no reason to suspect that the baby was sick. So when are we responsible$_2$ for our omissions?[28]

Can we keep faith with the rationale behind the Guidance Principle by relaxing it to say that one is responsible$_2$ for omissions that are either guided by one's powers of rational agency (as intentional omissions are), or can be guided by them? Should the test of 'can be guided' replace that of guidance for actions as well? To apply this test to actions is to hold one responsible$_2$ for any accidental action provided it could have been done intentionally. It is just about the same as dispensing with responsibility$_2$. But if this is a mistaken characterization of responsibility$_2$ for actions how could it be correct when applied to omissions? It would have a similar result. The parent would be responsible for not treating the baby. Making responsibility$_2$ for omissions turn not on the ability to omit intentionally, but on ability intentionally to perform the omitted action would have the same result. Besides, it is not clear why responsibility$_2$ should

example assumes that B (causing an accident) involves actions subsequent to A (driving), but the principle applies more generally to cases in which that is not so.

[28] For lack of a better term I use 'omitting to A' to mean 'not doing A'.

attach to acts and omissions that could be guided by the capacities for rational agency but were not.

4. The Rational Functioning Principle

Let us return to the Guidance Principle, and ask why it appears to fail to cover some acts and omissions for which we are responsible₂. The reason, it seems to me, is that it fails to capture conduct for which we are responsible₂ and in which our rational capacities *would have guided our conduct, but for the fact that they malfunctioned.*

Does it mean that we are responsible₂ for all actions we could and should have taken? No, for not all failures to do what we should have done are due to the malfunctioning of our capacities for rational agency. Think again of the case of the parents who did not save their baby.

Typical malfunction occurs when we intend to do something and then it slips our mind and we do not. Or, when someone fails to pick up his child from school, as he should have done, and you say to him: but you knew that they finish school early today, and he replies: yes but it did not occur to me, or I did not think of it at the time. These failures to connect, failures to do what we intended, or to intend what we would have intended had our background intentions and beliefs surfaced in consciousness at the right time, are typical of the ways in which our powers of rational agency sometimes malfunction. And, my suggestion is, we are responsible₂ for omissions due to the malfunctioning of our powers of rational agency.

I have instanced the malfunction of some of our mental capacities to explain which unintended omissions we are responsible₂ for. Naturally our ability physically to guide our movements can also fail us. We intentionally set out to perform actions of which we are masters, actions falling within our domain of secure competence, and fail to complete them as intended. For example, my foot may slip off the brake while driving. As Honoré reminded us, we are responsible for such actions, and for some of their consequences.

My suggestion differs, however, from his outcome-responsibility.

The only outcomes for which we are non-derivatively responsible₂ are either (a) intended or foreseen ones or, (b) ones that result from failure, due to the malfunctioning of our capacities of agency, to complete as intended an action within our domain of secure competence.

All these are united by being the outcomes of actions guided by our powers of rational agency, successfully or unsuccessfully. Non-derivative responsibility for omissions displays the same feature: intentional omissions are guided by our powers of rational agency, and we are responsible for those unintended omissions that result from the malfunctioning of our powers of rational agency. In sum, as the **Rational Functioning Principle** says:

conduct for which we are (non-derivatively) responsible is conduct that is the result of the functioning, successful or failed, of our powers of rational agency.

This unified account of basic responsibility meets the condition any such account must meet: it explains how capacity-responsibility is related to responsibility$_2$ for conduct, in the sense we are exploring. But we need more. We need an explanation of why this, rather than some alternative, relationship between powers of rational agency and actions determines responsibility$_2$. In part the answer is in the fact that this account matches the concept of responsibility$_2$, in particular it explains responsibility$_2$ for negligence. But the argument to that effect cannot be conclusive, given the multiplicity of senses and variations of senses in which 'responsibility' is used. The account has to, and can, be bolstered by an explanation of the significance of the actions for which we are responsible$_2$ in our life, a significance that depends on responsibility$_2$ having this sense.

That was what the discussion of the way responsibility$_2$ is crucial to our sense of Being in the World in the last chapter began doing. This is, probably, what Honoré and others had in mind when they asserted, without explanation, that responsibility for outcomes is necessary for the constitution of our identity. An explanation can start by noticing that our sense of who we are is shaped in part by our competence in using our capacities of rational agency. While as rational agents we share certain abilities, we also differ greatly in the range of capacities of rational agency that we master, regarding which we have secure competence. The abilities that we securely command determine the range of actions that fall within our domain of secure competence (and needless to say our abilities and the domain of secure competence vary over time, partly due to our deliberate efforts). The way we feel about ourselves, our self-esteem, our self-respect, the degree to which we are content to be what we are, or what we perceive ourselves to be, our pride in ourselves, our shame in how we are, or in how we conduct ourselves— all these and various other self-directed attitudes and emotions depend in part on competence in using our faculties of rational agency. Actions due to malfunction of our capacities of rational agency result from failure to perform acts of which we are masters. In acknowledging our responsibility for these unintentional acts and omissions we affirm our mastery of these abilities, deny that we are disabled in the relevant regards. When others attribute to us responsibilities for such actions they acknowledge our mastery of those abilities, and hold us responsible for these results of their use.

Much more needs to be said to do justice to this thought and to vindicate my suggestion that it underpins the concept of responsibility. Here I will end by examining the way in which this suggestion helps establish that liability for negligence is responsibility$_2$-based.

Take a simplified example: a driver who causes an accident. If he is a competent driver who caused the accident through momentary inattention he is responsible$_2$ because one is responsible$_2$ for actions within one's domain of competence even when, due to the malfunctioning of one's powers of agency, they accidentally go wrong. If he is not a competent driver then he should not have driven, and his responsibility$_2$ for the accident derives from his responsibility$_2$ for driving intentionally when he should not have done. A company that is liable to compensate workers injured at work because it failed to implement adequate safety measures is derivatively responsible$_2$ for the injury because it is directly responsible$_2$ for the omission, if it had the information that indicated that the workplace is dangerous. Alternatively, the company is indirectly responsible$_2$ for the omission, if it lacked this information, because it is responsible$_2$ for failing in its duty to attend to the need to secure the safety of the workplace, a duty that required it to find out which safety measures are needed.[29]

In brief: The content of the duties of care we are subject to is a matter of substantive principles. It is, as writers on the subject suggest, a matter of fair distribution of the risk of liability to damages. It is wrong to think that there are a priori principles of justice dictating the right distribution of the risk, or that some measure of economic efficiency dictates them. Both efficiency and abstract precepts of fairness need much assistance from prevailing practices to yield definite results. But that was not my topic. Furthermore, when it comes to legal duties of care the constraints of bureaucratized legal actions bring with them their own inevitable modification of the moral duties prevailing.

But none of this was my topic. Rather, I set out to explain how the very existence of moral duties that have the structure displayed by the Negligence Standard forces us to abandon some misguided ways of understanding responsibility$_2$, and lends support to the conception of responsibility$_2$ as vested in conduct which results from the functioning, good or faulty, of our capacities of rational agency, and in whatever else one is responsible$_2$ for in virtue of principles of derivative responsibility. I did not try to detail fully the content of the principles of responsibility$_2$, basic or derivative. My aim was to explain and partly defend the basic idea that animates those principles, and in the light of which we can proceed to establish their precise content. So long as we do not lose sight of the basic idea we are unlikely to go far wrong.

---

[29] An important aspect of the explanation of responsibility$_2$ offered here is that one may have to look closely at the background to an action for which the agent is responsible to establish the grounds of the responsibility: Suppose one fails to act as one has a duty to do (let us say to check that one's baby child is sleeping safely) through momentary laspe of memory. In that case one is responsible$_2$ for the omission because it is due to a malfunction of one's powers of rational agency. Imagine, however, that one fails one's duty because of feelings of hate and resentment towards the baby. In that case one's omission is not due to a malfunctioning of one's rational faculties. It is, however, intentional, and one is responsible$_2$ for it according to the Guidance Principle, which is an aspect of the Principle of Rational Functioning. Suppose, however, that the parent is merely ignorant of a duty to check on the baby. In that case the omission is neither due to a malfunction of the parent's powers, nor is it intentional. Is he not responsible$_2$? That would depend on whether not being aware of the duty is due to a malfunction of the parent's powers of agency. If the parent has normal competence and he lives in a society in which such duty is widely understood then he would be responsible$_2$ (derivatively) for not checking on the baby's condition. He will be responsible$_2$ for the ignorance (which is due to a malfunction of his rational powers) and derivatively responsible$_2$ for the omission that arises out of that malfunction. If, however, the parent is disabled (has limited mental powers) then he will not be responsible$_2$, for the omission will not be due to a malfunction of *his* powers. The same is true if he lives in an environment in which the duty is not generally understood and recognized. I am grateful to Jane Stapleton for bringing the example to my attention.

Bibliography

Adams, R. M., 'Involuntary Sins', *Philosophical Review* 94 (1985), 3.

Adler, J., *Belief's Own Ethics* (Cambridge, Mass.: MIT Press, 2002).

Anscombe, G. E. M., *Intention* (Oxford: Basil Blackwell, 1957).

Aquinas, T., *Summa Theologica* (etext).

Arpaly, N., *Unprincipled Virtue* (Oxford: OUP, 2004).

Augustine, *Confessions*, trans. Albert C. Outler (Philadelphia: Westminster Press, 1955).

Baker, G. P., and Hacker, P. M. S., *Wittgenstein: Rules, Grammar and Necessity: Essays and Exegesis of 185–242*, vol. 2 of *An Analytical Commentary on the Philosophical Investigations* (Malden, Mass.: Wiley-Blackwell), 2nd edn. extensively rev. P. M. S. Hacker (2010).

Bauman, P., and Belzler, M. (eds.), *Practical Conflicts* (New York: CUP, 2004).

Bermúdez, J., and Millar, A. (eds.), *Reason and Nature: Essays in the Theory of Rationality* (Oxford: Clarendon Press, 2002).

Bratman, M., *Intention, Plans and Practical Reason* (Cambridge, Mass.: Harvard UP, 1987).

Broome, J., 'Normative Requirements', *Ratio* 12 (1999), 398, and in Dancy (ed.), *Normativity*.

—— 'Practical Reasoning', in Bermúdez and Millar (eds.), *Reason and Nature*.

—— 'Reasons', in Wallace et al. (eds.), *Reason and Value*.

—— 'Have We Reason to Do as Rationality Requires: A Comment on Raz', *Journal of Ethics & Social Philosophy* 1/1 (2005) (http://www.jesp.org/).

——'Does Rationality Consist in Responding Correctly to Reasons?', *Journal of Moral Philosophy*, 4/3 (2007), 349–74.

Brudner, A., *The Unity of the Common Law* (Berkeley and Los Angeles: University of California Press, 1995).

Brunero, J., 'Two Approaches to Instrumental Rationality and Belief Consistency', *Journal of Ethics & Social Philosophy* 1/1 (2005) (http://www.jesp.org/).

Cane, P., *Responsibility in Law and Morality* (Oxford: Hart Publishing, 2002).

—— and Gardner J. (eds.), *Relating to Responsibility: Essays for Tony Honoré* (Oxford: Hart Publishing, 2001).

Chisholm, R., 'The Ethics of Requirement', *American Philosophical Quarterly* 1 (1964), 147.

—— 'Practical Reason and the Logic of Requirement', in Korner (ed.), *Practical Reason*.

Cullity, G., and Gaut, B. (eds.), *Ethics and Practical Reason* (Oxford: OUP, 1997).

Dan-Cohen, M., 'Luck & Identity', *Theoretical Inquiries in Law* 9/1 (2008).

Dancy, J., *Practical Reality* (Oxford: OUP, 2000).

—— (ed.), *Normativity* (Oxford: Blackwell, 2000).

—— 'Enticing Reasons', in Wallace et al. (eds.), *Reason and Value*.

—— *Ethics Without Principles* (Oxford: OUP, 2004).

—— 'How to Act—Disjunctively', in Haddock and Macpherson (eds.), *Disjunctivism* (2008).

D'Arms, J., and Jacobson, D., 'Sentiment and Value', *Ethics* 110 (2000), 722.

Darwall, S., *The Second-Person Standpoint: Morality, Respect, and Accountability* (Cambridge, Mass.: Harvard UP, 2006).

Davidson, D., 'Actions, Reasons and Causes' (1963), in Davidson, *Essays on Actions and Events*.

—— 'How is Weakness of the Will Possible?', in Feinberg (ed.), *Moral Concepts*, and in Davidson, *Essays on Actions and Events*.

—— *Essays on Actions and Events* (Oxford: OUP, 1980).

Dostoevsky, F., *Notes from the Underground* (Rockville, Md.: Serenity Publishers, 2008).

Dreier, J., 'Humean Doubts about the Practical Justification of Morality', in Cullity and Gaut (eds.), *Ethics and Practical Reason*.

Edgeley, R., *Reason in Theory and Practice* (London: Hutchinson University Library, 1969).

Egonsson, D., Josefsson, J., Petersson, B., and Rønnow-Rasmussen, T. (eds.), *Exploring Practical Philosophy* (Burlington, Vt.: Ashgate Press, 2001).

Enoch, D., 'Agency, Shmagency: Why Normativity Won't Come from What is Constitutive of Agency', *Philosophical Review* 115 (2006), 169.

—— and Marmor, A., 'The Case Against Moral Luck', *Law and Philosophy*, 26/4 (2007), 405.

Everson, S., 'What is a Reason for Action', in Sandis (ed.), *New Essays*.

Feinberg, J. (ed.), *Moral Concepts* (Oxford: OUP, 1970).

Forster, E. M., *A Room With a View* (London: Edward Arnold, 1908).

Frankfurt, H., 'The Problem of Action', in Frankfurt, *The Importance of What We Care About*.

—— 'Coercion and Moral Responsibility', in Frankfurt, *The Importance of What We Care About*.

—— *The Importance of What We Care About* (Cambridge: CUP, 1988).

Gardner, J., 'Obligations and Outcomes in the Law of Torts', in Cane and Gardner (eds.), *Relating to Responsibility*.

Gauthier, D., *Morals by Agreement* (Oxford: OUP, 1986).

Goldberg, J. C. P., and Zipursky, B. C., 'Tort Law and Moral Luck' (2007) 92, *Cornell Law Review* 1123.

Grice, P., *Aspects of Reason* (Oxford: OUP, 2001).

Haddock, A., and Macpherson, F. (eds.), *Disjunctivism* (Oxford: OUP, 2008).

—— Millar, A., and Pritchard, D. (eds.), *Epistemic Value* (Oxford: OUP, 2009).

Hampshire, S., *Justice is Conflict* (Princeton: Princeton UP, 2000).

Hampton, J., *The Authority of Reason* (Cambridge: CUP, 1998).

Harman, G., *The Nature of Morality* (New York: OUP, 1977).

—— *Change in View* (Cambridge, Mass.: MIT Press/Bradford Books, 1986).

—— 'Practical Reasoning', in Harman, *Reasoning, Meaning and Mind*.

—— 'Rationality', repr. in Harman, *Reasoning, Meaning and Mind*.

—— *Reasoning, Meaning and Mind* (Oxford: OUP 1999).

Hart, H. L. A., *Punishment and Responsiblity* (Oxford: OUP, 1968).

Heuer, U., 'Explaining Reasons: Where Does the Buck Stop?', *Journal of Ethics & Social Philosophy* 1/3 (2006) (http://www.jesp.org/).

—— and Lang, G. (eds.), *Themes from the Ethics of B. Williams* (Oxford: OUP, 2011).

Hieronymi, P., 'The Wrong Kind of Reason', *Journal of Philosophy* 102 (2005), 435.

Hohfeld, W. N., *Fundamental Legal Conceptions* (New Haven: Yale UP, 1919).

Honoré, A. M., *Making Law Bind* (Oxford: Clarendon Press, 1987).

—— *Responsibility and Fault* (Oxford: Hart Publishing, 1999).

Hornsby, J., 'A Disjunctive Conception of Acting for Reasons', in Haddock and Macpherson (eds.), *Disjunctivism*.

Hurley, S., *Natural Reasons* (Oxford: OUP, 1989).

Hyman, J., 'The Road to Larissa', *Ratio* 23 (2010), 323.

Jackson, F., 'Decision-theoretic Consequentialism and the Nearest and Dearest Objection', *Ethics* 101 (1991), 461–82.

James, W., 'The Will to Believe', *New World* 5 (1896), 327.

Kavka, G., 'The Toxin Puzzle', *Analysis* 43 (1983), 33.

Kenny, A., *The Metaphysics of Mind* (Oxford: Clarendon Press, 1989).

Kolodny, N., 'Why Be Rational?', *Mind* 114 (2005), 509.

—— 'How Does Coherence Matter?', *Proceedings of the Aristotelian Society* 107 (2007), 229.

—— 'The Myth of Practical Consistency', *European Journal of Philosophy* 16 (2008), 36.

—— 'Why Be Disposed to Be Coherent?', *Ethics* 118 (2008), 437.

—— and MacFarlane, J., '"Ifs" and "Oughts"', *Journal of Philosophy*, 107/3 (2010), 115–43.

Korner, S. (ed.), *Practical Reason* (Oxford: Basil Blackwell, 1974).

Korsgaard, C., 'The Normativity of Instrumental Reason', in Cullity and Gaut (eds.), *Ethics and Practical Reason*.

—— *Self-Constitution: Action, Identity and Integrity* (Oxford: OUP, 2009).

Lenman, J., 'Consequentialism and Cluelessness', *Philosophy & Public Affairs* 29 (2000), 342.

Mackie, J. L., *Ethics* (Harmondsworth: Penguin Books, 1977).

Marcus, R., 'Moral Dilemmas and Consistency', *Journal of Philosophy* 77 (1980), 121–36.

Morgenbesser, S., and Ullmann-Margalit, E., 'Picking and Choosing', *Social Research* 44 (1977), 757.

Nagel, T. 'Moral Luck', in Nagel, *Mortal Questions*.

—— *Mortal Questions* (Cambridge: CUP, 1979).

Nozick, R., *Anarchy, State and Utopia* (New York: Basic Books, 1974).

—— *The Nature of Rationality* (Princeton: Princeton UP, 1993).

Olson, J., 'Buck-Passing and the Wrong Kind of Reasons', *Philosophical Quarterly* 54 (2004), 295–300.

Owens, D., 'Epistemic Akrasia', *Monist* 85 (2002), 381.

—— 'Does Belief Have an Aim?', *Philosophical Studies* 115 (2003), 283–305.

—— 'Rationalism About Obligation', *European Journal of Philosophy* 16 (2008), 403.

Parfit, D., 'Rationality and Reasons', in Egonsson et al. (eds.), *Exploring Practical Philosophy*.

Pascal, B., *Pensées* (1670), trans. W. F. Trotter (London and New York: Dents/Dutton, 1943).

Perry, S., 'Responsibility for Outcomes, Risk, and the Law of Torts', in Postema (ed.), *Philosophy and the Law of Torts*.

Pettit, P., *The Common Mind* (Oxford: OUP, 1993).

Plato, *The Republic* (etext).

Pogge, T., 'What We Can Reasonably Reject', in Sosa and Villanueva (eds.), *Philosophical Issues* 11 (2001), 118–47.

Postema, G. J. (ed.), *Philosophy and the Law of Torts* (Cambridge: CUP, 2001).

Pritchard, D., 'Recent Work on Epistemic Value', *American Philosophical Quarterly* 44 (2007), 85.

Putnam, H., *Reason, Truth and History* (Cambridge: CUP, 1981).

—— *Realism With a Human Face* (Cambridge, Mass.: Harvard UP, 1990).

Rabinowitz, W., and Rønnow-Rasmussen, T., 'The Strike of the Demon: On Fitting Pro-Attitudes and Value', *Ethics* 114 (2004), 391–423.

Railton, P., 'How to Engage Reason: The Problem of Regress', in Wallace et al. (eds.), *Reason and Value*.

—— 'Practical Competence and Fluent Agency', in Sobel and Wall (eds.), *Reasons for Action.*

Rawls, J., *A Theory of Justice* (Cambridge: Harvard UP, 1971).

Raz, Joseph, *Practical Reason and Norms* (1975; current edn. Oxford: OUP, 1999).

—— 'Introduction', in Raz (ed.), *Practical Reasoning.*

—— (ed.), *Practical Reasoning* (Oxford: OUP, 1978).

—— *The Morality of Freedom* (Oxford: OUP, 1986).

—— *Engaging Reason* (Oxford: OUP, 1999).

—— *Value, Respect & Attachment* (Cambridge: CUP, 2000).

—— *The Practice of Value* (Oxford: OUP, 2003).

—— 'The Force of Numbers', *Royal Institute of Philosophy Lectures 2003* (Cambridge: CUP, 2004).

—— 'Personal Practical Conflicts', in Bauman and Belzler (eds.), *Practical Conflicts.*

—— 'The Myth of Instrumental Rationality', *Journal for Ethics and Social Philosophy* 1/1 (2005) (http://www.jesp.org/).

—— 'Numbers, With and Without Contractualism', in Stratton-Lake (ed.), *On What We Owe to Each Other.*

—— *Between Authority and Interpretation* (Oxford: OUP, 2009).

—— 'Reasons: Practical and Adaptive', in Sobel and Wall (eds.), *Reasons for Action.*

—— 'Responsibility and the Negligence Standard', *Oxford Journal of Legal Studies* 30 (2010), 1.

—— 'Being in the World', *Ratio*, ns 23 (2010), 43.

—— 'Agency and Luck', in Heuer and Lang (eds.), *Themes from the Ethics of B. Williams.*

Ridge, M., 'Saving Scanlon: Contractualism and Agent-Relativity', *Journal of Political Philosophy* 9 (2001), 472.

Ripstein, A., 'Equality, Luck, and Responsibility', *Philosophy and Public Affairs* 23/1 (1994), 3.

Sandis, C. (ed.), *New Essays on the Explanation of Action* (Basingstoke: Palgrave Macmillan, 2009).

Scanlon, T., 'Preference and Urgency', *Journal of Philosophy* 72 (1975), 655.

—— 'Contractualism and Utilitarianism', in Sen and Williams (eds.), *Utilitarianism and Beyond.*

—— *What We Owe to Each Other* (Cambridge, Mass.: Harvard UP 1998).

—— 'Reasons: A Puzzling Duality', in Wallace et al. (eds.), *Reason and Value.*

Schroeder, M., 'Instrumental Mythology', *Journal of Ethics & Social Philosophy*, 1/1 (2005) (http://www.jesp.org/).

Sen, A., 'Rights and Agency', *Philosophy & Public Affairs* 11 (1982), 3.

—— Williams, B. (eds.), *Utilitarianism and Beyond* (Cambridge: CUP, 1982).

Setiya, K., *Reasons Without Rationalism* (Princeton: Princeton UP, 2007).

Shafer-Landau, R. (ed.), *Oxford Studies in Meta Ethics*, vol. 5 (Oxford: OUP, 2010).

Shah, N., 'A New Argument for Evidentialism', *Philosophical Quarterly* 56 (2006), 481–98.

—— 'How Action Governs Intention', *Philosophers' Imprint* 8 (2008), 1–19 (http://hdl.handle.net/2027/spo.3521354.0008.005).

Smith, E. E., and Osherson, D. N (eds.), *Thinking: An Invitation for Cognitive Science* (Cambridge, Mass.: MIT Press, 2nd edn. 1995–8).

Sobel, D., 'Instrumental Rationality: Not Dead Yet', *Journal of Ethics & Social Philosophy* 1/1 (2005) (http://www.jesp.org/).

—— Wall, S. (eds.), *Reasons for Action* (Cambridge: CUP, 2009).

Sosa, E., *A Virtue Epistemology* (Oxford: OUP, 2007).

—— 'Value Matters in Epistemology', *Journal of Philosophy* 107 (2010), 167.

Sosa, E., Villanueva, E. (eds.), *Philosophical Issues* 11 (2001).

Statman, D. (ed), *Moral Luck* (Albany, N.Y.: State University of New York Press, 1993).

Stocker, M., 'Raz on the Intelligibility of Bad Acts', in Wallace et al. (eds.), *Reason and Value*.

Stratton-Lake, P. (ed.), *On What We Owe to Each Other* (Oxford: Blackwell Publishing, 2005).

Street, S., 'A Darwinian Dilemma for Realist Theories of Value', *Philosophical Studies* 127 (2006), 109.

Stroud, S., 'Epistemic Partiality in Friendship', *Ethics* 116 (2006), 498–524.

Tenenbaum, S., *Desire, Practical Reason, and the Good* (New York: OUP, 2010).

Thomson, J. J., *Normativity* (Chicago: Open Court, 2008).

Velleman, D., 'The Guise of the Good' *Noûs* 26/1 (1992), 3–26, repr. in Velleman (ed.), *The Possibility of Practical Reason*.

—— *The Possibility of Practical Reason* (New York: OUP, 2002).

Wallace, R. J., 'Normativity, Commitment, and Instrumental Reason', *Philosophers' Imprint* 1/3 (2001) (http://hdl.handle.net/2027/spo.3521354.0001.004); also in Wallace, *Normativity and the Will*.

—— 'Comment on Raz', *Journal of Ethics & Social Philosophy* 1/1 (2005) (http://www.jesp.org/).

—— *Normativity and the Will* (Oxford: OUP, 2006).

—— Pettit, P., Scheffler, S., and Smith, M. (eds.), *Reason and Value* (Oxford: OUP, 2004).

Williams, B., 'Internal and External Reasons', in Williams, *Moral Luck*.

—— 'Moral Luck', in Williams, *Moral Luck*.

—— *Moral Luck* (Cambridge: CUP, 1981).

—— 'Postscript' in Statman (ed.), *Moral Luck*.

—— *Shame and Necessity* (Cambridge: CUP, 1993).

Wittgenstein, L., *Philosophische Untersuchungen=Philosophical Investigations*, trans. G. E. M. Anscombe, P. M. S. Hacker, and J. Schulte (Chichester: Wiley-Blackwell); 4th edn., rev. P. M. S. Hacker and J. Schulte (2009).

von Wright, G. H.: *Norm and Action* (London: Routledge & Kegan Paul, 1963).

—— 'On the Logic of Norms and Actions' in von Wright, *Philosophical Papers*, vol. 1.

—— *Philosophical Papers*, vol. 1 (Oxford: Basil Blackwell, 1983).

Zimmerman, M. J., 'Luck & Moral Responsibility', in Statman (ed.), *Moral Luck*.

—— *Living With Uncertainty* (Cambridge: CUP 2009).

Index

Lightning Source UK Ltd.
Milton Keynes UK
UKOW04f1150221113

221581UK00001B/2/P